The National Institute of Economic and Social Research, London, is an independent, non-profit-making body founded in 1938. It always has had as its aim the promotion of realistic research, particularly in the field of economics. It conducts research by its own research staff and in co-operation with the universities and other academic bodies. The work done under the Institute's auspices is published by the Cambridge University Press in two series: *Studies* and *Occasional Papers*.

THE NATIONAL INSTITUTE OF
ECONOMIC AND SOCIAL RESEARCH

Economic and Social Studies
IX

THE DISTRIBUTION OF CONSUMER GOODS

THE NATIONAL INSTITUTE OF
ECONOMIC AND SOCIAL RESEARCH

Economic and Social Studies

I. Studies in the National Income, 1924–1938.
By A. L. Bowley, Sc.D.

II. The Burden of British Taxation.
By G. Findlay Shirras and L. Rostas, 1942.

III. Trade Regulations and Commercial Policy of the United Kingdom.
By the Research Staff of the Institute, 1943.

IV. National Health Insurance. A critical study.
By Hermann Levy, 1944.

V. The Development of the Soviet Economic System.
By Alexander Baykov, 1946.

VI. Studies in Financial Organization.
By T. Balogh, 1948.

VII. Investment, Location, and Size of Plant. A realistic enquiry into the structure of British and American industries.
By P. Sargant Florence, assisted by W. Baldamus, 1948.

VIII. A Statistical Analysis of Advertising Expenditure and of the Revenue of the Press.
By Nicholas Kaldor and Rodney Silverman, 1948.

THE DISTRIBUTION OF CONSUMER GOODS

A factual study of methods and costs in the United Kingdom in 1938

BY

JAMES B. JEFFERYS

ASSISTED BY

MARGARET MACCOLL

AND

G. L. LEVETT

CAMBRIDGE
AT THE UNIVERSITY PRESS
1950

CAMBRIDGE UNIVERSITY PRESS
Cambridge, New York, Melbourne, Madrid, Cape Town,
Singapore, São Paulo, Delhi, Tokyo, Mexico City

Cambridge University Press
The Edinburgh Building, Cambridge CB2 8RU, UK

Published in the United States of America by Cambridge University Press, New York

www.cambridge.org
Information on this title: www.cambridge.org/9781107602748

First published 1950
First paperback edition 2011

A catalogue record for this publication is available from the British Library

ISBN 978-1-107-60274-8 Paperback

Additional resources for this publication at www.cambridge.org/9781107602748

FOREWORD

The enquiry which led to the Study here presented had a double origin. Towards the end of the War the Executive Committee of the National Institute of Economic and Social Research, in reviewing its plans, decided that the most useful purpose to which it could devote the resources of the Institute was a series of studies in the structure of the economy of the United Kingdom. About the same time the Committee was approached by a group of businessmen, all concerned in one way or another with the distribution of consumer goods and all dissatisfied with the existing state of knowledge about distribution, with the suggestion that the Institute should undertake an enquiry into the existing organization and methods of distribution. They offered their help, but were concerned that the responsibility for and control of any enquiry should lie with an independent scientific body.

The Committee of the Institute welcomed this proposal, which fitted in so well with its plans. One of the most neglected tracts in the whole area of structural economic studies in this country is this field of distribution. It is perhaps less barren than it was a couple of decades ago, when Braithwaite and Dobbs' *Distribution of Consumable Goods* was published; but it is still comparatively neglected, still—possibly owing to the absence of a Census of Distribution—largely unexplored. At the same time interest in it has grown. In a period of general shortage of labour the continually rising number of persons employed in the distribution trades is bound to attract attention; in the wholesale and retail sectors alone they constitute the second largest industry, in terms of employment, in the country. Current policies designed to raise manufacturing productivity by increasing length of runs and reducing variety of products meet obstacles in the multiplicity of retail outlets and diverse methods of placing orders. And the hope of reducing the price of goods to the consumer is confronted with the realization, as shown in this enquiry, that between 35 and 40 per cent of the total expenditure on consumer goods is represented by the cost of distributing them, apart entirely from other distribution costs incurred at the raw material and semi-finished and importing stages.

An Advisory Committee was established, consisting of Mr. Hugh Weeks (Chairman), Mr. Paul Cadbury, Sir Geoffrey Heyworth, Mr. Frank Mitchell, the late Sir Frederick Ogilvie, Professor Sir Arnold Plant, Mr. W. B. Reddaway, Mr. Austin Robinson, Sir George Schuster, Mr. Richard Stone, the Secretary of the Institute, and myself.

This Committee felt that the most urgent task was to collect and record facts on distributive methods and costs, though the actual scope must depend on the data it was possible to obtain. The aim adopted was, briefly, to present in broad outline, in regard to consumer goods sold in the United Kingdom in 1938, the relative importance of different methods of distribution, the magnitude of different costs of distribution and an analysis of some of the main factors influencing these methods and costs; and alongside these general estimates to prepare a series of case studies on the distribution of individual commodities and commodity groups.

The results set forth in this volume are, I think, an ample justification of the enquiry. It is, however, important that the limitations of the results should be understood. They arise from the nature of the subject and the method of research used, and are, it is suggested, four in number.

In the first place, in order to undertake the study a division had to be made between production and distribution processes and somewhat arbitrary decisions had to be taken as to where the production of a particular good finished and where its distribution began. A breakdown of a continuous process into its component parts is necessary if closer inspection of the parts is to be made, but until they are re-assembled into a continuous whole the conclusions that may be drawn from the examination of individual components must be very guarded. Conclusions drawn, for example, from the total costs of distribution expressed as a proportion of the retail price of a commodity can be very misleading in the absence of data on the influence on the production costs of that commodity of the particular methods and costs of distribution employed.

In the second place the approach used in this enquiry has been the commodity approach; a study of the methods and costs of distribution of individual commodities and groups of commodities, of the ways in which the commodities passed from the producer to the consumer, the proportions sold by different types of outlet and the distributive costs incurred by manufacturers, wholesalers and retailers in selling the commodities. This approach contrasts with the approach of studying economic units, that is manufacturers, wholesalers and retailers, and their margins, costs, price policies, and profit on all the goods that they handled. While the difference between the two approaches may not be significant in the case of a manufacturer in that he tends to confine his production to one type of good, the difference is important in the case of wholesalers and retailers in as much as they handle, in most instances, a variety of products, each having different characteristics, different methods of distribution and yielding different margins. In order to construct a complete picture of distribution both approaches are necessary and the conclusions that can be drawn from the use of one method by itself are necessarily limited.

In the third place the information obtained relates to one year only, 1938, and can therefore give no indication of trends. The choice of 1938 as the focal point of the enquiry was influenced by the desire to present an outline of distribution practice as it existed in a relatively free economy and to avoid the complications and distortions introduced by governmental controls and the war and post-war scarcities. The decision was also influenced by the wish to obtain data which would, with the publication of the results of the forthcoming Census of Distribution, enable some trends in distribution practice to be traced and measured. But until such a comparison is possible the conclusions that can be drawn from the cross-section represented by one year are once again limited.

In the fourth place the survey does not claim to present precise figures or data relating to distributive methods and costs in 1938 as such figures, and the means of collecting them in relation to that year, do not exist. What has been attempted is a series of estimates based on information obtained from manufacturers, wholesalers, retailers, the trade associations and Government departments. Every effort has been made by thorough and painstaking research to check and cross-check the figures, but they remain estimates suggesting the approximate proportion of goods distributed in various ways and the order of magnitude of the various costs incurred. An explanation of the methods used to obtain the information and some assessment of the relative reliability of the estimates has been given in the Introduction, but the important margin of error attending these estimates is another reason why the conclusions that can be drawn from them are limited and it is important that a greater measure of accuracy should not be attributed to them than they claim to possess.

While recognizing these limitations, however, the Study does, I think, represent a substantial advance in our knowledge of distribution and an important contribution to structural economics. Limited though it is, it provides a starting-point which did not exist before for further research in its field; in particular, it should enable students to make a much more effective use of the data which will shortly be provided by the official Census of Distribution than would have been possible without it. It remains only to thank the many associations, firms and individuals who have helped the enquiry with information, criticism, and advice. The group which approached the Institute in the first instance, both as members of the Advisory Committee and as individuals, have responded to every appeal for facilities and aid, and it is only the number of others, and the expressed preference of some of them, that makes it impossible to thank them all by name.

The Executive Committee of the Institute and the Advisory Committee wish me also to record their high appreciation of the competence and devotion which Mr. Jefferys and his assistants have brought to the work of the enquiry.

HENRY CLAY

President

National Institute of Economic and Social Research

October 1949

AUTHOR'S PREFACE

James Boswell in his *Life of Samuel Johnson* quotes a letter from the Doctor written in 1776 to the Master of University College, Oxford, which discusses the methods and costs of the distribution of books.

"We will call our primary agent in London, Mr. Cadell, who receives our books from us, gives them room in his warehouse, and issues them on demand; by him they are sold to Mr. Dilly, a wholesale bookseller, who sends them into the country; and the last seller is the country bookseller. Here are three profits to be paid between the printer and the reader, or in the style of commerce, between the manufacturer and the consumer; and if any of these profits is too penuriously distributed, the process of commerce is interrupted.

"We are now come to the practical question, what is to be done? You will tell me, with reason, that I have said nothing, till I declare how much, according to my opinion, of the ultimate price ought to be distributed through the whole succession of sale.

"The deduction, I am afraid, will appear very great: but let it be considered before it is refused. We must allow, for profit, between thirty and thirty-five per cent, between six and seven shillings in the pound; that is, for every book which costs the last buyer twenty shillings, we must charge Mr. Cadell with something less than fourteen. We must set the copies at fourteen shillings each, and superadd what is called the quarterly-book; or for every hundred books so charged we must deliver an hundred and four.

"The profits will then stand thus:

"Mr. Cadell, who runs no hazard, and gives no credit, will be paid for warehouse room and attendance by a shilling profit on each book, and his chance of the quarterly-book.

"Mr. Dilly, who buys the book for fifteen shillings, and who will expect the quarterly-book if he takes five and twenty, will send it to his country-customer at sixteen and sixpence, by which, at the hazard of loss, and the certainty of long credit, he gains the regular profit of ten per cent which is expected in the wholesale trade.

"The country bookseller, buying at sixteen and sixpence, and commonly trusting a considerable time, gains but three and sixpence, and if he trusts a year, not much more than two and sixpence; otherwise than as he may, perhaps, take as long credit as he gives.

"With less profit than this, and more you see he cannot have, the country bookseller cannot live; for his receipts are small, and his debts somewhat bad."

While Boswell can conclude: "I am happy in giving this full and clear statement to the publick, to vindicate, by the authority of the greatest authour of his age, that respectable body of men, the Booksellers of London, from vulgar reflections, as if their profits were exorbitant", the less overawed reader might ask whether Johnson's own phrase in his second paragraph "I have said nothing" may not apply to the whole letter. A simple account of the ways of distributing books and of the margins obtained by the agent, wholesaler and bookseller, while valuable for many purposes, proves nothing regarding the nature of the profit earned even when the margins appear to be justified by such illustrative expressions as "the certainty of long credit", "trusting a year" and "debts somewhat bad" and when the total spread and particular allocation of costs are considered fair by no less a person than Dr. Johnson.

This volume is also confined to a recital of facts on the methods and gross margins of distribution, and while covering many more commodities than did Dr. Johnson is not, unfortunately, enlivened by his phrases. And similarly, as information on distributors' operating expenses and net profits and on the nature of consumer demand was not available, the material presented here can only be regarded as first statements of fact and cannot, by itself, be either a "vulgar reflection on" or a "vindication of" the producers, wholesalers and retailers engaged in the distribution of these goods.

For this reason, and this reason only, polemics, political and economic, are absent from this volume. This is also one of the reasons for the cautionary note which appears in the discussion of the estimates that have been made. But polemics will and should follow when the complementary data on costs and profits are available, as the efficiency of distribution is becoming an increasingly important factor both for the wellbeing of the nation and in our everyday lives.

At the same time, while not claiming with Boswell that this approach provides a full picture of the economics of distribution, I think sufficient material has been presented to enable producers and distributors to undertake a fair measure of self-criticism, to encourage specific enquiries into aspects of methods and costs, and to permit the drawing up of plans for further essential research.

Sir Henry Clay in his Foreword has thanked the very many individuals and associations who have co-operated to make an enquiry on this scale possible. I feel I must add my thanks to them for their courtesy, assistance and willingness to answer innumerable questions. I am particularly grateful to Mr. Hugh Weeks who was closely concerned with the designing of the enquiry, and should also like to acknowledge the considerable help given by the Advisory Committee in indicating the main lines of enquiry and, individually, by direct assistance in very many ways.

Mrs. Margaret Maccoll and Mr. G. L. Levett who assisted me are responsible for a number of the individual case studies. In this they showed themselves resourceful both in obtaining information and in piecing together the jigsaw to construct the whole picture. Further, Mrs. Maccoll was extremely helpful in the final stages of collating the mass of information obtained and in preparing the text. I should like also to thank Mr. R. Silverman who worked directly on the enquiry for some time and also gave us the benefit of his experience on the Advertising Enquiry undertaken by the Institute. Similarly Mr. D. A. Rowe of the National Income and Expenditure Enquiry was unfailingly helpful in his suggestions on the difficult territory of consumers' expenditure.

Finally my thanks are due to Miss H. M. Rogers, Librarian at the Institute, for her painstaking work on the proofs and in preparing the Index, and to Mrs. F. S. Stone, who, both as a member of the Advisory Committee and as Secretary of the Institute, was a real source of encouragement and advice throughout the whole period of the enquiry.

JAMES B. JEFFERYS

National Institute of Economic and Social Research

October 1949

CONTENTS

CHARTS

Charts I, III, IV and VI are available in colour for download from www.cambridge.org/9781107602748

TABLES

INTRODUCTION

THE SCOPE OF THE ENQUIRY AND THE METHODS OF RESEARCH

The aim of this study and the general limitations to which it is subject have been discussed in the Preface. But before proceeding further some description is necessary of the scope of the enquiry and, particularly, of the ways in which the information has been obtained and of the methods used in its presentation. As little or no published material exists on most of the aspects of distribution discussed in this study the methods used in the research have a considerable bearing on the reliability of the estimates made and the uses to which they can be put.

1. THE ENQUIRY LIMITED TO CONSUMER GOODS

The enquiry has been confined to the distribution of those consumer goods in their finished or near-finished state which were purchased by the private consumer in the United Kingdom in 1938. It does not cover purchases by industrial and trade users, by service trades, and by Government departments and institutions. It does not cover exports, or the methods used and costs incurred in distributing raw materials and semi-finished consumer goods.

The process of distribution has been considered to have started at the point at which the commodity reached the state in which it would finally be purchased by the private consumer; in other words the chocolates in their box, the soup in its can, the dress when made up or the furniture when polished or painted. The distribution of imported goods has been considered from their point of landing in the United Kingdom. Therefore no discussion has been attempted, for example, of the processes and costs involved in the distribution of cotton goods before reaching the maker-up or of the various markets, auctions and intermediaries through which imported fruit passed before reaching the United Kingdom. These definitions and exclusions, which in some instances have been rather arbitrary, for example the consideration of tea from the stage where it left the packers rather than from the point of landing in the United Kingdom, have been made solely in order to facilitate comparisons between commodities and to keep this particular research within manageable limits. An analysis of the methods and costs of distributing raw materials and semi-finished goods and the goods purchased by caterers or the on-costs represented by insurance and shipping, however, must form a part of any complete study of distribution.

Method of treatment of groups of commodities

The first stage of the enquiry consisted of obtaining information on individual consumer goods, the case studies setting out this information forming Part II of the volume. All goods could not be covered, but an effort was made to make the enquiry as fully representative of the private consumer's shopping list as possible, and in all approximately nine-tenths of estimated consumers' expenditure in 1938 has been included. This estimate, and a list of the main goods excluded owing to the difficulty of obtaining information or the inability of a particular trade to co-operate with the enquiry, are discussed later in the chapter. But it must be made clear that this somewhat ambitious coverage has only been made possible by dividing the consumers' expenditure up into general groups of goods and discussing the methods and costs of distribution of these groups as though they related to a single commodity or group of homogeneous commodities.

For example the estimates relating to men's outerwear, furniture, and pottery and glassware have been presented as if each of these groups of goods consisted of a number of homogeneous units. But in practice each of these commodities consists of a very large number of individual products, that is the many different types and qualities of men's suits, jackets and overcoats, the many different articles of furniture, and the various grades and forms of pottery and glass, and the methods and costs of distribution of each of these individual products making up the group vary. The ideal treatment of this problem would involve a discussion of every individual product, but such an undertaking would of course be impracticable. To reduce the discussion to manageable proportions the individual products have been grouped under general commodity headings and these groups have been described, perhaps somewhat loosely, as 'commodities' or 'groups of commodities'. These 'commodities' consist of a number of individual products which have certain characteristics in common though the degree of homogeneity varies between the different commodity groups discussed.

Similar conditions of production, methods of distribution and types of retail outlet have been the main considerations in mind when grouping individual products under a general commodity heading and these headings, such as bread and cakes, carpets, and radios and radiograms, correspond for the most part with the commodities enumerated in production and sales statistics and with the trades covered by associations of producers, wholesalers and retailers. In the individual case studies of commodities some indication has been given, where usable information was available, of the varied methods and costs of distribution of individual products or groups of products within the general commodity grouping. For example some information is given on the differences in margins between tobacco and cigarettes and in the methods of distribution of beauty preparations in different price ranges. But the estimates relating to the commodity as a whole are approximations which attempt to allow for and assess the particular variations of the products making up the group. The resulting figures therefore refer to somewhat hypothetical commodities, for example leather footwear, rather than to the constituent products of the group, that is men's boots and shoes in certain price ranges, women's fashion shoes, slippers, children's shoes and so on. In this case while, with the exception of women's fashion shoes, the retail margins do not vary greatly between one product and another, there are wide differences in the methods of distribution, in the proportion of each product handled by wholesalers and particularly in the distribution costs incurred by producers. In making the estimates relating to leather footwear as a commodity, an attempt has been made, as far as the information permitted, to take these variations into account.

The degree of homogeneity of the products constituting the final commodity or commodity groups chosen for study varies and the selection of the groups was influenced partly by the consumers' expenditure on individual products or groups of products but mainly by the availability of information on the particular products. A separate case study, for example, has been prepared on imported canned fruit and vegetables but not on imported cigars as the total consumers' expenditure on the latter hardly warranted a detailed analysis. On the other hand the imported canned fruit and vegetables group is not particularly homogeneous and, if the information had been available, could well have been split up into separate studies according to different countries of origin, as this influenced the methods of distribution, price ranges and products. The lack of homogeneity of the products making up a general commodity group is most conspicuous in the fresh fruit and vegetables group. This group, and to a lesser extent some of the other primary product groups, would really require a volume on its own to give the full details of the methods and costs of distribution of each of the individual products making up the group. The difficulty of obtaining in a reasonable time all the necessary information, and the limitations of space, made a summary of the main practices and features of the group as a whole the only practicable method of treatment.

The breakdown of total consumer purchases into commodity groups and the treatment of these groups as single commodities has therefore been influenced by the desire to split up the groups into sub-groups of homogeneous products on the one hand and by the limitations of information, of time and of space on the other. The result in the case of each commodity is a compromise, though a more satisfactory compromise in some cases, say, general service electric light lamps or jam and marmalade, than in others, say, general drapery goods or leather goods. The fact that compromise was necessary, that the commodities considered do not consist of entirely homogeneous units each distributed in the same way and with the same costs of distribution, must limit the use that can be made of the estimates as reflecting the distributive characteristics of an individual product in a commodity group. Where use has been made of the estimates in this way, for example in order to suggest factors influencing the methods of distribution, the approach is a tentative one and intended more to illustrate a method that can be used when fuller data are available than to draw hard and fast conclusions. The data, of course, will never be complete; every individual unit of a commodity, even in the case of apparently homogeneous commodities such as eggs, differs from the next though it may have the same name and production conditions, and a grouping of products which by some standards can be called heterogeneous is inevitable. But in the collection of data the aim must always be to provide as complete a breakdown of the groups as possible.

2. THE QUESTIONS ASKED AND THE SOURCES OF INFORMATION

The methods of distribution and the costs of distribution of each commodity or group of commodities in the sense discussed above formed the focal points of the enquiry. The definitions of the terms used and the classifications of the data adopted are discussed in some detail in the following chapters. Here it is only necessary to indicate that the methods of distribution relate to the proportions passing through different channels from the producer or port to the consumer and to the proportions of total sales undertaken by different types of retail outlet. The costs of distribution refer to the spread between the producers' selling price less their distribution expenses, or, in the case of imported goods, landed cost and the price paid by the consumer. In the case of goods sold under a hire purchase agreement or a similar system a notional retail price excluding the additional cost of hire purchase has been used. The total distribution costs of each commodity suggested, therefore, include producers' distribution costs and wholesalers' and retailers' gross realized margins.

The case studies and the estimates are based on information obtained mainly from individual producers, importers, wholesalers and retailers, their trade associations, market research and advertising organizations and Government departments. No attempt was made to undertake a full or sample survey, in the statistical sense, of the various firms engaged in the distribution of a particular commodity. A full survey was an impossibility and a sample could hardly be assessed until the universe was known. The approach was rather through trade associations and the larger firms engaged in the particular trade. These organizations were asked to assist and advise as to the most productive lines of research. Practically all the trade associations and leading manufacturers, wholesalers and retailing organizations handling the commodities studied were consulted except where information already available made further enquiry unnecessary. Part of the enquiry was conducted by personal interview, part by correspondence and in some instances a questionnaire was used either directly or with the co-operation of a trade association.

Considerable problems of assessment and analysis of the information obtained presented themselves. As was to be expected the passing of ten years was hardly sufficient time to make the enquiry seem only of academic and historical interest, and varying responses were met with in different trades. By some, questions as to what happened in 1938 were received with the same shocked reproaches as would the proposed disinterment of a deceased relative, by others 1938 was regarded as the pinnacle of a free economy and a wealth of detail was provided to illustrate the smooth functioning of the trade in those days. As far as possible allowance was made for the gloomy or enthusiastic perspectives which unconsciously tended to colour replies. In practically all trades the producers, wholesalers and retailers pursued varying selling, pricing and mark-up policies. In some, owing to the relatively small number of producers or retail outlets, these variations appear to have been small, but in many others widely differing practices were reported and assessments had to be made of the prevalence of particular policies based on the proportions of total output or of wholesale and retail trade estimated to have been undertaken by various firms and types of firm.

Presentation and meaning of the estimates

The estimates presented in the case studies have in almost all instances been given in the form of a range, with an upper and lower limit. For example in the discussion of the channels of distribution the estimates have been given as percentage ranges of total sales, viz. from producer to wholesaler and then to retailer, 60–70%, from producer direct to retailer, 30–40%. When discussing margins or costs of distribution a range has also been used, viz. retailers' margins are estimated at 30–33% on sales. These ranges are intended to indicate that on the basis of the information obtained and by careful checking it would appear unlikely but not impossible that the actual figure fell outside the range or limits. It would be misleading to attempt to present the 'unlikelihood' in terms of statistical probability as the data have not been obtained in a form that would warrant such an excursion. But it can be said in a general way that the objective was not to make the limits of the range so wide as to give a virtual certainty of the truth lying within them; it was rather to keep them narrow enough to make the results reasonably useful at the risk that some answers will really lie outside the limits shown. In view of the difficulty of the problem this is, indeed, bound to be the case in some instances though it is naturally impossible to say which.

3. THE RELIABILITY OF THE ESTIMATES

Much of the information was provided in confidence, and therefore a list of the firms, associations and individuals assisting the enquiry cannot be given. In arriving at the estimates some assistance has been obtained from unpublished data in the possession of market research and advertising organizations. The number of firms or associations providing information on individual commodities would be confusing as a test of the reliability of the data as in some instances one organization because of its size or concern with marketing was in a position to provide a more complete picture of the practices in a trade than some twenty-five firms and trade associations in another. Some suggestions as to the character of the different estimates can, however, be made.

Estimates of the methods of distribution

First in regard to the methods of distribution. This information was obtained for the most part from producers and importers and in some cases from their trade associations. The individual wholesaler was not, of course, in a position to say what proportion of the total trade in a given commodity he handled, though in one or two cases a strong wholesalers' trade association was in a position to give a general estimate of the total turnover of its members which could then be checked against the estimates of the proportions of goods passing through the various channels that had been suggested by the producers. Individual retailers in many cases were able to provide figures relating to their method of purchase, that is the proportion purchased, for example, from producer, wholesaler or agent, but apart from those provided by large national multiple organizations no use could be made of the figures provided by individual retailers except as background information. In each instance the aim has been to present a picture of the main channels, the less significant variations being omitted.

The reliability of the estimates tends to vary with the degree of concentration of production. In those instances where a few firms dominate the trade and where they co-operated with the enquiry, the possible error in the estimates is unlikely to be great, but in those cases where the bulk of the output was produced by a large number of small scale units the limits given are wider apart and even then the truth may lie outside the limits. In some instances of small scale production the usual method of distribution was through wholesalers and where the wholesalers were few in number or well organized some check was possible on the estimated proportions passing through wholesalers.

The sales by producers direct to consumers presented a particularly difficult problem of assessment. Such sales occurred in practically every trade and are largely made by the small firms about which little is known. While in the trades where the practice was widespread some estimates could, after considerable enquiry, be made of its significance, in those trades where the proportion appeared to be of the order of less than 5% of total sales no closer estimates have been attempted.

The estimates of the methods of distribution for each commodity and for the goods as a whole may understate the proportions passing through wholesalers and the proportions sold direct to the consumer, and consequently overstate the proportions passing from producers direct to retailers. This bias, if it exists, will have arisen from the tendency to consult the larger firms and the ability of the larger firms to provide far more information on methods than the smaller ones. The larger producers tended to sell direct and the larger retailers to purchase direct to a greater extent than did the smaller producers and retailers, who more frequently traded through wholesalers. In making the estimates in each case some allowance for this bias has been made but the possibility of underestimating the extent of wholesale trading remains. The underestimate of direct to consumer trading would arise from the difficulties, mentioned above, of obtaining reliable information from the small producers who in many cases undertook such sales.

Estimates of distribution costs

The reliability of the estimates made of the distribution costs incurred by producers is particularly difficult to assess. While the estimates are based in almost all cases on the data supplied by producers there must remain doubts as to their accuracy. Among the obstacles are the variety of definitions in use as to what constitutes these costs, the reluctance of some firms to provide a detailed breakdown of their expenditure, and the weakness of the methods of cross-checking the data obtained. Considerable care was taken to ensure as far as possible that the costs were comparable in all cases and the fullest use was made of the statistics available on freight and transport costs and advertising expenditure by producers, but the estimates of producers' costs are probably the least satisfactory of the cost estimates.

The estimates of wholesalers' and retailers' margins could be checked in some measure by asking similar questions at different stages in the chain of distribution. In the case of price-maintained articles fairly full information was available on the range of margins and discounts allowed and some estimates of averages within these ranges could be made, though the extent of 'price cutting' of these goods which resulted in both wholesalers and retailers earning lower gross margins was sometimes difficult to assess. In the case of non-price-maintained commodities, while a number of price lists and trade catalogues were available, the estimates had to be based on the experience of a large number of different distributors. The aim was to obtain estimates of the limits within which the average gross margin on a particular commodity or group lay. The approach by commodity rather than by trade presented a problem here inasmuch as a gross margin on total turnover or on the turnover of a department rather than a margin on particular commodities is the concept more familiar to wholesalers and retailers. But for the most part it has been possible to present a range, in the sense discussed above, of gross margins which fitted the experience of the trade associations and individual firms consulted. In many trades the necessities of price control during the war had led to a close examination and costing of pre-war experience, and these, when made available, threw some light on average pre-war margins.

In suggesting the range of gross margins for particular commodities an attempt has been made to allow for mark-downs and stock losses, or in other words the gross margin is presented as a gross realized margin. The incidence of mark-downs and losses varied between trades and—more than mark-ups—between individual distributive undertakings. This factor added to the difficulty of assessment, and for those commodities, for example fruit and vegetables, millinery and fish, where mark-downs or stock losses were of considerable importance, the estimates made of the average gross margins are probably less accurate than those made in respect of other commodities where such practices were insignificant. In the case of many home-produced primary foodstuffs and imported goods the average spread between the farmer's or grower's price or the landed value at the port and the price paid by the retailer proved very difficult to determine. The fluctuations in the prices of these commodities while they were in the course of being distributed, the practice of purchasing against a price rise and sometimes being forced to sell on a falling market, the number of intermediaries either handling or buying and selling these goods at the early stages of distribution, and the practice in some instances of stating margins as a money sum related to weight rather than as a percentage figure related to selling price combined to obscure the average gross margins earned by different distributors. Every effort has been made to allow for the influence of these factors and to assess average realized margins, but there will undoubtedly be a greater margin of error in the estimates relating to these goods than in those relating to home-manufactured goods.

Estimates of sales by different types of outlet

The estimates of the proportion of sales made by different types of retail outlet are based on information obtained from producers and market research and retailing organizations. As may be expected the information on the sales by co-operatives, department stores and multiple organizations was more plentiful than that relating to the sales of unit or independent retailers and the estimates of the proportion of total sales undertaken by the latter tend to be in a number of cases in the nature of residual estimates. The published and unpublished data on the operation of rationing schemes in the early war period provided a check in some cases on the estimates made of sales by different types of outlet. Population changes and other war-time influences had to be allowed for, but where comparisons were practicable there was a fair measure of agreement between the two sets of figures.

4. THE METHODS OF SUMMARIZING THE INFORMATION GIVEN IN THE CASE STUDIES

In Part I of the volume the information in the case studies relating to commodities and commodity groups has been brought together. To do this some assumptions have had to be made in regard to the separate estimates and a comment on the methods of presentation used and the assumptions made may be of use in interpreting the results.

The ranges of the estimated methods and costs of distribution and of the proportions sold by different types of outlet given in the case studies are, as suggested above, in the form of limits within which it is thought that the actual figure falls. But the limits are not so wide as virtually to exclude the possibility of the figure falling outside. In presenting the summary figures in Part I the middle point of the ranges given in the case studies has been used. This assumption would appear to be justified by the information to hand, but the possibility of error is somewhat greater than in the individual case studies in that in the first instance the suggestion is made that the truth probably lies somewhere within a range, whereas in the second instance the suggestion is made that it is the middle point of the range; and there is also the possibility that the truth may lie outside the range. Further the estimates relating to each commodity were made independently and there is no reason for assuming that the possible error made in relation to one commodity will, when the results are summed, be compensated by errors made in relation to other commodities. Indeed the similarity of the methods used to collect the data suggest, as in the case of sales through wholesalers discussed above, that a bias in one estimate may be paralleled by a similar bias in all estimates. All that can be said is that the assumptions made are based on the information obtained and that allowance has been made as far as possible for any bias that may have arisen from the methods of research used.

The summaries of the estimates of the total costs of distribution for each commodity which are given at the end of the case studies and which are discussed in Part I are based on the information given in the case studies but need a special note of interpretation. Again where the range, in the sense discussed above, of margins, discounts or bonuses has been given, the middle point of this range has normally been used in the calculations of total costs, but there are some exceptions to this. In the course of the enquiry a great deal of information was obtained relating to the practices of individual producers, wholesalers and retailers in regard to selling policies, mark-ups, settlement discounts and special discounts. Where these practices appear to have general application and where it was possible to summarize their operation in a reasonable space, this has been done in the case studies. In other cases where such practices influenced only a sector of the trade or could not be easily summarized, the information has not been presented in the case studies but has been used, where applicable, in addition to that already given, in calculating the total costs of distribution. The definitions used to break down the total costs into manufacturers', wholesalers' and retailers' costs are given in detail in the appropriate chapter.

5. THE ESTIMATES OF CONSUMERS' EXPENDITURE

The estimates of consumers' expenditure on the various commodities and groups of commodities are based in the main on the parallel research undertaken by the National Institute, *Consumers' Expenditure in the United Kingdom, 1920–1938*. In some cases estimates made by manufacturers and trade associations or calculations based on published figures of pre-war output and price levels have been used. An attempt has been made in arriving at the final estimates to exclude sales of second-hand goods, free gifts, purchases by employees on special terms and all purchases by trade and industrial users, by the catering trades, by institutions, schools and other public bodies and by Government departments. The value of the products consumed by self-suppliers, such as farmers, has also been excluded. These exclusions can only be made very approximately in some cases, for example stationery, flour confectionery and eggs, and the final figures of the private consumer's expenditure on individual commodities and groups of commodities, and the estimate of consumers' expenditure as a whole, must be regarded as subject to error. This error is, however, undoubtedly greater in the case of some commodities than in others. For example in those trades where production is very diversified and sales to trade users and public bodies at the manufacturing, wholesaling and retailing stages are common, as happens in proprietary and non-proprietary medicines and drugs, and in stationery, the error in the estimate of the private consumers' expenditure is likely to be greater than in the case of the estimates of the sales of newspapers, sewing machines or tobacco and cigarettes.

Proportion of total consumers' expenditure included in the enquiry and the commodities omitted

The total expenditure by the private consumer on the commodities and commodity groups covered in the enquiry is estimated at £2,582 millions. This could be compared with the £2,800 millions as the estimated total private expenditure in 1938 on all consumer goods, apart from services, given in the *National Income and Expenditure of the United Kingdom, 1946 to 1948* (Cmd. 7649).[1] Just over 90%, therefore, of the private consumers' expenditure on commodities and commodity groups in 1938 is estimated to have been covered in this enquiry.

The most important commodities on which no information was

[1] The comparison is made with the estimates given in Appendix I, Table 20, p. 26, Personal Expenditure on Consumers' Goods and Services at Current Market Prices. In order to make a reasonably accurate comparison the expenditure by private consumers on certain items included in the National Income White Paper estimates but which represent the purchase of services rather than commodities or which do not enter into normal retail trade have been excluded. For example in Group 1, *Food*, pork, bacon and egg self-suppliers have been excluded, in Group 5, *Fuel and Light*, miners' coal, electricity and gas and some firewood, in Group 6, *Durable Household Goods*, the sales of furniture, pottery and hollow-ware to the catering trades, in Group 8, *Clothing*, the costs of making-up consumers' own materials, in Group 9, *Books, Newspapers and Magazines*, the sale of educational and technical books to schools, in Group 10, *Private Motoring*, the cost of licences, upkeep and dealers' margins on second-hand cars, and in Group 15, *Other Goods*, dog and gun licences. Owing to the absence of detailed information on the expenditure in most of these instances the exclusions and the residual figures are subject to error. The commodities have been taken in both cases at their retail value and additional expenses due to purchasing under a hire purchase or similar system have been excluded.

obtained, for the various reasons given above, are:

- Sausages
- Meat pies
- Ice cream
- Soft drinks
- Certain manufactured foods such as custard powder
- Potato crisps
- Jellies and blancmanges
- Meat extracts and essences
- Suet
- Lard
- Cream
- Cake and bun mixtures
- Nuts
- Firewood
- Garden seeds
- Flowers
- Pianos
- Musical instruments
- Gramophone records
- Electrical fittings
- Domestic heating and cooking appliances other than small electric fires and toasters
- Certain household cleaning materials
- Retail bespoke clothing and footwear
- Weekly newspapers and trade journals
- Educational and technical books
- Bicycles and cycle accessories
- Certain manufactured toilet and fancy goods

The variations in the extent of the coverage in this enquiry compared with the estimates in the National Income White Paper (Cmd. 7649) are shown for broad commodity groups in the following Table.

Table 1. *Consumers' expenditure on main commodity classes included in the enquiry compared with the estimates of consumers' expenditure in the National Income White Paper (Cmd. 7649)*[1]

National Income White Paper commodity groups	Approximate proportion of National Income White Paper expenditure represented by goods covered in the enquiry
	%
Food, excluding sales in catering establishments	89
Alcoholic beverages	100
Tobacco and cigarettes	100
Household fuel	93
Durable household goods	85
Other household goods	86
Clothing and footwear	97
Books, newspapers and magazines	88
Private motoring	99
Other goods	65

[1] Owing to the difficulty of determining from the figures given in the National Income White Paper the exact expenditure on particular commodities, the goods included in particular commodity groups, and the exclusions to be made to render comparable the two sets of figures, these estimates can only be very approximate.

The variations in the degree of coverage between the main commodity groups are important when an attempt is made to construct from the evidence obtained in this study a picture of the distribution of all consumer goods. The fact, for example, that the coverage in the miscellaneous group of 'other goods' is relatively low has a bearing on the estimated proportions of all goods shown later to have been handled by wholesalers and sold by variety chain stores, inasmuch as these goods were handled by both wholesalers and variety chain stores to a greater extent than was the case in several other groups. And to make estimates relating to total sales of consumer goods and not merely the nine-tenths covered in this enquiry appropriate estimates have to be made for the missing commodity groups. In the final chapter of Part I where an attempt is made to give estimates relating to the total sales of consumer goods the appropriate adjustments are discussed. All estimates of the expenditure on goods subject to duty include the tax or duty.

These comments have attempted to give a general picture of the methods of research used in this enquiry and of the reliability of the estimates made. In the following chapters additional notes are given explaining the treatment of particular items. When the estimates and information given in this volume are considered it is hoped that their approximate nature and the broad aim of the enquiry will be borne in mind and that the estimates will not be used to decide some issue of detail or theory which by their nature they are unfitted to do.

PART I

THE METHODS, COSTS AND STRUCTURE OF DISTRIBUTION IN THE UNITED KINGDOM IN 1938

CHAPTER I

HOW THE GOODS WERE DISTRIBUTED

1. THE PROBLEM OF DEFINITION OF METHODS OF DISTRIBUTION

The three main ways of distributing consumer goods in their finished or near-finished state to the consumer can be described, simply, as follows: the manufacturer, grower or importer can sell directly to the consumer; the producer or importer can sell to a retail organization which sells the commodities to the consumer; or the producer or importer can sell to an intermediary who in turn re-sells to a retailer who sells to the consumer. But while the bulk of the commodities are distributed in one or other of these ways, there remain a proportion of the goods which pass through many variations of these channels, and these methods prove difficult to classify. In some instances the chain is lengthened by sales between similar types of organization such as producer-to-producer sales or, more commonly, wholesaler-to-wholesaler sales. In other instances while the methods of distribution used appear at first sight to correspond with one or other of the main channels suggested above, closer inspection shows that the actual functions undertaken by the organizations handling the commodities make it difficult to class them simply as producers, intermediaries or retailers. For example there are cases where the retailers do not actually handle and sell the commodities but introduce customers to the manufacturer, who does the selling while crediting the retailer with a commission, or where intermediaries sell on behalf of producers to wholesalers without taking either physical or financial possession of the goods being sold. The varied methods used to classify that proportion of the goods which do not readily fall under general headings have usually limited the value of comparisons which have been made between the distribution of different commodities.

Once the point of departure of the study has been fixed and the three main channels determined and defined, the type of problem faced is, in what category should the sales of finished goods by one manufacturer to a second manufacturer who in turn re-sells to a wholesaler or a retailer—as happens in the furniture and some branches of the clothing trades in the United Kingdom—be placed? In what category should sales by manufacturers to wholesale organizations controlled by retail units—as happens in the hardware and chemist trade—be placed? In what category should the sales of products in retail shops owned by the manufacturers of the goods—as happens in the footwear and men's clothing trades—be placed? In what category should goods imported directly from abroad by retail organizations—as happens in the fruit and vegetable and watch and clock trade—be placed? These are a few of the problems and to them may be added the varied and conflicting definitions and functions of wholesalers, factors, commission buyers and sellers, agents and higglers, to mention only the more common terms, and the fact that many of these intermediary organizations perform one function in relation to one consignment, say commission selling, and an entirely different function, say wholesaling, in relation to another consignment of the same goods and on the same day. Also there is the further problem of the treatment of the purchases, production and sales of co-operative wholesale societies.

Ideally a description of distribution processes should reveal these less defined and more intricate paths as well as the main highways. But in any enquiry—a full Census of Distribution or a general survey such as this—the tools of analysis are rarely sufficiently developed to capture all the detail, and the character of the finished study has to be dictated by its general purpose, the use to which the results are to be put and by the tools available.

The criteria adopted in this study in order to introduce some uniformity into the treatment of the flourishing variety of methods of distribution stress the factors of the physical movement of the goods and the transfer of ownership from one party to another. Attention has been focussed on the three main methods of distribution and in most instances it has been possible, by using these criteria, to allocate the proportion of goods passing through other types of channels to one or other of the three main channels. Where warranted by the volume of sales, however, some indication has been given of the use of alternatives to the three main channels.

Direct to consumer sales

All goods sold directly to the consumer by the grower or produce whether ex-factory or ex-farm, through a producer/retailer organization or by a manufacturers' mail order organization, have been classed as sales direct to the consumer. Sales by manufacturer-controlled multiple retail outlets have, however, been treated as sales to retailers as the retail organization often had a separate legal identity and further in most instances sold products in addition to those manufactured by the parent firm. Some indication of the proportion of total sales of a commodity represented by the output of concerns linked with retailers has been given.

Direct to retailer sales

Goods which changed hands financially and physically only once between the producer or the port and the final consumer have been defined as sales from producer direct to retailer. For example, sales by producers to multiple organizations, whether to the wholesaling company of a retail multiple firm or by split deliveries to individual shops, have been classed as sales direct to retailer; as have sales by producers or importers through agents, brokers or 'brass plate' merchants to retailers, as these brokers, agents and merchants were rarely responsible for the physical movement of the goods, nor did they take full financial ownership. Sales to retailers by importer/wholesalers, that is firms which combined the functions of importing and of stockholding, breaking bulk and distributing to retail, have been classed as sales direct to retailers since the goods only changed hands once, as have sales by importers to retailers and goods purchased abroad by retailers. There is a case for including the sales of goods purchased abroad by retailers as sales direct to the consumer if ownership at the time of entry into the United Kingdom is taken as the criterion, and some indication of the extent of such purchases has been given to enable the alternative definition to be used.

The sales by co-operative wholesale societies to the retail societies, irrespective of whether these goods were produced in co-operative manufacturing establishments or purchased from private manufacturers, have been listed as sales direct to retailer. This classification is not very satisfactory as it conceals the different functions performed by the co-operative wholesale societies in relation to different types of goods handled. Where the goods are produced by the productive establishments connected with the wholesale society the sales to retail societies are clearly direct to retail sales. In other instances the goods are purchased from outside manufacturers and the wholesale societies perform the normal wholesaling function of holding stock, breaking bulk and delivering to retail societies. But there are other instances where the goods are merely invoiced through the wholesale societies and actually pass direct from the manufacturers to the retail society. The information obtained did not, however, allow of separate treatment of these different methods in relation to individual commodities and all the goods sold by wholesale societies to retail societies have been classified in the same manner, as sales direct to retailer. In a later chapter a further examination of co-operative trading is attempted.

Sales through wholesalers

Goods which changed hands physically and financially twice between the producer or the port and the final consumer have been defined as goods passing from producer to wholesaler and then to retailer. The term 'wholesaler' has been used in every case to describe the intermediary to avoid the confusion entailed in using varying terms for each commodity. 'Changing hands physically and financially' relates to transactions between two independent parties. Transactions between producers and their linked or controlled wholesaling organization, for example, are not considered as wholesaling transactions. Similarly transactions between producers and a wholesaling organization linked with or controlled by a retailing organization (other than wholesaler/retailers) are not classed as wholesaling but as direct to retailer transactions. The operations of wholesaler/retailers, who are prominent in trades such as tobacco and confectionery, have been divided as far as possible and classed as direct to retailer sales where the goods were purchased from a manufacturer and sold by the retail section of the organization and as goods passing from manufacturer to wholesaler to retailer where they are sold to other retailers. Where goods changed hands physically and financially three times or more between the producer or port and the final consumer, these sales have been classed as sales through wholesalers, though some indication is given in the case studies of the extent of the practice in relation to particular commodities.

Naturally the process of fitting the evidence into the somewhat Procrustean bed prepared above has called for a measure of ingenuity though not, it is hoped, a disregard of fact. But the advantages of using the classification suggested here are that it does make possible a comparison of the methods of distribution of different commodities and also stresses the rôle played by the independent wholesaler, thus drawing a distinction between the wholesaling function when performed by a manufacturing or multiple organization or co-operative society and when performed by an independent wholesaling firm. Further, the need to give precise definitions of wholesaler, agent, broker, factor, merchant or dealer in each trade, a task of no mean magnitude, has been by-passed.[1] The terms themselves are used according to the practice in the particular trade, but organizations are classed as intermediaries between producer and retailer only in those cases where they are responsible for both the physical movement and ownership of the particular goods.

2. ESTIMATES OF THE USE OF THE DIFFERENT CHANNELS OF DISTRIBUTION

Using these principles[2] to classify the information obtained on the methods of distribution, the results of the enquiry are shown in the following Chart and Tables. The estimates relating to the individual commodities and commodity groups studied are set out in Chart I. The commodities have been arranged in the order of importance of the proportion passing from manufacturer, grower or port to wholesaler and then to retailer. In each instance the estimates are subject to error and the Chart is intended to illustrate the relative magnitude of the different methods of distribution with respect to individual commodities rather than to suggest the exact proportions flowing through each channel in 1938.

[1] While some general definitions have to be made, there is a strong case for avoiding detailed definitions in the distributive trade until the Census of Distribution throws some light on the statistical background into which the definitions will have to fit. Terms accepted in particular trades through long usage have quite often lost their original meaning, but until a revised definition can be prepared on the basis of ascertained fact, attempts to re-write the definitions of these traditional terms would lead to interminable discussions with little prospect of reaching a satisfactory conclusion. This problem arises not only in connection with the definition of intermediaries in distribution but, as is shown later, in respect of concepts of outlets and distributive costs.

[2] The allocations of particular types of sale to each of the three main channels are given in the Glossary.

Notes to Chart I

In some instances the titles of the commodities and commodity groups have, for convenience, been shortened in this and later Charts. The individual case studies should be consulted for full information on the goods included under each heading.

The figures given of consumers' expenditure and of the proportions of sales passing through the different channels are only approximate and the middle points of an estimated range rounded to the nearest ·5 have been used to simplify presentation. No attempt has been made to illustrate those instances where the proportion of total sales of a commodity passing through a particular channel are estimated at less than 5%.

Explanations are given in the case studies of the classifications used in the case of particular commodities, but the following comments may be necessary here.

Chart I is available for download from
www.cambridge.org/9781107602748

Bread and flour confectionery:	The sales direct to consumers refer to the sales by bakers who baked and sold in their own shops. Only a negligible quantity of bread and cakes was sold by the baker to a wholesaler who re-sold to a retailer. The 'wholesale bakers' baked and made bread and cakes for sale in their own multiple shops or for sale to retailers and these sales have been classed as direct to retailer.
Meat—home-killed:	The proportion of meat passing through wholesalers relates only to sales of dead meat. Sales of livestock are excluded. Sales direct to retailer comprise sales of meat by retailers who did their own slaughtering, including multiple and co-operative concerns. An alternative classification would be to define the sales by wholesalers as sales direct from 'processor' to retailer, 46·5%, sales by unit retailers who did their own slaughtering as sales direct to consumer, 29·5%, and sales by multiple and co-operative concerns where they did their own slaughtering as sales direct to retailer, 24%.
Meat—imported:	Sales through wholesalers refer only to sales by importers to wholesalers or jobbers who were not linked in any way either with the importing companies or with retailing organizations. The bulk of imported meat passed from the importer/wholesaling companies direct to retailers.
Eggs, butter, poultry, home-produced:	Sales through wholesalers are taken to include sales by higglers and dealers to retailers where the former bought outright, but exclude sales by producers to retailers through agents acting on commission.
Tea and coffee:	The term wholesaler in these trades is often applied to the packers and blenders. Here the sales through wholesalers refer to sales by 'secondary' wholesalers who usually purchased from packers or blenders and re-sold to retailers.
On-licence sales:	The purchases by brewers of wines and spirits for sale in their own or tied houses have been classed as sales direct to retailer. So have sales of the brewers' own beer in tied houses.
Vacuum cleaners:	Only sales of cleaners direct to consumer by door-to-door salesmen have been classed as direct to consumer sales. Orders taken by salesmen which were fulfilled by retail dealers have been classed as sales to retailers.
Clothing:	Sales of retail bespoke wear, e.g. made-to-measure suits, are excluded. Sales by manufacturing multiple concerns through their own retail shops have, by definition, been classed as sales direct to retailer.
	Dress materials. Sales of dress materials by manufacturers or wholesalers to makers-up are by definition excluded.
Watches:	The sales direct to consumer consist largely of the sales of watches assembled by retailers.

Methods of distribution by trade groups

The methods of distribution used in different trades are shown, to some extent, in Table 2. In this Table the information relating to individual commodities has been aggregated to form 25 roughly distinct trade groups.

Table 2. *Estimated methods of distribution in 1938 of commodities, by trade groups*[1]

Trade groups[2]	Estimated consumers' expenditure £ million	Estimated proportions passing from manufacturer, grower or port: To wholesaler and then to retailer %	Direct to retailer %	Direct to consumer %
Fish	35·5	88	12	—
Fruit and vegetables	141·0	79	21	—
Newspapers and magazines	48·0	69	31	—
Chocolates and sweets	55·0	64	36	—
Poultry, game and rabbits	19·0	62	38	—
Furnishings	59·0	52	48	—
Cigarettes and tobacco	177·0	52	48	—
Women's and children's wear	239·0	51	49	—
Provisions	206·0	50	50	—
Chemists' goods	55·0	46	54	—
Motor trade	114·5	41	59	—
Men's and boys' wear	121·5	38	62	—
Coal	97·5	37	63	—
Stationery, pens, pencils, inks	17·5	35	65	—
Groceries	262·0	35	65	—
Footwear	68·0	31	69	—
Pottery and ironmongers' goods	45·0	30	70	—
Meat	180·0	29	71	—
Jewellers' goods	24·5	28	72	—
Electrical goods	28·0	25	75	—
Other specialities	37·5	23	77	—
Milk	86·5	22	58	20
Beer, wines and spirits	297·0	20	80	—
Furniture	63·5	17	78	5
Bread and flour confectionery	104·5	—	54	46

[1] — indicates less than 5%.

[2] Included in the general trade groups are the following commodities:

Furnishings:	Household textiles, furnishing fabrics, carpets, linoleum.
Provisions:	Bacon and ham, margarine, butter, eggs, cheese.
Chemists' goods:	Beauty preparations, perfumes and toilet waters, sanitary towels, razors and blades, dental preparations, tooth-brushes, proprietary and non-proprietary medicines and drugs, infant and invalid foods, contraceptives, photographic goods, toilet and shaving soap.
Motor trade:	Motor cars, motor cycles and parts, accessories, tyres and tubes (including cycle tyres and tubes), petrol, oil.
Men's and boys' and women's and children's wear:	All clothing studied. Retail bespoke wear is excluded.
Groceries and household stores:	All groceries studied and matches, kerosene, household soap and polishes, candles and nightlights.
Pottery and ironmongers' goods:	Pottery, glassware, hollow-ware, hardware, cutlery, brooms and brushes, paints, varnishes and distemper, wallpaper.
Meat:	Home-killed and imported.
Jewellers' goods:	Real and imitation jewellery, silver and electro-plate, watches and clocks.
Electrical goods:	Electric fires, kettles and appliances, lamps, vacuum cleaners, radios and radiograms.
Other specialities:	Books, toys, sports goods, leather goods, sewing machines, perambulators, portable typewriters.

Methods of distribution of all commodities

Finally, Table 3 shows the estimates for the three broad classes of commodities, food and drink, clothing and footwear, and a residual 'other goods' class, and also for all commodities included in the enquiry.

Table 3. *Estimated methods of distribution in 1938 of commodities by three main classes and of all commodities included in the enquiry*[1]

Commodity division[3]	Estimated consumers' expenditure	Estimated proportions passing from manufacturer, grower or port		
		To wholesaler and then to retailer	Direct to retailer	Direct to consumer
	£ million	%	%	%
Food and drink[2]	1,386·0	37	58	5
Clothing and footwear	429·0	44	56	—
Other goods	767·0	41	59	—
All commodities[2]	2,582·0	39–40	57–58	3

[1] — signifies less than 5%. These proportions are not shown separately for two groups but have been allowed for in calculating the aggregate for all goods.

[2] If on-licence sales of beer, wines and spirits are excluded the proportion of food

and drink distributed through wholesalers is 42%, that distributed direct to retailers 52%, and that to consumers 6%. The proportions of total goods are 42–43%, 53–55% and 3–4%.

[3] Food and drink:	This comprises groceries and provisions (the constituents of which are listed in notes to Table 2, page 21), meat, poultry, game and rabbits, fish, fruit and vegetables, chocolates and sweets, fresh milk, bread and flour confectionery, and on- and off-licence sales of beer, wines and spirits.
Clothing and footwear:	This comprises all men's and boys' and women's and children's clothing and footwear studied. In addition to apparel, this division includes haberdashery, dress materials and general drapers' goods, but not retail bespoke wear.
Other goods:	This comprises all other goods studied: newspapers and magazines, furnishings, furniture, chemists' goods, cigarettes and tobacco, motor trade, coal, stationery, inks, pens and pencils, pottery and ironmongers' goods, jewellers' goods, electrical goods and other specialities. For a further breakdown of these groups see page 21.

Limitations of the data

Tables 2 and 3 and Chart I show the general pattern of the methods of distribution of consumer goods in 1938, but in many ways more is concealed than revealed. The proportions of each commodity shown as passing through the various channels are estimated averages for all sales of the commodity and conceal the very wide differences existing between the practices of individual manufacturers. Some biscuit manufacturers, to take one of many examples, distributed the bulk of their output through wholesalers while others sold only to retailers. Secondly the division of the sales direct to retailers and direct to consumers as made above fails to show the extent of the sales of goods produced or imported by establishments or organizations linked with the large-scale retailers. The sales direct to the consumer include individual producer/retailer sales but not the sales of manufacturing multiple organizations or co-operative societies. Thirdly, the relationship between the wholesaler and the unit retailer is revealed neither by Tables 2 or 3 nor by Chart I. The proportion of the total sales and of the sales of individual commodities passing direct to retailers shown in Chart I tends to reflect the importance of the large-scale retailing organizations, such as multiple shops and co-operative and department stores, which themselves in many cases perform the wholesaling function, rather than the importance of the different methods of purchase by the unit retailer.[1] Fourthly, no indication is given of the extent to

[1] The term unit retailer is used in this study in the place of the more familiar 'independent retailer' as it avoids the semi-political connotation which the familiar

which goods passed through three or more intermediaries before reaching the consumer. A further breakdown of this overall pattern is necessary before the factors influencing the methods of distribution can be discussed.

Some information has been given in the individual case studies on the varying distributive practices of producers. As suggested above the use of very broad commodity groups, such as home-produced fruit and vegetables, has helped to conceal some of the variations in the methods of distribution of individual commodities and even when the study is narrowed to a more homogeneous group there are important variations in methods, as shown in the case of toilet and beauty preparations, where similar goods in different price ranges are distributed in different ways. The differences in the methods of distribution used, in the proportions sold direct to retailers and through wholesalers by individual producers of the same type of commodity and the reasons for these differences form some of the most interesting aspects of distribution, and a close examination of this problem would be of considerable value. The information obtained on this subject in this study, however, hardly permits such detailed analysis and full data on the variation in methods of distribution employed by producers and retailers in relation to a single commodity must await a complete census.

3. PRODUCER/RETAILER SALES AND SALES BY OUTLETS LINKED WITH PRODUCERS

The importance of the producer/retailer link can be shown by a re-definition of the channels of distribution, though it must be emphasized that the original definition tended to be determined by the nature of the information collected and the re-casting of the definitions may increase the margin of error.

In order to distinguish the goods which remained in the hands of a single integrated or semi-integrated organization from the start of production, assembly, planting, or entry into the United Kingdom until sold to the consumer, from the other goods which changed hands within the country, direct to consumer sales can be re-defined as follows: the sales by producer/retailers, by manufacturers of their own products direct to the public; the sales by multiple retail organizations and retail co-operative societies of goods produced by establishments linked with the retailing group or by co-operative wholesale and productive societies and federations; the sales by retailers—usually multiple and co-opera-

term tends to evoke and as it is, logically, the opposite of the term multiple retailer. Further, the familiar term, in many trades, hardly gives an accurate description of his rôle as his independence tends to be circumscribed.

tive organizations—of goods purchased abroad and imported by them. When this definition is adopted the pattern of distribution appears as follows:

Proportion of all commodities studied passing from manufacturer, grower or port:

	%
To wholesaler and then to retailer	38–42
Direct to retailer	40–46
Direct to consumer	16–18

The importance of integrated production and distribution in respect of individual commodities and groups is discussed later, but to avoid any misreading of these estimates, the effect on these figures of the inclusion of the sales of beer, wines and spirits in on-licences should be noted. Between four-fifths and nine-tenths of the beer and smaller proportions of wines and spirits sold through on-licences in 1938 are estimated to have been sold in 'tied' houses, that is retail outlets controlled directly or indirectly by the brewers of the beer, and these sales have been included above in the sales direct to the consumer. If all sales of beer, wines and spirits in on-licences are excluded from the estimates, the proportions of total sales passing through the three channels are:

	%
To wholesaler and then to retailer	40–45
Direct to retailer	43–48
Direct to consumer	11–13

4. THE METHODS OF DISTRIBUTION OF GOODS SOLD BY UNIT RETAILERS

To show the importance of the relationship between the wholesaler and the unit retailer in a manner that is free from the distortion caused by the inclusion of the purchases of large-scale retailing organizations, their sales have to be excluded. For this purpose the definitions of the different economic types of retail organizations and units adopted require some explanation.

Definitions of different types of retail outlet

Four main types have been distinguished—the multiple organization and shop, the co-operative society and store, the department store and the unit retailer or shop.

The terms co-operative society and store and unit retailer are generally accepted and require little further definition. All that need be said is that co-operative society or store has been taken to mean a society or federation linked with the main co-operative movement in the United Kingdom, and a unit retailer is a residual term covering all retailing organizations or units which are not by definition co-operative stores, department stores or multiple shops.[1]

The selection of workable definitions of department stores and multiple organizations, on the other hand, is no easy problem in the absence of reliable information on numbers, size groupings, methods of purchase and range of goods sold. Some definition is, however, necessary and here department stores are taken to mean shops or stores possessing five or more departments under one roof, each department being treated from an accounting point of view as a separate unit, and usually having some physical barrier, a door or a passageway, separating the departments selling different types of goods. The range of goods sold almost always includes clothing, furnishings and furniture or household hardware and hollow-ware.

Multiple firms are defined as organizations owning or controlling five or more retail branches. This definition is not particularly satisfactory. A multiple organization is generally conceived of as a firm possessing the finance, managerial staff and turnover to maintain a business with units in different localities and able to secure economies in retailing compared with the unit retailer either by the scale of the purchases made or by undertaking all or part of the wholesaling function. But the number of retailing units and turnover required to allow the operation of these factors varies from trade to trade and while some of the advantages and problems of multiple organization may be reached in, say, the pottery and glass trade with as few as five shops, in, say, the meat and footwear trade, similar problems and advantages would not be reached until the organization possessed fifteen or more shops. Again national multiple organizations, that is organizations with retailing units in several counties, are faced with very different problems and have a different influence in the distributive system to that of local multiple organizations confined to shops in two or three towns in one county. The most useful way to present information regarding the scale of retailing organizations would be in a series of steps, that is 2–5 shops, 5–10 shops, 10–25 shops, and so on. Again this degree of refinement will have to await a full census. In this study the information obtained only allowed the use of a simple dividing line of five shops between unit retailers on the one hand and multiple organizations on the other. Variety chain stores are classed as multiple organizations.

Estimates of the proportion of total sales of the various commodities

[1] Included under unit retailers, therefore, are stalls in market places, barrows, delivery vehicles and other means of retailing as well as fixed shops.

and groups of commodities made by the different economic types of retail outlet were obtained in the same manner as the estimates of the methods of distribution. Their significance and reliability are discussed in a later chapter and here they will only be used indirectly to throw some light on the channels of distribution of goods sold by unit retailers.

To examine the part played by the unit retailer, the purchases and sales of the other types of retail outlet, multiple, co-operative and department store organizations, have to be eliminated from the picture. If the purchases by these organizations from producers, importers and wholesalers and the sales of goods produced by manufacturers linked with these retailing organizations are subtracted from the estimates given above, the residual estimates, apart from the sales by producer/retailers and by producers direct to consumers, can be assumed to relate to the methods of purchase and sales of unit retailers. This subtraction can be made, on the basis of present information, only very approximately, partly because the estimated proportions of total sales made by the different types of outlet are only intended to provide a picture of the relative significance of each organization in retail trade and cannot be claimed to be close estimates of actual purchases and sales, and partly because little is known of the purchases by multiple, co-operative and department store organizations from wholesalers. The incidence of such practices varied widely between different types of commodity and with the different sizes of orders placed, but it would appear that in the case of few commodities did the purchases from wholesalers by multiple, co-operative and department store organizations—excluding the purchases of retail co-operative societies from co-operative wholesale societies—exceed 20% of their total purchases, and for all commodities the average was considerably lower.

Methods of distribution of goods sold by unit retailers by commodities and by trades

In the following Tables 4, 4A and 5 an attempt has been made to eliminate the sales by multiple, co-operative and department store organizations and to show the methods of distribution of the goods sold by unit retailers. The sales of unit producer/retailers who, by definition, did not purchase either from producers or wholesalers and the sales of manufacturers direct to the consumer by mail order, door-to-door sales or other direct means are excluded.

As the error in the estimates relating to individual commodities is likely to be great, the most satisfactory way of presentation appeared to be to group the commodities into ten main divisions showing the approximate proportion of purchases estimated to have been made from wholesalers and, by difference, the proportion purchased direct from producers or importers. This is done in Table 4 and within each division the commodities are listed in the order of the estimated proportion of purchases made from wholesalers.

Table 4. *Approximate proportions of commodities sold by unit retailers which were purchased from wholesalers in 1938*[1]

Proportion of sales of unit retailers represented by purchases from wholesalers	Commodity division[3]		
	Food and drink	Clothing	Other goods
%			
90 and over	Potatoes Syrup and treacle Cheese Unpackaged breakfast cereals Sugar Fish Health food beverages Butter Imported canned fruit, vegetables and fish Packaged breakfast cereals Infant and invalid foods	Haberdashery and general drapers' goods Millinery Gloves Dress materials Women's and children's underwear and nightwear Men's handkerchiefs, ties, scarves and braces Men's and boys' hosiery Corsets and brassières Women's and children's stockings and socks Men's hats and caps	London morning newspapers Sunday newspapers Magazines and periodicals Imitation jewellery Household textiles and soft furnishings Furnishing fabrics Carpets Sanitary towels Non-proprietary medicines and drugs Household polishes Matches Razors and blades
80–90	Wines—on-licence sales Canned milk Sauces, soups and salad creams Fruit and vegetables Spirits—off-licence sales Eggs Fresh milk	Rubber footwear	Toothbrushes Proprietary medicines and drugs

Proportion of sales of unit retailers represented by purchases from wholesalers	Commodity division[3]		
	Food and drink	Clothing	Other goods
% 70–80	Sweets Bacon and ham Poultry, game and rabbits Canned fruit, vegetables—home-produced Wines—off-licence sales	Furs and fur garments Leather footwear Women's and children's outerwear	Dental preparations Motor car parts and accessories
60–70	Chocolates Margarine Salt	Men's and boys' shirts, collars and pyjamas	Motor cars Motor cycle accessories Candles Toys
50–60	Cocoa Jam and marmalade Spirits—on-licence sales Coffee		Cigarettes Cigars and snuff Tobacco Contraceptives Cutlery Cycle and motor cycle tyres and tubes Hardware, hollow-ware and general ironmongery Stationery, pens, pencils and accessories Coal Brooms and brushes Electric light lamps
40–50	Tea Meat[2]	Men's and boys' outerwear	Beauty preparations Watches and clocks Perfumes and toilet waters Leather goods Pottery and glassware Paints, varnishes and distemper Motor car tyres and tubes

Proportion of sales of unit retailers represented by purchases from wholesalers	Commodity division[3]		
	Food and drink	Clothing	Other goods
% 30–40	Beer and cider—off-licence sales Self-raising flour		Household and toilet soap Linoleum Electric fires, kettles and appliances Vacuum cleaners Furniture
20–30	Biscuits		Books Motor oil Radios and radio-grams London evening newspapers Wallpaper Photographic goods Silver and electro-plate Motor cycles
10–20	Plain flour		Provincial daily newspapers Sports goods Real jewellery

[1] Petrol, bread, flour confectionery, kerosene, portable typewriters, on-licence sales of beer, wines and spirits, perambulators and sewing machines, have been omitted from the Table as the proportions of these goods passing through wholesalers were very small. See Chart I.

[2] This is a weighted figure including both home-killed and imported meat. The proportion of imported meat purchased through wholesalers was very small as sales by the importer/wholesaling companies to unit retailers have been classed as direct sales.

[3] In some instances the titles of the commodities and commodity groups have, for convenience, been shortened in this and later Tables. The individual case studies should be consulted for full information on the goods included under each heading.

Table 4A presents the same information but with the commodities in main trade groups.

Table 4A. *Approximate proportions, by trade groups, of commodities sold by unit retailers which were purchased from wholesalers in 1938*[1]

Trade group	Estimated sales by unit retailers £ million	Proportions of unit retailers' sales represented by goods purchased from wholesalers %
Fish	31·0	90–100
Women's and children's wear	119·0	
Furnishings	31·5	
Provisions	113·0	80–90
Fruit and vegetables	125·5	
Milk	24·0	
Newspapers and magazines	41·5	
Chocolates and sweets	45·0	
Poultry, game and rabbits	14·0	70–80
Footwear	25·5	
Chemists' goods	33·0	
Men's and boys' wear	69·0	
Groceries and household stores	143·0	60–70
Cigarettes and tobacco	153·0	
Beer, wines and spirits	108·0	
Stationery, inks, pens and pencils	11·5	50–60
Coal	69·5	
Pottery and ironmongers' goods	27·5	
Motor trade	112·0	40–50
Meat	129·0	
Jewellers' goods	16·5	
Other specialities	23·5	
Electrical goods	23·0	30–40
Furniture	27·5	

[1] The individual commodities included in the different trade groups are given above on page 21.

Methods of distribution of all goods sold by unit retailers

Finally Table 5 shows the estimates for the three broad classes of commodities and also for all commodities included in the enquiry.

Table 5. *Estimated methods of distribution in 1938 of commodities sold by unit retailers by three main classes and of all commodities included in the enquiry*[1]

Commodity division	Estimated sales by unit retailers	Approximate proportions of unit retailers' sales represented by goods purchased from	
		Wholesalers	Producers or importers
	£ million	%	%
Food and drink[2]	750	66	34
Clothing and footwear	213	79	21
Other goods	570	52	48
All commodities	1,533	62–64	36–38

[1] If on-licence sales of beer, wines and spirits are excluded the approximate proportions of unit retailers' sales of food and drink represented by purchases from wholesalers is 68%, and of total goods 63–65%.

[2] Bread and flour confectionery sold by bakers to other retailers have been included in this total.

The factors influencing the position of the various commodities and classes of commodities in this Chart and Tables are to be examined later. Here all that is needed is a reminder that the figures relate to estimated averages of all the commodities in each group and that there were wide variations in the practice of individual manufacturers and retailers.

Of the total sales by wholesalers to retailers in the group of commodities studied it is estimated that just under 95% were made to unit retailers, and the remainder to multiple shops, retail co-operative societies and department stores. Viewed from the angle of the multiple, co-operative and department store organizations, some 6% of their purchases are estimated to have been made from wholesalers. The purchases by retail co-operative societies from wholesalers other than co-operative wholesale societies were, however, very small as a proportion of total co-operative sales. If the purchases and sales of co-operative societies are excluded from the estimates and also on-licence sales of beer, wines and spirits, about 10% of the total purchases of multiple and department store organizations, as defined above, are estimated to have been made from wholesalers.

5. COMMODITIES PASSING THROUGH TWO OR MORE WHOLESALERS

To complete the picture of the main outlines of distribution an estimate can be made of the proportion of goods handled by two or more intermediaries on their way from the manufacturer, producer or importer to the retailer. The information on this point was obtained in the manner described above but once again the problems of definitions and terminology arise. In the estimates already given of the proportion of goods passing through wholesalers, the wholesaler has been defined, briefly, as an intermediary who took full physical and financial possession of the goods in their finished state from the producer and importer and re-sold to either another intermediary or to a retailer. The second intermediary, therefore, can be defined as one who purchased consumer goods outright other than from a producer or importer, and who re-sold outright either to a third intermediary or to a retailer. From this follow the definitions of a third, fourth and fifth intermediary. The terms primary wholesaler and secondary wholesaler or first-hand buyer and second-hand buyer, or factor and second wholesaler which are customarily used in many of the trades where sales through two or more intermediaries are common, are not, in all cases, co-incident with the above definition and therefore have not been used. Frequently, for example, the primary wholesaler—as the term is commonly used—is indistinguishable from the importer, or from the producer, as in the case of imported canned goods and blended and packaged tea and butter.

Using the definition suggested above approximately 5–6% of the purchases of retailers were made from intermediaries who in turn had purchased from other intermediaries. And, approximately, a further 1% of the goods purchased by retailers had passed through three intermediaries from the producer or importer. Sales through two or more intermediaries were most prominent in the greengrocery trade, the fish trade, the egg trade, and the imported canned goods, milk, wines and spirits and motor car trades.

6. SUMMARY OF THE METHODS OF DISTRIBUTION

A re-assembly of the sections of the distributive process can now be made in order to present a general view of the methods of distribution of the commodities and commodity groups studied, and this is presented in Chart II. Determination to reduce the great variety of methods of distribution to the five or so main ones as defined above accounts for the somewhat austere character of the chart. A more detailed interpretation of the methods in use would have produced many additional lines and routes, and would have put clothing on the skeleton, though certainly at the expense of accuracy and probably at the risk of confusing the eye. The conclusions which can tentatively be drawn from the Chart as it stands can be summarized as follows:

Approximately 17% of the goods are estimated to have remained

Chart II THE METHODS OF DISTRIBUTION OF ALL COMMODITIES

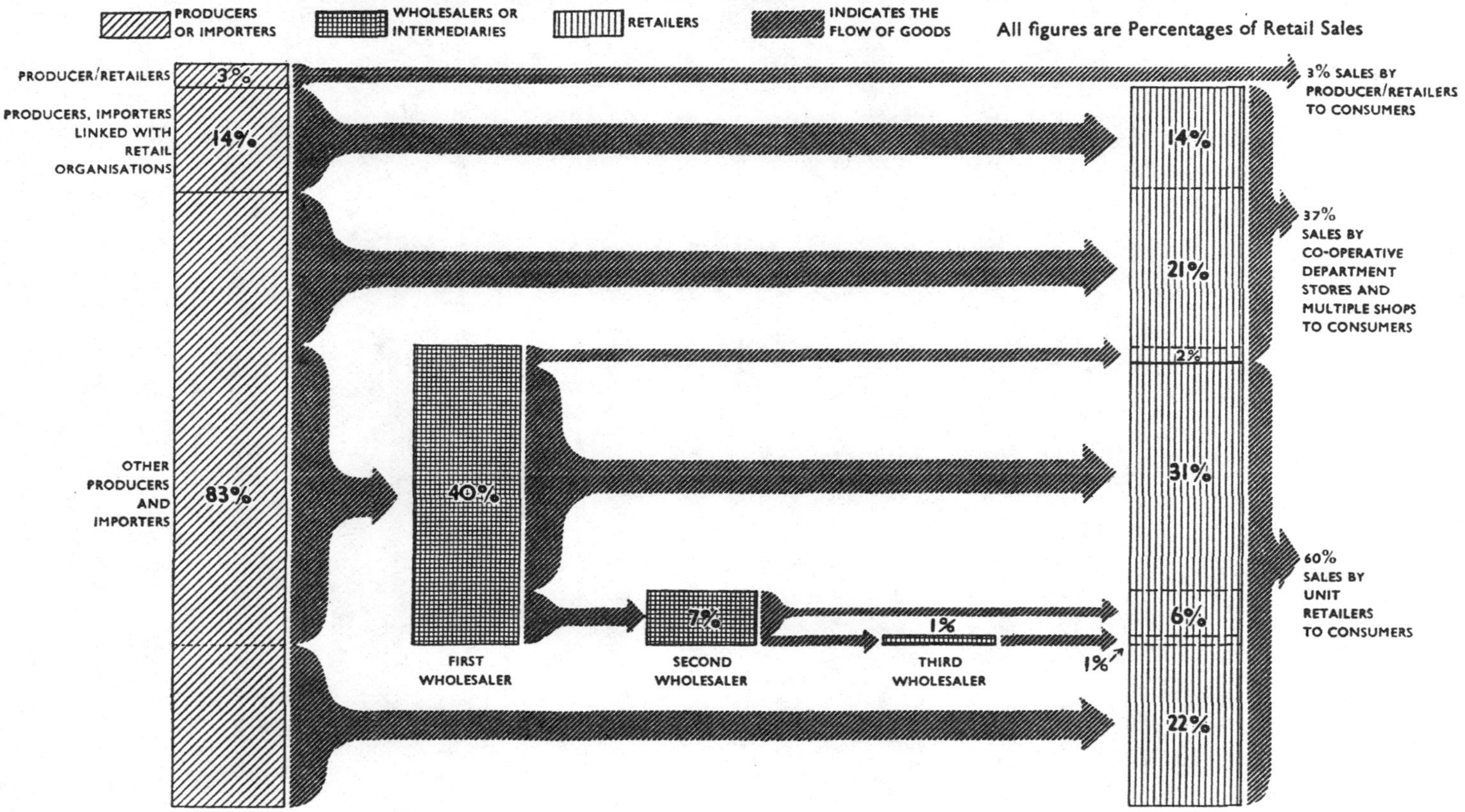

in the same hands, that is either stayed in the possession of one firm or passed only between linked firms, from the start of production or assembly or entry into the United Kingdom until sold to the consumer.

Approximately 43% of the goods are estimated to have passed directly from the producer or importer to the retailer and then to the consumer.

Approximately 33% of the goods are estimated to have passed from producer or importer to an intermediary, from him to a retailer and then to the consumer.

Approximately 6% of the goods are estimated to have passed through two intermediaries after leaving the producer or importer before going to the retailer to be sold to the consumer.

Approximately 1% of the goods is estimated to have passed through three or more intermediaries before going to the retailer to be sold to the consumer.

CHAPTER II

FACTORS INFLUENCING THE METHODS OF DISTRIBUTION

I. THE MAIN CONSIDERATIONS INFLUENCING THE METHODS OF DISTRIBUTION

Three methods of distribution have been discussed. They are, briefly, direct sale by the producer or importer to the public, direct sale by producers or importers to retailers, and the sale by producers or importers to intermediaries who re-sell to the retailer. In each case the service rendered to the consumer by the distributors as a whole is the same. The same functions of obtaining information about the requirements of consumers and telling consumers of the goods available, of transporting, of providing credit and stockholding against demand, of breaking bulk, of sorting, grading and preparing for sale and of physically selling the goods, have to be performed by the distributors. In the third instance they are performed by three or more separate economic units, in the second shared between two, and in the first wholly performed by one unit. This is not to suggest that the cost of undertaking these functions in all three cases will be identical, but that the same essential distributive functions have to be undertaken in one degree or another whatever method be adopted. The failure fully to grasp this somewhat simple and obvious fact has led to much confused thinking in popular discussions of distribution.

The differences in methods of distribution between commodities and between countries arise not so much from the ingenuity or lack of ingenuity displayed in avoiding performance of these essential functions by one set of distributors compared with another or one nation of shopkeepers compared with another, as from the structure of the economy and character of the economic conditions in which the distribution takes place. In making comparisons of methods of distribution between countries obviously such factors as the extent of urbanization, the degree of dependence on imported goods, the measure of concentration of production and of retailing and the particular economic conditions, such as the presence of full employment or unemployment, of a sellers' or a buyers' market, existing at the time of the comparison, all influence the relative proportions of the goods flowing through each of the three main channels in the different countries. Similarly in making comparisons of the distribution of commodities within a country these and other factors, such as the nature of the commodity itself, influence the methods of distribution used. And the changes in the processes of distribution over time, where they can be measured, in turn throw light on the economic climate and structure of a country and the tempo of economic change and development.

This approach to the distribution process as a reflection, in the main, of the state of the productive processes must not, however, be pressed too far. Distribution has, of course, a logic and dynamic of its own and in its turn influences the character of production. There are two main ways in which this influence may be exerted. In the first place the methods of distribution may affect directly the productive process and organization. The degree of influence which can be exerted varies widely between particular commodities. The size of the production unit and the length of the run in the manufacture of fashion goods or goods produced in a wide range of qualities and patterns, for example, can be strongly influenced by the methods of distribution and the extent of wholesaling, of large or small retailing units, and of bulk buying and ordering in the trade, while the production methods of, say, matches may be influenced only slightly by these factors. Many examples of the pressure of distribution methods on productive organization, both speeding up and distorting trends and policies evolved by the consideration of productive problems alone, could be given. In the second place, and less directly, the distributive processes may affect the methods of production because the reaction of the distributive trades to new factors, problems and needs may be slow and uneven. The sluggishness where it develops is probably due to the pervading influence of tradition and traditional methods. The reasons for this are many. The three most important are probably the relatively small scale of operation of most units making up the distributive trades, the individual and national lack of economic facts and usable yardsticks except in the crudest form, by which policies can be determined and progress measured, and lastly the close relationship of these trades with the consumer, who in many respects is an incorrigibly conservative force. The effect of this sluggishness is that often the distributive system of to-day may be reflecting, albeit in a blurred fashion, and with variations between commodities, the productive changes of yesterday or even the day before.

A discussion of the factors influencing the methods of distribution of the different main commodities and commodity groups studied cannot therefore hope to be conclusive unless all the variables relating to the particular commodity are closely examined. This task cannot be attempted within the limits of one volume. All that can be done is to isolate some of the main influences and discuss them in the light of the information collected on the methods of distribution obtaining in 1938.

Before this is done one further aspect of the problem must be mentioned. In the above discussion the phrase 'methods of distribution' has been used in its narrower sense as synonymous with the channels of distribution; that is, the volume of goods passing through one channel or another. This is an over-simplification of the matter. While the distributive functions which have to be performed are roughly the same irrespective of the number of different distributive units taking part in the process, the actual division of the tasks between the units is not necessarily the same in the case of different commodities even though the number of units be the same. For example, while packaged cereal breakfast foods and unpackaged cereal breakfast foods might both pass from manufacturer to wholesaler and then to retailer, the distributive functions undertaken by the manufacturers in the first case, by advertising, packaging and breaking bulk are much greater, and those of the wholesalers and retailers correspondingly less, than in the second case. Or again, the division of the distributive functions between a producer and a retailer when the sales are made direct to a multiple organization and when the sales are made to a unit retailer, differs widely although both types of sale can be classed as producer direct to retailers. Such a qualitative assessment of the part played by the different units in the distribution of the various commodities cannot be made so readily as the quantitative assessments given above, though the gross margins earned by wholesalers and retailers and the distribution costs incurred by producers, which are considered later, do throw some light on the matter. In the following discussion of the main factors influencing the methods of distribution, while most use is made of the quantitative factors an attempt has been made to indicate the cases in which the qualitative factors exert an important influence.

The three basic considerations affecting methods are firstly the nature of the commodity, secondly the organization of production, and thirdly the existing structure of retail trading. Under the heading of the nature of the commodity fall such questions as its perishability, its unit value, whether it is a necessity or 'fashion' good, imported or home produced, and the character of consumer demand for the product. Under the heading of organization of production fall such questions as the size groupings of the productive units, the degree of concentration existing, the location of production in relation to demand, and the cost structures of the units *vis à vis* existing and potential demand. Under the heading of the structure of retail trading fall such questions as the number of shops mainly selling the commodity and the total number of outlets, the proportions of total sales made by different size groupings of shops, the importance of different economic types of outlet, that is multiple, co-operative, department store or unit retail outlet, the rate of stock turn of the retailer and the location of the retailers in relation to production and to consumers.

These are the main considerations to be borne in mind when examining a static picture of distribution. To make the picture come alive attention has to be paid to the efforts of both producers and distributors to change their cost structures and their size, thus influencing the methods of distribution, and also to the fact that the commodity being considered can itself change its character, for example from being a fashion good of yesterday to a necessity of to-day.

To assess the relative importance of these various considerations in determining the methods of distribution, an attempt will be made to distinguish the features of the goods using the different channels.

2. FACTORS INFLUENCING THE SALES OF GOODS DIRECT TO CONSUMERS

The sales of goods by the producers directly to the consumers and of goods remaining in the same hands from time of entry into the United Kingdom until sold to the consumer can be grouped under two headings: firstly, sales by unit producer/retailers and by mail order and other direct means employed by the producer; secondly, sales of goods produced by manufacturing units linked with multiple or co-operative retailing organizations and the sales of goods purchased abroad and imported by such organizations.

Producer/retailer and mail order sales

The value of the goods sold directly to the consumer by producer/retailers, by mail order methods organized by the producers or by other means such as door-to-door sales and direct sales promoted by club agents acting for manufacturers, is difficult to estimate closely. Some sales direct to the consumers were made by practically all producers. In the course of this enquiry estimates were obtained for those trades where such selling was significant and the total estimate at retail prices of about £80 millions must be regarded as only a minimum figure.[1]

Indication has been given in Chart I of those commodities where the

[1] In some respects the slaughtering and preparation of meat by unit retail butchers, estimated at £13–15 millions at retail prices, comes within the producer/retailer category. But as the butcher is not responsible for the production of the livestock and the final operation he performs on the product represents only a small addition to the value of that product, that is, a pre-distributive service rather than production, these sales have been excluded from the producer/retailer category.

proportion of total sales made direct to the consumer was over 5%. For convenience these commodities can be listed here in order of the importance of sales made direct to consumer.

Flour confectionery	Watches and clocks
Bread	Eggs—home-produced
Fresh milk	Books
Brooms and brushes	Domestic hollow-ware, hardware and ironmongery
Vacuum cleaners	
Perambulators	Fresh fruit and vegetables
Furs and fur garments	Furniture

These commodities can be grouped according to three main types of sale. First, the sales of unprocessed goods by producer/retailers direct to the consumer—milk, eggs, and fruit and vegetables. Second, the direct sales to the consumer of processed or manufactured goods by producer/retailers—flour confectionery, bread, watches and clocks, and some furniture. Third, the sales of manufactured goods by mail order, door-to-door sales and other means—brooms and brushes, vacuum cleaners, perambulators, furs and fur garments, books, domestic hollow-ware, hardware and ironmongery and some furniture. Other examples of direct to consumer sales which spring to mind and which are not listed above, such as potatoes, real jewellery and sweets, will be seen to fall into one or other of the groups.

The first two groups are, in terms of consumers' expenditure, by far the most important, representing over 90% of the estimated expenditure by consumers on goods purchased in this way. The significant common features of the commodities in these two groups which, it is suggested, influence the extent of direct to consumer sales, are the small scale and scattered nature of the productive units in the different trades and the location of the points of production near to the consumers. Variation in the degree to which the latter qualification is fulfilled appears to have the greatest influence on the proportion of total sales made in this manner. In the case of flour confectionery or bread, for example, these goods are produced in practically all urban and country districts and the potential consumer is on the doorstep. In the case of eggs, fruit and vegetables and watches and clocks on the other hand, only a small proportion of the potential demand for the particular product is located within easy reach of the point of production, farm, market garden or workshop, and the direct to consumer sales as a proportion of total sales are smaller. The differences in the location of production in relation to demand affect, along with other influences, the methods of distribution of that proportion of the sales made otherwise than direct to the consumer. In the case of flour confectionery and bread, wholesalers, as defined above, are not used at all and the remainder of the sales pass from producer direct to retailer. In the case of fruit and vegetables, on the other hand, nearly one-half of the remaining sales pass through two wholesalers before reaching the retailer.

The factors influencing the sales of the other 10% of the goods passing direct from manufacturers to consumer by mail order or other direct channels are somewhat complex. Each good, practically, has certain characteristics of its own. Furs and fur garments, for example, are made up to customers' specifications, the books distributed direct are mainly sold through book clubs and door-to-door canvassers, the domestic hardware and hollow-ware sales are manufacturers' mail order sales of advertised and branded goods, the sales of furniture are partly by mail order and partly arranged through local agents of manufacturers, and the sales of brooms, brushes and vacuum cleaners direct to the consumer are almost all undertaken by door-to-door canvassers. The common denominators in this group of goods are the relatively high unit value, except in the case of brooms and brushes, and the infrequent demand of consumers for the product, except in the case of books issued by book clubs.

Sales of goods imported directly by or produced by concerns linked with large scale retailing organizations

The total retail sales of the commodities which were produced by or imported directly by concerns linked with multiple shops, department stores and co-operative organizations, have been estimated at approximately £450 millions. In these instances one organization performed all the distributive functions, from those of the manufacturer or importer to those of the retailer. The list of the commodities of which approximately 10% or more of total sales were distributed in this way is given on the next page.

Table 6. *Commodities produced by or purchased abroad by concerns linked with multiple shop, department store, or co-operative organizations in 1938*[1]

Commodity or commodity group	Consumers' expenditure	Estimated proportion of total sales produced by or purchased abroad by concerns linked with retail outlet
	£ million	
Sewing machines	1·3	80–90
Beer—on-licence sales	190·0	80–90
Portable typewriters	0·3	55–65
Bread	67·0	25–35
Tea	45·0	25–35
Men's and boys' outerwear	68·5	25–35
Flour confectionery	37·5	25–35
Flour	22·5	15–25
Coffee	2·2	15–25
Butter	64·5	15–25
Canned fruit, vegetables and fish—imported	33·0	15–25
Jam and marmalade	14·5	15–25
Corsets	9·5	15–25
Soap	27·5	5–15
Cheese	19·5	5–15
Bacon	70·5	5–15
Milk	86·5	5–15
Leather footwear	63·0	5–15
Meat—imported	86·0	5–15
Furs	10·0	5–15
Medicines and drugs	23·0	5–15
Men's and boys' shirts, collars and pyjamas	13·5	5–15
Margarine	11·5	5–15

[1] In the case of corsets, sales made by agents appointed by the manufacturer and handling only his products have been classed as sales through manufacturer-controlled retail outlets. In the case of meat, only imported meat has been considered. In the case of home-killed meat practically all the larger multiple and co-operative organizations did their own slaughtering and preparation for sale.

The cases in which direct overseas purchasing is important are butter, imported canned fruit, vegetables and fish, cheese, meat and bacon. In the remaining instances the goods were grown, manufactured or processed in the United Kingdom by concerns integrated with retailing organizations.

Both the co-operative societies and the larger multiple organizations had a large retail turnover in the imported goods listed and with an assured market there were direct economies to be obtained in by-passing the importer and purchasing a proportion of their supplies overseas. In some instances the co-operative wholesale societies purchased from overseas co-operative producers.

The factors leading to the inclusion of the various home grown manufactured or processed goods in the list are much more complex. In some cases multiple and co-operative organizations have followed or taken the place of the unit producer/retailer, as in the production and distribution of bread, flour confectionery and milk, but not in the case of fresh fruit and vegetables. The other manufactured goods can be divided roughly into two groups, one group where the value of net output added in the course of manufacturing or processing is below one-fifth of the factory selling value, the second group where the value of net output added is more than one-fifth. Butter blending, bacon curing, tea blending and packing, coffee roasting and grinding and cheese processing and maturing can be placed in the former category and products such as sewing machines, clothing, boots and shoes and medicines and drugs in the latter category.

In the former cases the size and evenness of the demand for the product, the guarantee of retail outlets and the relatively simple processing operation required has made some control over production advantageous to the larger retailing organizations. It is very difficult to generalize about the characteristics of the commodities in the second category and the reasons for the link between production and distribution are a part of the history of the production and distribution of each commodity. Only a close examination along these lines would reveal the determining factors. The development of a particular patent, as in the case of sewing machines, the bias of the early co-operative movement towards particular types of productive enterprise, the existence of severe competition between a dozen or so leading brewers coupled with the increase in the capital required to undertake beer, wines and spirits retailing, are three examples of particular factors influencing the presence of individual commodities on this list. The only safe generalizations that can be made about the products, each of which applies to a number, though not all, are firstly, the durability of the products and the importance of an element of reliability in manufacture rather than an element of fashion, for example medicines and drugs, boots and shoes, sewing machines, and men's and boys' outerwear; secondly, the relatively small number of retail outlets for the products which enables the manufacturers to reach the public without developing a chain of retail outlets on too large a scale to enable both productive and retailing processes to be undertaken under one management.

3. THE SALE OF GOODS THROUGH WHOLESALERS

The importance of the wholesaler in relation to the distribution of various products, and the factors influencing his importance, can best be discussed, as suggested above, in relation to the sales and methods of purchase of the unit retailer. While the information obtained on these purchases and sales is somewhat less reliable than the information relating to all types of retail outlet, the rôle of the wholesaler does not appear with any clarity unless the direct to consumer sales of manufacturers and producer/retailers and the purchases and sales of multiple, co-operative and department store organizations are excluded from the discussion. Estimates of the proportion of purchases of individual commodities and groups made by unit retailers from wholesalers have been presented above in Tables 4, 4A and 5.

The position of the commodities and of the different trade groups in these Tables confirms, by and large, the general economic propositions that have been made regarding the use of varied methods of distribution.[1] In Table 4 for example, the commodity groups falling into the top sector of the Table, that is 80% or more purchased from wholesalers, possessed some or all of the following characteristics: small-scale, scattered production, inability of producers and retailers to hold large stocks or undertake the necessary grading, a retail demand for a range of goods greater than can be supplied by any single producer. Further an important proportion of the goods is imported, most of the goods have a low unit value and tend to be unbranded and unadvertised, some are relatively perishable, and in many cases the supply of the products fluctuates necessitating continuous marketing. The commodity groups in the bottom sector of the Table, say 40% or less purchased through wholesalers, similarly reveal all or some of the expected characteristics: for example, the unit value of the goods is high, the number of retail outlets small, the goods are durable, only a small proportion is imported (except in the case of meat where the low proportion passing through wholesalers is due to the fact that the bulk of the imported trade is in the hands of importer/wholesalers and distribution through these firms has been classed as direct to retailers), producers and retailers tend to hold large stocks and the scale of production is either large or concentrated in particular areas.

The more interesting questions to be asked are what factors influence

[1] For example, the full-length discussion in D. Braithwaite and S. P. Dobbs' *The Distribution of Consumable Goods*, London, 1932.

the relative positions of the trade groups in the middle of the Table and what factors influence different firms in the same trade to pursue entirely different policies in regard to their method of sales. Information on the second question is not, unfortunately, available in sufficient detail to provide material for discussion but an attempt can be made to deal with the first.

4. TESTS FOR THE CHARACTERISTICS OF COMMODITIES SOLD BY UNIT RETAILERS

The most promising approach appears to be to analyse all the commodities studied by reference to five factors: the proportion of purchases made by unit retailers from wholesalers as against the proportion purchased direct from producers, the degree of concentration of production of the commodity, the extent to which the commodity was advertised, branded and price-maintained by the producer, the character of the unit price of the commodity, and the number and type of its retail outlets.

The estimates given above in Table 4 have been used to indicate the proportions of commodities purchased by unit retailers from wholesalers. In estimating the degree of concentration of production of particular goods, the analysis made by H. Leak and A. Maizels of the Census of Production returns for 1935 has been drawn upon heavily.[1] This analysis used in the main the concept of the ratio between the employment in the three largest units and total numbers employed in the production of a commodity or group as an index of the concentration of production. This principle has, as far as possible, been followed, but many difficulties arise. In the first place the estimates made by Leak and Maizels refer to the conditions existing in 1935. No attempt has been made, owing to the absence of information, to revise the figures. Secondly, in many instances the commodity groups identified do not correspond exactly with the commodity groups studied in this enquiry. In these instances estimates of concentration based partly on the Census of Production figures and partly on information obtained from the trade have been made. Thirdly, where an important proportion of the goods was imported the degree of concentration of home production is of little value as a criterion influencing the methods of distribution of both home-manufactured and imported goods. In these instances a new estimate of concentration has been made based on the concentration of home production and on the proportion of total sales that was imported. Fourthly, the estimates made by Leak and Maizels

[1] H. Leak and A. Maizels, 'The Structure of British Industry', *Journal of the Royal Statistical Society*, vol. CVIII, pt. 2, 1945.

are themselves, as stated in their paper, subject to error. Fifthly, no evidence at all on the concentration of production is given by Leak and Maizels for some commodities and groups included in this enquiry. In these cases other sources have had to be used such as estimates provided by individual firms and trade associations. The figures showing the degree of concentration of production can, therefore, only be approximate, and to indicate this a range rather than a single figure has been used.

The estimates of the extent of branding and price-maintenance by the producer for different commodities have been based on information obtained from the trade. There has been no attempt to narrow the estimate to close limits, but a single division has been made between significant branding and price-maintenance—indicated by S—meaning half or more of the commodity or group was branded or price-maintained, and insignificant—indicated by I—meaning less than half was branded and price-maintained. The particular methods employed to price-maintain the product or the extent of sales made below the suggested or fixed price do not have a direct relevance here and no allowance for them has been made. The unit price of the commodity is taken as the price of the unit normally purchased by the private consumer in 1938, and three divisions have been made; low unit price —indicated by L—as 2s. 6d. or under per unit; medium unit price—indicated by M—as between 2s. 6d. and 40s.; and high unit price—indicated by H—as approximately £2 and over per unit.

Estimates of the number and character of the retail outlets for the commodities have been based on information obtained from the various trades and shown in the case studies. Use of the number of outlets for each commodity is not, however, an entirely satisfactory way of showing the different retailing structure characteristic of different commodities as, in relation to the unit value of the product or total consumers' expenditure, 50,000 outlets, for example, would be considered small in some trades and very large in others. Further it is important to establish whether the sales of the commodity are limited to one particular trade type of shop, for example grocers, or whether it is sold in two or more different trade types of shop, for example grocers and chemists. The actual number of outlets provides an answer when the number rises above, say 200,000, where at least two trade types of shop must be in use, but this is not necessarily the case where the total number is, say 100,000. Without further indication these outlets could be of one, two or more trade types. To bring out these characteristics as well as the numbers of outlets involved, a somewhat flexible system of definitions has been adopted. First, the commodities mainly sold by specialist retailers numbering less than approximately 30,000 have been described as sold by a small number of specialists or SS, for example, furniture or motor cars. Second, the commodities mainly sold by specialist retailers numbering up to 75,000 have been described as sold by a large number of specialists or LS, for example, most women's wear. Third, the commodities sold both by specialist shops and by general shops with total outlets from 50–200,000 have been described as sold by general shops or G, for example, most groceries and provisions. In those instances where the commodities are sold by specialist and general shops in two or more different trades with total outlets numbering over 50,000 and up to 200,000, the sales have been described as general in two or more trades or G2, for example, canned fruit and vegetables, which are sold by both grocers and greengrocers. The overlap between the top limit of specialist shops and lower limit of general shops has been introduced in order to include in general distribution such goods as toys or stationery which are not sold by a small or large number of specialists alone. Fourth, the commodities sold by specialist, general and other shops totalling roughly 200,000 or over, have been described as sold by a widespread number of outlets or W, for example, matches.

The characteristics of the commodities sold by unit retailers

Using these terms, which are summarized below, Table 7 showing the characteristics of the individual commodities and commodity groups sold by unit retailers has been constructed.

TERMS USED IN THE TABLE

Extent of branding and price maintenance:	Estimated proportions of the goods in each group which were branded and price-maintained by manufacturers and producers.	
	Where significant, 50% and over, shown as	S
	Where insignificant, under 50%, shown as	I
Type of retail outlet:	Where sold mainly by a small number of specialist shops, under 30,000, shown as	SS
	Where sold mainly by a large number of specialist shops, up to 75,000, shown as	LS
	Where sold mainly by specialist and general shops, 50–200,000, in one trade, shown as	G
	Where sold mainly by specialist and general shops, 50–200,000, in more than one trade, shown as	G2
	Where sold by widespread outlets, over 200,000, shown as	W
Price group:	Low unit price, under 2s. 6d., shown as	L
	Medium unit price, 2s. 6d.–40s., shown as	M
	High unit price, over 40s., shown as	H

Table 7. *Price, type of retail outlet, extent of branding and organization of production of different commodities sold by unit retailers in 1938*[1]

Commodity or commodity group	Estimated sales in unit retail shops £ million	Proportion of purchases of unit retailers made from wholesalers %	Degree of concentration of production %	Branding and price maintenance	Type of retail outlet	Price group
Furnishing fabrics	5·0	90–100	0–10	I	SS	M
Imitation jewellery	2·0	90–100	0–10	I	G2	L
Household furnishings	13·5	90–100	0–10	I	SS	M
Millinery	13·0	90–100	10–20	I	LS	M
Gloves	4·5	90–100	10–20	I	LS	M
Men's and boys' hosiery	14·5	90–100	0–10	I	SS	M
Sanitary towels	1·5	90–100	30–40	S	G2	L
General drapers' goods	20·0	90–100	0–10	I	G	L
Cheese	10·5	90–100	0–10	I	G	L
Butter	33·5	90–100	10–20	I	G	L
Sugar	12·5	90–100	80–90	I	G	L
Dress materials	4·5	90–100	0–10	I	SS	M
Underwear, nightwear	10·0	90–100	0–10	I	LS	M
Unpackaged cereals	1·0	90–100	0–10	I	G	L
Syrup and treacle	2·0	90–100	70–80	S	G	L
Carpets	8·5	90–100	10–20	I	SS	H
Fish	31·0	90–100	0–10	I	SS	L
Potatoes	21·0	90–100	0–10	I	LS	L
Health food beverages	1·0	90–100	70–80	S	G2	L
Corsets and brassières	5·0	90–100	30–40	S	SS	M
Household polishes	5·0	90–100	40–50	S	G2	L
Matches	7·5	90–100	40–50	S	W	L
Men's hats and caps	4·0	90–100	0–10	I	SS	M
Razors and blades	2·0	90–100	50–60	S	G2	L
Handkerchiefs, ties, braces	6·0	90–100	0–10	I	LS	L
Stockings and socks	18·5	90–100	10–20	I	LS	M
Medicines and drugs	13·5	90–100	10–20	S	G2	L
Packaged breakfast cereals	3·0	90–100	60–70	S	G	L
Infant and invalid foods	2·0	90–100	60–70	S	LS	L
Canned milk	4·5	80–90	50–60	S	G2	L
Sauces, soups, salad creams	6·0	80–90	40–50	S	G2	L
Fruit and vegetables	104·5	80–90	0–10	I	LS	L
Canned fruit, vegetables	23·0	80–90	20–30	S	G2	L
Toothbrushes	0·8	80–90	30–40	S	G2	L
Rubber footwear	2·5	80–90	20–30	I	SS	L
Eggs	25·0	80–90	0–10	I	G	L
Fresh milk	24·0	80–90	0–10	I	LS	L

Commodity or commodity group	Estimated sales in unit retail shops £ million	Proportion of purchases of unit retailers made from wholesalers %	Degree of concentration of production %	Branding and price maintenance	Type of retail outlet	Price group
Sweets	16·5	70–80	10–20	S	SS	L
Poultry, game and rabbits	14·0	70–80	0–10	I	G2	L
Newspapers and magazines	41·5	70–80	20–30	S	G2	L
Dental preparations	2·0	70–80	50–60	S	G2	L
Furs and fur garments	3·0	70–80	10–20	I	SS	H
Motor accessories, parts	9·5	70–80	60–70	S	SS	M
Leather footwear	23·0	70–80	10–20	I	SS	M
Women's outerwear	40·0	70–80	0–10	I	LS	M
Chocolates	28·5	60–70	50–60	S	W	L
Motor cars	50·5	60–70	40–50	S	SS	H
Meat—home-killed	67·0	60–70	0–10	I	LS	L
Salt	1·0	60–70	80–90	S	G	L
Margarine	5·5	60–70	70–80	S	G	L
Candles and nightlights	0·5	60–70	50–60	I	G2	L
Shirts, collars and pyjamas	8·0	60–70	0–10	I	SS	M
Toys	3·5	60–70	10–20	I	G2	M
Cocoa	1·0	50–60	50–60	S	G	L
Jam and marmalade	8·5	50–60	30–40	S	G	L
Contraceptives	1·5	50–60	20–30	S	SS	L
Cutlery	0·8	50–60	10–20	I	SS	M
Tobacco and cigarettes	153·0	50–60	60–70	S	W	L
Stationery	11·5	50–60	20–30	S	G2	L
Hardware, hollow-ware	13·0	50–60	10–20	I	LS	M
Coal	69·5	50–60	0–10	I	LS	M
Coffee	1·5	50–60	10–20	I	G	L
Brooms and brushes	1·5	50–60	20–30	I	SS	M
Electric light lamps	1·0	50–60	50–60	S	SS	L
Watches and clocks	5·5	40–50	10–20	I	SS	H
Beauty, toilet preparations	4·5	40–50	10–20	S	LS	M
Leather goods	6·0	40–50	0–10	I	SS	M
Pottery and glassware	8·5	40–50	10–20	I	LS	M
Tea	22·0	40–50	50–60	S	G	L
Paints, varnishes	2·0	40–50	20–30	S	SS	M
Men's and boys' outerwear	37·0	40–50	0–10	I	SS	M
Motor car and cycle tyres	6·0	40–50	70–80	S	SS	M
Motor cycles, accessories	5·0	30–40	50–60	S	SS	H
Household and toilet soap	15·0	30–40	60–70	S	W	L
Linoleum	4·5	30–40	80–90	I	SS	M
Electric fires, appliances	4·5	30–40	40–50	S	SS	H
Self-raising flour	7·5	30–40	50–60	S	G	L

Commodity or commodity group	Estimated sales in unit retail shops £ million	Proportion of purchases of unit retailers made from wholesalers %	Degree of concentration of production %	Branding and price maintenance	Type of retail outlet	Price group
Bacon—home-produced	11·5	30–40	40–50	I	G	L
Vacuum cleaners	4·5	30–40	80–90	S	SS	H
Furniture	27·5	30–40	0–10	I	SS	H
Books	6·0	20–30	20–30	S	SS	M
Motor oil	4·5	20–30	30–40	S	SS	M
Radios and radiograms	13·0	20–30	30–40	S	SS	H
Wallpaper	1·5	20–30	80–90	S	SS	M
Biscuits	13·0	20–30	30–40	S	G	L
Photographic goods	2·0	20–30	60–70	S	SS	L
Jewellery	9·5	10–20	10–20	I	SS	H
Sports goods	7·0	10–20	20–30	I	SS	H
Plain flour	4·0	10–20	60–70	I	G	L
Perambulators	1·0	0–10	20–30	S	SS	H
Kerosene	4·5	0–10	50–60	I	LS	L
Portable typewriters	0·1	0–10	60–70	S	SS	H
Petrol	36·5	0–10	80–90	S	SS	M

[1] The sales of beer, wines and spirits and of bread and flour confectionery have been excluded from the Table, as, in the former instance, very special conditions obtained in the trade which have been given separate treatment in the case study, and in the latter instance, the purchases by unit retailers of bread and flour confectionery from wholesalers were negligible.

Home-produced commodities have been listed separately from imported commodities only in those cases where the methods of distribution were very different. In all other cases home-produced and imported goods have been considered together. The sales of imported meat and bacon have been excluded altogether. Just over 85% of the estimated total sales of unit retailers are considered in this Table and the subsequent discussion.

In estimating the degree of concentration of production of the various commodities, an attempt has been made in certain cases to exclude the output of firms which sold the bulk of their output to multiple retail units. Here only the sales to unit retailers are considered. This makes a significant change in the estimated degree of concentration of production of men's and boys' outerwear which, when production for multiple and co-operative retail shopsi s excluded, drops from approximately 30–40% to 0–10%.

Limitations of the data

This Table is somewhat crude of construction owing to the incompleteness of the information on which the various figures are based. Moreover although a wide range has been given for both the method of distribution used and the degree of concentration of production it is possible that in some cases the actual figure will fall outside the limits given, and some may quarrel with the estimates made of the degree of branding or the price grouping of particular commodities. There is a further, and in some ways more serious limitation. The character of the Table and the association that can be observed between different factors is dependent, to no small extent, on the composition of the so-called commodities and commodity groups. For example the actual number of commodities listed as showing a more than average proportion being purchased from wholesalers means little, as with more information some of the larger commodity groups, such as fresh fruit and vegetables, could be broken down into six or so separate commodities all displaying, perhaps, differing methods of distribution and different degrees of concentration or unit price. The use of consumers' expenditure as the guide or weight is open to similar objections except in so far as the estimates given for a commodity group are an attempt at a weighted average for the constituents of that group. Such weighting is practicable, within limits, in considering the method of distribution or the degree of concentration, but means little in considering the simple alternatives of significant or insignificant branding or the unit price or type of outlet. Some non-proprietary medicines, for example, have a very specialist type of distribution, a high degree of concentration of production and a high price, while for other products in the same general group the reverse is true. Finally, it will be recognized that the price divisions are fairly arbitrary, though a variation in the steps, while altering the position of the classification of the medium group, would probably not affect very much the main groups at either end of the scale.

The conclusions that can be drawn from the Table, therefore, have to be used with considerable care, but the analysis does, it is believed, indicate an approach which with more accurate and detailed evidence could be fruitfully pursued and, even in this somewhat crude form, throws a certain amount of light on the factors influencing methods of distribution.

5. AN ANALYSIS OF THE RELATIONSHIP BETWEEN CHARACTERISTICS AND METHOD OF DISTRIBUTION OF COMMODITIES

The average proportion of all commodities, excluding beer, wines and spirits, purchased by the unit retailers from wholesalers was 63–65%.[1] An estimate of the average degree of concentration of production of all commodities in the Table can only be made very approximately. Information on total employment is lacking in many trades, the use of consumers' expenditure to weight the various commodities suffers from the inclusion of tax and wholesale and retail margins, although an attempt has been made in the calculation to deduct these, and there is the further error arising from the use of the middle point of the 10% steps—particularly serious in the groups of commodities listed as 0–10%. The average for all commodities works out at just about 20%. This compares with the 26% estimated by Leak and Maizels for the groups of commodities and trades covered by them.

Using these averages as guides an elementary pattern can be traced in this Table. Taking 65% purchased through wholesalers as the dividing line, the commodities can be arranged in two groups—Group I showing in every case more than 65% and Group II less than 65% purchased through wholesalers.[2] The characteristics of the commodities in each group in regard to concentration of production and branding and price maintenance are shown in the following Table.

[1] The concept of the average proportion of purchases made by unit retailers from wholesalers is sound enough when all commodities are considered but is less satisfactory when applied as a yardstick for judging the methods of distribution of individual commodities or groups. The criterion in this case should be the average practice of the particular trade group of which the commodity is a member. For example, in the above Table both electric light lamps and electric fires and appliances are listed as showing less than the general average of all goods passing through wholesalers. But the 40–50% of electric light lamps passing through wholesalers is considerably higher than the 20–30% of electric fires and appliances, and if the electrical trade alone were considered electric light lamps would have to be classed in the higher than average group. The question could then be asked: What are the characteristics of the individual commodities, making up a particular trade, that are associated with more or less than average sales through wholesalers? The immediate obstacle to this procedure is definition of a trade. The tendency of retailers in the majority of trades to sell goods other than those of their main trade has made usable definitions almost impossible but has also rendered the general average concept more meaningful. In the absence of a workable alternative the general average of all goods has been used and broadly it is effective in distinguishing between those commodities sold mainly through wholesalers and those sold mainly direct to retailers. It is less effective in distinguishing between the commodities listed as having methods of distribution near the general average and in distinguishing between different practices in the same trade group.

[2] Although the average proportion of purchases from wholesalers by unit retailers, for all goods except beer, wines and spirits, is estimated in Table 5 as 63–65%, an

Table 8. *Characteristics of commodities sold by unit retailers*

Number of commodities	Degree of concentration of production			
	More than 20%		Less than 20%	
	Number of commodities	Proportion of group expenditure	Number of commodities	Proportion of group expenditure
		%		%
Group I 50	22	28	28	72
Group II 43	30	64	13	36

Number of commodities	Incidence of branding and price maintenance			
	Significant		Insignificant	
	Number of commodities	Proportion of group expenditure	Number of commodities	Proportion of group expenditure
		%		%
Group I 50	22	30	28	70
Group II 43	24	59	19	41

The differences in the method of retail sale and in the unit price between the two groups cannot be shown in relation to the consumers' expenditure on each commodity. The method of classification and the evidence is not sufficiently reliable to allow this to be done but it is of some interest to show the difference between the groups by reference to numbers of commodities as above. This is done in Table 8A.

average of 65% has been used here to allow for the underestimation of sales through wholesalers discussed previously. Of the goods listed as showing 60–70% distributed through wholesalers in Table 7, motor cars, meat, salt, margarine and chocolates have been taken as falling above the average for all goods, and candles and night-lights, shirts, collars and pyjamas as below.

Table 8A. *Characteristics of commodities sold by unit retailers*

Number of commodities	Type of retail outlet: Small number of specialists	Large number of specialists	Total specialists	General shops in one trade	General shops in two trades	Total general shops	Wide-spread outlets
Group I 50	14	11	25	10	13	23	2
Group II 43	25	5	30	8	3	11	2

Number of commodities	Price group: Low price	Medium price	High price
Group I 50	34	13	3
Group II 43	16	17	10

From these Tables the general pattern which emerges quite clearly, allowing for the crudity of the analysis, is that the goods purchased by unit retailers from wholesalers, Group I, tended to have a less than average degree of concentration of production, were usually unbranded, were sold widely, the number of outlets averaging between 75,000 and 200,000, and were of low unit value. The commodities purchased directly from producers, on the other hand, Group II, tended to have almost exactly opposite characteristics. They had a more than average measure of concentration of production, a high proportion was branded and price-maintained, the number of outlets was usually under 75,000, and they were of medium to high unit price.

Relationship between characteristics and methods of distribution by groups of commodities

The analysis can be carried a stage further. By grouping the individual commodities which exhibit similar characteristics together, six main groups emerge and a further two miscellaneous groups. The two miscellaneous groups, one distributed mainly through wholesalers and the other mainly direct to retailers and together representing some 15% of sales by unit retailers considered, are not listed as having the characteristics of any of the six groups discussed later. The first of these miscellaneous groups comprises the following commodities or commodity groups: Sugar, sweets, proprietary and non-proprietary medicines and drugs, infant and invalid foods, corsets and brassières, furs, carpets, rubber footwear, motor car parts and accessories, motor cars. The motor trade commodities form a separate sub-group having a high degree of concentration of production, being significantly branded and sold by a small number of specialists. Into the second of these miscellaneous groups fall candles and nightlights, electric light lamps, toys, coffee, brooms and brushes, contraceptives, beauty preparations and toilet waters, photographic goods, linoleum, bacon and ham, sports goods and plain flour.

The incompleteness of the data available has prevented a closer analysis of many of the commodities in these two groups. For example in the proprietary and non-proprietary medicine and drug trade, sports goods trade and sweets trade, many of the individual commodities included in these general commodity groups, for example health salts, golf balls, toffee, have production and retailing features entirely different from those listed as belonging to the respective group as a whole, and if these commodities could be disentangled they would probably fall into one or another of the six main groups. The presence of some of these commodities in the miscellaneous groups is the result of summing the characteristics of a number of unlike and heterogeneous products. Other commodities in the miscellaneous groups such as sugar, home-produced bacon and ham or plain flour are, however, sufficiently homogeneous to avoid this confusion and they clearly represent exceptions. The practices adopted in these cases with respect to method of distribution and branding and price maintenance do not follow the general lines adopted in the case of other commodities having similar characteristics of production and retailing.

The six groups into which goods having a number of characteristics in common can be divided are shown in Table 9. The characteristics of the groups are indicated by letters, the explanation of which has been given on page 45. The method of distribution has been shown as W where the proportion purchased from wholesalers was more than the average for all commodities, 65%, and as D where it was less. The degree of concentration is indicated by H where it was high, over 20%, and L where under 20%.

Table 9. *Relationship of characteristics of commodities and methods of distribution by group*

Group of commodities		Degree of concentration	Extent of branding and price maintenance	Type of retail outlet	Price group	Method of distribution	Proportion of total sales of unit retailers
	A						%
Electric fires, kettles and appliances Vacuum cleaners Radios and radiograms Paints, varnishes and distemper Wallpaper Books	Perambulators Portable typewriters Petrol Motor car and motor cycle tyres and tubes Motor cycles and accessories Motor oil	H	S	SS	M–H	D	6
	B						
Cocoa Jam and marmalade Self-raising flour Biscuits	Tea Household and toilet soap Stationery, inks, pens Tobacco and cigarettes	H	S	G–W	L	D	17
	C						
Syrup and treacle Health food beverages Packaged breakfast cereals Canned milk Sauces, pickles and salad creams Canned fruit, vegetables, fish Salt	Matches Household polishes Newspapers and magazines Dental preparations Sanitary towels Toothbrushes Margarine Razors and blades Chocolates	H	S	G–W	L	W	10
	D						
Men's and boys' outerwear Men's and boys' shirts, collars and pyjamas Leather goods Cutlery Watches and clocks	Jewellery and silver and electro-plate Furniture Pottery and glassware Domestic hardware, hollow-ware and general ironmongery Coal	L	I	SS–LS	M–H	D	14

Group of commodities		Degree of concentration	Extent of branding and price maintenance	Type of retail outlet	Price group	Method of distribution	Proportion of total sales of unit retailers
	E						%
Furnishing fabrics Household textiles and soft furnishings Men's and boys' hosiery Men's and boys' hats and caps Men's and boys' handkerchiefs, ties, scarves and braces Women's and children's outerwear Women's and children's underwear and nightwear	Dress materials Leather footwear Fish Fruit and vegetables Potatoes Fresh milk Women's and children's stockings and socks Millinery Gloves Meat—home-killed	L	I	SS–LS	L–M	W	30
	F						
Imitation jewellery Haberdashery and general drapers' goods Unpackaged breakfast cereals	Cheese Butter Eggs Poultry	L	I	G	L	W	8

6. GENERAL CONCLUSIONS ON THE FACTORS INFLUENCING THE METHODS OF DISTRIBUTION TO UNIT RETAILERS

Some of the general conclusions which are suggested by an examination of these six groups, which together cover some 85% of the estimated sales by unit retailers here considered, are discussed below and illustrated by a few examples from the list of commodities in each group.

It would appear from this Table that where the goods are significantly branded and price maintained, have a higher than average concentration of production and are of high unit price, as in Group A, representing approximately 6% of total unit retailers' sales, they tend to be distributed largely direct to retailers, usually to a small number of specialists. For example, radios and radiograms and books are commodities having these features. However, goods having similar characteristics in regard to branding and price maintenance and concentration, but which are of low unit price, Groups B and C, are shown in one case, Group B, as having a more than average proportion distributed direct to retailers and in the other, Group C, a more than average proportion through wholesalers. Biscuits and self-raising flour (Group B), for example, are sold largely direct to retailers, while syrup and treacle and packaged breakfast cereals (Group C) are mainly distributed through wholesalers. The commodities in both B and C Groups were sold by a large number of outlets in one or more trades. Group B represented 17% of total sales by unit retailers and Group C 10%.

Of the groups which are insignificantly branded and have a low concentration of production, the group in the medium to high price category, Group D, representing 14% of the total sales, shows a higher than average distribution direct to retailers, while the groups with the same characteristics but which fall in the low and low to medium price ranges, E and F, representing 38% of total sales, tend to be distributed mainly through wholesalers. Group D goods were usually sold in either a small or large number of specialist shops, as were those in Group E, while Group F goods had a more general distribution.

To sum up, this analysis, although admittedly over-simplified, confirms the conclusions drawn from Tables 8 and 8A. It suggests that, so far as the methods of distribution from producers to unit retailers are concerned, goods which are significantly branded and price maintained, have a higher than average concentration of production and are of high unit price tend to be distributed direct to retailers, Group A, while those which are insignificantly branded and price maintained and have a low concentration of production are mainly distributed through wholesalers, Groups E and F, except where they are of high unit price when they tend to be sold mainly direct to retailers, Group D. In the case of goods with a higher than average concentration of production, significant branding and price maintenance and a low unit price, there appears to be a choice as to the method of distribution adopted, as these two Groups, B and C, have similar characteristics in all respects other than this. In the case of these two Groups the method of distribution employed would appear to depend more on the producer's decision than on the characteristics of the commodity. Owing to the scale of production, the character of the commodities and the type of retail outlets through which they are sold, sales through wholesalers or sales direct to retailers both appear possible and practicable policies. The degree of reliance on credit by the unit retailers in these trades, the average size or groupings of the orders they place, the amount of stock they hold and the frequency of delivery required are elements to be considered by the manufacturer when determining sales policy, as is the tradition in the particular trade. But the deciding factor is the manufacturer's estimate of the potential market to be gained by direct selling as against the costs of organizing and sustaining such a policy. Some of the factors influencing a decision to distribute direct to retailers are the characteristics of the retail trade in the commodity, the extent of the potential market in relation to the unit price of the goods and to competitors' price and sales policy, and the estimated effects of possible greater output on costs of production. Also to be considered are the need and cost of advertising, the number of salesmen required to cover the territory and the size of the economic delivery load. Against these must be set the costs and potential market associated with distribution through wholesalers.

The information obtained in the course of this enquiry has not been sufficiently detailed to warrant an elaboration of the general problem here. The evidence collected would appear to show a considerable diversity in practice. In some instances very extensive estimates are made by the producers of the gain and loss involved in pursuing the existing distribution policy or changing that policy. In other instances belief in the traditional method of distribution tends to outweigh any statistical evidence that might be produced in favour of a change of policy and in yet others the personality and opinions of the sales manager are the deciding factors. One firm consulted, for example, changed its sales policy three times in the eight years before 1939, each change coinciding with the appointment of a new sales manager. Somewhat concealed in the above groupings is a second point which must be borne in mind when considering the policies of producers and the methods of distribution employed. Very few of the commodities are distributed entirely through wholesalers or entirely direct to retailers. Most producers combine the two methods and a change in the methods of sale can sometimes be effected by such a simple means as altering the minimum value of the parcel or consignment which may be ordered direct from the producer.

7. SUMMARY OF FACTORS INFLUENCING METHODS OF DISTRIBUTION

Some assessments can now be made of the incidence of the various factors in order to determine the overall pattern of distribution for all commodities studied. Three main factors were suggested—the characteristics of the commodity, the organization of production and the organization of retailing. In the case of the 3% of total retail sales estimated to have been represented by the output of unit producer/

retailers, the important factor is the second, the organization of production in relation to demand, that is, the existence of small scattered producing units located close to the consumer.

In the case of the commodities passing directly from producer to multiple, co-operative or department store organizations, representing about 37% of total sales, it is the organization of retailing that appears largely to determine the channels used. Whether the production is on a small or large scale, whether the commodity is of high or low unit value, perishable or durable, the goods tended to be wholesaled by concerns linked with the retailers rather than by independent wholesalers. The extent to which these large-scale retailers exerted direct control over the production of the goods as well as over their distribution appears to depend rather more on the character of the commodities. Two main types of good in which there was a close link between retailing and production were noted; firstly, goods requiring processing rather than manufacturing and sold widely and regularly by the retailing organizations, such as butter, bacon and tea; secondly, goods of a durable or semi-durable nature, of medium to high unit price, and retailed through a limited number of outlets, for example men's ready-to-wear clothing and footwear. Many other commodities, such as breakfast cereals and radio, exhibit characteristics similar to those suggested for the two groups, but show no similar integration of their production and distribution. The process of integration is, in fact, very much circumscribed by the existing organization of production and retailing. Integration takes the form of mergers between existing production and retailing organizations rather than the development of entirely new enterprises, and such mergers do not always occur at the rate that economic consideration alone would appear to suggest. And there are further problems of optimum size and ranges of products to be faced by firms already controlling production establishments and considering expansion.

In the case of sales by unit retailers, other than unit producer/retailers, representing just over 60% of total sales, the number of instances where the producer had a genuine choice of alternative methods of distribution appeared to be limited. The characteristics and the methods of distribution of these goods have been discussed in some detail above and there is no need to repeat in full that discussion. But leaving aside the groups of commodities that were noted as possessing miscellaneous characteristics—this heterogeneity may result from the bluntness of the tools of analysis or these commodities may be the exceptions to the generalizations suggested below—the method of distribution used by the producers in four of the six groups distinguished appeared to be readily explained by a reference to the type of production, the number of outlets and the unit price. For example, producers of commodities which showed a low degree of concentration of production; were sold by a large number of outlets, and which were of low unit price, tended to sell their goods through wholesalers, while producers of commodities which showed a high degree of concentration of production, were sold by a small number of outlets, and which were of high unit price, tended to sell their goods direct to retailers. But in the remaining two groups, representing just under a quarter of the total sales of unit retailers, the producers of the commodities, which were subject to practically identical production and retailing conditions, and which possessed many of the same characteristics, appeared to have a choice as to methods of distribution. In these cases the decisions of the producers based on their assumptions regarding the potential market to be gained by the adoption of different methods and the relative costs involved appeared to be more important than the organization of production, the structure of the retail trade in the commodity or the characteristics of that commodity.

This discussion of the factors influencing the methods of distribution has begged a number of questions and has presented a somewhat oversimplified analysis. For example, among the questions which have not been fully answered is why and not merely what goods were distributed in particular ways. While the list of their characteristics has supplied a part of the answer the economic effects of these characteristics have not been fully explored. The analysis too has suffered in some degree from the need to generalize. This had led, for example, to an underemphasis in some cases of the extent of variations in the methods of distribution of the individual products comprising the broader commodities or commodity groups. In the same way the fact that most unit retailers have a number of sources of supply, that they may purchase the same type of good from two or three wholesalers as well as direct from manufacturers, has not been fully brought out in the discussion of the methods of distribution. But most of the questions begged and refinements omitted relate to individual commodities or types of retail trading each calling for a monograph on their own. What has been attempted is a general summary of the relative importance of the main factors influencing the methods of distribution, and, in the process, the administration of a mild correction to the suggestion that the most important problem facing producers was how to distribute their goods. In practice the decision appeared to be scarcely of their making in the case of more than four-fifths of the commodities—three-quarters if imported goods be excluded—although it was a significant and important one for the producers of the remaining one-fifth of the commodities.

But this subject cannot be left without a brief glance at some of the other factors influencing the methods of distribution. These are more sociological and traditional in character than economic and their incidence, accordingly, is far more difficult to measure. As examples of the influence of tradition may be mentioned the tendency of retailers to continue to buy goods from a particular wholesaler, and of producers to continue to deliver direct to a particular retailer, long after the original reason, say, the quality of the service provided or the size of the order placed, has ceased to operate. Personal ties and reluctance to change in such cases often preclude a fully rational approach to the question of the most efficient and economic method of distribution. Or to obtain additional credit the retailer may have opened accounts with four or five separate wholesalers and two or three producers all delivering the same or similar types of goods. The immediate aim is achieved but the multiplicity of sources of supply may continue to be maintained long after the original need for credit has passed. Pressure from the representatives of the different wholesalers and producers, the safety-first wish of the retailer to avoid 'keeping all his eggs in one basket', and the desire to keep 'good will' similarly delay or prevent a reconsideration of the methods of purchase. Other factors influencing the methods of distribution are more overt, such as the influence of unwritten 'principles of trading' and the direct limitation by trade associations. An example of the former is the generally accepted condemnation in many trades of the 'brass-plate' merchant who buys and sells without handling the goods, and the suggestion that unless a wholesaler has a stock-room and a broken-package room he cannot be considered to be a bona fide wholesaler. While this almost unanimous condemnation was not successful in eliminating the 'brass-plater' in many trades, the outspokenness may have limited the preparedness of both established traders and new entrants to consider in a rational way the possibility of alternative and more efficient methods of linking supply and demand. An example of influence exerted on the methods of distribution by trade associations is the effort made in some trades to limit direct trading between producers and retailers by stop lists and other sanctions and to forbid direct trading by the producer with the public.

Many of these traditions and limitations may in practice coincide and not conflict with economic influences affecting methods of distribution, but until their incidence has been carefully studied such an assumption can hardly be justified and they must be listed as additional factors influencing the methods of distribution of consumer goods.

CHAPTER III

THE COSTS OF DISTRIBUTION

I. THE PROBLEM OF DEFINITION OF COSTS OF DISTRIBUTION

The costs of distribution are here considered as the total outlay and expenses involved, including profit, in the performance of the distributive function, that is, in getting goods to the consumer at the right time, in the right place, in the right quantities and at the right price. This concept includes, of course, the costs incurred by the manufacturers or importers in preparing for sale, selling and transporting the finished or near finished goods as well as the costs of wholesaling and retailing. But after general agreement is reached on what is to be included in distribution costs, there remain problems of definition, terminology and of the allocation of costs to different parties. These problems must be briefly discussed and some indication given of the system of classification used before the estimates of the costs can be presented.

Producers' distribution costs

The definition of manufacturers' or producers' distribution costs is one of the most disputed problems, and once this has been overcome it remains a difficult concept to handle without giving misleading impressions when making comparisons between trades or within the same trade. There is a wide divergence of practice between firms as to what should be included in or excluded from their distribution costs. One of the most important questions is how far back into the production process distribution costs should go. For example, should container costs be excluded or included? Some firms include outer packing as a distribution cost but exclude inner packing and inner container cost; others exclude both and yet others include both. In particular trades the decision appears to rest on whether the packing is actually done in the factory as a part of the production process or in a separate packing and despatch department. A second problem which makes comparisons between trades misleading is the allocation of carriage and transport costs. In some trades it is usual for the whole cost to be borne by the wholesaler or by the retailer or, as in the case of motor cars, transport costs take the form of a special addition to the retail price and are paid by the consumer. In other trades, for example the newspaper trade, the organization and maintenance by the producers of a costly and elaborate transport network is an integral part of their business.

There are further issues such as the inclusion or exclusion from producers' distribution costs of the settlement discounts and rebates of various types given. Many firms include these as a part of distribution costs but others deduct them from the net production value of the goods exclusive of distribution costs. Similarly the allocation of profit varies. Some firms take the difference between warehouse value of the goods, excluding profit, and total sales revenue as the distribution costs of the product, thereby including profit on both production and distribution in this figure. Some allocate a percentage of total profits to distribution and others none. This variable practice is one of the many pitfalls that attend comparisons between the distribution costs of a manufacturer selling his goods direct to retailer and the margin allowed to wholesalers on similar goods.

Expenditure on all forms of advertising appears at first sight clearly to be a distribution cost. But reasons can be offered why it should not be so included and there is the further problem of a satisfactory definition. For example, advertising is regarded by some firms as capital expenditure, an addition to the good will of the undertaking, and as having little relationship to the expenses incurred in distributing the product of the firm at any one period of time. The problem of finding a satisfactory definition can be illustrated by the following question: should the elaborate packing and branding of articles, such as toilet preparations, be considered as advertising and therefore a part of distribution costs or as a part of the production costs of the article?

On safer ground is the allocation to producers' distribution costs of warehousing charges and expenses of maintaining depots, salesmen's salaries, and the administrative costs involved in checking, invoicing, receiving and despatching orders. The chief difficulty here lies in the exact definition of some of these costs and the inevitably arbitrary division which has to be made by a great number of firms in the allocation of administrative expenses, materials and labour costs as between production and sales departments.

These comments indicate some of the difficulties involved in finding a satisfactory definition of manufacturers' distribution costs. There can be little doubt that the core of the problem lies in the attempt to split a continuous physical and economic process into separate water-tight compartments, but some division has to be made. In the ensuing discussion of producers' distribution costs, therefore, these costs are taken as including the following items: first, the expenses connected directly with selling and sales promotion, that is salesmen's salaries, commission and other payments, travelling expenses, advertising and sales promotion including free gifts, samples, catalogues and other material, market research, general selling office expenses including invoicing and stock control, and all payments made to agents, brokers and other intermediaries selling on behalf of the producer; second, the expenses connected with handling the finished goods, that is warehousing and storage costs including the cost of maintaining depots, the packing of the finished goods and the carriage and transport costs whether provided by the producer or by an outside contractor; third, the indirect selling costs, that is general administrative costs and the costs of providing finance and credit.

Wholesalers' and retailers' costs

Intermediaries' or wholesalers' and retailers' distribution costs appear to present less difficulty of definition in that they can be described as the difference between the outlay on the goods and the revenue from their sale. In practice some difficulties are met with in the treatment of settlement discounts and mark-downs, wastage, pilferage and other stock losses. The book-keeping methods of wholesalers and retailers vary but the actual cost of performing the wholesaling or retailing function is represented by the realized gross margin after allowing for discounts received and discounts given and stock losses. A somewhat different problem arises in the case of hire purchase or credit trading when undertaken by retailers. These selling arrangements increase the spread between the outlay on goods by the retailer and his revenue. The increase in the spread actually represents the price the consumer pays for borrowing money in order to buy now what would otherwise have to be purchased in the future out of accumulated personal savings. Or to put it another way, the additional payment made is payment for a service rather than a good, and there is a case for excluding it from the cost of distribution of the product. Another problem of definition arises where the wholesaler or retailer performs some processing operation on the goods in his possession before re-sale, for example maturing cheese, blending tea or coffee or slaughtering and cutting meat. Productive functions can never be completely separated from distributive functions and in these instances all that can be done is to narrow the overlap as far as possible and note where it occurs. A further problem is the combination of functions in one unit such as the producer/retailer, the importer/wholesaler or the wholesaler/retailer. In order to discuss distribution costs at all some division has to be made, on an arbitrary basis in many cases, between the cost of the products and the cost of their distribution by the producer/retailer, whether the organization be a unit retailer or multiple or co-operative concern, but in the other instances of joint functions, the importer/wholesaler and wholesaler/retailer, the costs of performing each function need not be arbitrarily separated as they are both distribution costs.

2. THE CLASSIFICATION OF DISTRIBUTION COSTS USED AND THE RELIABILITY OF THE ESTIMATES

The different elements constituting distribution costs having been agreed upon in general, the grouping of the costs under main headings, the methods of calculation and the reliability of the evidence can be discussed.

The main headings used are firstly producers' distribution costs, secondly wholesalers' and importers' distribution costs, including net profit, and thirdly retailers' distribution costs, including net profit. Under the first heading come the manufacturers' distribution costs proper, as discussed above, and also the costs and net profit involved in selling direct to the consumer by mail order, door-to-door selling and similar direct means but excluding producer/retailer trading and the retail margin earned when selling through a shop or outlet linked with the producer. Under the second heading are included all costs and net profit represented by the difference, after allowing for stock losses, between the manufacturers' selling price and the price paid by the retailer where the goods pass through an intermediary who takes financial possession of the goods or the difference between the landed price plus duty and the price paid by the retailer whether the goods pass through an intermediary or not. Under the third heading are included all costs and net profit represented by the difference, after allowing for stock losses, between the outlay by the retailer and the revenue from sale. The costs and net profit of firms performing two or more distributive functions in relation to the same consignment of goods such as wholesaling and retailing or importing, wholesaling and retailing, are included under this heading. The category of retailers' distribution cost or gross margin therefore covers the wholesaling and the retailing costs of multiple, department store and co-operative organizations, as no attempt has been made to distinguish between the two types of costs. The retailing costs and net retailing profit of producer/retailers likewise are included here, as are also the retailing costs and profits of multiple retailers selling commodities produced in linked manufacturing units. In some instances, to distinguish the retailing from the manufacturing costs of goods produced by manufacturing concerns linked with multiple retailers, a notional figure has had to be used as the price at which the retail units purchase the products. This is somewhat unsatisfactory but rather less so than the alternative of including the total costs and profit in the category of producers' distribution costs.[1]

The information obtained on distribution costs was collected in the same way as that relating to methods of distribution and therefore must be viewed in the same light. There are, however, particular problems of interpretation. The information on manufacturers' distribution costs is in some ways the least reliable, owing in part to the difficulties and differences of definition discussed above and in part to the reluctance of many manufacturers to disclose their costs. This latter feature added to the problem of estimating an average for any particular commodity and, of course, increased the possibility of error. A further problem arose in some trades where the product was sold generally to industrial as well as private users or where a wide variety of products was made, some of which were sold only to industrial users and others only to private users. In most of these instances the firms concerned did not separate their costs of sale to industrial and private users and the allocation of distribution costs on sales to private users has been made somewhat arbitrarily.

In estimating the distribution costs of wholesalers and retailers the concept of gross realized margin was used. The make-up of the margins of wholesalers and other intermediaries and of retailers on the sale of the various commodities is discussed in the case studies; here all that need be said is that the estimates of gross realized margins include not only the basic margins earned after allowing for stock losses but also the difference between discounts, rebates, bonuses and other allowances, if any, earned and given. No allowance in the estimated distribution costs of retailers has been made for the additional revenue that might be earned by them for club trading and for sales on hire purchase, though some indication of the extent of hire purchase trading is given, where information exists, in the particular case studies. No allowance, either, has been made for the dividends distributed to consumers by the retail co-operative societies, though these undoubtedly lower the total cost of distribution on certain commodities to certain purchasers.

The estimates of total distribution costs and of the distribution costs of producers, wholesalers and retailers used in the following tables are based on the information given in the case studies. The assumptions made in calculating these costs and margins have been briefly discussed in the Introduction. All that need be said here is that the estimates do not claim to be closely accurate but are rather intended to

[1] The classification used for the different costs of distribution is set out in the Glossary.

show the order of magnitude of different costs. As far as any judgment on their accuracy can be made, it is thought that the producers' distribution costs in a number of instances are understated. This has arisen from the difficulty mentioned above of obtaining full information on this aspect of distribution cost. Further the combined wholesale and retail margins of large-scale retailing organizations earned on purchases direct from producers, which are included in retail margins, may also be slightly understated. This has arisen from the difficulty of obtaining exact information on the actual terms given to such organizations by producers.

3. ESTIMATES OF THE TOTAL COSTS OF DISTRIBUTION OF THE COMMODITIES STUDIED

The variations in the total distribution costs of individual commodities are presented in Chart III. The commodities have been arranged in order of magnitude of distribution costs, though it will be clear that comparisons of the costs of distribution of different commodities mean little without information on the comparative functions performed by the distributors of the different commodities. A further warning may be necessary. The method employed of presenting the spreads as percentages of the retail price or as percentages of estimated

NOTES TO CHART III

The figures given of consumers' expenditure and of total costs of distribution are, as in the case of figures used in the other Charts, the middle points of estimated ranges rounded off to the nearest ·5. The division of the total costs of distribution in each case between producers', wholesalers' and retailers' costs and margins is presented visually as the data hardly warrants the use of single figures, but the information on the estimated ranges in each case is given in the case studies in Chart IV and Tables 12 and 16.

In those cases where the goods were imported and sold to the consumer without further processing, other than breaking bulk, no producers' distribution costs have been given. Petrol and motor oil form a borderline case where the importer/distributor companies undertake some processing, but these costs including those of advertising have been classed as importing and wholesaling costs.

Duty is an important constituent of consumers' expenditure in the case of the following commodities: cigarettes and tobacco, beer, wines and spirits, matches, petrol and motor oil and tea. If the duty paid is excluded from the estimate of consumers' expenditure in each case, while the actual cost of distribution remains the same, this cost expressed as a percentage of consumers' expenditure less duty would increase in each case.

Producers' distribution costs on sugar, sewing machines and plain flour have been based on indirect information and may be less reliable than the other estimates. See page 164.

Chart III is available for download from
www.cambridge.org/9781107602748

consumers' expenditure can be very misleading. While comparisons between the total figures are possible, the division of the total costs between producer, wholesaler and retailer reflects the methods of distribution in use in each commodity and shows only the relative share of the total costs borne by each participant. Some of the pitfalls inherent in this manner of presentation are obvious. For example, the small share of the total costs borne by wholesalers in the distribution of some commodities clearly reflects the insignificance of the sales of those commodities through wholesalers and has no relation whatsoever to the size of the wholesalers' gross margin on those goods. Others are more obscure. For example, where mail order or door-to-door sales are significant, producers' distribution costs appear as a relatively larger and wholesalers' and retailers' costs a relatively smaller proportion of total sales. When producer/retailer sales are significant both producers' and wholesalers' costs appear as relatively smaller proportions. Where retailers' or wholesalers' gross margins are large, producers' distribution costs tend relatively to be small and vice versa. Conclusions as to the comparative distribution costs of producers or gross margins of wholesalers or retailers cannot, therefore, be drawn from this chart. Here all that is presented is the estimated total distribution costs of the various commodities and the share of the producer, wholesaler and retailer in those costs.

Costs of distribution by trade groups

The estimates of total distribution costs can also be presented for the commodities aggregated in trade groups as follows:

Table 10. *Estimated total distribution costs in 1938 of commodities by trade groups*[1]

Trade group	Consumers' expenditure	Total distribution costs as proportion of consumers' expenditure	Producers', wholesalers' and importers', and retailers' distribution costs or gross margins as a proportion of consumers' expenditure		
			Producers	Wholesalers and importers	Retailers
	£ million	%	%	%	%
Newspapers and magazines	48·0	58·5	22·5	6·5	29·5
Chemists' goods	55·0	53·0	15·0	5·0	33·0
Stationery, pens and inks	17·5	52·0	6·0	6·0	40·0

Trade group	Consumers' expenditure	Total distribution costs as proportion of consumers' expenditure	Producers', wholesalers' and importers', and retailers' distribution costs or gross margins as a proportion of consumers' expenditure		
			Producers	Wholesalers' and importers	Retailers
	£ million	%	%	%	%
Jewellers' goods	24·5	51·5	2·5	8·0	41·0
Furniture	63·5	50·0	7·0	2·5	40·5
Coal	97·5	49·5	18·0	1·5	30·0
Chocolates and sweets	55·0	49·5	8·5	5·0	36·0
Pottery and ironmongers' goods	45·0	48·5	7·0	5·0	36·5
Electrical goods	28·0	48·0	13·0	3·0	32·0
Other specialities	37·5	48·0	9·0	3·5	35·5
Fish	35·5	47·5	3·0	16·0	28·5
Milk	86·5	47·5	3·5	3·0	41·0
Fruit and vegetables	141·0	46·0	3·5	13·5	29·0
Furnishings	59·0	45·0	4·0	6·0	35·0
Women's and children's wear	239·0	44·0	4·0	6·0	34·0
Men's and boys' wear	121·5	43·0	4·5	4·5	34·0
Footwear	68·0	37·0	4·0	3·5	29·5
Motor trade	114·5	33·0	4·5	7·0	21·5
Groceries	262·0	31·0	8·0	3·0	20·0
Beer, wines and spirits	297·0	30·0	3·0	1·5	25·5
Meat	180·0	29·5	1·0	3·5	25·0
Poultry, game and rabbits	19·0	27·0	1·0	3·0	23·0
Cigarettes and tobacco	177·0	25·0	5·0	2·0	18·0
Bread and flour confectionery	104·5	23·0	3·0	—	20·0
Provisions	206·0	22·0	1·5	3·5	17·0

[1] The individual commodities included in the various trade groups have been given above, p. 21.

Costs of distribution of all commodities

Finally the costs of distribution can be shown for three broad classes of commodities and for all commodities included in the enquiry.

Table 11. *Estimated total distribution costs of commodities by three main classes and of all commodities included in the enquiry*

Commodity division	Consumers' expenditure	Total distribution costs as proportion of consumers' expenditure	Producers', wholesalers' and importers', and retailers' distribution costs or gross margins as a proportion of consumers' expenditure		
			Producers	Wholesalers and importers	Retailers
	£ million	%	%	%	%
Food and drink[1]	1,386·0	32	3·5	4·0	24·5
Clothing and footwear	429·0	42·5	4·0	5·0	33·5
Other goods	767·0	42·0	9·0	4·0	29·0
All commodities[1]	2,582·0	35–39	5–6	4–5	26–28

[1] If on-licence sales of beer, wines and spirits are excluded, the distribution costs of the food group, using middle points and not ranges would be: Total distribution costs 32·6%, producers' distribution costs 3·8%, wholesalers' margins 4·8%, retailers' margins 24·0%. The distribution costs for all commodities would be, again using middle points: Total distribution costs 37·4%, producers' distribution costs 5·5%, wholesalers' margins 4·6%, retailers' margins 27·3%.

Limitations of the data

In considering these estimates the limitations of the evidence discussed above and also the particular methods used in allocating different costs under the different headings must be borne in mind. Taking the costs as a whole it is possible that the total spread has been underestimated. This may have arisen partly from the difficulty of obtaining full information on producers' distribution costs and partly from an underestimate of the total spread between the purchase and selling price of goods sold by the large scale retailing organizations which undertook their own wholesaling. A further factor which should perhaps be mentioned is the possibility that in view of the general suggestions that distribution costs are too high, producers, wholesalers and retailers may, in providing information, have understated their costs and margins. This possibility exists though every effort has been made by cross-checking in various ways the information received to counter any underestimate due to this factor.

But from Chart III and Tables 10 and 11 a general pattern of the main features of distribution costs begins to emerge. Of the main trade groups foodstuffs, except fish, milk, and fruit and vegetables, show the lowest total distribution costs, and specialities except the motor trade and household goods show the highest total costs, with clothing and footwear in the middle. A closer analysis, however, cannot be made until the constituent parts of the total cost—producers' costs and wholesalers' and retailers' gross margins—are examined.

Taking retailers and wholesalers first, the gross retail margins given include the joint wholesaling and retailing margins earned by multiple, co-operative and department store organizations as well as the retail margin earned by unit retailers. The gross margins, as such, obtained by wholesalers are not shown in any way and, further, the proportion of total consumers' expenditure represented by the returns to wholesalers includes the margins of importers and other intermediaries. In the case studies information has been given of the margins obtained by wholesalers and of the margins obtained by retailers when purchasing from wholesalers. By using this information and considering only that portion of the sales made through wholesalers and eliminating the margins earned by importers and other intermediaries, a more accurate picture of wholesale and retail gross margins is obtained.

This alternative picture cannot, however, be freed entirely from distortion. Multiple, department store and co-operative organizations all purchase to some extent through wholesalers and in some instances split margins with wholesalers. Further no effective attempt can be made to distinguish the component parts of the importer/wholesalers' margin, a combination which is usual in some trades. These problems are, however, of relatively small statistical significance and should not seriously affect the figures relating to all commodities and to commodities arranged in trade groups.

4. THE MARGINS OF WHOLESALERS AND RETAILERS ON GOODS SOLD THROUGH WHOLESALERS

The gross margins earned by wholesalers and retailers on the goods sold through wholesalers can be shown as percentages of consumers' expenditure. It is not possible with the information available to show the producers' distribution costs incurred on sales to wholesalers. The costs for individual commodities are shown in Chart IV; in each case the margins relate to realized margins after allowing for mark-downs, stock losses, and discounts obtained and given. The size of the retail margin determined the order of the commodities in the Chart.

Chart IV is available for download from
www.cambridge.org/9781107602748

NOTES TO CHART IV

The figures given of consumers' expenditure and of wholesalers' and retailers' percentage margins are very approximate and the middle point of ranges, rounded off in the latter instances to the nearest ·5%, have been used.

The wholesale margins given in this Chart, or rather the estimated spread between wholesalers' outlay and revenue expressed as a percentage of consumers' expenditure, while reflecting the cost of wholesaling in relation to the final price do not give any direct indication of the margin of wholesalers in relation to turnover. The estimated margin earned by wholesalers expressed as a percentage of their sales is shown in the following Table. In each division the commodities are arranged in ascending order of estimated margins: that is, in the 4% to 6% division for example, wholesalers' margins on household soap are the highest and on poultry the lowest.

Table 12. *Estimated wholesalers' margins in 1938 as a percentage of sales, by commodities*

Estimated wholesalers' margin as a percentage of sales[1] %	Commodity or commodity group	
2–4	Sugar	Spirits—on-licence sales
4–6	Poultry, game and rabbits Coal Motor cars[2] Butter Meat	Eggs[2] Cigarettes and tobacco Spirits—off-licence sales Household soap
6–8	Bacon London evening newspapers Canned milk Cheese	Syrup and treacle Matches Provincial daily newspapers
8–10	Unpackaged cereals Beer—off-licence sales Beer—on-licence sales Tea Candles and nightlights Imported canned fruit and vegetables[2]	Cocoa Jam and marmalade Salt Margarine Plain flour

Estimated wholesalers' margin as a percentage of sales[1] %	Commodity or commodity group	
10–12	Kerosene	Home-canned fruit and vegetables
	Sauces, soups and salad creams	Biscuits
	Packaged cereals	London morning newspapers
	Coffee	Motor cycles
	Toilet and shaving soap	Chocolates and sweets
	Books	
12–14	Self-raising flour	Linoleum
	Motor car tyres and tubes	Sports goods
	Perambulators	Infant and invalid foods
	Cutlery	Wines—off-licence sales[2]
	Sewing machines	Photographic goods
	Rubber footwear	Proprietary medicines and drugs
14–16	Wallpaper	Household polishes and cleaners
	Electric light lamps	Sunday newspapers
	Health food beverages	Vacuum cleaners
	Non-proprietary medicines	Men's and boys' hosiery
	Dental preparations	Carpets
	Magazines	
16–18	Household textiles	Wines—on-licence sales[2]
	Dress materials	Other drapers' goods
	Sunday newspapers	Men's handkerchiefs, braces
	Leather footwear	Watches
	Women's underwear and night-wear	Clocks
	Perfumes and toilet waters	Women's stockings and socks
	Shirts, collars and pyjamas	Furnishing fabrics
	Gloves	Motor car mechanical components
	Men's and boys' outerwear	
	Women's outerwear	
18–20	Radios	Sanitary towels
	Beauty preparations	Milk[2]
	Razors and blades	Motor oil
	Corsets	Pens and pencils
	Electric fires and appliances	

Estimated wholesalers' margin as a percentage of sales[1] %	Commodity or commodity group	
20–22	Motor cycle accessories Contraceptives Furs and fur garments Toys	Millinery Furniture Fruit and vegetables[2] Brooms and brushes
22–24	Leather goods Inks and accessories Real jewellery Potatoes[2] Toothbrushes	Motor car ignition equipment and batteries Paints and varnish Motor cycle and cycle tyres and tubes Silver and electro-plate
24–26	Motor car accessories Fish[2] Hardware and hollow-ware Hats and caps	Pottery and glassware Stationery and other paper products Imitation jewellery

[1] In these steps the range includes the first figure and up to the second.

[2] The estimated wholesalers' gross margin in these instances is overstated, as a proportion of these goods pass through two or more wholesalers and the wholesalers' margin given here is the sum of their margins. In some cases the usual wholesalers' margin is split between two wholesalers, but in other instances the sales through two wholesalers represent an addition to the total costs.

Margins of wholesalers and retailers by trade groups

The estimated margins of wholesalers and retailers on goods passing through wholesalers expressed as percentages of consumers' expenditure and arranged in trade groups are shown in Table 13.

Table 13. *Estimated margins of wholesalers and retailers in 1938 on goods passing through wholesalers, by trade groups*

Trade group	Consumers' expenditure on commodities passing through wholesalers £ million	Wholesalers' gross margin as percentage of retail sales %	Retailers' gross margin as percentage of retail sales %
Jewellers' goods	7·0	13·0	42·5
Furniture	11·0	13·5	36·0
Beer, wines and spirits—on-licence sales	27·0	7·0	35·5
Stationery, inks, pens and pencils	6·0	16·0	34·0
Chocolates and sweets	35·0	8·0	33·5
Men's and boys' wear	46·5	11·5	33·0
Women's and children's wear	122·0	11·5	32·5
Furnishing	30·5	10·5	32·5
Other specialities	8·5	12·0	32·0
Electrical goods	7·0	13·0	32·0
Pottery and ironmongers' goods	14·0	16·5	31·0
Milk	19·5	14·0	30·5
Newspapers and magazines	33·0	9·5	28·5
Footwear	21·0	11·5	28·0
Fruit and vegetables	111·5	16·0	27·0
Fish	31·0	18·0	27·0
Chemists' goods	25·5	10·5	27·0
Coal	36·0	3·5	27·0
Meat	52·0	4·0	25·0
Motor trade	47·5	6·5	21·5
Poultry, game and rabbits	12·0	3·5	21·0
Beer, wines and spirits—off-licence sales	32·0	6·0	18·0
Cigarettes and tobacco	93·0	4·0	16·5
Groceries and household stores	93·0	7·0	16·5
Provisions	104·0	5·0	15·0

The estimated margins of wholesalers expressed as a percentage of turnover require separate presentation and they are given for commodities by trade groups in the following Table:

Table 14. *Estimated margins of wholesalers in 1938 as a percentage of sales, by trade groups*

Gross margin of wholesalers as a percentage of wholesalers' sales %	Trade group	
3–5	Coal	Poultry, game and rabbits Cigarettes and tobacco
5–7	Provisions	Meat
7–9	Groceries and household stores Beer, wines and spirits—off-licence sales	Motor trade[1]
9–11	Beer, wines and spirits—on-licence sales	
11–13	Chocolates and sweets	
13–15	Chemists' goods	Newspapers and magazines
15–17	Footwear	Furnishings
17–19	Electrical goods Other specialities	Women's and children's wear Men's and boys' wear
19–21	Milk[1]	
21–23	Jewellers' goods Fresh fruit and vegetables[1]	Furniture
23–25	Fish[1] Stationery, pens and inks	Pottery and ironmongers' goods

[1] In these trade groups, owing to a proportion of the goods passing through two wholesalers, the estimated margin of wholesalers on sales is overstated by the addition of two or more margins.

Margins of wholesalers and retailers on all commodities

Finally the estimated margins of wholesalers and retailers on goods passing through wholesalers by three main classes and for all commodities are presented in Table 15. The estimated margins of wholesalers as a percentage of turnover are also shown.

Table 15. *Estimated margins of wholesalers and retailers in 1938 on goods passing through wholesalers, by three main divisions and for all commodities*

Commodity or group	Estimated consumers' expenditure	Gross margins as a percentage of consumers' expenditure		Gross margin of wholesalers as a percentage of wholesale sales
		Wholesalers	Retailers	
	£ million	%	%	%
Food and drink	518·0	9·0	23·0	11·5
Clothing	189·0	11·5	32·0	17·0
Other goods	319·0	8·0	25·5	10·5
All commodities	1,026·0	9–9·5	25–25·5	12–12·5

The total turnover of wholesalers, using wholesalers in the sense defined above, was in the region of £750 millions for the commodities included in the enquiry. This figure can only be approximate owing to the difficulty of isolating the wholesalers' turnover entirely from the turnover of other distributors. The wholesalers' gross margin, on these figures, amounted to just over £90 millions.

5. THE MARGINS EARNED BY DIFFERENT TYPES OF DISTRIBUTOR

The factors influencing the costs of distribution of the various commodities and groups of commodities are discussed in the following chapter. But here some suggestions based on the above Tables can be made regarding the wholesale and retail margins earned by the different types of distributor.

A comparison of Tables 11 and 15 shows that the gross margin of retailers on all commodities covered in the survey is estimated at 26–28%, while the gross margin of retailers on all goods purchased from wholesalers is estimated at 25–25·5%.[1] The gross margin of retailers on all goods purchased direct from producers, estimated from these figures, is 28–29%. Approximately 60% of the sales classed as sales direct to retailers were sales to multiple, department store and co-operative organizations, the remaining 40% being sales direct to unit retailers. The gross margins earned by unit retailers purchasing direct from manufacturers were slightly higher than the gross margins earned by unit retailers purchasing from wholesalers, and the type of commodities purchased direct carried, usually, a slightly higher retail margin than the commodities purchased from wholesalers. The gross margin earned on all commodities by unit retailers purchasing direct from manufacturers was, it is estimated, about 1–1·5% higher than that earned by the unit retailer purchasing from wholesalers. Direct selling, as is shown in the case studies, was effected by the producer's undertaking the wholesaler's function and not—so far as unit retailers were concerned—splitting the function and margin with the retailer. If the margin of unit retailers when purchasing direct from producers be accepted as 26–27%, the gross margin earned by multiple, department store and co-operative organizations on their retail sales was approximately 29–30% or about 4–4·5% higher than that earned by the unit retailer purchasing from wholesalers. This figure is not, of course, even allowing for the crudity of the estimates, strictly comparable with the 9–9·5% given in Table 15 as the gross margin of wholesalers as a percentage of consumers' expenditure. This wholesale margin is almost certainly overestimated by comparison with the other figures owing to the failure to exclude other than 'pure' wholesaling margins and to a certain amount of double counting where two wholesalers were engaged in the distribution of the product. On the other hand the suggested 4–4·5% margin for 'wholesaling' of the multiple, co-operative

[1] Such a comparison while it can be made, for some purposes, in relation to all commodities can only be made between groups of commodities with considerable caution. For example, a comparison of the retail gross margins earned on other goods in Tables 11 and 15, 29% in the case of total sales and 25·5% in the case of purchases from wholesalers, may give the impression that the terms allowed to retailers purchasing direct from producers were very much more favourable than those obtained by retailers purchasing from wholesalers, or that trading by co-operative, multiple and department store organizations was very significant in this group of goods, thus inflating the retail margin with the combined wholesale and retail margins earned by these organizations. Both these impressions are incorrect and the chief reason for the wide difference in the two estimates of retail margin is the tendency of the goods in this group which have a low retail margin to be sold through wholesalers, while those with a high retail margin are sold direct to retailer. In the other two groups, food and drink and clothing, the commodities included are rather more homogeneous and the estimates in the Tables, therefore, less misleading.

and department store organizations is understated owing to the fact that the retail margins considered by themselves in these organizations tend to be slightly lower than those in unit retail shops in similar trades owing to a deliberate pricing policy in many instances and to a higher rate of stock turn. A further difficulty in making any comparison is the bias of the multiple and co-operative organizations towards the foodstuffs trades, trades which, certainly on the provisions side, carry a low wholesale margin. If the evidence were sufficiently detailed to permit some weighting to be given to these factors, the gap between the 4–4·5% and the 9–9·5% suggested above would be narrowed, but there would still, on the information obtained in this survey, remain a gap indicating a lower total wholesaling and retailing cost on goods distributed through these multiple, co-operative and department store organizations than on goods purchased by unit retailers from wholesalers.

6. PRODUCERS' DISTRIBUTION COSTS

Finally the estimates of producers' distribution costs can be presented in a similar fashion as a percentage of producers' sales revenue to enable some comparisons to be made of the functions undertaken by producers in the distribution of various commodities.

Separate figures of the costs incurred by producers when distributing to unit retailers as distinct from distributing to all retailers cannot be given and therefore all sales by producers are included. The average producers' distribution costs on all commodities are estimated at about 8% of producers' sales revenue. This includes the sales of finished imported goods on which, by the definitions adopted above, no producers' distribution costs were incurred. If the imported goods which did not undergo any process of manufacturing after landing are excluded, producers' distribution costs as a percentage of sales revenue rise to 9–9·5%. The estimates relating to individual commodities are subject to an important margin of error and the most satisfactory manner of presentation was considered to be by a series of steps as in Table 16. Within each step the commodities are arranged in descending order, for example in the 30–25% division sewing machines are estimated to have a higher producers' distribution cost than coal.

Table 16. *Estimated producers' distribution costs shown as proportion of producers' sales revenue for each commodity in 1938*

Producers' distribution costs as a proportion of producers' sales revenue %	Commodity or commodity group	
45–35	Newspapers	Toilet and shaving soap Health food beverages
35–30	Dental preparations	Proprietary medicines and drugs
30–25	Sewing machines[1] Beauty preparations Perfumes and toilet waters Packaged cereals	Vacuum cleaners Kerosene Salt Coal
25–20	Infant and invalid foods Cocoa Candles and nightlights Household soap, powder and flakes	Radios and radiograms Wallpaper Magazines and periodicals
20–15	Perambulators Books Biscuits Self-raising flour Margarine Household polishes Toys	Paints, varnishes and distempers Contraceptives Razors and blades Motor car tyres and tubes Photographic goods[1] Motor car parts and accessories Portable typewriters
15–10	Chocolates and sweets Electric fires, kettles and appliances Motor cycle accessories Toothbrushes Brooms and brushes Domestic hardware, hollow-ware and ironmongery Stationery, inks, pens and pencils Plain flour[1]	Sports goods[1] Cutlery Sanitary towels Motor cycles Cycle tyres and tubes Home-canned fruit and vegetables Sauces, pickles and salad creams Jam and marmalade

Producers' distribution costs as a proportion of producers' sales revenue %	Commodity or commodity group	
10–5	Linoleum	Cigarettes and tobacco
	Men's and boys' outerwear	Syrup and treacle
	Pottery and glassware	Women's and children's underwear and nightwear
	Electric light lamps	Clocks
	Leather goods	Fish
	Potatoes	Canned milk
	Motor cars	Rubber footwear
	Women's and children's outerwear	Non-proprietary medicines and drugs
	Stockings and socks	Leather footwear
	Dress materials	Fresh fruit and vegetables
	Corsets	Furnishing fabrics
	Carpets	Silver and electro-plate
	Shirts, collars and pyjamas	Household textiles and soft furnishings
	Fresh milk	
	Tea	
	Coffee	
Under 5	Men's and boys' hats and caps	Gloves
	Spirits—on-licence sales	Haberdashery and general drapers' goods
	Real jewellery	Flour confectionery
	Unpackaged cereals	Poultry, game and rabbits
	Spirits—off-licence sales	Fish
	Beer—on-licence sales	Bacon and ham
	Sugar[1]	Cheese
	Men's and boys' hosiery	Imitation jewellery
	Beer—off-licence sales	Watches
	Millinery	Meat
	Matches	Wines—off-licence sales
	Bread	Wines—on-licence sales
	Men's handkerchiefs, ties, braces, scarves	Butter
		Eggs

[1] The estimates of the costs of distribution incurred by producers of these commodities are based on indirect information and may be less reliable than the other estimates. See page 164.

Producers' distribution costs by trade groups

Again, to show the pattern more clearly the commodities can be grouped into main trade categories as follows:

Table 17. *Estimated producers' distribution costs as proportion of producers' sales revenue, by trade groups in 1938*

Trade group	Consumers' expenditure £ million	Producers' distribution costs as a proportion of producers' sales revenue %
Newspapers and magazines	48·0	33–37
Coal	97·5	25–28
Chemists' goods	55·0	23–25
Electrical goods	28·0	19–21
Chocolates and sweets	55·0	14–15
Other specialities	37·5	14–15
Furniture	63·5	12–13
Stationery, inks, pens and pencils	17·5	11–12
Pottery and ironmongers' goods	45·0	11–12
Groceries and household stores	262·0	10–11
Women's and children's wear	239·0	7–8
Men's and boys' wear	121·5	6–7
Furnishings	59·0	6–7
Milk	86·5	6–7
Cigarettes and tobacco	177·0	6–7
Motor trade	114·5	6–7
Fruit and vegetables	141·0	6–7
Footwear	68·0	5–6
Fish	35·5	5–6
Beer, wines and spirits—on-licence sales	237·5	4
Jewellers' goods	24·5	4
Beer, wines and spirits—off-licence sales	59·5	4
Bread and flour confectionery	104·5	3
Provisions	206·0	2
Poultry, game and rabbits	19·0	2
Meat	180·0	1

Incompleteness of information on producers' distribution costs and the relative costs of different methods of distribution

The estimates of producers' distribution costs are, as suggested above, not very reliable owing to the difficulties of securing a common definition and of obtaining information, and they are also unsatisfactory on a further count. To reach the core of the problem of the efficiency or inefficiency, the economy or waste of different methods and practices of distribution, the expenditure of money and manpower on the different methods needs to be accurately costed. An approximation to the answer can be obtained in those trades where some producers sell all their goods to wholesalers and then to retailers and where other producers sell all their goods direct to retailers, but where individual producers pursue a mixed policy a usable answer under the present system of costing is almost impossible to obtain. Many producers concern themselves solely with the total costs of distribution incurred irrespective of the method of distribution. Others, usually the larger ones, attempt some estimates of the cost of the various methods of distribution in operation. But to the initial differences between producers as to what constitutes distribution costs in general are added differences as to the allocation of costs to the different methods. If an attempt is made to distinguish between the cost of distribution through wholesalers as against the cost of distribution direct to retailers, problems such as how to allocate advertising costs, the salaries of salesmen who call on both wholesalers and retailers, and market research costs immediately arise. Different methods are used to serve the purpose in hand of the particular firm, but these results can hardly be used to draw conclusions regarding the trade as a whole. However, what is probably required is not so much agreement on the method of allocating costs as information on the proportions of total costs incurred under each heading by each firm along with some measurement of the methods of distribution used by that firm. Until this kind of statistical material is available, the experiences of one unit based on the costing methods employed by that unit have a very limited application.

The information obtained in the course of this enquiry does not fulfil these requirements and therefore only partial light is thrown on the problem of the relative costs of different methods of distribution. An attempt has been made on the basis of information given by various firms and associations and by using what other information exists on producers' distribution costs such as advertising expenditure, to present figures relating to the particular trade as a whole. But at the same time, as shown in many of the individual case studies, there is no question but that there were marked differences in costs involved in selling direct to retailers as against selling through wholesalers, or selling direct to multiple and department store organizations as against selling direct to unit retailers. The total producers' distribution costs on all commodities studied is estimated above at 5–6% of consumers' expenditure and at about 8% of producers' sales revenue. In the instances where

Chart V THE COSTS OF DISTRIBUTION OF ALL COMMODITIES

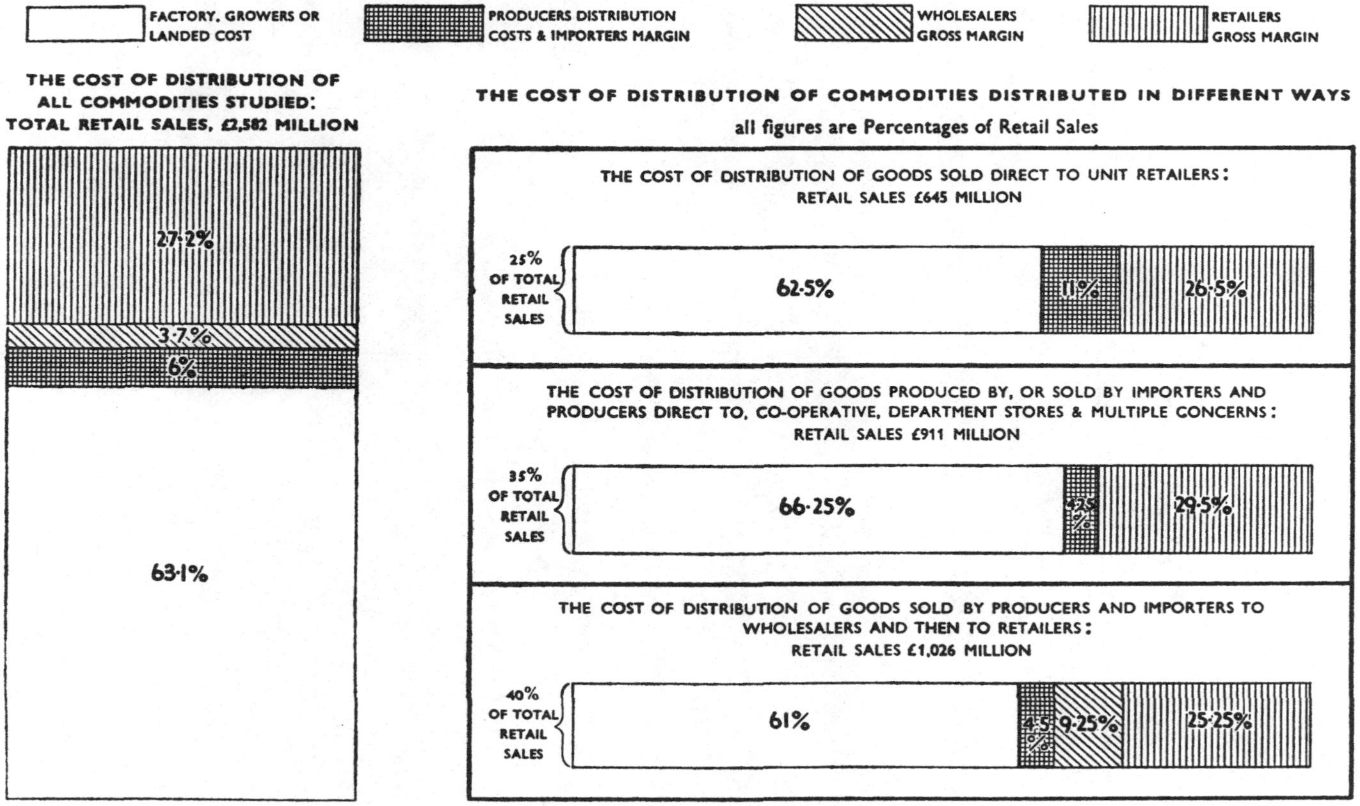

FACTORY, GROWERS OR LANDED COST
PRODUCERS DISTRIBUTION COSTS & IMPORTERS MARGIN
WHOLESALERS GROSS MARGIN
RETAILERS GROSS MARGIN
THE COST OF DISTRIBUTION OF ALL COMMODITIES STUDIED: TOTAL RETAIL SALES, £2,582 MILLION
27·2%
3·7%
6%
63·1%
THE COST OF DISTRIBUTION OF COMMODITIES DISTRIBUTED IN DIFFERENT WAYS
all figures are Percentages of Retail Sales
THE COST OF DISTRIBUTION OF GOODS SOLD DIRECT TO UNIT RETAILERS: RETAIL SALES £645 MILLION
25% OF TOTAL RETAIL SALES
62·5%
11%
26·5%
THE COST OF DISTRIBUTION OF GOODS PRODUCED BY, OR SOLD BY IMPORTERS AND PRODUCERS DIRECT TO, CO-OPERATIVE, DEPARTMENT STORES & MULTIPLE CONCERNS: RETAIL SALES £911 MILLION
35% OF TOTAL RETAIL SALES
66·25%
4·25%
29·5%
THE COST OF DISTRIBUTION OF GOODS SOLD BY PRODUCERS AND IMPORTERS TO WHOLESALERS AND THEN TO RETAILERS: RETAIL SALES £1,026 MILLION
40% OF TOTAL RETAIL SALES
61%
4·5%
9·25%
25·25%

two estimates of producers' distribution costs on the one commodity were obtained, one relating to sales entirely through wholesalers and to the wholesale depots of multiple, co-operative and department store organizations and the other relating to sales entirely direct to unit retailers, the cost incurred in the former case averaged 5–6% of sales revenue and in the latter case 18–20% of sales revenue. These figures cannot be applied to all commodities, as the sample is unrepresentative in that the commodities selected were all manufactured goods, about half were branded and no imported goods were included, the result being an overstatement of producers' distribution costs. On the other hand, as suggested above, producers' distribution costs as a whole are probably underestimated. The ratio between the two estimates does, however, give a rough indication of the variation concealed in the overall average of 8% given above.

7. SUMMARY OF THE COSTS OF DISTRIBUTION

A diagrammatic presentation of the estimates of total distribution costs of the commodities included in the enquiry is given in Chart V. Goods in their finished state valued at some £1,630 millions at the factory, farm or port cost the domestic consumer some £2,582 millions. Producers' distribution costs represented about 5·4% of the retail price of the goods, the margin of wholesalers, importers and other intermediaries about 4·3% and the margins of retailers about 27·2%. A breakdown of these estimates to show the cost of selling goods in different ways and through different types of outlet can only be of a very tentative nature. Generally, on the goods sold direct to co-operative, multiple and department store retailing organizations, producers' distribution costs were of the order of 4·5%, and retail margins, including the cost of wholesaling, 29–30% of the retail price. These sales represented about 35% of total sales. On the goods sold through wholesalers to retailers, producers' distribution costs were of the order of 4–5%, wholesalers' margins 9–9·5% and retailers' margins 25–25·5% of the retail price. These goods represented some 40% of total sales. On the goods sold direct to unit retailers, producers' distribution costs were of the order of 10–12%, and retailers' margins 26–27% of the retail price. These goods represented some 25% of total sales. In this breakdown and in Chart V importers' margins are grouped with producers' distribution costs, and sales direct to consumers and the margins of producer/retailers are grouped with the sales direct to, and the margins of, unit retailers.

This summary cannot be other than very tentative on the basis of facts at present available, and further it may be necessary to point out that as different types of commodities each having different total costs of distribution are not distributed in equal proportions in each of the different ways, the low or high total costs of distribution associated with a particular method of distribution are not necessarily a measure of efficiency or its opposite.

CHAPTER IV

THE FACTORS INFLUENCING THE COST OF DISTRIBUTION

I. THE SIGNIFICANCE OF THE COST OF DISTRIBUTION

'Does distribution cost too much?' is a twentieth century question. It also appears to be a well-meaning but mistaken question. The virtual disappearance of the producer/retailer in all developed industrial countries in the twentieth century, widespread division of labour in production, and urbanization, date the question. With the growing separation of the producer and the consumer in time and space, the cost of distribution obviously increases, and growing general awareness of this fact leads to the question being asked. The relative inability of the consumer in the 'twenties and 'thirties of this century to purchase the goods produced at the price at which they were offered added practical point to the question. The mistakenness arises from the simplicity of the question. The cost of distribution, in the sense of the proportion of the price paid by the consumer represented by other than production costs, is higher to-day than, say, half a century ago, and will probably be higher still fifty years hence. The significant question to ask is, Do consumer goods cost too much in relation to the earnings or purchasing power available and the type of goods and services demanded by the consumers? The division of that cost between production and distribution is a reflection, in general, of the character of the economy and, in particular, of the commodity under discussion and the demands of the consumer. A small mixed agricultural and industrial economy might show an 80 : 20 division between production and distribution costs whereas in a large industrial economy the proportion might be 50 : 50. A commodity produced by small units located near consumers might show a 75 : 25 proportion while an imported product or commodities manufactured in one area only but widely sold throughout the country might show a 45 : 55 proportion.

There is a further consideration. The cost of distribution in a given economy can also reflect the standard of living of that economy. This may be obscured by the operation of the above influences in that the volume of goods exchanged or distributed as a proportion of total output would tend to be lower in a less developed country, but the distribution requirements of the consumer in a country with a high standard of living contrast with those in countries with a lower standard of living. The economies in time and labour obtained by the consumer through the replacement of bartering or higgling by retail price fixing, of trying and testing by retail guarantees and name branding, and of market days by fixed shops with regular opening hours, add to the cost of distribution. The greater the refinement of these services, such as shops close to hand instead of only in town centres, storage in the shops and supplies in small packages instead of storage in the home and monthly bulk supplies, delivery to the house instead of carriage by the consumer, and greater choice of goods, the greater the absolute cost of distribution. The consumers in countries with a high standard of living were able to demand and obtain increased distributive services, thus influencing the ratio of total production to total distributive costs. This factor similarly influences the ratio of the production and distribution costs of individual commodities in that the consumer demanded and paid for greater services in respect of some goods such as milk or coal than in respect of others such as cigarettes or sugar, though the difference between the distributive services provided on different commodities in one country is less when all aspects of the services are considered, than the difference between the general level of services provided in countries with different standards of living.

To analyse the costs in one country both production and distribution costs in relation to effective consumer demand for the joint goods and distributive services need to be examined, and, in general, the higher the relative costs of distribution the closer should be the examination of this sector of the costs. But the list of comparative distribution costs of different commodities, as set out, for example, in Chart III, is more in the nature of an agenda of different items calling for discussion than a list of relative priorities. Further, in discussing the cost of different commodities, care must be taken to see that the subjects are 'likes'. A difference in the unit price of the commodities can result in a difference in the relative proportion of total cost represented by distribution costs even though the absolute money cost of distribution may be the same. A similar problem arises in relation to the rate of stock turn of wholesalers and retailers of a particular commodity in that this directly influences the proportion of the retail price represented by wholesalers' and retailers' gross margins.

Even in the consideration of one commodity these factors have an important bearing on the conclusions regarding efficiency. For example, for one unit or a series of similar units of the commodity the production-distribution cost ratio as a proportion of the retail price might be 60 : 40 while for another unit or series of units of the same commodity produced by a different firm the ratio might be 70 : 30. Yet both products might be sold at the same retail price owing to the economies in production secured by the greater sales and longer production runs developed by the more costly distributive organization. The ratio for a third firm might be 50 : 50 and yet the unit might be sold at a lower retail price than that fixed by the first or second firm, owing to the increased expenditure on the marketing organization making possible yet greater economies of production. This is really another way of emphasizing the incompleteness of a discussion of distribution costs by themselves and, particularly, the care that must be taken when drawing conclusions or making comparisons based on these costs.

Another aspect of distribution costs must be mentioned. In the foregoing discussion these costs have been treated as a single whole, but there is a strong case for distinguishing between different types of distribution costs. Some of the costs, for example transport from the point of production to the point of sale, whether undertaken by the producer, wholesaler or retailer, can be regarded as unavoidable distribution costs. Even if the product was purchased by the consumer at the factory or farm he would have to pay the cost of transport to his home. But other costs, for example sales promotion costs, advertising, window display, fall into a somewhat different category. Firstly, while to some extent these costs would appear to be unavoidable in the sense that the consumer must be informed of the goods that are available, they also take the form of promoting the sale of a particular type or brand rather than merely informing the consumer of the goods for sale. Secondly, as suggested above, while these selling costs can and do lower the production cost of an article by making longer production runs possible, since the demand for all products is limited the overall effect of the costs of providing such services may be to keep the actual prices of consumer goods higher than would be the case if the purchasers, be they wholesalers, retailers or consumers, were in a position to choose between goods involving different degrees of service at different prices. This is not the place to enter into a theoretical discussion of this problem, but the operation of these factors, as well as the character of the economy as a whole and the conditions of production and distribution of individual commodities, influences the ratio of distribution to production costs.

If the different services provided with commodities were separately priced at all stages of distribution some attempt could be made to distinguish between the different costs making up total distribution costs, but in practically no instance is this done for all distribution costs. That is the purchaser, wholesaler, retailer or consumer usually has no choice of different services at different prices. A possible approach lies in the separation of the costs of distribution along the lines discussed above between unavoidable and avoidable costs, that is classing transport costs as unavoidable and advertising as avoidable costs. But this course will not be pursued here. The main obstacle is the absence of information on the breakdown of producers' costs and distributors' margins into the constituent costs, and a second obstacle, which would remain even were the information available, is the difficulty of allocating the costs between these two categories. For example, while all transport costs might appear to fall in the first category, in practice deliveries twice weekly by producers or wholesalers to retailers may be just as much sales promotion as are visits by travelling salesmen. Again in practice the distinction between unavoidable informational advertising and avoidable brand or name advertising is almost impossible to make on the basis of present evidence.

2. THE METHODS OF ANALYSIS OF THE COSTS OF DISTRIBUTION

Some of the general factors influencing distribution costs and their relative importance in the case of different commodities can, however, be delineated, and such a procedure is an essential preliminary to a closer inspection of the total costs and prices of any commodity.

The total distribution costs, expressed as percentages of the retail price or of consumers' expenditure on individual commodities and commodity groups, can be considered from two angles: firstly, from that of the factors that influence the relative size of the total costs of distributing particular goods and secondly, from that of the factors influencing the relative proportions which producers', wholesalers' and retailers' costs bear to the total cost of distributing a commodity.

Under the first heading fall such factors as the conditions of production and retailing, the relative perishability or durability of the commodity, its unit price and its size or bulk. Under the second heading fall such factors as the division of the distributive functions between the three main participants, and the extent to which the producer takes over all or part of the wholesalers' and retailers' functions, the retailer part or all of the wholesalers' function, or the wholesaler part of the producers' and retailers' functions. For example a commodity which is produced by small scattered units, is heavy and bulky, is of low unit price and is sold by a large number of outlets, such as home-produced fruit and vegetables, will clearly tend to have a higher total distribution cost expressed as a percentage of consumers' expenditure on the group than will a high unit priced good produced in one location by few firms, sold by a limited number of outlets and easily transportable, such as a motor car. And in regard to the relative cost of producers, wholesalers and retailers, where the producer takes over the wholesaler's function of stock holding and transporting the goods by selling direct to retailers and where the producer also takes over part of the retailer's function of informing the consumer what goods are available and their quality and price by extensive advertising, branding and price maintenance, the producer's share of total distribution costs can be expected to be higher than in cases where the producer merely sells the product ex-works to wholesalers who hold stocks, break bulk and re-sell to retailers who advertise, determine price and inform the consumer of the quality of the goods. These contrasts could be expanded by reference to the other distributive functions which have to be performed, such as estimating future demand, forward ordering and the bulking of orders.

The information obtained in this enquiry has made it possible to show the operation of these factors, but only in a very general way. Detailed information is required on all the characteristics of the commodity or commodity group to indicate the full reasons for the total costs incurred in distributing the good and the relationship of these costs to those incurred in other cases. Some incomplete evidence can however be used. But the different functions performed by producers, wholesalers and retailers and the changing relative share in distribution costs which accompanies changes of function can only be shown by comparing commodities which are 'likes' in every respect except in the functions undertaken by the producer, the wholesalers and the retailers. For example, comparisons can be made between two types of biscuits which have a somewhat similar unit price, bulk, rate of stock turn and number of retail outlets but one of which is advertised, branded and distributed direct to retailers while the second is unadvertised and sold largely through wholesalers. Such comparisons would show the degree to which the proportion represented by producer's distribution costs in the first instance reflected his undertaking functions performed by the wholesaler and retailer in the second instance. Comparison cannot, however, be made between commodities with different characteristics such as a widely different unit price or wholesale and retail rate of stock turn, for example radios and biscuits, as these factors exert a stronger influence on the relative share of producers, wholesalers and retailers in the total distribution costs than such factors as the different functions performed by the particular distributors when different methods of distribution are used. As only groups of commodities and not units of the groups have been considered in this enquiry the limitations are evident. However, by considering the distribution costs incurred by producers, wholesalers and retailers as a proportion of their respective sales revenues, or turnover, the influence of some of the 'unlike' characteristics is removed, particularly in relation to producers' distribution costs, and some general comparisons are possible.

The operation of these factors on producers', wholesalers' and retailers' costs will be discussed first and then some consideration can be given to the total distribution costs of individual commodities and commodity groups.

3. PRODUCERS' COSTS AND THE METHOD OF DISTRIBUTION

The outlay by producers on the distribution of a commodity is influenced both by the type of commodity in question and by the extent to which the producer undertakes functions that would otherwise be performed, wholly or in part, by wholesalers and retailers. The first step towards showing the influence of these factors can be taken by relating the costs of distribution incurred by producers to the methods of distribution used. For this purpose only home-produced or processed commodities are considered. The costs of selling imported goods which do not undergo any processing before sale, for example the advertising of imported products, have been included in the importers' or wholesalers' costs and margin. Producers' distribution costs on home-produced goods are best taken as a percentage of producers' sales revenue and the method of distribution is best related to the method of purchase by unit retailers. The method of distribution to this group of retailers is taken as the criterion so as to exclude the sales to multiple, co-operative and department store organizations, since these concerns, for the most part, undertake the wholesaling function themselves. The question therefore of whether the producer should undertake all or part of the wholesale or retail function does not usually arise. There are exceptions to this. A number of department stores rely on producers to perform any wholesaling functions, such as stockholding, which may be necessary for the goods they sell. Also multiple concerns handle a proportion—but not so large a proportion as the unit retailer—of nationally advertised commodities and some producers make split deliveries to the retail branches of multiple and co-operative organizations instead of delivery to the central depots of those concerns; but in general the distinction holds good. Only on the sales made direct to unit retailers does the producer usually undertake the full or nearly the full wholesale functions. In other cases, whether the sale is made to wholesalers or to large-scale retailing organizations, the producer usually performs either no part or a small part of the wholesaler's rôle.

The distribution costs incurred by producers selling goods manufactured or processed in the United Kingdom have been estimated above as 9–9·5% of producers' sales revenue. The proportion of total sales of home-produced commodities made by producers direct to unit retailers is estimated at 22–24%. These two averages can be used as guides to test the degree of correspondence between the size of the producers' expenditure on distribution and the method of distribution used. Information is available for some 109 of the commodities and commodity groups covered in the enquiry, and, considering the commodities grouped by trades, those which show a higher than average producers' distribution cost and a higher than average proportion sold direct to unit retailers are:

Pottery and ironmongers' goods	Stationery, pens and inks
Furniture	Coal
Electrical goods	Groceries

The trade groups which show a lower than average producers' distribution cost and a lower than average proportion sold direct to unit retailers are:

Furnishings	Fish
Footwear	Provisions
Women's and children's wear	Poultry, game and rabbits
Milk	Men's and boy's wear
Fresh fruit and vegetables	Bread and flour confectionery

Two further categories appear: one is where the producers' distribution costs are higher than the average but the proportion of goods sold direct to unit retailers is lower than the average. The trade groups in this category are:

Chemists' goods	Newspapers and periodicals
Chocolates and sweets	

The second category is where the producers' distribution costs are lower than the average and the proportion of sales direct to unit retailers higher than the average. The trade groups in this category are:

Jewellers' goods	Motor trade
Meat	Cigarettes and tobacco

In considering these categories the small proportion of total sales made by unit retailers of the particular trade group must be borne in mind.

Association between producers' distribution costs and methods of distribution by commodities

The averages for trade groups conceal some important differences between the commodities making up the trade group. The individual commodities and commodity groups in the four main categories are set out in Table 18. As in some instances the estimated producers' distribution costs and the methods of sale were very close to the average, other factors, such as the evidence on related commodities and the probable underestimation of producers' distribution costs, have been taken into account in allocating the commodity to a particular group.

Table 18. *Associations between producers' distribution costs and the method of distribution by commodities*

Type of association	Commodity or commodity group	
GROUP I Higher than average producers' distribution costs and higher than average sales direct to unit retailers	*Food and drink*	
	Self-raising flour	Chocolates
	Plain flour	Jam and marmalade
	Biscuits	
	Clothing	
	Nil	
	Other goods	
	Radios and radiograms	Toilet soap
	Books	Candles
	Coal	Furniture
	Kerosene	Linoleum
	Domestic hollow-ware and hardware	Motor mechanical parts, accessories, ignition equipment and batteries
	Brooms and brushes	
	Paint and varnishes	Motor cycles
	Wallpaper	Motor cycle accessories
	Cutlery	Motor car tyres
	Electric fires and appliances	Motor cycle and cycle tyres
	Electric light lamps	Sports goods
	Vacuum cleaners	Beauty preparations
	Stationery and paper products	Perfumes and table waters
		Contraceptives
	Pens and pencils	Perambulators
	Ink and accessories	Portable typewriters
	Household soap	Photographic goods
GROUP II Lower than average producers' distribution costs and lower than average sales direct to unit retailers	*Food and drink*	
	Bread	Eggs
	Flour confectionery	Cheese
	Unpackaged breakfast cereals	Sugar
		Syrup and treacle
	Poultry, game and rabbits	Potatoes
	Fish	Beer—on-licence sales
	Butter	Spirits—on-licence sales
	Fresh fruit and vegetables	Wines—on-licence sales
	Milk	Spirits—off-licence sales
	Canned milk	Wines—off-licence sales
	Clothing	
	Leather footwear	Men's and boys' hats and caps
	Rubber footwear	
	Men's and boys' outerwear	Men's and boys' handkerchiefs, ties and braces
	Shirts, collars and pyjamas	

Type of association	Commodity or commodity group	
GROUP II (*continued*)	*Clothing*	
	Men's and boys' hosiery	Women's and girls' outerwear
	Stockings and socks	Women's and girls' underwear and nightwear
	Millinery	Dress materials
	Corsets and brassières	Gloves
		General haberdashery
	Other goods	
	Matches	Carpets
	Furnishing fabrics	Imitation jewellery
	Household textiles and soft furnishings	Non-proprietary medicines and drugs
GROUP III Higher than average producers' distribution costs and lower than average sales direct to unit retailers	*Food and drink*	
	Packaged cereals	Cocoa
	Margarine	Salt
	Canned fruit, vegetables and fish	Health food beverages
	Sauces, pickles, soups and salad creams	
	Clothing	
	Furs and fur garments	
	Other goods	
	Household polishes and cleaners	Dental preparations
	Newspapers and magazines	Toothbrushes
	Toys	Proprietary medicines and drugs
	Sanitary towels	Infant and invalid foods
	Razors and blades	Sewing machines
GROUP IV Lower than average producers' distribution costs and higher than average sales direct to unit retailers	*Food and drink*	
	Meat	Coffee
	Bacon and ham	Beer—off-licence sales
	Tea	
	Clothing	
	Men's and boys' outerwear	
	Other goods	
	Pottery and glass	Silver and electro-plate
	Leather goods	Watches
	Motor cars	Clocks
	Real jewellery	Cigarettes and tobacco

This Table suggests that in the case of 37 commodities, Group I, high producers' distribution costs went with a high proportion of sales direct to retailers, and in the case of 40 commodities, Group II, low producers' distribution costs went with a low proportion of sales direct to retailers. Together these 77 commodities represent some 60% of total consumers' expenditure on home-produced goods covered in the enquiry. In the case of 18 commodities, Group III, representing about 20% of total consumers' expenditure, high producers' distribution costs were matched with a low proportion of goods sold direct to retailers and in the case of 14 commodities, Group IV, representing about 20% of total consumers' expenditure, low producers' distribution costs were matched with a high proportion of goods sold direct to retailers.

Variations in the constituents of producers' distribution costs for different groups of commodities

To carry the analysis a stage further, information is needed on the type of distributive function undertaken by producers in each instance and on the characteristics of the commodities in each of these four groups. Some light is thrown on these questions by an examination of the relative importance in each case of the individual constituents of the producers' distribution costs, and of the degree of branding and price maintenance and the unit price of the commodity. The most useful division of producers' distribution costs is by four main constituents: carriage, packing and transport; salesmen's salaries and costs; advertising costs; and general warehousing and administrative costs. Unfortunately, for the reasons explained above the information on these points is very general and a breakdown of distribution costs under these different headings has not been possible in some instances, while in others the division is very approximate. However, for those commodities on which some information does exist an estimate of the importance of the different factors can be made.

Of the commodities listed for Group I above, the most important single element in the producers' distribution costs in 20 instances for which a breakdown exists is advertising. In all these cases advertising is estimated as accounting for a quarter or more of producers' distribution costs. In 19 instances out of the 20, advertising accounts for more than one-third of the total costs. And this Group I contains 10 of the commodities specified by the authors of *A Statistical Analysis of Advertising Expenditure* as 'substantially advertised commodities', that is, where 5% or more of manufacturers' sales revenue is spent on advertising.[1] The

[1] N. Kaldor and R. Silverman, *A Statistical Analysis of Advertising Expenditure and of the Revenue of the Press*, N.I.E.S.R., Economic and Social Studies, VIII, 1948, p. 21.

most important single element in the producers' distribution costs of a further 5 commodities in Group I was transport costs. In each case, this cost is estimated as accounting for over one-third of total costs. In the remaining 13 instances the costs are either evenly spread among the four main categories, or no breakdown of the costs is available. Some 27 of the 37 commodities can be classed as significantly branded and price maintained, as defined above, and in all the instances where advertising is the most important element in costs the goods are branded. The degree of concentration of production, as estimated above, of 31 of these 37 commodities is higher than the average for all commodities.

This information suggests that within the Group I three sub-groups can be distinguished: first, the large group of commodities with high producers' distribution costs due in a large part to expenditure on advertising by producers—this group includes commodities such as soap, chocolates, motor car tyres, electrical goods, stationers' goods and photographic goods; second, a smaller group with high producers' distribution costs due mainly to the bulk, size or number of retail outlets for the goods leading to heavy carriage, packing and transport costs—this group includes commodities such as coal, furniture and biscuits; third, a small number of heterogeneous commodity groups such as domestic hardware, hollow-ware and ironmongery and sports goods, which reveal no outstanding detail on any one item of producers' distribution costs. In the second and third sub-groups the producer, for reasons discussed above, can be said to be undertaking the normal distributive functions of a wholesaler and the costs involved in so doing are similar in most instances to the gross margins earned by wholesalers when and if they handle the goods. These functions consist mainly of holding stocks, breaking bulk, preparing catalogues and information for retailers on the goods for sale and transporting the goods to retailers. In the first sub-group, however, the producers are undertaking on a significant scale a function which the wholesaler usually performs to only a limited extent, that of advertising or making information available to the consumer on the qualities, character and price of goods available for sale. And it is the cost of this item, rather than the cost of holding stocks, or selling, or packing and transporting the goods, that tends to be the largest single cost. The difference in the functions undertaken by the producers and those undertaken by the wholesalers in relation to the commodities in the first sub-group is reflected in the difference between

The enquiry related to conditions obtaining in 1935. The commodities and commodity groups are household and toilet soap, paint and varnishes, electric light lamps, radios, pens and pencils, tyres and tubes, beauty preparations, perfumes and toilet waters, and photographic goods.

producers' distribution costs and the gross margins earned by wholesalers when and if they handle the goods. In practically every case the gross margin of the wholesalers expressed as a percentage of sales is lower than the producers' distribution costs expressed as a percentage of sales.

The break-down of producers' distribution costs is less complete for Group II, but again there would appear to be three sub-groups. Firstly, the unprocessed and semi-processed foodstuffs, where the most important item in producers' distribution costs is transport. Secondly, a group of manufactured goods, in particular clothing, where producers' distribution costs are spread relatively evenly between the four main categories, though advertising costs in most instances are the lowest of the four and selling costs, that is salesmen's salaries and general administrative selling costs, the highest. Thirdly, there is a small group of manufactured goods where advertising represents a significant element in producers' distribution costs. The important commodities in this group are canned milk, cheese, stockings and socks, corsets, and beer and spirits.

For practically all the commodities in this Group II the gross margin of wholesalers on sales is very much higher than the distribution costs incurred by producers expressed as a percentage of sales. The presence of beer, wines and spirits in this group is influenced by the particular methods of distribution used in the on- and off-licence trades, but in the case of spirits the most important single element in producers' distribution costs was advertising.

The commodities listed in Group III show very close parallels with those listed in Group I, the main difference being the method of distribution. Sixteen of the 18 commodities in the Group were significantly branded and price maintained, and of these 16 the authors of *A Statistical Analysis of Advertising Expenditure* list 10 as substantially advertised.[1] The producers' distribution costs as a percentage of sales are higher than the gross margin earned by wholesalers on sales in 13 instances. Information on the make-up of producers' distribution costs is far from complete, but for 10 of the 18 commodities advertising costs accounted for one-third or more of the total distribution costs incurred by producers. In these instances, more clearly than in the case of commodities in Group I, can be seen the rôle which the producer sometimes plays in distribution as against that undertaken by the wholesaler and retailer. The producer, in these 10 cases, which include packaged cereals, cocoa,

[1] Ibid., p. 21. The commodities and commodity groups are packaged breakfast cereals, margarine, sauces, pickles, soups and salad creams, household polishes and cleaners, razors and blades, dental preparations, proprietary medicines and drugs, health food beverages, toothbrushes and cocoa.

health food beverages, razors and blades, dental preparations and proprietary medicines and drugs, would appear to rely on the wholesaler to perform the functions of breaking bulk and redistributing to retailers, but undertakes the function of informing retailers and consumers of the quantity, quality and price of the goods available almost entirely by himself. The demand for the product is created and developed by the producer but the actual distribution of the commodities is left to the wholesaler and retailer. In some of these trades, however, the process goes further and producers undertake the task of determining in detail the volume and character of consumer demand and will also, through representatives, make 'courtesy' calls on retailers and having secured orders pass them on to wholesalers for fulfilment.

Of the commodities listed in Group IV one sub-group stands out very clearly, that is the goods which are of high unit value. Among these are jewellery and watches and clocks and motor cars. In these cases producers' distribution costs expressed as a percentage of sales revenue tend to be small. A second feature of this sub-group is that although sales are made by producers direct to retailers, transport, carriage and packing costs are low, for example in the case of jewellery and watches, owing to the small bulk and high price of the commodities, and in the case of motor cars owing to the practice of charging delivery costs—a small charge in relation to retail price—to consumers. For some of the other commodities in this group both producers' distribution costs and methods of distribution are very close to the average in each case. But in the case of tea and coffee, the reasons for the lower than average producers' distribution costs associated with higher than average sales direct to retailers were probably the relatively small amount of advertising undertaken compared with total sales of the product, minimum stockholding, the low transport costs arising from the small bulk of the goods and the spread of selling and administrative costs between these and other commodities produced by the same manufacturers or producers.

4. THE RELATION BETWEEN STOCK TURN AND WHOLESALERS' AND RETAILERS' GROSS MARGINS

Turning to wholesalers' and retailers' gross margins, the variation in size as between different commodities is, of course, a reflection of the difference in wholesalers' and retailers' operating costs plus net profits. Assuming for the moment that variations in net margins or profit as a percentage of gross margins were not very great between different commodities, operating costs expressed as a percentage of sales revenue can be said to be influenced by two main factors: first the nature of the commodity, particularly its unit price and perishability, and the rate of wholesale and retail stock turn; second the nature of the distributive functions undertaken by the wholesalers and retailers in relation to the commodity. The rate of stock turn clearly influences holding costs and, over time, a smaller gross margin on a fast moving commodity can yield the same gross return as a high margin on a slow moving commodity, though the unit price is significant in that the margins and stock turn of articles of widely varying unit price cannot strictly be compared. The functions performed by the wholesaler and retailer influence both the relative gross margins earned by them on the sale of different commodities and also the division of the total distribution costs of a single commodity between the producer, the wholesaler, if used, and the retailer. Starting with the rate of stock turn some indication can be given of the influence of these factors on wholesale and retail gross margins.

Information was obtained from wholesalers and retailers on the rate of stock turn of different goods in 1938, but the estimates suggested in the case studies can only be approximations. In the first place, over a wide range of commodities the rates of stock turn that are usually quoted refer to total turnover of broad groups of commodities rather than individual commodities. In the second place there are often wide differences between the rates of stock turn of different retailers of the same commodity. Only a complete census can produce reliable average figures. A third, though less important difficulty is the use of different methods for calculating stock turn. As far as possible the estimates used here relate to both sales and stock at selling price. This method enables a greater measure of comparison to be made between trades than does the alternative method of calculating stock at cost price and turnover at selling price.

The absence of precise information on stock turn gives rise to difficulties in the presentation of what material is available. A simple time series such as a stock turn of less than once a year, between once and twice a year, between twice and three times a year, does not meet the case as the commodities are 'unlikes', and while a variation in months in some instances is relatively unimportant a variation of days in other cases is vital to the wholesaler or retailer. The most suitable time series to use cannot be decided in the absence of more detailed information, and the grouping adopted in the following Table is therefore open to some objections, but it does throw some light on the general relationship between stock turn and gross unit margin. The rate of stock turn is shown as a range for each group, the goods in each group being shown approximately in the order in which they fall between the limits given for each range.

Table 19. *Estimated rates of retail stock turn of commodities in 1938*

Group and rate of stock turn	Commodity or commodity group	
GROUP I Twice a year or less	Real jewellery	Watches and clocks
	Silver and electro-plate	Toys
	Imitation jewellery	Books
GROUP II From 2 to 4 times a year	Carpets	Cutlery
	Pottery and glass	Motor cars
	Sports goods	Motor car and cycle tyres and tubes
	Perfumes and table waters	Leather goods
	Furniture	Photographic goods
	Furs and fur garments	Household textiles
	Leather footwear	Vacuum cleaners
	Health food beverages	Furnishing fabrics
	Domestic hollow-ware and hardware	Dress materials
	Brooms and brushes	
GROUP III From 4 to 6 times a year	Gloves	Cocoa
	Household polishes	Stationery
	Rubber footwear	Linoleum
	Men's and boys' outerwear	Electric light lamps
	Men's hats and caps	Radios
	Men's ties, braces, handkerchiefs	Unpackaged cereal breakfast foods
	Men's and boys' hosiery	Women's (non-fashion) outerwear
	Proprietary medicines and drugs	Women's and children's underwear
	Men's shirts, collars and pyjamas	Corsets and brassières
GROUP IV From 6 to 9 times a year	Haberdashery	Pickles, sauces, soups and salad creams
	Infant and invalid foods	Motor oil
	Electric fires and appliances	Sanitary towels
	Soap and soap powder	Women's and children's stockings and socks
	Razors and blades	Women's fashion outerwear
	Beauty preparations	
	Coal	
	Chocolates and sweets	

Group and rate of stock turn	Commodity or commodity group	
GROUP V From 9 to 12 times a year	Salt Canned fruit, vegetables and fish	Flour Jam and marmalade Packaged breakfast cereals
GROUP VI From once a month to twice a month	Syrup and treacle Canned milk Millinery Biscuits Contraceptives	Cheese Coffee Cigarettes and tobacco Kerosene Tea
GROUP VII From once a fortnight to once a week	Sugar Petrol	Margarine Magazines and periodicals
GROUP VIII More than once a week	Butter Fruit and vegetables Potatoes Eggs Meat Poultry, game and rabbits	Bacon and ham Fish Bread Cakes Newspapers Milk

This Table is not complete as information on the stock turn of all commodities is not available, but a comparison of the order of commodities in this Table with the estimated gross margins of unit retailers presented in Chart IV shows the elementary relationship between stock turn and gross margins. The gross margins of unit retailers are used here rather than the gross margins of all retailers, as the latter figures include, as has been made clear above, the margins earned by concerns such as multiple and department store organizations in the performance of a wholesaling function. Nearly all the commodities with a stock turn of less than 9 times a year have a retail gross margin higher than the average estimated above for all commodities, that is 25–25·5%, and similarly those commodities with a stock turn higher than 9 times a year have in most cases a lower than the average retail gross margin. Taking the eight main Groups which are distinguished, this correspondence is not very marked in the last Group, VIII, but the average margin for all of the commodities in each of the first seven Groups declines, though not evenly, from about 40% in the case of Group I to 15% in the case of Group VII. It has not been possible to obtain sufficient reliable information on the stock turn of wholesalers of these commodities, but in the case of some 34 commodities and commodity groups for which some figures of wholesale stock turn exist there is, in most cases, a similar inverse relationship between the rate of stock turn and the size of the gross margin of wholesalers on sales.

Cases where there is no relation between gross margins and stock turn

These figures confirm the generally accepted axiom that the relative rate of stock turn, or in other words the holding cost, is the strongest factor in determining the relative wholesale and retail gross margins earned on different commodities, but at the same time the exceptions make it clear that this is not the only factor operating. The exceptions to the generalization, that is commodities which had a low stock turn and a low retail margin and vice versa, in Table 19 are as follows: of the commodities with a retail stock turn slower than 9 times a year, those with a lower than the average retail gross margin are books, health food beverages, motor cars, cocoa, infant and invalid foods, household and toilet soap, and pickles, sauces, soups and salad creams. The commodities having a retail stock turn faster than 9 times a year but with a retail gross margin higher than the average are millinery, contraceptives, magazines, fresh fruit and vegetables, fish, newspapers and milk. The wholesale exceptions appear, from the limited evidence, to be practically the same as the retail exceptions. This does not constitute a complete list but includes only those commodities for which information is available. Further the use of a stock turn of 9 times and of the average retail gross margin for all commodities as guides reveals only the major exceptions. This method for example does not show up those commodities which may have the same average stock turn —either below or above 9 times a year—but different margins, if the margins are both above or both below the average, but discloses only the commodities with directly contrasting margin and stock turn characteristics.

The exceptions listed above are examples of those commodities where the other factors suggested as influencing gross margins—such as unit price, perishability, or bulkiness of the goods or the distributive functions undertaken by producers, wholesalers and retailers—may singly or in combination have counteracted the influence of stock turn by itself. In other instances, not listed as exceptions, the influence of these factors has probably played some part in determining the gross margin but has not completely counteracted the stock turn factor, while in yet others the influence on margins may have been exerted in the same direction as the rate of stock turn. The degree of association shown between the size of the gross margin and the rate of stock turn is, in fact, mainly a reflection of the relative 'likeness' of the commodities listed. If the evidence on which the Table is based had been more detailed and the commodities included had shown greater variations in unit price and in the nature of the wholesaling and retailing functions which had to be undertaken, it is doubtful whether any consistent correspondence would appear at all. For example many commodities with a high unit price and a slow rate of stock turn nevertheless have a low gross margin expressed as a percentage of this price although the cash margin may be considerable. And other commodities with a high rate of stock turn have a high gross margin since they incur considerable storage and handling costs. Association between gross margins and stock turn depends on comparing 'like' with 'like' commodities. The value of the comparison remains, however, when the rates of stock turn of the same commodity in different shops are considered. Although other factors operate here, the comparison of rates of stock turn on the same commodity in different retail outlets is one of the sharpest tools in distributive efficiency analysis.

To carry further the examination of the reasons for variations in margins between commodities, a breakdown of the main groups of commodities listed above, showing the individual gross margins and the individual rates of stock turn, would be necessary. Here, however, this will not be attempted for two reasons. In the first place the incompleteness of the data relating to the stock turn of a number of commodities and the probable errors in the data collected make the sample unsatisfactory. In the second place there is little point in measuring one set of facts with care when the other set of facts required to test for correlation cannot, as yet, be measured with any degree of accuracy. Margins and stock turn mean little by themselves unless evidence is also available on the characteristics of the commodity and the tasks involved in its distribution.

While some approximations to standards of unit price and perishability could be made, the measurement of the relative functions performed by wholesalers and retailers in the distribution of different commodities requires a complete census or a wide sample of the detailed operating expenses of the distributors, and this is not available. Measurement of the relative shares of the distributive functions undertaken by producers, wholesalers and retailers in relation to an individual commodity depends similarly on a detailed breakdown of the type of costs incurred by these units in the distribution of that commodity. Again these types of data are not available. Finally, comparable data on the net profits earned on the distribution of particular commodities by wholesalers and retailers are necessary. This involves not only collection of data but also some standardization in the methods of calculating profits. Without information on these aspects of the problem no elaborate analysis can be made, but by using such material as does exist illustrations can be given of the influence of factors other than stock turn on gross margins, and these also give an indication of the type of material which is required if this aspect of distribution cost is to be examined in detail.

5. THE RELATION BETWEEN UNIT PRICE, COMMODITY CHARACTERISTICS, THE NATURE OF THE DISTRIBUTIVE FUNCTION AND GROSS MARGINS

The influence of the unit price of one commodity compared with other commodities can be readily seen in the case of motor cars. This commodity, one of the exceptions, had a relatively slow rate of stock turn and also a lower than the average gross margin on sales for both wholesalers or distributors, 4–5%, and retailers or dealers, 18–19%. These margins were not very different from those on cigarettes or eggs, which had very much higher rates of stock turn. The explanation clearly lies in the difference in average retail price, that of a motor car in 1938 being, say, £200, and that of cigarettes 6d. for 10 or eggs 1s. a dozen. The effect of unit price differences, however, while influencing all relative gross margins expressed as a percentage on sales, can only be clearly distinguished in extreme instances. For there are many other instances of commodities which have a relatively high unit price, a slow rate of stock turn but a high gross margin, such as real jewellery, or on the other hand of commodities with opposite characteristics, such as bread. Here other factors counteract the single influence of unit price on gross margins expressed as a percentage of sales. In a closer analysis of distribution costs, the variations in unit price would have to be taken into account.

The nature of the commodity in some cases makes the rate of stock turn unimportant as a factor in gross margins. For example, in the case of highly perishable commodities such as fruit and vegetables, fish, milk and newspapers, again exceptions listed above, the stock turn is determined not so much by consumer demand or wholesaling and retailing efficiency as by the perishable nature of the commodity in question. In these instances the costs of rapid handling and selling, including the loss through fluctuating demand and deterioration, are more significant than the costs of stock holding. While the risk element in selling newspapers is less than in selling fish or vegetables owing to the system of 'returns', the unit price of newspapers is lower than that of fish or vegetables and influences the gross margin. A second illustration of the influence of the nature of the commodity on gross margins is to be found in the case of heavy or bulky goods involving wholesalers, especially, in high transport costs compared to the unit value of the articles. Both fish and fruit and vegetables fall into this category, as do other commodities such as motor oil, radios and electrical goods. A comparison of Tables 19 and 12 shows that these commodities, among others, have fairly high rates of stock turn—the wholesalers' stock turn follows, in these instances, that of the retailers—and relatively high wholesale margins in relation to the stock turn. But this factor is closely linked with the influence on gross margins of the different distributive functions undertaken by wholesalers and retailers in relation to different goods.

Variations in the distributive function undertaken in different trades

The variation in distributive functions can be seen from a few examples. The wholesalers of hollow-ware, hardware and ironmongery and of stationery have a stock turn equal to or usually faster than that of electrical wholesalers carrying radios, electric fires and appliances and electric light lamps, but the gross margins of the former wholesalers are higher than those of electrical wholesalers. The difference in unit price, that of electrical goods being usually higher than that of hardware and stationery, is important, but so also is the fact that the electrical wholesalers are dealing in branded goods for the most part and have smaller selling and transport costs expressed as a percentage of their turnover than ironmongery and stationery wholesalers, as these costs directly influence the size of the gross margins on sales. The distributive functions of breaking bulk, preparing assorted orders and issuing catalogues and informational material were relatively less important in the case of electrical wholesalers than in that of stationery or hardware wholesalers.

The variations in the distributive functions undertaken by retailers in relation to different commodities are much more marked even when all the commodities are assumed to have been purchased from wholesalers. For example, some goods require selection, weighing and packaging by retailers, others can be sold already packaged. Some require special knowledge and demonstration by the retailer, others can be sold by untrained juveniles. Some goods must be delivered to the consumer's house, others are taken away by the purchaser. In many instances the goods sold are consumed within a short period of time, in others extensive after-sales service is expected of the retailer. The influence of these different functions on relative gross margins compared with the influence of stock turn can readily be illustrated. Millinery and tea have a somewhat similar rate of stock turn, but the gross margin on millinery, which has to be stocked in a wide range, involves personal sales and carries a risk of unsaleability, is much higher than that on the packaged, branded, price maintained and easily sold tea. Milk, requiring bottling and house-to-house delivery, has a faster stock turn and higher gross margin than butter or eggs, which require little packaging by the retailer and are usually collected by the purchaser. Radios and small electric fires and appliances also have a somewhat similar rate of retail stock turn; both require skilled retailing and both are usually branded and price maintained, but the retail margin on radios, although they are usually of a higher unit value, is greater than that on small electric appliances. The difference springs mainly from the very much greater after-sales service expected of the retailer of radios. This list need not be extended, as in the case of practically all commodities obvious differences in the distributive function and therefore cost of retailing spring to mind. What is required, to go beyond the stage of generalization, is measurement, by means of a detailed breakdown of operating costs of wholesalers and retailers, of the proportion of total costs represented by expenditure on each different function, for example on warehousing or on after-sales service, and along with this an analysis of the relative share in distribution costs undertaken by the producers, wholesalers and retailers of the different commodities.

6. THE RELATIVE SHARES IN TOTAL COSTS OF PRODUCER, WHOLESALER AND RETAILER

In discussing the relative shares of producers, wholesalers and retailers in the total distribution costs of one commodity, the clearest transference of function and therefore of cost occurs where the wholesaler as such does not participate at all and his function is undertaken wholly or partly by the producer or by the retailer. In the latter case the retailers are usually large-scale concerns such as multiple or department store organizations. The particular division of wholesaling costs made between producer and retailer in these instances is reflected, along with the incidence of other factors discussed above, in the relative size of producers' costs and retail gross margins of the commodities.

Transference of function, however, also takes place where both wholesalers and retailers participate in the chain of distribution as separate units, and the most marked case of transference relates to the function of informing the consumer of the quality and price of the goods that are for sale, or advertising. Examples have been given above, in the discussion of producers' distribution costs, of those commodities where the producer took an active part in sales promotion, and all the commodities listed by the authors of *A Statistical Analysis of Advertising*[1] as 'substantially advertised', such as cocoa, cigarettes and tobacco, soap, electrical appliances, packaged cereals, margarine, sauces, pickles,

[1] Kaldor and Silverman, op. cit., p. 21 foll.

soups and salad creams, health food beverages, photographic goods and razors and blades certainly fall into this category. The sales promotion of this type of product is largely undertaken by the producer, leaving the wholesaler and retailer with the more limited functions of meeting a created demand. Producers also usually undertake the packaging and re-sale price fixing of these commodities, functions which would otherwise have to be performed by the wholesaler and/or retailer. All the exceptions listed above as having a stock turn slower than 9 times a year but a lower than the average retail margin are commodities widely advertised by producers and usually price maintained, and 5 of these 7 exceptions are classed as 'substantially advertised'. While the other factors mentioned above, such as the small bulk of many of the goods in relation to price, contributed to the lower than average gross margin, the transference of the sales promotion function from wholesaler and retailer to producer was clearly significant. On the other hand there are commodities on which the producers' advertising expenditure was either nil or very small. In these instances sales promotion had to be undertaken by the wholesaler and retailer, adding to their costs and gross margins. The performance of this function by retailers is to some extent reflected in the amounts spent by them on advertising. In 1935 advertising by retailers was significant in the case of drapery and women's and girls' clothing, furniture, men's and boys' clothing, jewellery and chemists' goods.[1] With the exception of the last-named group of commodities, these goods were rarely advertised directly by producers, though this contrast is somewhat offset by the fact that an important proportion of the retail advertising of furniture and men's and boys' wear was undertaken by organizations linked with producers, for example the multiple manufacturing retailers of men's and boys' wear.

A detailed breakdown of the distribution costs and operating expenses of producers, wholesalers and retailers would bring out more clearly the contrasts in the share of general sales promotion undertaken by the retailers in the latter group of commodities and the producers in the former group and the consequent influence on gross margins. But the particular division of the distributive functions obtaining in relation to a single commodity will not necessarily influence the position of that commodity in any scale of wholesale and retail gross margins. For example, while the retailer may be responsible for some 90% of the total advertising of men's and boys' wear but only 10% of the total advertising of chemists' goods, the relative insignificance of total advertising of the former goods compared with the latter in relation to total consumers' expenditure in each case may mean that the expenditure

[1] Ibid., p. 10.

on this form of sales promotion, or the cost of undertaking this particular distributive function, has a greater influence on the size of the gross margin of chemists than on that of outfitters or tailors.

This applies also to the particular division between the two or three participants of the other distributive functions. Some of these divisions of functions have been mentioned above, such as grading, sorting and preparing goods for sale, weighing and labelling and price fixing, others include the division of transport costs, which in some trades tend to be borne by the wholesaler and retailer and in others, the majority, by the producer, and the division of stock holding, of risk bearing, of credit provision and of bulking orders.

The influence on gross margins of the division of these latter functions can in some cases be measured, inasmuch as they are linked in a number of trades with special discounts, volume rebates and cash discounts. The producers of some commodities, for example electric light lamps, give special discounts to wholesalers and retailers for forward ordering, others give bonuses for goods purchased in the slack seasons. Bulk orders are encouraged in a large number of trades by the operation of fixed volume discount schemes or *ad hoc* agreements having a similar result. Practically all producers, and in their turn wholesalers, encourage prompt payment for goods, thus reducing the cost of credit provision, by offering settlement discounts, in effect, a reduction of the selling price. The size of these settlement discounts varies between trades, being highest in footwear and some clothing trades, 5–6¼%, and lowest in the provisions trades, 1d. and 2d. in the £, for payment in 7 days, though in some trades, for example eggs and motor cars, there are no settlement discounts at all. The most usual settlement discount is 2½% for payment in the month. The size of the settlement discount offered also varied in some trades with the size of the order placed. In these instances the producer or wholesaler in offering terms was hoping to reduce his holding costs as well as costs incurred in providing credit. The scale of these bonus, discount and settlement terms in different trades and the extent to which wholesalers and retailers are able or willing to take advantage of them influence both the relative share of distributive costs incurred and the functions undertaken by the different parties handling the goods.

Assumption on net margins or profit

A further factor which may have an important bearing on individual wholesalers' and retailers' gross margins is the net profit earned by them. As between trades, an implied assumption has been made above that net profits as a percentage of gross margins were approximately the same in all cases and therefore do not have an important effect on the size of gross margins earned on different commodities. This assumption, which has to be based more on economic theory than on empirical data, proceeds from a further assumption of existence of competition in the distributive trades and freedom of entry into those trades. This is not meant to suggest that variations in net profits did not exist between concerns in the same trade handling the same commodities; they varied widely from the marginal firm to the firm earning windfall profits. Nor is this statement meant to imply that, as net profits in different trades bore a similar relationship to one another, total distribution costs were at a minimum. Net profits as a percentage of gross margins can be the same in an inefficient as in an efficient distributive system if in the former case there are other factors arising from the methods of production or consumption which prevent distributors adopting alternative systems or costs of distribution. But if competition existed between the wholesalers and retailers and entry to the trades was relatively easy, these factors, it is suggested, would keep variations in the net profits earned in different trades, expressed as a percentage of gross margins, within close limits. The evidence obtained in the course of this survey and the methods of research used, however, do not permit of any judgment on the validity of these assumptions. The influence of net profit on gross margins in different trades must remain a subject for further investigation.

7. SUMMARY OF THE FACTORS INFLUENCING THE COSTS OF DISTRIBUTION

An attempt has been made to indicate some of the main factors affecting the distribution costs of various commodities, and therefore the total costs of distribution, by analysing the costs incurred by the various intermediaries in the chain of distribution. The relative size of total distribution costs of one commodity compared with another of not greatly dissimilar unit price is determined by a variety of factors, one of which may be dominant in the case of a particular commodity whilst in other commodities this influence may be offset by the operation of other factors. Differences in total distribution costs may be affected on the one hand by the nature of the commodities—their relative size, weight, perishability—and by differences in the conditions of their production—whether produced in large, centralized units or small, scattered units, whether home-produced or imported. On the other hand, differences in the character of the service required by the consumer obviously influence the cost of distributing particular commodities. For example, transport and stockholding costs are directly affected by the method of sale of the commodity, depending on whether it is sold locally in small shops or only in large centres, is collected by the consumer or delivered to his home, whether the retailer or producer provides after-sales service or not and on the range of selection expected by the consumer.

The division of total costs between producers' distribution costs and wholesalers' and retailers' gross margins in relation to individual commodities reflects by and large the division of the distributive functions undertaken. The distributive functions ordinarily associated with producers, wholesalers and retailers respectively may be and often are transferred to one or another in varying degrees. The functions most frequently transferred in this way are, first, the entire wholesaling function, which may be shared by producers and retailers or may be wholly performed by producer or retailer, and second, that of informing the consumer of the quality and price of the commodity in question, originally a retailers' function but often taken over by producers, especially, as has been shown, where there is a high degree of concentration of production of the particular commodity. Other functions such as providing the finance to enable stocks to be held before sale, collecting, bulking and placing forward orders and estimating future demand trends are similarly shared between the three participants in different ways for different commodities.

Other factors influencing the costs of distribution

For the most part the influence of these factors is measurable, given possession of the economic and statistical data on the distributive trades comparable to those which are already available on production in the United Kingdom. But there are a number of other factors influencing costs which are not easily measurable. These factors are sociological and institutional as well as economic in character, and an adequate discussion of them must await further research; but some indication of their possible effects and incidence can be given here.

As in the case of the methods of distribution, traditional practices can influence the costs of distribution. Here tradition can take the form of an accepted margin or mark-up for a particular class of goods irrespective of the differences that may exist between the individual commodities composing the group and of the changes taking place over time. Practically all the old and established distributive trades such as clothing, furniture, ironmongery, chemists' goods, greengrocery, and many of the new trades such as radios and bicycles which have grown out of older trades, have traditional wholesale and retail mark-ups or margins. The extent to which the margins or mark-ups of individual commodities in a particular trade range above or below the traditional figure varies. For example, the chemists' trade experiments with different margins to a greater extent than does the furniture or clothing trade. But in all these instances there appears to be a tendency to accept a certain figure, say 20%, 25% or 33⅓% as being the normal margin in a trade, and practically all commodities handled, irrespective of their particular characteristics, are offered for sale with margins at or around these figures. Further, there would appear to be some evidence that the traditional mark-ups or margins have been maintained in certain trades over time without close reference to the changes that may have taken place in the character of the goods sold, in the proportions of the goods of home or foreign origin, and in the relationship between wage rates and rents and margins and prices; though this is not the same as saying that the cost of distributing a certain weight of goods or a certain number of units has remained the same. Lower money costs of distribution may lead to a lower retail price although the margin earned by distributors as a percentage of retail sales may remain at the traditional figure.

One of the reasons for the use of the same or a traditional on-cost for a group of somewhat dissimilar goods is the difficulty, if not impossibility, of isolating the actual costs of distribution of an individual product. That is, a grocer or a draper is not usually able to determine exactly the cost of selling, say, imported canned fish or men's handkerchiefs compared with the cost of selling home-canned peas or girls' scarves. Even if the rate of stock turn, or holding costs, has been calculated in each instance, most of the other costs, that is rent and rates, wages, credit charges and general overhead costs, have to be allocated according to the total turnover in the different classes of goods rather than by making a separate estimate in the case of each commodity. This, by and large, is the common-sense approach to the problem, provided the groups of commodities are not too diverse in their nature. But such an approach by groups of commodities rather than by individual commodities will almost certainly result in discrepancies between the economic characteristics of certain commodities and the gross realized margin on those commodities. In conditions of free competition, of course, such discrepancies would tend to be compensatory and the overall gross margin earned by one retailer on a particular group of commodities would vary little from that carried by a second retailer on a similar group of commodities.

'Sales' and mark-downs are one way in which the influence of a traditional mark-up may be tempered. While, for example, the on-cost of retailers in a particular trade on certain groups of commodities may be practically identical, mark-downs, with the exception of those goods which were price maintained, took place in practically all trades, especially in trades such as clothing. The extent of the mark-downs or of the price reductions offered at sales appeared to vary between individual retailers, and therefore the realized gross margins on the same type of commodities earned by individual retailers would also differ. But whether the actual variations in gross realized margins were as great as the publicity given to mark-downs and price reductions would lead one to suppose and therefore whether this practice in fact countered the influence of traditional margins and mark-ups is a matter of conjecture.

To a certain extent and in certain trades the influence of tradition on margins and mark-ups is also offset by variations in settlement discounts. These discounts, while in theory relating to the cost of providing credit, are shown in the case studies to vary quite widely between trades, suggesting that factors other than the cost of providing credit are taken into account in determining the scale offered. These variations in the rates of settlement discounts may result in changes in the realized margin earned by wholesalers and retailers, even though the traditional mark-up or margin may continue to be used.

A third practice which may offset the operation of a traditional mark-up or margin is the use of price steps. In 1938 particular trades, such as the chemists' trade, used price steps of 3d., 6d. and 1s. on round figures, and the drapery, dress materials and furnishing fabric trades used steps of 6d. and 1s. on $\frac{1}{4}$d. under the round figure, for example 1s. 11$\frac{3}{4}$d., 2s. 11$\frac{3}{4}$d. This practice sometimes had the effect of forcing the retailer to adopt some mark-up other than the traditional one, though in most cases the producers and wholesalers adjusted their selling price to conform exactly with the traditional retail mark-up or margin and price step.

An example of the operation of traditional margins is to be seen in the sale of canned fruit and vegetables—relatively new products—which are sold in both the grocery and greengrocery trades. The same or similar types or brands of canned goods were frequently sold at different prices in grocers and greengrocers, owing to each trade aiming at the traditional gross margin, which was lower for grocers than for greengrocers. Certainly the rate of stock turn and the actual selling costs of the same goods were not the same in the different types of retail outlet, but it would appear that the different gross margins earned on the same goods by the retailers in different trades were determined by traditional rather than economic factors.

Re-sale price maintenance

Re-sale price maintenance also had an influence on the gross margin earned by wholesalers and retailers and in some cases may have led to higher or lower costs of distribution than would have been the case if wholesalers and retailers had been free to sell at prices dictated solely by the economic structure of their particular organizations. A rough calculation suggests—the information available does not permit of closer estimates—that between 27% and 35% of all consumer goods sold to the private domestic consumer in the United Kingdom in 1938 were sold at prices fixed or recommended by the producers. While the margins allowed to wholesalers and retailers on price maintained articles must at some stage bear a close relationship to the actual costs of selling, there may be a tendency for these margins to change at a slower rate than the changes in the circumstances of the particular trade concerned or in the demand for the individual commodity.

Two factors operate here. In the first place producers may fix margins and prices without consultation with wholesalers and retailers, and as they have little accurate knowledge of the selling costs of individual traders, the producers' selling and price policies react slowly to changes taking place in the trade. In the second place where producers may have consulted with distributors' trade associations the resulting agreement tends to be 'sticky'—easier to make than to alter—and few producers without concerted action by their competitors will attempt on their own to alter the margins allowed on price maintained articles.

As in the case of traditional mark-ups and margins, the influence of re-sale price maintenance is of particular interest where the same type of product is sold in different trades, each of which tends to operate on traditional margins. For example, boot and shoe polish and some chemists' goods were both sold to some extent by grocers, but the retail margin fixed by the producers of these goods tended in the former case to conform with the traditional footwear margin and in the latter case with the traditional chemists' margin, whereas the grocer worked to a lower margin than either boot and shoe retailers or chemists. As these goods were price maintained the grocer in selling these goods therefore either earned a gross margin higher than was common in his trade or occasionally used some of the articles as free gifts to attract custom for his groceries. Again, while the rate of stock turn and the cost of selling consumer goods were not the same in the different types of retail outlet, it would appear that the actual margin earned either by the grocer or by the chemist or boot and shoe retailer was, owing to re-sale price maintenance, not directly in accord with actual costs.

The stability of margins on price maintained articles may not be, however, as great as would appear, owing, as in the case of traditional margins and mark-ups, to the operation of special discounts of one sort or another. The actual rates of discount earned by individual retailers for settlement, for volume purchases, for purchases on special offers, and under other such schemes, varied widely and therefore may have influenced the realized gross margins in each case.

These are some of the factors which in addition to the more directly economic factors which have been discussed above may influence the cost of distribution of particular commodities. There remains a further important group of factors whose influence on costs is even more difficult to measure but whose actual effect may be very much greater. These factors are related to the character of the distributive system itself. Among them may be mentioned the type of competition existing between distributors, that is whether the distributors competed directly in price or whether competition in price was secondary to competition in providing services, and whether in the case of particular commodities, producers, wholesalers and retailers undertook 'unnecessary' distributive functions, that is functions which, if he had the choice, the consumer would have preferred to forego in return for the same commodity at a lower price.

Sufficient information has not been collected in the course of this enquiry to assess the influence of these additional factors on the cost of distribution as a whole and on the cost of the distribution of individual commodities. Nevertheless it is evident that these factors, in addition to those such as the rate of stock turn, the organization of production and distribution and the characteristics of individual commodities, influence costs and therefore have a bearing on the relative order of magnitude of the costs of distributing the individual commodities and commodity groups discussed in the previous chapter.

CHAPTER V

THE STRUCTURE OF THE DISTRIBUTIVE TRADES

Any attempt to present an outline of the pre-war structure of the distributive trades faces at the outset three main obstacles: firstly, the amazing variation in the estimates made of the number of units in these trades and the difficulty of devising any methods by which these estimates can be checked; secondly—and probably more important—the absence of qualitative information on turnover, employment and size groupings of different units; thirdly, the difficulties of terminology and definition, for example the exact meaning of terms such as grocer or provision dealer, or the exact line to be drawn between tobacconist, tobacconist/confectioner and confectioner, difficulties which detract greatly from the value of the information which is available on the numbers of units and on employment. Only a full Census of Distribution can provide the information that can be used to solve these problems. There is a further drawback, of a different type, to an analysis of the structure of the distributive trades in one particular year. Information on the trends over time is essential if an account of the structure of the distributive trades in one year is to be of value, and only a series of full or sample censuses can provide this.

The limitations of the information presented in this chapter are mentioned at the outset as, to a greater degree than in the earlier discussions, the evidence was obtained at second hand and but little cross-checking was possible. No sample census of the number, type and turnover of wholesalers and retailers in different trades was possible and, with the exception of the co-operative movement and the Retail Distributors' Association, no distributive organizations or trade associations published figures of the turnover of their members and sales by groups of commodities. Many producers have, however, collected a good deal of information relating to the number and types of outlet for their particular products. Trade associations of wholesalers and retailers have also attempted, for the purposes of negotiation, to estimate the number of firms engaged in their particular trade, and some market research organizations have made fairly careful enquiries into and surveys of the methods of distribution and of retail outlets for certain commodities and trades. Further the introduction of rationing of some commodities in the early war years has provided some data on the number of shops handling certain types of goods. By the use of this information, with cross-checks wherever possible, an elementary picture of the structure of the distributive trades in 1938 has been constructed. But the figures are estimates only and there remain a number of important gaps in the information.

1. ESTIMATES OF THE NUMBER OF WHOLESALERS IN DIFFERENT TRADES

Estimates of both the total number of wholesalers and the numbers engaged in the different trades are difficult to present in a wholly satisfactory manner owing to the varying use of the word wholesaler, the absence of widely accepted definitions of the trades, the overlapping of wholesalers between trades and the existence of wholesaler/retailers. In these estimates wholesalers have been defined, following the discussion above, as firms or organizations taking physical and financial possession of the goods and re-selling to retailers or to second wholesalers. As far as possible the estimates refer to the number of firms and not the number of establishments. That is, one firm with six or so depots in different parts of the country is classed as one wholesaler. Agents, brokers, commission houses, commission buyers and sellers and importers who did not undertake wholesaling in this sense are excluded and so are those firms doing all or most of their trade in goods which were not in a completed state or which were not sold to the private domestic consumer. The wholesaling organizations of multiple and co-operative organizations are also excluded. The problem of distinctions between trades is an almost insuperable one, partly because the nature of a particular trade changes over time, and so the definition of 'main turnover in an identifiable group of commodities' has been used as the basis of classification. This method does not completely solve the problem and there remains a group of wholesalers who deal in such a wide range of products that they cannot be identified with any single group of commodities. These firms have been classed as 'other wholesalers'.

The number and rôle of wholesaler/retailers varies widely between different trades. In the tobacco and cigarettes and sugar confectionery trades, for example, the wholesaler/retailer is an accepted and fundamental part of the structure of distribution. This is only slightly less true of the newspaper trade. In the small towns and country districts one of the larger retailers undertakes the job of holding stock and delivering as a wholesaler to his smaller neighbours and competitors. In the large towns wholesaler/retailers also exist in these trades but often the retailing side of the business takes the form of a small chain of shops. The wholesaling of milk is almost always undertaken by firms who also sell on retail terms to the public, and again in the motor car trade all distributors or main dealers are wholesaler/retailers selling cars to other dealers and to the public, while a large number of the dealers perform a similar double function of selling to retail dealers and casual traders as well as to the public. In contrast to these trades there were others where the number of wholesaler/retailers was very few, for example furniture or clothing, or where any attempt to combine both functions in one firm was strictly opposed by existing producers, wholesalers and retailers, for example in the electrical goods trades and the tyre trade. The solution to this problem is, of course, to divide the number of wholesalers into two classes, wholesalers only and wholesaler/retailers. But while some estimates can be made of the number of wholesalers, this cannot be done, with any measure of accuracy, for the number of wholesaler/retailers. The larger producers and wholesale trade associations were able to make some estimates of the number of firms engaged in wholesaling as a main occupation in various trades, but little reliable information was available on the number of wholesaler/retailers. Most of these firms were very small, their wholesaling activities often formed only a minor part of their turnover and identification was also made difficult by the practice of allowing, in some trades, special terms to retailers who did no wholesaling as well as to wholesaler/retailers proper. Wholesaler/retailers have therefore been excluded from the following Table except in the case of motor cars, where the number of distributors or main dealers is known within reasonable limits.

Owing mainly to the attempt to exclude wholesaler/retailers and partly to the source of the estimates, that is individual producers and trade associations, and to the method of classifying by trades, the number of wholesalers estimated in the following Table for each trade and for all trades is certain to be less than the total number of firms engaged in the wholesaling of finished consumer goods in 1938. The membership of trade associations was in almost every case less than the number of wholesalers in the trade and the estimates made by the associations of the number of non-members were most probably on the conservative side. Similarly the information from producers tended to understate the actual number, as few producers had accounts with all the wholesalers in the country. While allowance has been made, as far as possible, for this bias toward under-estimation, some double counting between similar trades may also have taken place resulting in an over-estimate of the number of wholesalers in individual trades. These qualifications are important if an attempt is made to compare the number of wholesalers and retailers in a particular trade and to estimate the turnover of wholesalers.

In the following Table the ranges given in each case are meant to indicate that on the basis of present information the actual number of wholesalers, in the sense defined above, probably falls somewhere within the range. At the same time the possibility that the actual figure lies outside the range is by no means excluded. The policy in constructing the ranges has been to keep them within sufficiently narrow limits to be meaningful at the risk of the truth falling outside, rather than to make them so wide as to be virtually certain that the actual figure is included.

Table 20. *Estimated number of wholesalers in different trades in the United Kingdom in 1938*

Commodity or group of commodities handled	Estimated number of wholesalers doing their main trade in the commodity
Meat and livestock	1,000–1,100
Fish	2,100–2,400
Greengrocery	5,500–6,500
Groceries and provisions	2,500–3,000
Foodstuffs handled by general wholesalers as main trade	750–1,000
Beer, wines and spirits	2,500–3,000
Clothing and household textiles	400–500
Footwear	250–300
Confectionery and tobacco	3,500–4,500
Newspapers and magazines	375–425
Stationery and books	325–375
Furniture and floor coverings	250–300
Ironmongery, hardware, hollow-ware and oils and colours	300–350
Pottery and glass	150–200
Chemists' and toilet goods, photographic goods and sundries	300–400
Cycles and accessories and associated goods	250–300
Electrical goods including radio	400–500
Jewellery, watches and clocks	400–500
Motor cars (distributors)	900–1,000
Tyres (distributors)	200–250
Fancy and leather goods	150–200
Toys and sports goods	150–200
Coal (factors and wholesalers)	300–400
Other consumer goods (wholesalers dealing in a wide range of products)	2,000–2,500

The total number of wholesalers

This Table suggests that there were in 1938 25–30,000 wholesalers, as defined above, engaged in handling consumer goods in the United Kingdom. In making these estimates all consumer goods have been considered and not merely the goods included in the enquiry. If wholesaler/retailers were included, the total would probably rise to over 50,000. The tobacco trade had the greatest number of wholesaler/retailers, approximately 10,000, followed by the confectionery and grocery trades. No information was available on the size grouping by turnover of the wholesalers, although in the case studies some indication is given of the number of wholesalers responsible for the bulk of the sales in each trade. Nor was any information available on the regional distribution of these wholesalers. In relation to individual commodities the number of wholesalers listed as doing their main trade in the commodity does not, in most cases, suggest that this was the total number of wholesalers handling the good in question. Stationery, for example, is handled by far more than 325–375 wholesalers, though it tends to be a subsidiary trade for the other wholesalers who also stock and sell these goods. Some ambiguity also arises in grouping two commodities together, for example furniture and floor coverings and toys and sports goods. While some wholesalers handled both classes of goods, the numbers given represent an estimate of the total number of wholesalers whose main trade is in one or other of the two commodities and they do not represent, necessarily, the number handling both commodities.

2. ESTIMATES OF THE NUMBER OF RETAILERS IN DIFFERENT TRADES

The information on the number of retailers in the United Kingdom in 1938 is somewhat more plentiful than on wholesalers, as this aspect of the structure of distribution has received closer attention from producers, market research organizations and other bodies than has the rôle of wholesalers. Some information is also available in Government returns relating to the number of retailers dealing in certain rationed commodities in the early war years. The total information obtained allows some attempt to be made not only to estimate the number of retail outlets but also to classify them according to the four main economic types: unit shops, multiple branches, co-operative shops and department stores.

The following Table 21 relates to fixed shops only, except for the co-operative column which includes travelling shops, and the main classifications have been made according to the usual trade divisions, though some of the smaller trades have been grouped together. In each case a brief description of the type of traders included in each classification has been given. The definition of multiple organizations used is that suggested above, a concern controlling five or more retail branches, and co-operative shops or stores are those belonging to the national co-operative movement. Department stores and variety chain stores are also classed according to the definitions already given. Multiple department stores, that is groups of five or more stores under the control of one organization, are not considered separately but are listed with department stores. Second-hand dealers are excluded in all cases.

The policy adopted in constructing the ranges in each case is the same as that adopted in Table 20 and has been discussed above. Some mention must be made however of the variations in the individual ranges. The information obtained on the number of shops in some trades, for example pharmacy, was very much more reliable than that obtained on other trades, for example arts and crafts and hobbies, and this difference is reflected in the size of the range. Further while the total number of shops dealing mainly in a mixed group of related goods, such as men's and boys' and women's and girls' clothing, can be estimated within limits, the division of the total into different trade classes is somewhat arbitrary. With regard to the estimated number of shops of different economic types in each trade classification, the number of co-operative stores or shops is more reliable than the number of multiple branches and unit retailers suggested. Estimates of the number of branches of multiple organizations proved particularly difficult to make. Among the difficulties met with in obtaining this information were the different definitions adopted as to what constitutes a multiple organization and the use, in cases where private traders' shops were bought by a multiple organization, of the original name rather than the name of the multiple concern. Again the reliability of the evidence regarding the number of multiple branches varied from trade to trade, but the difficulties in making the estimates have led to the use in some cases of a rather wider proportional range for the number of multiple branches than for the number of unit retailers. This somewhat inconsistent position arises from the fact that the two sets of figures were estimated independently, from, in part, different sources. The sum of the number of unit and multiple shops in a trade must therefore include the sum of the errors, though there will undoubtedly be instances where the errors are compensatory.

Table 21. *Estimated number of retail shops grouped by main trades and economic types in the United Kingdom in 1938*[1]

Type of trade	Definition	Estimated number: Unit retail shops	Multiple branches	Co-operative shops or stores
BAKERS	Bakers, pastrycooks and shops selling mainly bread and/or cakes	24,000–28,000	2,500–3,000	*
DAIRIES	Retail shops only, not distributing dairies or travelling sales vehicles	16,000–19,000	2,000–2,500	*
BUTCHERS	Butchers, pork butchers and tripe dealers	35,000–41,000	5,500–6,500	5,000–5,200
FISHMONGERS	Fishmongers and poulterers but not fried fish shops or travelling sales vehicles	9,000–11,000	750–1,000	1,240–1,260 (Fishmongers and Greengrocers together)
GREENGROCERS	Greengrocers and fruiterers, excluding barrow-men and hawkers	39,000–44,000	900–1,100	
GROCERS	Grocers and provision dealers, corn and seed merchants, corn chandlers, tea and coffee retailers	65,000–75,000	18,000–20,000	11,200–11,500
GENERAL FOOD DEALERS	Village general and other general dealers selling mainly food	65,000–85,000	—	—
BEER, WINE AND SPIRIT DEALERS	Off-licences selling mainly beer, wines and spirits	5,000–6,000	1,500–2,000	*
RETAILERS OF WOMEN'S AND CHILDREN'S WEAR	Outfitters and tailors, gown shops, furriers, wool shops, milliners and drapers	60,000–70,000	1,500–2,000	2,500–3,000 (Retailers of women's and children's wear and Men's and boys' tailors and outfitters together)
MEN'S AND BOYS' TAILORS AND OUTFITTERS	Outfitters, ready-to-wear tailors, hatters, speciality men's clothing retailers	13,000–16,000	3,000–4,000	
BOOT AND SHOE RETAILERS	Shops specializing in the sale of boots and shoes	8,000–9,500	4,500–5,000	1,200–1,225
GENERAL CLOTHING RETAILERS	General and other shops selling mainly clothing, other than second-hand clothes shops	15,000–20,000	—	—

Type of trade	Definition	Estimated number		
		Unit retail shops	Multiple branches	Co-operative shops or stores
CONFECTIONERS	These trades overlap to a considerable extent and the numbers in each category are very approximate	45,000–53,000	2,500–3,000	*
TOBACCONISTS		20,000–24,000	1,750–2,250	*
NEWSAGENTS		19,000–22,000	2,000–2,250	—
STATIONERS		4,500–5,500	400–500	*
FURNITURE DEALERS	Furniture and furnishings, carpet and linoleum dealers but not second-hand furniture dealers	10,000–12,500	1,500–2,000	650–700
IRONMONGERY, HARDWARE AND CHINA AND GLASS DEALERS	Including shops selling domestic stores and cutlery	12,500–15,000	1,250–1,500	210–220
OIL AND COLOURMEN	Oil and colourmen and shops mainly selling wallpaper, paints and other builders' materials to the public	3,000–4,000	*	*
CHEMISTS AND DRUGGISTS	Chemists, drug-stores, herbalists, retailers of surgical appliances and photographic goods, but not photographers	15,000–16,000	3,250–3,750	500–600
CYCLE AND MOTOR CYCLE DEALERS	Cycle and cycle accessory dealers, not cycle repairers	9,000–11,000	1,000–1,250	*
ELECTRICAL AND RADIO DEALERS	Electrical contractors with retail shops, radio dealers, not public utility showrooms	19,000–23,000	1,250–1,500	*
JEWELLERS, SILVERSMITHS AND WATCHMAKERS	Excluding shops doing repairs only	7,000–8,000	1,250–1,500	*
BOOKSELLERS	Retailers selling new books as main trade, not circulating and other libraries	4,000–4,500	700–800	*
LEATHER AND FANCY GOODS DEALERS	Dealers in handbags, travel goods and fancy goods	4,000–5,000	*	*

Type of trade	Definition	Estimated number		
		Unit retail shops	Multiple branches	Co-operative shops or stores
SPORTS GOODS AND TOY RETAILERS	Specialist dealers in sports goods and toys only	2,000–2,500	*	*
MOTOR VEHICLE DEALERS	Stockists of new motor vehicles only	7,000–7,400	*	—
FLORISTS, NURSERYMEN AND SEEDSMEN	Dealers doing a main trade in these goods and also often selling greengroceries	6,000–8,000	*	*
RETAILERS OF PIANOS AND MUSICAL INSTRUMENTS	Shops engaged principally in the sale of these goods including the sale of sheet music, gramophones and records	2,500–3,000	*	*
ARTS AND CRAFTS DEALERS	Art dealers, hobbies specialists	3,000–4,000	*	*
SPECIALITY RETAILERS	Perambulator, sewing machine, umbrella and marine stores dealers, dealers in live animals, office furniture, typewriters, and other speciality retailers	8,000–12,000	2,000–2,500	*
GARAGES AND TYRE DEALERS	Garages and other dealers selling oil, petrol and/or tyres	20,000–25,000	*	—
GENERAL DEALERS	Village general and other general shops not included above, excluding second-hand dealers	20,000–30,000	—	—
VARIETY CHAIN STORES	Five or more branches of one concern, each shop selling a wide variety of commodities	—	1,300–1,400	—
DEPARTMENT STORES	A store with five or more separate departments each selling different commodities or commodity groups	400–450	—	—

[1] In this Table:

— indicates nil or a negligible number of shops in this trade.

* indicates that multiple branches and co-operative shops or stores sold these commodities but either such outlets have already been included in the numbers given for other trades or it has not been possible to give the number of shops owing to the difficulty of classification.

The total number of multiple branches selling consumer goods, therefore, that must be added to the total shown in the Table is approximately 200 and the number of co-operative shops or stores to be added is approximately 1,000, of which dairies and tobacconists were the most important.

The number of shops shown in the different trades does not, of course, indicate the total number of outlets for particular commodities or commodity groups but merely the number of shops that could by the composition of their sales be classified as belonging primarily to that trade.

Total number of retailers

These estimates suggest that there were in the region of 750,000 fixed shops selling finished consumer goods in 1938. Of this number approximately 66,000 were branches of multiple organizations, 24,000 were co-operative stores and travelling shops, 450 were department stores and about 657,000 unit retailers. Some estimates have also been made of the number of other fixed shops not included in this list which were engaged primarily in selling goods and services or only services. The distinction drawn between shops selling finished consumer goods and shops selling services or goods and services is as follows: in the first group are shops whose turnover was mainly in goods sold 'over the counter' in the condition, except for breaking bulk, in which they were received from the wholesaler or producer and without any service to the consumer being undertaken beyond that of transport or delivery or elementary installation; in the second group are included those shops whose turnover was represented by the sale of services or the sale of joint services and goods which involved some change in the character of the goods by the retailer. For example a shop selling mainly bread and cakes and serving lunches and teas as a sideline has been classed as belonging to the first group whereas a teashop whose main revenue was obtained from the sale of meals but which also sold some groceries has been placed in the second group.

The number of shops in the United Kingdom in 1938 estimated to fall in the second group is about 250,000. The largest single group was public houses, about 80,000, followed by restaurants, cafés, teashops and milk bars, about 50,000, men's and women's hairdressers and beauty salons, about 37,000, and fish fryers, about 23,000. The remaining shops include those of second-hand dealers of all kinds, pawnbrokers, coal merchants and those engaged in service trades such as dyers, cleaners, launderers, photographers, opticians and undertakers. Also included are post offices and circulating libraries. The estimates of the number of shops selling services is very approximate, as a special study has not been made of this aspect of distribution.

Taking the two groups together, the total number of shops selling consumer goods and providing services for the consumer in the United Kingdom in 1938 was probably in the region of 1,000,000. This estimate must be a very approximate one and almost certainly understates the total number of retailers of various sorts, as producer/retailers without shops, delivery vehicles, market stalls and barrows, and agents, pedlars and individual salesmen are excluded. The number of branches of multiple organizations is probably slightly higher as a proportion of all shops than the proportion suggested for shops selling consumer goods only, as multiple branches were relatively prominent in a number of service trades such as catering, dyeing, cleaning, laundering and circulating libraries, and further, as suggested above, a large number of public houses can be classed as multiple branches.

3. SALES BY DIFFERENT ECONOMIC TYPES OF RETAIL OUTLET

Estimates of the sales made by the different economic types of retail outlet of the individual commodities and commodity groups covered in the enquiry are given in Chart VI. These estimates are based in the same fashion as the other estimates on the information obtained from individual producers and retail organizations, trade associations and market research and advertising agencies, and on data available in official and non-official publications. On the whole, the estimates relating to sales by department stores and co-operative stores are probably more reliable than the estimates relating to the sales by multiple branches and unit retailers. This is mainly due to the existence of far more statistical data on the first two types of retailing and partly to easier identification of sales made by producers to these organizations. The estimates of sales by unit retailers tend to be residual figures. When presented in terms of turnover, the estimates of the sales by unit retailers may therefore be subject to error as a result of an error in the estimates of the proportion of trade handled by other types of outlet as well as by the possible error in the estimate of consumers' expenditure.

In this Chart the sales by producer/retailers and the sales from delivery vehicles, barrows and market stalls and all sales made other than through a fixed shop have been included in the sales of unit retailers except in those instances were the delivery vehicle or stall was owned by a multiple or co-operative organization.

The importance of the sales by different types of economic outlet of commodities in main trade groups is shown in the following Table 22.

NOTES TO CHART VI

The estimated consumers' expenditure on each of these commodities has been given in Charts I and III.

The figures given are the middle points of the estimated ranges shown in the case studies.

The estimates in this Chart of the proportions of total sales of individual commodities and commodity groups that were undertaken by unit retailers differ in some instances from those given in the case studies. The differences arise from the attempt to distinguish in the Chart the sales of the four economic types of outlet while in the case studies the sales by department stores are frequently included with the sales by unit retailers. The sales by supply authorities have been included in sales by unit retailers.

Chart VI is available for download from
www.cambridge.org/9781107602748

Table 22. *Estimated proportions of total sales in 1938 made by different economic types of retail outlet, by trade groups*[1]

Trade group	Consumers' expenditure £ million	Unit retailers %	Co-operative shops %	Department stores %	Multiple shops %
Motor trade	114·5	98·0	—	—	2·0
Fresh fruit and vegetables	141·0	91·0	3·5	—	5·5
Fish	35·5	88·5	4·0	—	7·5
Newspapers and magazines	48·0	87·0	—	—	13·0
Cigarettes and tobacco	177·0	86·0	8·0	—	6·0
Chocolates and sweets	55·0	83·5	2·5	—	14·0
Electrical goods	26·5	83·0	1·0	4·0	12·0
Poultry, game and rabbits	19·0	75·0	4·0	—	21·0
Beer, wines and spirits, off-licence sales	59·5	73·0	1·0	1·5	24·5
Jewellers' goods	24·0	72·5	1·0	6·0	20·5
Meat	180·0	71·5	12·5	—	16·0
Coal[2]	97·5	71·5	13·5	—	15·0
Other specialities	36·5	66·0	2·0	16·0	16·0
Stationery, pens, inks, pencils	17·5	66·0	—	4·5	29·5
Bread and flour confectionery	104·5	64·5	19·0	—	16·5
Pottery and ironmongers' goods	43·5	63·5	5·0	12·5	19·0
Chemists' goods	55·0	61·0	4·0	4·0	31·0
Men's and boys' wear	121·0	57·0	6·5	7·5	29·0
Provisions	206·0	56·0	20·5	1·5	22·0
Groceries and household stores	262·0	54·5	20·5	1·5	23·5
Furnishings	58·5	53·5	4·5	25·0	17·0
Women's and children's wear	238·0	50·5	7·5	27·5	14·5
Furniture	62·0	48·0	7·0	15·0	30·0
Fresh milk	86·5	47·0	25·5	—	27·5
Leather and rubber footwear	68·0	38·0	10·0	6·0	46·0
Beer, wines and spirits—on-licence sales	237·5	27·0	—	—	73·0

[1] — indicates less than 1% of total sales estimated to have been undertaken by the particular type of outlet.

The individual commodities comprising the trade groups have been given above on p. 21.

Sales by unit producer/retailers are included in sales by unit retailers.

Sales by producers to consumers by mail order and other direct means have been excluded.

The sales of variety chain stores are included in the sales of multiple shops.

Beer, wines and spirits, on- and off-licence sales: 'Tied' on- and off-licences have been included in multiple shops. The proportion of on-licences tied was very much higher than the proportion of off-licences tied, and the proportion of on-licences tied for beer very much higher than the proportion tied for wines.

[2] Coal: The sales of coal by merchants possessing five or more depots or order offices and by colliery selling networks have been classed as sales by multiple shops.

Finally an estimate can be made of the proportion of total sales undertaken by the different economic types of retail outlet. The on-licence sales of beer, wines and spirits have been omitted from this Table, as classification of public houses owned by or tied to breweries as multiple shops is an unusual one and this inclusion might be misleading.

Table 23. *Estimated proportions of consumer goods studied sold by the four main types of retail outlet in 1938*[1]

Commodity	Consumers' expenditure	Proportion of total sales made by different types of retail outlet			
	£ million	Unit retailers %	Co-operative shops %	Multiple shops %	Department stores %
All commodities studied	2,336·0	64·5–67·0	10–10·5	17·5–19·0	5·5–6

[1] Estimated sales by producers direct to consumers by mail order have been excluded.

Significant sales of individual commodities by multiple branches, co-operative stores and department stores

The use of the proportion of sales by unit retailers as the guide for constructing Chart VI and Table 22 brings out clearly the variation in the proportion of individual commodities and of commodities grouped by trades sold by these retailers. But the variations in the case of the other economic types of retail outlet are less readily seen, and a rearrangement of the data is necessary to show at a glance the particular commodities having a significant sale in co-operative, multiple or department stores. In Table 23 the average proportion of all goods represented by sales by co-operative shops has been estimated as 10–10·5%, by multiple shops as 17·5–19% and by department stores as 5·5–6%. Using these averages as guides to the trading pattern of each of these outlets, the following Table lists those commodities of which more than the average proportion of national sales was undertaken.

Table 24. *Commodities and commodity groups with significant sales by co-operative shops, department stores and multiple shops in 1938*

1. Commodities or commodity groups with significant sales in co-operative shops		
Food and drink	Margarine Cocoa Fresh milk Sugar Syrup and treacle Tea Cheese Packaged and unpackaged breakfast cereals Plain and self-raising flour Butter Sauces, pickles and salad cream Salt	Imported canned fruit, vegetables and fish Jam and marmalade Bacon and ham Bread and flour confectionery Biscuits Home-produced canned fruit and vegetables Canned milk Health food beverages Eggs Meat Coffee
Clothing	Corsets and brassières Women's and children's stockings and socks	Men's and boys' shirts, collars, pyjamas and hosiery
Other goods	Coal Candles and nightlights Household soap	Toilet soap Household polishes
2. Commodities or commodity groups with significant sales in department stores		
Food and drink	Nil	
Clothing	Dress materials Furs and fur garments Women's and children's outerwear Gloves Women's and children's underwear and nightwear Haberdashery and general drapers' goods Millinery	Corsets and brassières Women's and children's stockings and socks Men's and boys' shirts, collars, pyjamas and hosiery Men's and boys' handkerchiefs, ties, scarves and braces Men's and boys' outerwear Men's and boys' hats and caps Leather footwear
Other goods	Toys Furnishing fabrics Household textiles and soft furnishings	Furniture Perambulators Domestic hardware, hollow-ware and ironmongery

	Carpets	Beauty preparations
	Leather goods	Imitation jewellery
	Cutlery	Perfumes and toilet waters
	Linoleum	Electric fires, kettles and appliances
	Brooms and brushes	Real jewellery and silver and electro-plate
	Pottery and glassware	
	Sports goods	
	Clocks	
3. Commodities or commodity groups with significant sales in multiple shops		
Food and drink	Beer—on-licence sales	Plain and self-raising flour
	Spirits—on-licence sales	Butter
	Beer—off-licence sales	Home-produced canned fruit and vegetables
	Biscuits	Bacon and ham
	Cocoa	Wines and spirits—off-licence sales
	Fresh milk	Canned milk
	Imported canned fruit, vegetables and fish	Poultry, game and rabbits
	Wine—on-licence sales	Cheese
	Sauces, pickles and salad creams	Sugar
	Tea	Salt
	Margarine	
Clothing	Leather footwear	Men's and boys' shirts, collars, pyjamas and hosiery
	Rubber footwear	Men's and boys' handkerchiefs, ties, scarves and braces
	Men's and boys' outerwear	Haberdashery and general drapers' goods
	Men's and boys' hats and caps	Corsets and brassières
	Women's and children's underwear and nightwear	
Other goods	Sewing machines	Stationery, inks, pens and pencils
	Portable typewriters	Perfumes and toilet waters
	Imitation jewellery	Watches
	Electric light lamps	Razors and blades
	Non-proprietary medicines and drugs	Toys
	Dental preparations	Household soap
	Proprietary medicines and drugs	Linoleum
	Beauty preparations	Domestic hardware, hollow-ware and general ironmongery
	Toilet soap	Pottery and glassware
	Furniture	Carpets
	Infant and invalid foods	Candles and nightlights
	Contraceptives	Sanitary towels
		Furnishing fabrics

Share of the different economic types of outlet in the total national trade

A further estimate can be made of the share of the different economic types of retail outlet in the total national trade in consumer goods in the United Kingdom in 1938. To do this allowance must be made for the commodities and commodity groups which have not been covered in the enquiry and appropriate estimates made for each. In a number of instances, for example lard, pianos, bicycles, ice cream, sausages and manufactured food preparations, a certain amount of information was collected in the course of this enquiry on the methods and costs of distribution but this was not sufficiently complete to warrant a separate case study. In other cases, such as local weekly newspapers and electrical fittings, an assumption has been made that goods were distributed in much the same manner as the fairly similar commodities studied such as magazines and daily newspapers and household electrical goods. There remain some commodities where the methods of distribution could only be estimated very approximately.

Table 25. *Estimated national retail sales of consumer goods in 1938 made by different economic types of retail outlet and the estimated numbers of each type of outlet in the United Kingdom*[1]

Type of shop or outlet	Estimated sales £ million	% of total sales	Estimated number of shops	% of total number of shops
Unit retailers	1,681·0	66·0	657,000	88·0
Multiple shops	480·0	18·5	66,000	9·0
Co-operative shops	258·0	10·0	24,000	3·0
Department stores	136·0	5·5	425	—
Total	2,555·0	100·0	748,000	100·0

[1] These estimates exclude the on-licence sales of beer, wines and spirits, mail order sales and also the estimated number of public houses. The estimated sales and percentages have been rounded off.

In interpreting the above Table it should be borne in mind that the number of shops given relates to fixed shops only, whereas the sales by retailers relate to total sales whether made in a fixed shop or not. The types of retail outlets excluded from the Table are producer/retailers other than those with a fixed shop, delivery vehicles operating independently of a fixed shop, market stalls, barrows, and other outlets of this nature. The number of outlets of this type cannot be estimated closely but it is thought that there were, possibly, over 100,000. The proportion of the total national sales undertaken by these outlets was not, of course, very great. Ten per cent would probably represent the very outside limit, five per cent being nearer the truth. And as most of these outlets could be classified as unit retailers the effect of their inclusion, if the numbers were known, would be to increase the proportion of unit retail outlets as a percentage of total outlets, with a corresponding decrease in the proportion represented by the other three types of outlet. A second qualification to the Table, which also applies to the subsequent discussion of multiple, co-operative and department store trading, is that the estimates of turnover of these types of outlet do not correspond to the actual turnover, as all three types of outlet provided services in one degree or another, such as cafés and restaurants. Receipts from the sale of services have been excluded from these estimates.

4. MULTIPLE SHOP AND VARIETY CHAIN STORE TRADING

The different types of retailing organization can now be examined in some detail. The number of multiple shop organizations controlling the 60,000–70,000 retail branches is estimated at 2,100–2,500. But wide variations existed in the size and turnover of both the branches and the organizations. Of the 2,100–2,500 organizations some 300–350 are estimated to have controlled 35,000–40,000 of the retail branches and these branches were responsible for about three-quarters of the total turnover of multiple shops in consumer goods. Within this smaller group there was a further concentration in that some half-a-dozen organizations in the variety chain store, grocery, chemists' goods and meat trades controlled some 9,000 shops with a total turnover of approximately £170 millions or just over one-third of the estimated total multiple sales and 6–7% of the national retail trade. In the case of variety chain stores, which are treated as a sub-section of multiple trading, the total turnover in consumer goods of the 1,300–1,400 branches in 1938 is estimated at £98–106 millions. Three organizations controlled just under 1,000 of these branches, and this group is estimated to have been responsible for nearly 90% of the total turnover by variety chain stores. While no information is at present available to show the number of multiple shops by different turnover groupings or the variations between the turnover of multiple shops in different trades, the above figures illustrate the wide divergencies in the size and turnover of different organizations. About 10% of the total number of organizations in 1938 are estimated to have controlled approximately 60% of the total number of branches, and these branches had an average turnover in the neighbourhood of over £9,000 per annum compared with an average turnover of about £4,000 per annum for the remaining 40% of the branches. The average turnover of variety chain stores is estimated at approximately £80,000 per annum compared with an average of £6,000 per annum for all the remaining multiple branches.

The estimated number of multiple branches in different trades and the estimated proportion of total sales of various commodities undertaken by multiple shops have been given above in Tables 21 and 22 and Chart VI, but the numbers in each trade cannot strictly be related to multiple sales in that trade since the sales of variety chain stores, covering a wide range of goods, are included in multiple shop sales.

Variety chain stores

The goods sold by variety chain stores can be roughly divided into three main groups: foodstuffs, including certain groceries and provisions, fruit and vegetables, sugar and flour confectionery, ice cream and soft drinks; clothing including footwear and men's and boys' and women's and girls' clothing and miscellaneous drapery; and a general group covering a wide range of goods. The division of the total turnover of variety chain stores between these three groups in 1938 is estimated as follows:

Foodstuffs	18–22%
Clothing	30–32%
General	46–52%

The relative importance of these groups varied widely between different organizations. In some organizations the sales of clothing were responsible for nearly two-thirds of the total sales while in others their importance dropped to less than one-fifth. The sales in the general group tended to vary inversely with the sales of clothing, as the proportion of total sales represented by foodstuffs varied relatively slightly—from 15% to 25%—between different organizations, though there were variations in the type of foodstuffs sold. For example, in some organizations the sales emphasis was on canned goods, flour confectionery, fruit and provisions while in others the emphasis was on biscuits, sugar confectionery, ice-cream and soft drinks.

Variety chain stores are estimated to have undertaken some 3–4% of total retail sales of consumer goods in 1938. The commodities of which more than 10% of total sales are estimated to have been made by variety chain stores are as follows:

Electric light lamps	Beauty and toilet preparations and requisites
Imitation jewellery	Women's and girls' stockings and socks
Haberdashery and general drapers' goods	

Toys	Dental preparations
Pottery and glassware	Hardware, hollow-ware and general ironmongery
Women's underwear and nightwear	Razors and blades
Biscuits	Watches
Stationery, pens, pencils and ink	

Linked production and retailing by multiple organizations

Vertical integration of production and distribution was a prominent feature of some multiple organizations. Further many of the imported commodities not requiring further processing which were sold by multiple organizations were purchased abroad by such concerns and thus remained in their hands from the point of landing in the United Kingdom until sold to the final consumer. Altogether it is estimated that between 17–20% of the commodities sold by multiple retail branches were either manufactured or processed in the United Kingdom by concerns linked with these retailing organizations or were imported directly from abroad by these organizations. Of this proportion some three-quarters were goods processed or manufactured in the United Kingdom and the remainder were direct imports.

The following were the most important commodities and commodity groups, measured by the value of their retail sales, manufactured or processed by concerns linked with multiple retailing organizations:

Men's and boys' outerwear	Milk
Bread and flour confectionery	Chocolates and sweets
Leather footwear	Stationery
Tea	Watches and clocks
Proprietary and non-proprietary medicines and drugs	Sewing machines

Only a small number of multiple organizations were engaged in manufacturing or processing and the extent to which the retail branches sold only the products of linked manufacturing or processing concerns varied with the commodity. Multiple branches which had linked production units and which retailed sewing machines, typewriters, men's and boys' outerwear, bread and flour confectionery and tea, for example, sold almost entirely only their own products. Multiple branches selling proprietary and non-proprietary medicines and drugs, stationery, watches and clocks, chocolates and sweets and leather footwear, on the other hand, sold an important proportion of goods of other than their own manufacture, sometimes as much as two-thirds to three-quarters of their sales being represented by such goods. The demand by the consumer for a wide range of goods and the impracticability of one manufacturing unit producing such a range was the main factor operating in the case of the second group of commodities. The position however is far from static. Decisions are continuously being made either to limit or increase the range of products offered by multiple retail branches or to contract or expand the range produced by the linked manufacturing establishment, thus influencing the proportion of bought-out purchases in any trade.

5. CO-OPERATIVE TRADING

The extent and character of co-operative trading in the United Kingdom is more fully documented than any other sector of the distributive trades.[1] The co-operative movement regularly publishes statistics and these have been subjected to detailed analysis both inside and outside the movement. Here no attempt will be made to discuss the principles or the problems of co-operative trading; the discussion will be confined to estimates, based on the information obtained in the course of the enquiry and on the published figures, of the main methods of distribution within the co-operative movement and the importance of co-operative trading in consumer goods. The arrangement of the statistics of co-operative trading as at present published does not allow of a definite answer to many of the questions asked regarding methods of distribution, such as what proportion of the consumer goods sold by retail societies are produced within the co-operative organization, and therefore the attempts made below to answer this and some related questions must be regarded as estimates subject to error.

The total sales of 1,085 retail co-operative societies in 1938 amounted to £263 millions. In order to estimate the sales of consumer goods alone services must be excluded. Hairdressing, catering, laundering, funeral furnishing, boot and shoe repairing and other service sales in 1938 are estimated at between £4–5 millions. This leaves a retail turnover in consumer goods of approximately £258 millions.

The consumer goods sold by the retail societies were obtained in one or more of four main ways. The retail society could purchase the products from a co-operative wholesale society, the three main societies being the Co-operative Wholesale Society Ltd., the Scottish Co-operative Wholesale Society Ltd. and the English and Scottish Joint Wholesale Society Ltd. Secondly the retail society could purchase the goods from an independent co-operative productive society, that is a society or federation not linked either with the three main wholesale societies

[1] The main sources used are the *Annual Congress Reports* of the Co-operative Union, 1939, 1940 and 1941, and *The People's Year Book*, 1939 and 1940. Other books are given in the Bibliography.

or with the particular retail society. Thirdly, the retail society could sell the goods produced in its own production section. Fourthly, the retail society could purchase the goods directly from a manufacturer, producer, importer or wholesaler who was completely unconnected with the co-operative movement.

In order to estimate the proportion of goods sold by the retail societies passing through each of these four main channels, a number of adjustments have to be made to the published figures of the sales of the various co-operative organizations.

The sales, at wholesale prices, of the three main co-operative wholesale societies in 1938 were £147 millions. But the figure includes items such as exports or re-exports by these societies, duplication of sales between different productive establishments and between the societies, capital goods sold to retail societies, and raw materials and semi-processed goods sold to independent productive societies and retail productive societies. Excluding such sales, the purchases by retail societies from co-operative wholesale societies of products requiring no further process of manufacture before their sale to the public are estimated at about £114 millions at wholesale prices.

The sales, at wholesale prices, of independent productive societies and productive federations in 1938 were £7·2 millions. But again this figure includes such items as capital goods and printing, and semi-finished goods which were sold to retail productive societies to undergo a further process of manufacture, as well as the sales of services, particularly laundry. Further, a part of the sales of these societies is included at retail prices. Excluding non-consumer goods and adjusting prices, the purchases by retail societies of finished consumer goods from independent productive societies or federations are estimated at about £4 millions at wholesale prices.

The output of the productive departments of retail societies in 1938 was valued at £42·3 millions. This figure includes the value of output, such as building or transport, which did not enter directly into retail sales and the sales of services such as laundering and boot and shoe repairing. Again there is a complication, in that part of the value of the production is expressed in terms of retail prices and part at wholesale prices. If these sales of services and non-consumer goods are excluded and adjustment made in the prices, the value at wholesale prices of the finished consumer goods produced or processed by the productive departments of retail societies is estimated at approximately £36 millions. This total includes a large proportion of goods on which only 'pre-retailing services' were performed rather than productive operations.

Methods of distribution of goods sold by retail societies

The sales can be approximately translated into retail prices by using the average margins for the different types of goods, and the following Table constructed:

Table 26. *Sources of purchases of consumer goods by retail co-operative societies in 1938*

Estimated total retail sales of consumer goods by retail societies	Estimated proportions of goods sold by retail societies purchased from			
	Co-operative wholesale societies	Independent productive societies and federations	Productive departments of retail societies	Other manufacturers, wholesalers or importers (by difference)
£ million	%	%	%	%
258	56–59	2	17–18	21–25

The second question of interest is the proportion of total sales by retail societies represented by goods produced or processed by co-operative organizations in the United Kingdom, and, following the approach developed earlier, the proportion represented by imported goods which remained in the hands of co-operative organizations from the moment of landing in the country until sold to the consumer.

The sales at wholesale prices of goods manufactured or processed (this includes the packing of tea) by productive departments of the co-operative wholesale societies were approximately £61 millions in 1938. This figure includes the sale of capital goods and raw and semi-finished materials to productive and retail societies as well as the sales of other goods which were not sold to the consumer. If these are deducted, the estimated sales at wholesale prices of finished consumer goods produced or processed by the productive departments of the wholesale societies is estimated at approximately £43 millions.

Estimates of the sales of finished consumer goods to retail societies by independent productive societies and the productive departments of retail societies have already been made and, translating the figures into retail prices, the following Table 27 can be constructed:

Table 27. *Source of production or processing of goods sold by retail co-operative societies in 1938*

Estimated total sales of consumer goods by retail co-operative societies	Estimated proportions of total goods produced or processed by			
	Co-operative wholesale societies	Independent productive societies	Productive departments of retail societies	Other producers or importers
£ million	%	%	%	%
258	21–23	2	17–18	57–60

Tables 26 and 27 can now be combined to show the main channels of distribution of goods sold by co-operative retail societies.

Table 28. *Main methods of distribution of consumer goods sold by co-operative retail societies in 1938*

Estimated total retail sales of consumer goods by retail societies	Estimated proportions of goods sold by co-operative retail societies purchased from				
	Co-operative wholesale societies		Independent productive societies	Productive departments of retail societies	Other producers, wholesalers and importers (by difference)
	Goods purchased by the societies from other producers and importers	Goods produced by the societies themselves			
£ million	%	%	%	%	%
258	35–36	21–23	2	17–18	21–25

Of the goods purchased by the co-operative wholesale societies from other producers and from importers about one-fifth is estimated to be represented by goods purchased abroad by the societies and re-sold, through the retail societies, to the consumer without undergoing any further stage of manufacturing or processing.

Co-operative production and retail sales

These estimates relate to the trade of the co-operative organizations as a whole in the United Kingdom. There were important differences in respect of individual commodities and commodity groups and in respect of different retail societies. The information obtained in the course of this enquiry has not thrown much light on the latter differences save that the larger the retail society the less it relied on co-operative sources for its purchases.[1] Some estimates of the importance of co-operative production and of the sources of purchase by retail societies of groups of commodities can, however, be made.

Of the goods with an estimated value at wholesale prices of £43 millions which were produced or processed by the co-operative wholesale societies in 1938 for sale in the stores of retail societies without undergoing a further process of manufacture, 70–80% can be classed as foodstuffs, about 9% as clothing, 5% as boots and shoes, 6% as furniture, furnishings and hardware and 2% other miscellaneous goods including leather goods, coal and drugs. Included in the foodstuffs group are the goods usually sold in the grocery and provision departments such as soap, tobacco, matches, candles and household stores, amounting to about 12% of the total production. Of the goods with an estimated value at wholesale prices of £36 millions which were produced or processed by the production departments of retail societies for sale in the retail shops, over 90% was represented by foodstuffs, about 5% by clothing and footwear and 4–5% by furniture, furnishings and other goods. The bulk of the foodstuffs production and processing represented the baking of bread and cakes, livestock slaughtering and meat preparation, and milk processing. Of the goods with an estimated wholesale value of £4 millions produced or processed by independent productive societies for sale in the stores of retail societies, about one-half was represented by foodstuffs, 35–40% by clothing and the remainder by boots and shoes and miscellaneous goods.

Therefore, of the total goods manufactured or processed by the co-operative movement and passed to retail societies for sale without undergoing further manufacture or processing, estimated at £83 millions at wholesale prices, approximately 80–82% can be classed as foodstuffs, 8–9% as clothing, 3–4% as boots and shoes, 4–5% as furniture, hardware and ironmongery and 2–3% as other miscellaneous goods. If tobacco, soap, candles, polishes and general stores are deducted from the foodstuffs group, so that it consists in the main of bread and cakes, meat, tea, milk and milk products, margarine, butter, bacon and ham, self-raising and plain flour, preserves, fish, fruit and vegetables and other general groceries and provisions, the proportion for this group drops to about 75%.

[1] For a useful discussion of this problem see A. M. Carr-Saunders, P. Sargant Florence and R. Peers, *Consumers' Co-operation in Great Britain*, London, 1942, third, revised edition, pp. 158 foll.

In the case of a number of commodities some estimates can be made of the proportion of total retail sales by co-operative retail stores represented by goods processed or manufactured by co-operative organizations. Total retail sales by co-operative stores in 1938 of foodstuffs, including groceries and provisions, bread and cakes, sales in the butchers', dairy, greengrocery and fish shops and also the sales of soap, tobacco, confectionery and household stores, were approximately £195–200 millions at retail prices. The value of the foodstuffs produced or processed within the co-operative movement was approximately £85 millions at retail prices or 43–44% of the total retail sales of this group. To this figure can be added the value of the foodstuffs imported directly from abroad by co-operative organizations, excluding, of course, those imported products which were processed in the United Kingdom. If this is done the proportion rises to 54–55%. There were wide variations between commodities. Practically all of the bread, cakes, plain and self-raising flour, home-killed meat and meat products, margarine, lard, tea, coffee, and candles were processed or produced within the co-operative movement, and a high proportion of the milk, preserves, canned goods and soap. At the other end of the scale, a relatively small proportion of the total co-operative retail sales of the following products were produced or processed within the movement: home-produced and imported butter and cheese, biscuits, sugar confectionery, cocoa and eggs. An important proportion of some of these goods was, of course, imported. Some goods, such as sugar and treacle, were not manufactured at all by the co-operative movement.

Total retail sales by co-operative societies of clothing, excluding boots and shoes, were £25–28 millions in 1938. The value of the clothing produced within the co-operative movement in 1938 was, at retail prices, approximately £10–11 millions or 38–41% of retail sales. The proportion of the men's and boys' wear sold by retail societies that was produced within the movement, representing about 66%, was higher than that of women's, girls' and children's wear, representing about 33%. In the case of the sales of some goods such as men's ready-to-wear outer clothing, hats and caps, and shirts, collars and pyjamas, a very high proportion was of co-operative manufacture. Of the sales of men's hosiery, women's underwear, corsets, and millinery, between one-half and two-thirds were of co-operative manufacture. A much lower proportion of the sales of women's and children's outerwear and stockings, general haberdashery and drapers' goods consisted of co-operative manufactured goods. Co-operative retail sales of boots and shoes, including rubber footwear, are estimated at £6–7 millions in 1938, of which approximately 60–66% were goods of co-operative manufacture.

Total retail sales by co-operative societies of furniture, furnishings, pottery and glassware, hardware and hollow-ware, brooms and brushes and general electrical goods in 1938 are estimated at £9–10 millions. The total value at retail prices of co-operative production of these goods is estimated at £5–6 millions or 56–60% of retail sales. Practically all the brooms and brushes, cutlery, paints, electric light lamps and linoleum and floorcloth sold by retail societies were of co-operative manufacture and also a high proportion of the furniture, household textiles, and hollow-ware, hardware and general ironmongers' goods. On the other hand only a small proportion of the furnishing fabrics, carpets, pottery and glass and general electrical goods were so produced.

The sales of other goods by retail co-operative societies in 1938 are estimated at £17–19 millions, of which coal was the most important, £13·2 millions, the remainder being chemists' goods and sundries. Co-operative coal production was insignificant, less than 5% of the retail sales, and in the remaining group the co-operative production of such goods as drugs and medicines, toys and leather and fancy goods amounted to just over one-third of total sales in these groups.

Sources of purchase by retail societies of commodities by main trade classes

Some information on the parallel question of the proportion of particular groups of commodities purchased by retail societies from the co-operative wholesale societies or from other manufacturers, wholesalers or importers, can be obtained by a closer examination of the sales of the wholesale societies. Of the total sales estimated above at £114 millions at wholesale prices, approximately 73–76% was foodstuffs, 9–10% clothing, 3–4% boots and shoes, 4–5% furniture and hardware, 6% coal and 2–4% miscellaneous other goods. To these estimates can be added the estimates made above of the sales to retail societies by the independent productive societies and the productive departments of retail societies, to give the total purchases by retail societies from co-operative sources. Taking the main commodity groups, retail societies purchased approximately 75% (expressed in terms of retail sales) of their foodstuffs from co-operative wholesale societies, the productive departments of retail societies or independent productive societies, just over 85% of their clothing, over 90% of their boots and shoes, furniture, hardware and ironmongery, and 80% and 70% respectively of their coal, and sundries and chemists' goods.

6. DEPARTMENT STORE TRADING

There were 400–450 department stores in the United Kingdom in 1938 and their total turnover—excluding café and restaurant sales and other revenue from services—is estimated at £135–140,000,000. A number of the stores were branches of a central organization and of the 400–450 stores it is estimated that about 110–120 were multiple department stores. This group of multiple department stores was controlled by five organizations and they accounted for approximately 30–40% of the total turnover of department stores. In many instances, however, while the individual stores were financially a part of a larger organization they operated as separate trading units.

The commodities sold by department stores can be roughly divided into four main groups: foodstuffs, including off-licence sales, tobacco and household stores other than hardware; clothing, including footwear and men's and boys' and women's and girls' wear; furniture and ironmongery including furniture and furnishings, radio and electrical goods, pottery, glassware and ironmongery; and a miscellaneous group including books, jewellery, toys, sports goods and chemists' goods.

The division of the total sales of department stores between these four groups of commodities in 1938 is estimated as follows:

	%
Foodstuffs and associated goods	7–9
Clothing, footwear and general drapery	57–62
Furniture and ironmongery	23–27
Miscellaneous	6–9

There were, of course, important variations between individual stores as to the proportion of total turnover represented by each of these groups. Some stores, for example, had no food department except a restaurant while in others an extensive grocery and provisions department was responsible for up to one-fifth of the total sales. There were similar variations in the importance of the sales of the miscellaneous group but in practically all department stores the major proportion of the total sales was represented by clothing, followed by furniture, furnishings, and hardware, hollow-ware, ironmongery and pottery and glass.

In very few cases did department store organizations have any links with producing units though some direct purchases were made from abroad of commodities such as toys and fancy goods.

7. COMPARISONS OF THE DIFFERENT ECONOMIC TYPES OF TRADING

Some comparisons can now be made of the sales by different economic types of retail outlet to illustrate the differing rôles they played in distribution. This can best be done by dividing the total national retail sales into three broad commodity classes, food and drink,[1] clothing and footwear, and a residual other goods class.[2] Some comments on this

[1] The on-licence sales of beer, wines and spirits have been excluded in this and in all subsequent estimates.

[2] The commodities forming the three classes are listed above, p. 22.

division and on the treatment of the different economic types of retailing are necessary. In the first place these classes of commodities, particularly the residual class of other goods, are heterogeneous and cannot be used to give more than a broad indication of the different types of goods sold. In the second place, while the methods of trading and types of commodities sold in different co-operative stores and shops tended to be similar in character, and the same could be said of the trading by most department stores, there were wide variations in the methods used and goods sold by the different shops and organizations making up the multiple shop group and by the heterogeneous group of unit retailers.

A case can be made out for distinguishing multiple and unit retailers from one another and from the other two groups of retailers inasmuch as each of the four types of retailer has some well defined characteristics. But generalizations on the methods of trading and the types of goods sold when related to the unit retailer group, which includes barrows as well as very large and established retailers, and the multiple shop group, which includes some organizations with 6 branches and others with 2,000, some shops dealing mainly in convenience goods and others in specialities, can be of limited application only. The estimates relating to the trading of unit and multiple retailers therefore are of less value than those relating to co-operative and department store trading.

The estimated proportions of the total national retail sales represented by each of the three broad classes of commodity and the proportion each class represented of the total sales of each of the four economic types of outlet are as follows:

Table 29. *Estimated proportions of sales by the four economic types of retail outlet and of national sales in 1938 represented by the sales of food, clothing and other goods*

Commodity division	Proportion of total sales by				Proportion of total sales made by all outlets
	Multiple shops	Co-operative shops	Department stores	Unit retailers	
	%	%	%	%	%
Food and drink	51·0	72·5	8·5	50·0	50·0
Clothing and footwear	22·0	13·0	59·5	13·0	17·5
Other goods	27·0	14·5	32·0	37·0	32·5
All goods	100	100	100	100	100

The number of fixed retail shops can also be divided approximately according to their sales of food and drink, clothing and footwear and other goods and, with the exception of department stores, this division can be made for the total number of shops of each economic type.

Table 30. *Estimated proportion of all shops and of the total shops of each economic type selling food, clothing and other goods in 1938*

Commodity division	Number of shops with main trade in a particular commodity class as a proportion of total shops of each economic type			
	Multiple branches %	Co-operative shops %	Unit shops %	All shops %
Food and drink	55·5	75·5	51·0	52·0
Clothing and footwear	15·5	16·5	14·5	15·0
Other goods	29·0	8·0	34·5	33·0

Department stores and variety chain stores are not included as, by definition, it cannot be said that their main trade was in any one of these commodity classes. Unit retailers classed as general dealers have been allocated to the commodity division estimated to have been responsible for the biggest part of their turnover. This Table is not strictly comparable with Table 29 showing the proportions of total sales as there are difficulties of allocation arising from shops selling in nearly equal proportions goods in two categories and also because the sales figures include all sales of retailers whether in fixed shops or not, while the above Table relates to fixed shops only and excludes barrows and market stalls.

Using the same broad commodity classes the following Table 31 shows the approximate proportions of total sales in each class undertaken by the different economic types of retail outlet.

Sales emphasis of different economic types of retailer

Tables 29, 30 and 31 show the main features of the type of retail trading undertaken by the different economic outlets. Of the total national retail sales of consumer goods about one-half was represented by the sale of food, just under one-fifth by the sale of clothing and the

Table 31. *Estimated proportions of national sales of food, of clothing and of other goods in 1938 undertaken by the four main economic types of retail outlet*

Commodity division	Proportion of national sales of each commodity class undertaken by				National sales of each commodity class
	Multiple branches %	Co-operative shops %	Department stores %	Unit retailers %	%
Food and drink	19·0	14·5	1·0	65·5	100
Clothing and footwear	24·0	7·5	18·5	50·0	100
Other goods	15·0	4·5	5·5	75·0	100
All goods	18·5	10·0	5·5	66·0	100

remainder by the miscellaneous other goods class. The number of fixed shops selling each class of good was roughly proportional to the division of total sales. However, if the outlets not included in Table 30, such as barrows, market stalls and delivery vehicles, were brought into the picture, the number of shops or outlets for food and for other goods would increase and would represent a greater proportion of the total number of outlets than that given in Table 30, while the shops or outlets for clothing would represent a smaller proportion. A comparison of Tables 29 and 30 already suggests that the average turnover of clothing shops is slightly higher than the average for food and other shops and this bias—influenced in a large measure by the prominence of department stores in this trade—would be more marked if it were possible to include all outlets.

The features of the trading of the different types of outlet can now be summarized. About three-quarters of the total turnover of the co-operative shops and stores was represented by the sale of food and approximately the same proportion of the total number of co-operative stores were shops or stores selling mainly food. Co-operative sales of food are estimated to have represented just under 15% of the total national sales of food. The remaining sales by co-operative organizations were divided about equally between clothing and footwear and other goods, though the sales of clothing by these organizations represented a higher proportion, 7·5% of national sales, than the sales of other goods, 4·5%.

About 60% of the turnover of department stores was represented by clothing and footwear and these sales are estimated to have represented just under one-fifth of total sales of clothing and footwear. The sales of foodstuffs by these organizations were very small, the remainder of the turnover being in the other goods class.

About one-half of the turnover of multiple organizations of various sorts was represented by the sale of foodstuffs, a proportion corresponding to the division of total national sales suggested above. Multiple organizations are estimated to have undertaken about one-fifth of the total sales of foodstuffs. The number of multiple branches selling mainly foodstuffs was similarly about one-half of the total number of multiple branches. The remaining turnover of multiple branches was divided between clothing and footwear and other goods, the proportion of other goods sold being slightly higher. In terms of national sales, multiple branches are estimated to have been responsible for nearly one-quarter of total sales of clothing but only 15% of other goods.

The sales of food and drink represented about one-half of the total turnover of unit retailers and the number of unit shops whose main trade was in these goods was also about one-half of the total number of unit shops. The remaining turnover of unit retailers was divided in the ratio of 1 : 3 between clothing and footwear and other goods. The relatively smaller proportion of national sales represented by the sales of clothing and footwear by unit retailers compared with their sales of the other classes of commodity can be readily seen in Table 31. Unit retail sales are here suggested as representing some 66% of total national sales, and while this proportion is equalled in the case of food and drink, in the case of clothing and footwear unit retailers are suggested as accounting for only one-half of total national sales. The important proportion of the total sales of these goods undertaken by multiple branches and department stores, together accounting for over 40% of total sales, is of significance here in bringing down the proportion represented by unit retailers' sales. On the other hand unit retailers were responsible for some three-quarters of the total sales of other goods. This class is a very heterogeneous one and the conclusions that can be drawn from the Tables are limited, but the importance of sales by unit retailers of this group of goods is also a reflection of the relative weakness of co-operative and multiple shop trading in this class.

Integration of production and distribution by the different economic types of distributor

The integration of the production and distribution of certain commodities by single economic organizations has been discussed above in respect of producer/retailers and multiple and co-operative organizations. Some indication has been given of the circumstances leading to such integration in the case of particular commodities. Here a summary of the position can be presented showing the extent of integration in each of the three main commodity classes and in respect of the different economic types of retailing organizations. As such integration was of only minor importance in department store trading these concerns have been grouped with unit retailers.

Table 32. *Estimated proportions of their total sales of food, of clothing and of other goods in 1938 which were produced or processed by concerns linked with the different types of retailing organizations*

Commodity division	Proportions of total sales of each commodity division made by each type of outlet, estimated to have been produced or processed by firms linked with the retailer			
	Multiple organizations %	Co-operative organizations %	Unit retailers %	All retail organizations %
Food and drink	13·0	44·0	9·0	15·0
Clothing and footwear	27·0	45·0	1·0	10·5
Other goods	6·0	19·0	2·0	3·5
All goods	14·0	40·5	5·0	10·5

These figures can be presented in another fashion. Of the 10·5%, or approximately £265 millions, estimated to have been produced or processed by concerns linked with the retailers, some 72% was food and drink, 17·5% clothing and footwear and 10·5% other goods. Of the 14.0%, or approximately £68 millions, of the total sales of multiple organizations estimated to have been produced or processed by concerns linked with the retailers, 46·5% was food, 42% clothing and 11·5% other goods. Of the 40.5%, or approximately £108 millions, of the total sales by co-operative organizations estimated to have been produced or processed within the co-operative movement, 78% was represented by food, 15·0% by clothing and 7·0% by other goods. Of the 5%, or approximately £92 millions, of the total sales by unit retailers estimated to have been produced or processed and sold by producer/retailers or by firms linked with retailers, some 84% was represented by food, about 3% by clothing and 13% by other goods.

If the goods imported directly by retail organizations are added to these figures, the proportion of all goods sold by multiple organizations which was produced, processed or directly imported by linked firms is estimated at about 18%, the proportion for co-operative organizations at about 48%, the proportion for unit retailers including department stores at about 5% and for all retail organizations at about 12%. Such imports were only of significance in relation to food and the proportion for this class for all retail organizations is estimated at about 18%. This Table and these figures show clearly the importance of the linked production and distribution of clothing and footwear by multiple organizations, the emphasis on the production and processing of food in the case of the co-operative movement, and the fact that producer/retailers, as has already been shown, were of importance only in the case of food.

8. FACTORS INFLUENCING THE DIVISION OF RETAIL TRADE AMONG DIFFERENT TYPES OF OUTLET

The main factors influencing the relative importance of the sales of different commodities by the different economic types of shop have been discussed at length elsewhere.[1] A résumé can be given. Department stores, in most instances, have developed from drapery stores and have pursued a twofold policy of providing the consumer with convenient and attractive surroundings in which to shop and with a wide selection of clothing, furnishings and general household goods. They have developed and maintained their significant sales in this group of goods against the competition of the unit retailer by offering greater services for which the consumer has been prepared to pay both the extra transport cost of shopping centrally and, for some lines, a slightly higher retail price than that of the unit retailer. The goods sold are in the main durable and the sales made to the individual consumer tend to be occasional rather than regular. The co-operative stores, on the other hand, have catered primarily for the day-to-day demands of their class of customer, selling mainly food followed by clothing. An attempt has been and is being made to broaden the basis of sale to include household durable goods having an occasional sale, but strong competition from both multiple and unit retailers exists in this field and the headway made has been relatively small. Multiple shop trading exists in practically every trade. There is no marked bias in the total

[1] For example, H. Levy, *The Shops of Britain*, London, 1948, H. Smith, *Retail Distribution*, Oxford, 1948 (second revised edition), L. Neal, *Retailing and the Public*, London, 1932, and various books on co-operative trading listed in the Bibliography.

sales of these organizations towards either 'convenience goods', 'shopping goods' or 'specialities'[1] as is the case with co-operative and department store trading, though some commodities have a relatively small sale by multiple organizations and there are important regional differences in the incidence of multiple trading.[2] Unit retailers are similarly present in every trade, though as shown above they are faced with severe competition in the food and clothing trade.

Of considerable interest is the reason for the comparative weakness of multiple and, to a lesser extent, of co-operative trading in certain commodities. This question does not arise in relation to department stores as their type of organization restricts them clearly to shopping goods. The trades in which multiple and co-operative sales are small as a proportion of total sales are the motor trade, greengrocery trade, fish trade, newspaper trade, cigarette and tobacco trade,[3] sugar confectionery trade and electrical goods trade.

For three of these trades, newspapers, cigarettes and tobacco and sugar confectionery, the suggestion of small or negligible multiple and co-operative sales is misleading. Each of these commodities has a large number of selling points and each is usually sold by a mixed shop rather than by a specialist. Owing to the number of selling points only a limited number of shops can secure sufficient turnover to warrant specialization. But specialists exist in each of these trades and the number and turnover of multiple specialists as a proportion of the number and turnover of all specialists in these trades is very much higher than the proportion they represent of total numbers and turnover of both specialists and non-specialists. For example, the number of specialist tobacconist shops is estimated at 10–15,000 of which 2,000–2,500, or 18%, were multiple and co-operative shops, and these multiple and co-operative shops are estimated to have undertaken some 25%

[1] The usual definition of these terms is adopted here, that is, convenience goods are commodities sold at the same quality and price in most outlets and areas, such as soap or chocolates, shopping goods are goods requiring personal inspection and choice by the consumer, such as drapery, and speciality goods are goods with limited outlets not sold by the general retailer and goods requiring trained selling, such as radios.

[2] No reliable pre-war figures exist to show regional difference in trading, but returns of sugar registrations in 1946 can be used to illustrate these differences. Multiple shops, organizations with 10 or more branches, held 35·6% of the sugar registrations in London in October 1946 but only 18·3% in Scotland and 13·1% in the North Midlands. The share held by the co-operative branches similarly varied, being 15·2% in London, 41·3% in Scotland and 35·8% in the North Midlands. Ministry of Food, memorandum on *Analysis of the Grocery and Provisions Retail Distributive Trade*, October 1947.

[3] The sale of cigarettes and tobacco by tied on-licences has not been considered as a sale by multiple organizations.

of the total turnover of specialist shops, but only 14% of the total trade. A similar though less marked position of importance was held by multiple and co-operative shop sales in the specialist sugar confectionery trade and, in the case of multiple shops only, in the newspaper trade.[1]

The motor trade and electrical goods trade, two of the other exceptions, have certain characteristics in common, in that both require specialist knowledge and the provision of after-sales service and that the degree of concentration of production is high in both cases. The producers have, in relation to most motor trade commodities, for example motor cars, and many electrical goods, for example radios, pursued a policy of distribution through appointed agents. These agents have to possess certain qualifications and in turn are granted a local sales monopoly of the particular make of goods. This type of distributive organization springs in part from the relative 'newness' of these commodities and from the problem facing the producers in the earlier stages of the sales history of the goods, of finding outlets and trained retailers who could demonstrate and provide after-sales service. Once this network of appointed agents had become established and successful there was little room for multiple or co-operative trading. This position will not necessarily continue to obtain: multiple, co-operative and department store trading may well develop greatly in some of these goods, particularly household electrical goods, though there is further and somewhat privileged competition in this field from the supply undertakings. However, the system of appointed agents and the characteristics of the goods do in part explain the relatively small trading by multiple and co-operative organizations in these goods as shown in Chart VI. An additional factor which should perhaps be mentioned is the existence of price maintenance and branding of these products by manufacturers. Both multiple and co-operative organizations were reluctant to handle such goods as in the one case it limited the price reductions that could be offered and in the other limitations were placed on the payment of a dividend.

The relatively small proportion of total sales of fruit and vegetables

[1] An additional factor operating in the case of these three commodity groups and in the case of fruit and vegetables is that these goods are sold in a large number of outlets and nearness and convenience to the purchaser is an important factor determining the choice of outlet. While multiple trading is for the most part carried on in shops only slightly larger than that of the unit retailer, such shops tend to be located in or near the main shopping centres, thus losing some of the 'convenience shopping' trade. In the case of co-operative stores there is no question of catering for 'convenience shopping'. The number of stores is relatively few and they are, for the most part, large and located near main shopping districts. Multiple and co-operative shop trading in these goods is limited by the habits of the consumer and by the location of the multiple and co-operative shops.

and fish that was undertaken by multiple branches and co-operative shops appears to arise mainly from the particular problems involved in the distribution of these goods.[1] They are highly perishable for the most part, require considerable selection and grading, are subject in the earlier distributive stages to wide price fluctuations, and are produced or marketed by small units in different areas, no one area or port providing the full selection of goods that is required daily by the retail shop; and both the supply and demand for them are highly variable. These circumstances are not a barrier to significant multiple and co-operative trading in these commodities but they are a barrier to the gradual development of such trading. If a multiple or co-operative organization having close contacts with the producers, ports and markets throughout the country and possessing assembling, sorting and grading depots in each producing area, a centralized intelligence system with full information on present and estimated production, landings and demand and a network of well situated retail outlets, could come into existence in one step, the organization would probably show sufficient superiority over the existing atomized and individual methods of distribution to be a success. But a small-scale version of such an organization, confined to particular areas or types of product, or a network of retail shops by themselves, would be unlikely to show any great superiority in efficiency or economy in costs. Multiple and co-operative trading in these products certainly exists—though in the greengrocery trade it is imported fruit and vegetables, which do not present the same distributive problems, rather than home-produced fruit and vegetables, that play the most important part in such trading. The transition to larger-scale trading in these commodities by such organizations however would appear to lie not in a gradual increase from year to year, by the growth of the number of shops from 20 to 30 and then to 50 and so on, but in the introduction of a fully fledged distributive machinery. To some extent this has been done in the fish trade, and vertical multiple organization in that trade may expand, but taking the two commodities together the relative absence of large-scale trading can be ascribed to the initial size, vertical organization and finance required.

[1] See footnote on p. 148.

CHAPTER VI

SUMMARY AND SUGGESTIONS FOR FURTHER RESEARCH

Two aspects of distribution have been outlined in the foregoing chapters: firstly, an account has been given of the methods and costs of distribution of a wide range of consumer goods in the United Kingdom in 1938, and, more generally, of the structure of the distributive trades: secondly, some of the main factors influencing these methods, costs and structure have been discussed. An attempt can now be made to summarize the discussion and the estimates and to relate them to the total national trade in consumer goods.

With the exception of the discussion on the structure of the distributive trades, all figures and estimates given so far relate to the commodities and commodity groups included in the enquiry. In the following summary the estimates given relate to the total national sales of consumer goods. To enable this to be done, as discussed above in the chapter on the structure of the distributive trades, estimates have been made of the methods and costs of distribution of the commodities and commodity groups which were not included in the enquiry and added with appropriate weighting to the estimates already made. In some cases a certain amount of information was available on the commodities not included, or 'missing' commodities, in others the estimates for missing commodities have been based on information already available for similar commodities, and in yet others only approximations could be made. The missing groups are estimated to represent some 10% of total expenditure by the private consumer on all commodities in 1938. The possible error in the final estimates is of course increased by this method but there is reason to believe that the increased error is not very great.

The following estimates have been presented as single figures, instead of the range which has been used hitherto in most instances. The middle point of each range has been used, rounded off to the nearest whole number. This method has been used purely for convenience in the summary and is not in any way meant to suggest greater accuracy than the preceding estimates.

I. SUMMARY OF THE METHODS AND COSTS OF DISTRIBUTION OF ALL CONSUMER GOODS

Of all consumer goods sold in the United Kingdom in 1938, excluding the on-licence sales of beer, wines and spirits, approximately 43% by value is estimated to have passed through one or more wholesalers (excluding the co-operative wholesale societies) on the way from the producer or importer to the retailer, approximately 4% was sold by producer/retailers or by producers using mail order or other direct means of sale, and the remainder passed directly from the producer or importer to the retailer. Approximately 28,000 wholesalers and a further 20,000 wholesaler/retailers handled the wholesale trade and some 750,000 shops and a further number of barrows, stalls and delivery vehicles the retail trade in consumer goods. The total turnover of all types of wholesalers, excluding co-operative wholesale societies, is estimated at approximately £800–850 millions and the total turnover of all retailers, excluding sales by producers to the public by mail order and other direct means, at £2,555 millions.

About 34% or approximately £850–900 millions of total sales to consumers was handled by multiple, co-operative and department store organizations, the remainder being undertaken by unit retailers, by producer/retailers, and by producers selling direct to the public. The proportion of total sales undertaken by multiple, co-operative and department store organizations varied between commodities. Dividing the commodities into three main classes, these organizations were responsible for about 35% of total sales of food, 50% of clothing and 25% of other goods. Multiple organizations, defined as organizations controlling five or more retail shops, and controlling in all some 66,000 shops, are estimated to have undertaken 19% of total sales or approximately £470–490 millions. One-half of these sales was represented by food. Co-operative shops and travelling shops, numbering some 24,000, are estimated to have undertaken approximately 10% of total retail trade, or £256–260 millions. Food represented nearly three-quarters of these sales. Department stores, numbering some 450, are estimated to have handled approximately 5% of total retail sales, or £130–140 millions. Clothing represented nearly 60% of these sales. Unit retailers, numbering approximately 650,000, and an unknown number of barrows, stalls and delivery vehicles, handled approximately 62% of total retail sales, or £1,560–1,600 millions, of which just under one-half was foodstuffs and one-third other goods. Producer/retailers handled about 3·5%, or approximately £90 millions, of which 90% was food. Mail order and other forms of direct sales by producers to the public were responsible for something less than one-half per cent of national sales or in the region of £10 millions.[1]

There are no reliable data relating to retail trade as a whole before the war which show the variations in employment or turnover of shops of different type and shops in different trades. But using the figures given above along with unpublished estimates of market research organizations relating to particular trades, and figures published by Government departments relating to the wartime distribution of rationed and controlled goods, some suggestions can be made. Of an approximate total of some 850,000 retail outlets selling mainly consumer goods (including the number of barrows, stalls and sales vehicles estimated above as upwards of 100,000), about 90,000 or about 10% of the total number of outlets were multiple shops, co-operatives and department stores, and this group undertook about one-third of the total trade. These shops and stores were almost always located in shopping centres and main streets. There were a further 150–170,000 unit retailers, or about 20% of the total number of outlets, located chiefly in the shopping centres and main streets, which undertook another third of the total retail trade. And there were 570–620,000 unit shops, barrows, stalls and sales vehicles, or about 70% of the total number of outlets, which undertook the remaining third of retail sales. The unit shops in this group were located chiefly in the side streets and include the 'parlour-type' of shop. The barrows, stalls and delivery vehicles were ubiquitous. The average turnover in 1938 of the different groups of shop or outlet—from which few conclusions can be drawn as they cover shops in different trades and each type of shop has a different cost structure—can be suggested as follows: unit retailers in side streets and stalls, barrows and sales vehicles averaged £1,500 per annum, unit retailers in main streets £5,000–5,500 per annum, multiple shops and vehicles, excluding variety chain stores, £6,000 per annum, co-operative stores and vehicles £10,000–11,000 per annum, variety chain stores £75,000–85,000 per annum, and department stores approximately £300,000 per annum.

Of all the commodities sold by unit retailers, other than producer/retailers, just under two-thirds, by value, were purchased from wholesalers and the remainder were purchased direct from the producer or importer. There were marked variations between different commodities, and of the three main groups the unit retailer purchased about two-thirds of the food he sold from wholesalers, about 80% of clothing and footwear and just over one-half of other goods. Of all the commodities

[1] These estimates of producer/retailer and mail order sales can only be very approximate and probably are an understatement in both instances.

sold by multiple, co-operative and department store organizations, 20% or approximately £175 millions was produced or processed by firms linked with the retailers. Nearly 65% of this total was represented by food and one-quarter by clothing, and some 60% of the total was co-operative production and processing, the remainder being undertaken by multiple organizations. These organizations also purchased goods abroad and imported directly, thus controlling the goods from the point of entry in the United Kingdom until sold to the consumer. Some 5% by value of the total goods sold by these organizations was purchased in this way. Another 5–6% was purchased from wholesalers and the remainder purchased direct from producer or importer. The variations in the proportions purchased in different ways by these three types of organization have been discussed in some detail above.

The cost of distribution of all finished consumer goods in the United Kingdom in 1938 is estimated at just under 38% of the retail value of the goods sold, or approximately £970 millions.[1] The distribution costs incurred by producers represented nearly 6% of the retail value of goods sold, or £150–160 millions. The gross margins of wholesalers, importers and other intermediaries represented nearly 5% of the retail value of the goods sold, or £110–120 millions, and the gross margin of retailers represented just over 27% of the retail value of the goods sold, or approximately £700 millions. The size of the total spread between production or landed cost and consumers' expenditure and the share of the costs incurred by producers, wholesalers and retailers varied widely between commodities. For example, taking the three main commodity classes, the total cost of the distribution of food was about 33% of the total consumer expenditure, made up of producers' distribution costs 4%, wholesalers' margins 5%, and retailers' margins 24%. The total cost of distribution of clothing was about 43%, made up of producers' distribution costs 4%, wholesalers' margins 5% and retailers' margins 34%. The total cost of distribution of other goods was about 42%, made up of producers' distribution costs 9%, wholesalers' margins 4% and retailers' margins 29%.

The definitions adopted to distinguish between the costs incurred by producers, wholesalers and retailers are, of necessity, somewhat arbitrary, and it should be noted that producers' costs above include the costs of selling direct to the public, that wholesalers' margins include importers' margins and that retailers' margins include the wholesale and retail margins earned by retailers performing the wholesaling function and also the margins of producer/retailers. A further clarifica-

[1] The total disposable surplus of co-operative societies paid in dividends amounted to nearly £26 millions in 1938 or just under 10% of retail co-operative sales.

tion regarding wholesalers' margins may be necessary. The above figures of wholesalers' margins relate, of course, to that part of the total cost of distribution borne by wholesalers and not to the margin earned by the wholesaler on the goods he handled. To show this only those goods passing through wholesalers must be considered, and on these the wholesalers' margin represented 9% of the total consumers' expenditure on these goods or 12% of the wholesalers' turnover. The retailers' margin on goods purchased from wholesalers was just over 25% of retail sales.

Information on the constituents of the total cost of distribution is scanty and only tentative estimates can be made. Of the total producers' distribution costs, £150–160 millions, advertising would appear to represent about one-quarter and packing, transport and delivery costs between one-fifth and one-quarter.[1] The remaining costs were represented by warehousing, salesmen's salaries, and general sales promotion and administrative selling costs. There were wide variations between commodities and between firms in the apportionment of these costs.

Information that has been obtained on wholesalers' costs suggests that the important constituents of their costs were wages and salaries, averaging between 50–60% of total costs, followed by transport and occupancy costs, the former between 10–15% and the latter 8–13%. The most important constituent of retailers' costs was also wages and salaries, averaging between 45–55% of total costs, followed by occupancy costs, 15–20% of total costs. The remaining costs of wholesalers and retailers are spread over a large number of miscellaneous items including publicity and advertising, general administration, depreciation, bad debts and so on. These estimates of costs, which are based on information from some 150 wholesalers in 12 trades and 2–3,000 retail shops, including multiple branches, in 18 trades, can only be regarded as showing the possible order of magnitude of different costs. Again wide variations between retailers and between trades are usual.

Some of the main factors influencing the methods, costs and structure of distribution have been discussed. In relation to method these can be summarized as the nature of the commodity, the organization of its production and the type and number of retail selling points. A fair measure of association was shown between the methods of distribution

[1] Total expenditure by manufacturers on the advertising of consumer goods in 1935 is estimated at £45·1 millions. To make this figure comparable with the estimate given in the text, the advertising expenditure on beer, wines and spirits sold in on-licences, on petrol and motor oil and on certain goods sold to commercial users would have to be excluded. Kaldor and Silverman, op. cit., p. 10.

of different commodities which had common characteristics in the above three respects. For example, commodities produced by small and scattered units, of a relatively perishable nature and sold widely through unit shops, tended to pass through wholesalers on their way to these retailers, and the proportion of total trade undertaken by unit retailers bore a close relation to the volume of trade handled by wholesalers. Commodities produced by a small number of units, of a durable and bulky nature and sold by a small number of specialist shops, on the other hand, tended to pass direct from producers to the retailer. A number of variations were seen to be possible and a number of exceptions were noted.

In relation to the cost of distribution, the main factors can be summarized as, again, the nature of the commodity, the organization of its production and the type of distributive services required by the consumer. The relative share in the total costs undertaken by producer, wholesaler, if any, and retailer was shown to be influenced by the respective distributive functions undertaken. Again a fair measure of association was shown between the costs of distribution of different commodities and the similarities or contrasts between commodities in the above three respects. The gross margins earned by wholesalers and retailers on different commodities were shown to be related to these three and sometimes more factors and not to one factor, for example the rate of stock turn, alone. The relative shares in the total costs undertaken by producer, wholesaler and retailer appeared in general to vary with the manner in which the total distributive function performed was divided between the two or three participants. For example, where a producer or a retailer undertook the wholesaling function, his costs or margins were higher than those of other producers or retailers selling or buying similar commodities through a wholesaler who performed this function. Or again in those cases where the wholesaler usually collected the commodities from a large number of small producers, selected, graded, packed and sometimes branded and price-maintained them, the margin of the wholesaler represented a higher proportion of the total costs of distribution than it did in the case of similar commodities which were, for example, graded by the producer and advertised or price-fixed by the retailer. Variations and exceptions were again noted.

To complete the discussion of the factors affecting the methods and costs of distribution, reference was made to other factors, mainly sociological and institutional in character, which appeared to exert some influence on the ways in which commodities were distributed and on the costs incurred, but insufficient data were available to measure their incidence.

2. SUGGESTIONS FOR FURTHER RESEARCH

The general conclusion suggested by the information obtained in the course of this enquiry and by the discussion of the factors influencing the methods, costs and structure of distribution, is that given the data, the jungle of distribution can be mapped, the operative forces delineated and the trends measured. The immediate need, therefore, is for more facts, and some suggestions can be made regarding the sort of facts and research required. The examples given will relate mainly to the subject-matter of this study, the distribution of consumer goods in the home market, but the need applies equally to the distribution of raw materials, capital goods and exports.

Information derived from the new questions on distribution and advertising in the Census of Production and the first Census of Distribution will fill a major gap in existing knowledge of the distributive trades, but this can only be regarded as the first step. A number of important questions will not be asked in the censuses. For example the censuses will only be concerned with particular distribution costs incurred by manufacturers or producers, that is advertising and certain transport costs, and not with the producers' distribution costs as a whole. And again the censuses will seek information on the margins earned by wholesalers and retailers on broad commodity groups and not on the margins earned on particular commodities. Further, little or no information will be available in the census returns on the extent or re-sale price maintenance, of retail price competition, and of the number, type and size of purchasing accounts maintained by individual wholesalers and retailers of different sizes and in different trades.

The results of the censuses that are made available will be of only general value unless research is undertaken with the object of linking the results with such information as already exists on the methods and costs of distribution and of translating them into terms appropriate and helpful to producers, wholesalers and retailers of various sizes in the different trades. At the best the censuses will not do very much more than provide information on the framework of distribution and facilitate sampling and research in particular fields.

Some of the lines of research that call for consideration are suggested below. Firstly, a concerted effort is needed to reduce the confusion arising from questions of definitions in distribution. While some steps in this direction have been taken in the formulation of questions for the Census of Distribution, though their value cannot be estimated until the results are tested in practice, there is a great need, particularly in relation to costings, for uniformity. Both the methods of costing and the breakdown of costs call for closer scrutiny if they are to be of use in answering such questions as the relative cost to producers of direct-to-retailer distribution as against distribution through wholesalers and the relative costs of stockholding by wholesalers as against retailers and of the provision by wholesalers and retailers of different distributive services on different goods. The present individualistic methods of costing are an obstacle to such research and will be of direct disadvantage to individual concerns when attempts are made to use the results of the census to measure the strength or weakness of their own performance. A report on the principles used and the obstacles encountered by the experts undertaking the many costings on behalf of various Government departments during the war and post-war period, and the establishment of a joint committee of professional and trade associations and economists to study the problem, would be of value in this respect.

Secondly, there is need to encourage the publication of the mass of information relating to distribution at present in the hands of trade associations and other bodies and individual firms. There is no doubt that a great deal of this information may be of limited value owing to the particular circumstances surrounding its collection, but the sifting cannot begin until the material is available. The value of such information collected by individual concerns and trade associations has already been shown by the publications of Cadbury Brothers and the British National Committee of the International Chamber of Commerce and by the Retail Distributors' Association.[1] In most instances the material may not be as complete as in the examples cited, but data relating to more limited problems are of value. And here a plea might be made for the publication by particular Government departments of the material collected under rationing and price control schemes on distribution and distributive problems in the last nine years. While this information relates to unusual conditions of trading it would provide a part of the background needed for interpretation of the results of the Census of Distribution and also would throw some light on trends in the distributive trades.

A leading part in the development of this research can be taken by trade associations and professional associations, and the distribution section of the British Institute of Management can play a valuable rôle in encouraging and co-ordinating the work. Trade associations which in many cases during the war had economics 'thrust upon them' can also help to ensure that this becomes a permanent side of their

[1] Cadbury Brothers Ltd., *Industrial Record, 1919–39*, 1939 ; British National Committee of the International Chamber of Commerce, *Trial Census of Distribution in Six Towns*, 1937 ; and A. Plant and R. F. Fowler, *An Analysis of the Costs of Retail Distribution* based on data supplied by the Retail Distributors' Association, Transactions of the Manchester Statistical Society, Session 1938–39.

activities. The recent formation of standing 'economic and statistical' sub-committees by many trade associations and the increase in the comprehensiveness of the statistics of retail trade collected by the Board of Trade are encouraging signs in this respect. If co-operation by individual firms and trade associations in providing economic data is to develop, the results of the work will have to be shown to be of direct value to the members as, for example, are the Board of Trade returns, and not merely of theoretical interest. At the same time, in the interests of national and not merely sectional gain the shibboleth of secrecy which has long dominated the wholesaling and retailing trades must be discarded. The associations and firms that have hitherto published appear, on balance, to have gained rather than lost.

There remain the more individual research projects which can be undertaken by firms, institutions or individuals. The list is far too long to be detailed here and many indications have been given in the course of this study of particular problems requiring investigation. Two may however be mentioned. First the need for direct experiments and investigations into the technique of distribution and the application to these fields of the methods of scientific management, re-deployment of labour and improvements of lay-out and work organization already used in production. The operation of self-service stores for different types of commodity and in different areas, the limitation of the number of different lines handled by wholesalers and retailers, re-arrangement of counters and service based on time and motion studies of selling operations, suggestions to consumers as to how they can reduce distribution costs and retail prices and the separate pricing of goods and services in certain trades are examples of these. The personal contact *vis-à-vis* the consumer that is characteristic of these trades is an element not encountered in the same way in the organization of production, but this factor, surely, is merely an additional problem to be solved rather than a barrier to the use of scientific or near-scientific techniques. A limited number of investigations in large-scale retailing organizations have already shown the value of this approach, but it is important that future work should be directed towards the more difficult medium and small size units constituting the bulk of the retail trade. In undertaking these investigations the views and co-operation of the workers employed in these trades can prove as useful and instructive as they have been in the factory trades. And the wishes of the consumer must not be taken as known without further investigation.

A second field of individual research lies in the preparation of monographs on the distribution of particular commodities and the operation of particular types of distributive unit. A few of the many examples which could be cited are studies of the distribution of household hardware and ironmongery, of certain types of clothing and branded groceries, an analysis of the retail price changes of comparable price-maintained and non-price-maintained products, an investigation of the transport methods and costs involved in the distribution of some commodities such as fruit and vegetables, coal and furniture, and of the extent of cross hauling when wholesalers are used, economic histories of small retailers in different areas selling the same range of goods and detailed studies of wholesale operations, costs and efficiency in different trades. Whenever possible such studies should be partly historical in nature, showing the trends and changes that have taken place as well as the facts at a given point in time. A few studies already exist, but in most trades the scattered and private nature of the material has restricted research. Again individual concerns and trade associations can greatly assist independent research in this direction. And perhaps a plea can be made that when such projects are undertaken some uniformity of approach should be used so that it will be possible to make some comparisons of the results.

The list of problems requiring investigation need not be expanded. All concerned with the part that distribution plays in the national economy and with developing the most efficient methods and techniques will readily agree on the vital and urgent nature of this task. But at this stage of economic research in distribution problems the active co-operation and initiative of all those engaged in distribution, be they producers, wholesalers, retailers, trade associations or Government departments, is essential if any progress is to be made. And it is hoped that the example of this volume, which has only been made possible by such co-operation, will encourage further efforts in this field.

PART II

CASE STUDIES OF THE METHODS AND COSTS OF DISTRIBUTION OF COMMODITIES AND COMMODITY GROUPS IN THE UNITED KINGDOM IN 1938

CHAPTER VII

THE METHOD OF PRESENTATION AND THE DEFINITIONS USED IN THE CASE STUDIES

The following chapters consist of case studies of the methods and costs of distribution of nearly one hundred commodities and commodity groups. Limitations of time and space have precluded an analysis of the many variations and complexities characteristic of the different commodities, but an attempt has been made to outline the main methods and costs of distribution in each case. The reasons for and disadvantages of grouping a number of individual products together and treating them under the general heading of a commodity or commodity group have been discussed in the Introduction. Homogeneity in the methods and costs of distribution has been the aim when grouping the products together, but lack of information has in some cases made a heterogeneous grouping inevitable. But where possible some account has been given of the significant variations in the methods and costs of distribution of individual products constituting a commodity or commodity group.

To enable comparisons between commodities to be made, each of the case studies is constructed on the same general lines, and uses for the most part the same or similar terminology. The way in which the information has been collected has also been explained in the Introduction and the meaning of the terms used has been discussed in the chapters relating to the ways in which the goods were distributed and the costs of distribution. A summary of the definitions used for most of the common terms is given in the Glossary. But to avoid misunderstanding and the necessity of repeating explanations in each case study some of the general principles on which the case studies are based and some of the more important definitions are restated here.

The order in which the case studies of commodities are presented follows, generally, the order used in the tables relating to personal expenditure on various goods in the White Paper on National Income and Expenditure.[1] Estimates of consumers' expenditure on particular commodities, which can only be approximate, exclude in all cases the purchases by industrial users and caterers and consumption by producers, and are based on published statistics, estimates made by the trades concerned and estimates made in the parallel research being undertaken by the National Institute, *Consumers' Expenditure in the United Kingdom, 1920–1938*.

I. THE METHODS OF DISTRIBUTION

In the discussion of methods of distribution attention has been focused in each case study on three main methods of distribution; from producer or importer to wholesaler and then to retailer, from producer or importer direct to retailer, and, where significant, sales by producer/retailers. The wholesaler is defined as a concern which takes physical and financial possession of the goods and re-sells either to other wholesalers or to retailers. Goods passing through the co-operative wholesale societies to retail co-operative societies and through wholesaling organizations linked with producers and with multiple and department stores have been classed as passing direct to retailers. Producer/retailers are defined as firms selling direct to the public through a retail shop or by retail round, but exclude multiple and co-operative organizations selling goods produced or processed by linked concerns. Sales by such concerns are classed as sales by producers direct to retailers, though some separate estimate of these sales is given. In most instances an indication has been given of the importance of methods of distribution other than those listed above.

The meaning of the percentage ranges given relating to the estimated methods of distribution has already been discussed. Very briefly the ranges are intended to indicate that on the basis of present information the actual figures fall somewhere within the range. At the same time the ranges have not been made so wide as for it to be virtually certain that the truth will be within the limits, and the possibility of its lying outside is not excluded.

In each case study an attempt has been made to estimate the proportion of total sales of the particular commodities made by different economic types of retail outlet. The four main types distinguished, multiple shops, co-operative shops, department stores and unit retailers

[1] The White Paper used is the *National Income and Expenditure of the United Kingdom, 1946 to 1948* (Cmd. 7649).

can be defined briefly as follows: multiple shops are shops controlled by organizations possessing five or more branches and include variety chain stores; co-operative shops are shops belonging to the national co-operative movement; department stores are stores possessing five or more separate departments under one roof with each department selling a different class of commodity; unit retailers embrace all other retailers including barrows, market stalls and delivery vehicles.

2. THE COSTS OF DISTRIBUTION

In the discussion of the costs of distribution, wholesalers' and retailers' margins or mark-ups always refer to the gross margin on that particular commodity. According to the practice in particular trades these have been expressed as a percentage of turnover or a percentage on cost, that is on purchase price, but the final estimate made relates in every case to the realized gross margin, that is the margin earned by the wholesaler and retailer expressed as a percentage of sales or on cost after allowing for markdowns, waste, pilferage and other stock losses. Once again in presenting the range of realized gross margins in each case the aim has been to give the limits within which, it is estimated, most of the transactions took place. The extremes, that is sales at or below cost or at a very high gross margin, have been given only in a few instances. Where the information permitted, an average margin within the wider range has been suggested. Naturally, the possibility that the actual figure does not correspond with this average, which is usually presented in the form of a small range, is greater than the possibility that the actual figure is outside the wider range given, but there appeared to be some advantage in using the information obtained to narrow the limits of the wider range and present an estimate of the average gross margin. Wherever possible the transactions of multiple, co-operative and department store retailing organizations have been treated separately from those of unit retailers.

The information provided in the case studies on the average rates of wholesale and retail stock turn represents estimates based on as wide a sample as possible and relates to shops with a main trade in the particular commodity or group of commodities discussed. The average rates for all shops cannot of course be determined with any accuracy in the absence of a complete census, as the variations between firms are so great. The estimates given must therefore be treated as very approximate.

The problem of reaching a satisfactory definition of producers' distribution costs applicable to all trades has been discussed at some length above. All that need be said here is that these costs have been taken to include all charges incurred under the heading of warehousing and storage of finished goods, all charges incurred under the heading of packing, carriage and transport to the purchaser whether wholesaler or retailer, all charges incurred under the heading of sales promotion including advertising, sales material, market research and salesmen's salaries, and all charges incurred under the heading of administrative selling costs including general overhead costs of the sales department, stock control costs and invoicing and general clerical costs. Where the information allowed, a breakdown of the total costs under one or more of the above headings has been made, and in some instances a distinction has been possible between the producers' costs incurred on sales direct to retailers and those incurred on sales through wholesalers. The ranges given of estimated producers' distribution costs for the whole trade are, as in the case of other ranges, intended to indicate that on the basis of the information obtained the actual figure should be somewhere within the range. But the limits have been made sufficiently narrow to be meaningful and because of this policy the possibility that the truth lies outside the range is not excluded. It must be emphasized that these estimates, while as accurate as careful investigation could make them, remain approximations.

In the case of some commodities, indicated by a footnote in the individual case study, estimates of producers' distribution costs could not, for various reasons, be calculated directly from information provided by producers and their associations. Indirect and partial evidence had to be used and some assumptions made. The estimates given therefore in these instances are likely to be less reliable than those given for other commodities.

At the end of each case study an estimate has been made of the total distribution cost of the commodity including producers', wholesalers' and retailers' costs and margins. These estimates, given in every case in the form of a range within which it is thought the actual figure lies, are based on the information given in the case study of the proportions passing through different channels and of the costs and margins of producers and distributors. In some instances additional information which was obtained in the course of the enquiry but which has not been presented in full in the case study has been used in the calculation of total costs. Such information, usually relating only to a portion or section of the trade or a particular practice of some producers or distributors has influenced the particular point within the various ranges used in the calculations.

These studies provide little more than the 'bare bones' of the methods and costs of distribution of each commodity or commodity group. Many of the refinements of practice, such as 'accommodation' sales from one wholesaler to another, conditional sales, double handling by merchants and agents, stock holding against price rises, price cutting, limitation of retail selling points, 'fancy' discounts to outsell competitors, and the offer of free samples, one or more of which was a feature of the distribution of almost all commodities, receive only cursory treatment. Not that these practices are without significance; while the proportion of the total trade of a commodity characterized by one or other of these and similar refinements appears to be small, the refinements of yesterday, the exceptional methods and discounts, may become the 'bare bones' of to-day. But quantitative and qualitative measurement of the exceptions, the most difficult and in some ways the most important task of empirical research, cannot begin until a norm, a framework has been established, and this is the task that these case studies have attempted to fulfil.

CHAPTER VIII

BREAD AND CEREALS

1. BREAD

Consumers' expenditure and methods of distribution

Consumers' expenditure on bread in 1938 is estimated at £66–68 millions. This estimate excludes the purchases of bread by the catering trade and institutions which represented approximately 5% of the total production of bread. The expenditure on home-baked bread is also excluded.

Types and numbers of bakers. A rough distinction can be drawn between three main types of firm baking and selling bread in 1938:

> The master baker, usually baking on a small scale for sale mainly in premises attached to the bakery or by local retail round: there were 23–25,000 bakers of this type in the United Kingdom in 1938 and they produced 53–57% of the total bread baked.
>
> The multiple and wholesale baker, baking on a large scale for sale both through their own or tied retail shops and by wholesale round: there were under one thousand firms of this type in 1938, though many of them controlled subsidiary companies, and they produced 24–26% of the total bread baked.
>
> The co-operative bakery, usually baking on a large scale and connected either with a retail co-operative society or operated by a federal society: there were some 800 bakeries operated by 600 retail societies and 14 federal societies in 1938 and they produced 19–21% of the total bread baked.

All three types of baker sold a proportion of their output on wholesale terms to other distributors, to institutions and to the catering trade. There were variations in the extent of wholesale trading by individual firms within the main groups suggested above. This variation was particularly marked in the case of the small master bakers. The average figures suggest that the master bakers sold about a quarter of their total output on wholesale terms, the multiple and wholesale bakers just over one-half of their output on wholesale terms and the co-operative bakeries less than one-twentieth of their output on wholesale terms, usually to co-operative cafés and restaurants and on contract to institutions.

The methods of distribution. The proportions of the total sales of bread to the private domestic consumer, excluding sales to institutions and to the catering trade, passing through the different channels of distribution in 1938 are estimated as follows:

	%
From baker through own shop or retail rounds to consumer	74–78
From wholesale baker to retailer to consumer	22–26

Included in the sales direct to the consumer are sales by wholesale and multiple bakers through their own and tied retail outlets and sales by co-operative bakeries through retail co-operative shops.

Number of retail outlets. The total number of outlets for the retail sale of bread in 1938 is not known with any accuracy but is estimated at 50–75,000. Of these 28–30,000 were shops designated as bakers or pastry-cooks though in some instances they did not bake but only retailed bread and flour confectionery. Included in this total are the 600 co-operative bread and cake shops, and 2,500–3,000 multiple bakers' shops. The other outlets were dairies, grocers and general shops. Bread was sold both in retail shops and by retail round. The proportion sold in the different ways varied between urban and country districts and also between the North and the South. A far higher proportion of the bread sold in Scotland and the North of England was sold in retail shops than in the South. Of the total retail sales of bread between one-half and two-thirds is estimated to have been sold on retail rounds.

Sales by different types of retail outlet. Estimates of the proportions of total sales to the domestic consumer made by the different economic and trade types of distributor are as follows:

	%
Independent master baker in retail shops and by retail rounds	42–45
Wholesale and multiple baker in own or tied retail shops and by retail rounds	10–15
Co-operative retail shops and by retail rounds	19–21
Shops that were mainly dairies and by retail milk rounds	8–12
Shops that were mainly grocers	10–13
Other retail shops	2–3

The estimated proportion of the total trade undertaken by multiple firms, including multiple grocers and dairies as well as multiple bakers, was 16–18%.

The cost of distribution

The gross retail margin earned by the baker in selling bread is difficult to distinguish, except in the case of shops selling bread bought on wholesale terms, from the gross margin earned by the baker on the complete cycle of bread baking and selling. A further problem arises in that almost all master bakers produced and sold flour confectionery as well as bread and a somewhat arbitrary allocation of total distribution costs to each commodity has to be made in order to consider the bread distribution costs separately.

The distributive margins and costs on the sales of bread to the domestic consumer in 1938 were approximately as follows:

Multiple and wholesale bakers selling to other distributors, retail bakers, dairies, grocers, for re-sale to the public gave a discount ranging from ·85 pence per quartern on a 2-lb. loaf to 1 penny per quartern on a 1-lb. loaf. This was the usual range of discounts irrespective of the particular retail price of bread. The retail prices in different areas were fixed by agreement between the Food Council and the trade. The average discount was nearer to 1 penny per quartern than ·85 pence per quartern and this represented a retail margin varying from 10–13% according to local retail price of bread, which, for example, was 8d. to 8½d. per quartern in London and 9d. to 10d. in the Midlands and the North-East. In some instances an additional discount of 2½–5% was given by wholesale bakers in the case of regular bulk orders. The average retail margin was 11–12% on sales. *Master bakers* selling on wholesale terms gave discounts similar to those of multiple and wholesale bakers. *Federal co-operative bakeries* in many cases gave slightly lower discounts to the retail co-operative societies.

The distribution costs incurred by bakers on the wholesale section of their trade are, as suggested above, difficult to disentangle from other costs, but it would appear from returns made by the trade that they averaged about 13% of wholesale turnover or just under 12% of the retail price. When the wholesale profit is included these figures suggest that the total gross distribution cost, wholesale and retail, of bread sold on wholesale terms to other distributors was about 25% of the retail selling price.

Margins of bakers, baking and retailing. In the case of bakers baking and selling their own bread, including multiple bakers selling to their own or tied retail shops as well as independent bakers, selling or distribution costs varied greatly between one firm and another. One baker may do the bulk of his trade over the counter and incur very small delivery costs; another may have built his business round a door-to-door delivery. Further, in the case of multiple bakers selling to their own retail shops, the delivery from bakery to retail shop often represented an additional cost. From returns made by the trade, selling costs appear to have varied from 13–14% to 25–26% of the retail selling price with an average (making an allocation of total net profit to distribution) of 19–20%. Viewing the picture as a whole, the larger the baker, the greater the distribution cost expressed as a percentage of retail sales. This is particularly marked in the case of multiple bakers but production costs of these firms were usually correspondingly lower than those of the smaller baker.

The make-up of costs. Taking 20% as the average total margin of master and multiple bakers baking and selling bread through their own shops, the chief constituents of distribution costs were delivery costs, upkeep and overheads of vehicles 6–7½%, salesmen's and roundsmen's wages 8–9%, occupancy costs 1–2%. The relatively higher retail margins of bakers making and selling their bread compared with those of retailers buying wholesale and not baking is partly to be explained by the practice of the latter outlets of selling over the counter rather than by retail round, and partly by the joint sale of bread and other commodities.

Stock turn. Bread was baked daily and had a practically daily rate of stock turn. Wholesale bakers usually sold on a sale or return basis. Allowing for public holidays the average rate of stock turn was approximately 305–310 times a year.

The total costs of distribution are estimated at 20–21% of retail sales.

2. FLOUR

Consumers' expenditure and methods of distribution

Consumers' expenditure on flour in 1938 is estimated at £22–23 millions. This estimate attempts to exclude the purchase of flour by trade users, by institutions and by the catering trade. About two-thirds of the total was represented by the sale of self-raising flour, the remainder by the sale of plain flour. There was a very wide variation in the consumption of plain and self-raising flour in different areas of the country. Relatively little self-raising flour was sold, for example, in Yorkshire and Scotland, and plain flour had a heavy sale, while the position was reversed in the South of England.

The methods of distribution. Estimates of the proportions of total sales of flour, plain and self-raising, passing through the various channels of distribution in 1938 are as follows:

	%
From miller or packer or importer to retailer	80–90
From miller or packer or importer to wholesaler to retailer	10–20

Included in the sales direct to retailer are the sales by the co-operative wholesale societies to retail co-operative societies. These sales represented some 15–20% of the total retail sales of flour, and just over four-fifths of the flour sold by retail societies was produced by co-operative wholesale societies.

A slightly higher proportion of self-raising flour went through wholesalers, probably 15–20% of total sales of this type of flour.

Number of wholesalers and retailers. The number of wholesalers handling flour, for the most part grocery and provision wholesalers, is estimated at 1,500–2,000 and the total number of retail outlets at 80–90,000.

Sales by different types of retail outlet. The proportions of total sales made through the different trade and economic types of retail outlet are estimated as follows:

	%
Shops that were primarily grocers and provision dealers	60–70
Dairies	15–20
Bakers	10–15
Other shops, mainly general shops	5

The sales of retail co-operative shops are included in the sales of grocers and provision dealers.

The division of the total sales between the different economic types of retail outlet in 1938 is estimated as follows:

	%
Multiple shops	23–26
Co-operative shops	21–24
Unit retailers	50–56

Included in the sales of multiple shops are sales by multiple grocers, dairies and bakers and a small sale, 1–2%, by variety chain stores.

The cost of distribution

Almost all self-raising flour and a large proportion of plain flour sold to the domestic consumer was branded in 1938 but, excluding co-operative production, only about a quarter to a third of the flour sold, mainly self-raising, was price-maintained or carried a recommended retail price.

The margins earned by various distributors in 1938 are estimated as follows:

Wholesalers. The margins earned by or allowed to wholesalers on both plain and self-raising flour ranged from 7–17½% on sales. The usual discount off the invoice price allowed was 9–12% but many firms gave additional discounts according to the quantities purchased.

Retailers buying from wholesalers earned a margin of 11–12% on plain flour and 13–17% on self-raising flour. Wholesalers sometimes allowed a further 2½–5% discount to retailers in order to give terms which were competitive with those offered by millers and bakers.

Unit retailers purchasing direct from the miller or baker earned a margin of 12–15% on plain flour and 14–21% on self-raising flour. It was the usual practice for additional discounts to be granted to retailers purchasing in a large quantity direct from the miller.

The multiple organizations usually purchased at wholesale terms where bulk delivery was taken and just under wholesale terms where split deliveries to retail branches were made by the miller or baker. In some instances this provided the multiple firm with a gross margin of 30% of the retail selling price, but the more usual margin was 20–25% on self-raising flour and 15–20% on plain flour.

Settlement terms. In addition many millers, bakers and wholesalers granted discounts both to wholesalers and to retailers varying from 4d. in the £ for payment within 7 days to 2d. in the £ for payment in 21 days.

Some firms earned margins on the sale of flour very much lower than the averages suggested above, as flour was sometimes sold both by wholesalers and retailers at or near the cost price.

Stock turn. The average retail stock turn of flour was 10–12 times a year.

Producers' distribution costs. The distribution costs incurred by millers and bakers on the sale of self-raising flour ranged from 15–20% of sales revenue. Some 3–6% was represented by advertising costs, 5–7% by packing, 3–4% by carriage and transport, and the remainder by salesmen's salaries and administrative selling costs. There were, of course, important variations between different millers and bakers. The distribution costs on plain flour were of the order of 9–13% of sales revenue.[1]

The total costs of distribution of all flour are estimated at 32–34% of retail sales.

3. CAKES AND FLOUR CONFECTIONERY

Consumers' expenditure and methods of distribution

Consumers' expenditure on cakes, buns and pastries in 1938 is estimated at £35–40 millions. This figure excludes the expenditure on flour con-

[1] See p. 164

fectionery by the catering trade and institutions, and the expenditure on home-made cakes and flour confectionery.

Numbers and types of producers. Practically all the bakers making bread also made cakes and flour confectionery and in addition many firms made flour confectionery only. Some of the latter were caterers who made for sale in their own restaurants. The total number of producers of cakes and flour confectionery in 1938 is estimated at 40–43,000.

Of the total production of cakes and flour confectionery, including the output of catering establishments, multiple and wholesale bakers are estimated to have been responsible for approximately one-fifth of the total, co-operative bakeries for 15%, and master bakers, pastry-cooks, confectioners and catering establishments for the remainder.

Multiple and wholesale bakers sold approximately one-third of their output to the catering trade and institutions, the co-operative bakeries less than 5%, usually to co-operative cafés and restaurants, and the master bakers and pastry-cooks sold about 10% of their output to the catering trade and institutions. The remaining supply of flour confectionery used by the catering trade was produced by catering establishments themselves.

The methods of distribution. The distribution of flour confectionery was similar to that of bread, and, excluding the sales by the different types of producers to the catering trade, the main channels of distribution in 1938 were as follows:

Multiple and wholesale bakers sold approximately one-half of their output to their own or tied retail shops or by retail round and one-half on wholesale terms to other distributors. Some wholesale cake manufacturers who did not control retail outlets sold their entire output to other distributors.

Co-operative bakers sold practically all their flour confectionery to retail co-operative societies or on retail rounds.

Master bakers, confectioners and pastry-cooks sold approximately three-quarters of their output of flour confectionery in their own retail shops or on retail rounds, and the remainder was sold on wholesale terms to other shops.

The proportions of total sales of cake and flour confectionery passing through the main channels of distribution in 1938 are estimated as follows:

	%
Sales by baker or pastry-cook in own or tied retail shop, including sales by co-operative retail societies	75–80
Sales by baker, cake manufacturer and pastry-cook to other retailers	20–25

Numbers and type of retail outlet. Just over one-third of the sales to other retailers were made to shops that were primarily grocers, a quarter to shops that were primarily dairies and the remainder to general shops, cafés and restaurants selling retail to the public, to retail bakers and to variety chain stores. The total number of outlets for flour confectionery is estimated at between 75–100,000. Flour confectionery was sold on retail rounds as well as in retail shops, but sales by the latter type of outlet are extimated to have represented over two-thirds of total sales.

Sales by different types of retail outlet. Of the total retail sales of cake and flour confectionery in 1938, the proportions sold by the different types of outlet were, approximately, as follows:

	%
Multiple and wholesale bakers in their own or tied retail outlets and on retail rounds	8–10
Co-operative shops and on retail rounds	17–18
Master bakers, pastry-cooks and confectioners in their own shops and on retail rounds	47–55
Other retail outlets, mostly grocers, dairies and variety chain stores	20–25

Multiple shops, including multiple bakers, grocers, dairies and variety chain stores are estimated to have undertaken 15–17% of the total sales of flour confectionery. Variety chain stores are estimated to have undertaken approximately 5–7% of total retail sales.

The cost of distribution

The distributive margins on flour confectionery are difficult to calculate with accuracy owing to the fact that in the majority of instances cake was sold alongside bread, and it is not always easy to distinguish the distribution costs on the sale of flour confectionery from those on the sale of bread.

The retail prices of different types of cake and flour confectionery in 1938 were not fixed or suggested by agreement in the trade, nevertheless there was a marked degree of similarity in the retail prices charged for the same type of cake in given areas.

The margins earned by different distributors on the sale of flour confectionery in 1938 are estimated as follows:

> *The wholesale margin* on the cake and flour confectionery sold by wholesale cake manufacturers, multiple bakers and master bakers to retailers, that is the spread between the production cost and the price charged to the retailer, was in the region of 11–12% of sales.

Retailers. The margins earned by retailers who bought from wholesalers ranged from 20–33% on sales, the average margin being 25%. Some retail firms, owing to bulk purchases, would obtain additional discounts averaging 2–3%.

Retailers making own cakes. The baker and pastry-cook selling cakes and flour confectionery made in his own shop normally put 33⅓% on cost; that is, obtained a margin of 25% on returns. In the case of pastries and fancy cakes the on-cost was approximately 50%.

The sale of cakes and flour confectionery was usually considered to be somewhat more profitable than the sale of bread and it is suggested that distribution costs in the case of wholesale sales would not average more than 8% of sales, and on retail sales and rounds not more than 16–17% of sales. However, while the initial gross margin on cakes and flour confectionery was usually higher than that on bread, mark-downs or losses due to damaged and stale flour confectionery were higher than those of bread and were thought to be in the region of 2–3% of sales. The average margin of the master baker and pastry-cook after allowing for mark-downs and losses was 23–26% on sales.

Stock turn. The stock held by retailers of cakes and flour confectionery was not more than one day of the perishable varieties and not more than one week of the non-perishable varieties.

The total costs of distribution are estimated at 25–28% of retail sales.

4. BISCUITS

Consumers' expenditure and methods of distribution

Consumers' expenditure on biscuits in 1938 excluding purchases by institutions and caterers is estimated at £26–27 millions.

The methods of distribution. The proportions of total sales represented by distribution direct to retailer and through wholesalers are estimated as follows:

	%
From manufacturer direct to retailer	85–90
From manufacturer to wholesaler to retailer	10–15

Goods passing through the wholesale departments of multiple organizations to retail branches and from the co-operative wholesale societies to retail co-operatives are included above in sales direct to retailer, as is also the very small quantity of biscuits produced by bakers and pastry-cooks for sale in their own shops.

This overall picture conceals two different methods of distribution. A group of large manufacturers (referred to in this study as Group A), which did approximately 40–45% of the total trade, sold almost exclusively direct to retailers throughout the country, using the wholesaler only for the specialized hotel and restaurant trade. One of these firms might deal with as many as 100,000 retailers. Other manufacturers sold mainly in bulk direct to multiple concerns, to large unit retailers and to wholesalers.

Number of wholesalers and retailers. Wholesalers, where used, were mainly the general grocery wholesalers, but biscuits were also handled by on- and off-licence suppliers and wholesale confectioners. The total number of wholesalers handling biscuits was in the region of 2,000. Retailers selling biscuits included grocery and provision dealers, dairies, confectioners, cafés and variety chain stores. The total number of retail outlets was approximately 175–190,000.

Sales by different types of outlet. The estimated proportions sold by the different economic types of retail outlet in 1938 are as follows:

	%
Multiple shops and variety chain stores	28–32
Co-operative stores	16–20
Unit retailers	48–56

Between one-quarter and one-third of the biscuits sold in retail co-operative stores were produced in co-operative manufacturing establishments. The sales of biscuits by variety chain stores are estimated at nearly £4 millions, or 13–15% of total sales of biscuits in 1938.

The cost of distribution

The proportion of the total trade represented by biscuits sold at retail prices suggested by the manufacturers is estimated at 60–65%. There was a wide difference in retail selling price as between the products of the manufacturers in Group A and those of the manufacturers who distributed largely in bulk to large retailers and to wholesalers. The former were sold retail at from 8d. to 2s. 6d. a lb., whereas the latter rarely rose above 1s. a lb. and averaged 6d.

The margins and discounts earned by the various distributors in 1938 are estimated as follows:

Wholesalers' margins ranged from 5–15% on sales, the usual margin in the trade being 10–12½%. Where wholesalers purchased from manufacturers in Group A, most of whom sold direct to retailers and had no set terms to wholesalers, they were often obliged to buy on the same terms as retailers.

Retailers' margins averaged 23–25% on sales of loose biscuits, after allowing for breakages, and 22½% on factory-packaged biscuits. Of the total sales of biscuits, approximately 20–25% were factory-packaged.

Multiple and co-operative organizations, like wholesalers, received no special terms if they bought from the manufacturers in Group A, although they sometimes received a 1¼% bonus at the end of the year. Bulk discounts were not given by these manufacturers on the ground that this practice might lead to price cutting. Multiple organizations and other large retailers purchasing from manufacturers other than those in Group A were frequently allowed discounts of 5, 10 or 15% off wholesale price, that is wholesale selling price.

Settlement discounts varied considerably in the trade, some manufacturers giving none at all and others the usual grocery trade discount of 1d. in the £. The manufacturers in Group A gave 1¼% for payment in the month. This is included in the margins quoted above.

The stock turn of retailers averaged 12–14 times a year. In the case of some multiple shops, however, for example the variety chain stores, stock was turned over weekly. The larger manufacturers trading direct with retailers throughout the country delivered once a week in most provincial towns and daily in some parts of London. They were frequently prepared to deliver an order as small as a single tin of biscuits.

Manufacturers' distribution costs varied considerably as between the manufacturers in Group A and those selling largely in bulk to multiple organizations and to wholesalers. The distribution costs of manufacturers in Group A are estimated to have averaged 25–30% on their sales revenue, salesmen's salaries and expenses representing 7–10%, warehousing, carriage and despatch 8–10%, advertising 3–5%, and other selling costs 5–7% on sales revenue. There were variations in the distribution costs of the manufacturers outside this group depending on particular sales policies, the estimated range being 7–12% on sales revenue.

The total costs of distribution are estimated at 39–42% of retail sales.

5. CEREAL BREAKFAST FOODS

Consumers' expenditure and methods of distribution

Consumers' expenditure in 1938 on cereal breakfast foods, both factory-packaged and unpackaged, is estimated at approximately £7 millions, of which just under three-quarters represented expenditure on the branded packaged cereals, and the remainder expenditure on loose cereals, mostly unpackaged oatmeal. An attempt has been made in this estimate to exclude purchases by institutions and the catering trades.

The methods of distribution. The proportions of the total sales passing through the main channels of distribution in 1938 are estimated as follows:

	%
From manufacturer direct to retailer	40–45
From manufacturer to wholesaler to retailer	55–60

Both packaged and unpackaged cereals were distributed to unit retailers almost entirely through wholesalers, only the multiple and co-operative organizations, large unit retailers and retail buying groups purchasing direct from manufacturers.

Number of wholesalers and retailers. Wholesalers handling breakfast cereals numbered approximately 1,500–2,000 and were, for the most part, general grocery wholesalers. The principal retail outlets for breakfast cereals were grocers and provision dealers and dairies, but these goods were also sold by a large number of small general shops and by variety chain stores. Total retail outlets are estimated at approximately 125–150,000.

Sales by different types of retail outlet. The proportions sold by different retail outlets classified according to economic type are estimated as follows:

	%
Multiple shops and variety chain stores	17–19
Co-operative stores	20–24
Unit retailers	57–63

The cost of distribution

Practically all the branded packaged cereals carried retail prices recommended by the manufacturers, but sales below the 'recommended' price were common.

The margins earned by the various distributors were approximately as follows:

Wholesalers' margins on branded cereals ranged from 9–11% on sales, varying slightly with the brand and the amount purchased. On some lines it was slightly higher and on others lower than the limits of this range. On bulk cereals, that is loose, unpackaged cereals, the wholesalers' margin was approximately 5–10% on sales, being nearer the upper limit where he had to break bulk. Certain *multiple organizations* and the co-operative wholesale societies received similar terms to those given to wholesalers on both packaged and unpackaged cereals.

Retailers' margins on packaged cereals ranged from 12½–20% on sales varying with the brand, and averaged 16–17%. The margin on loose cereals, which the retailer had to weigh out and bag, varied widely, the average being in the region of 30% on sales.

Settlement discounts. Most manufacturers gave a settlement discount of 1¼% for payment in 10–14 days. Some allowed 1d. in the £ for payment in 14 days, net for payment in the month.

The stock turn of retailers of packaged cereals averaged 12 times a year and of loose cereals 5–6 times a year. Wholesalers' stock turn was slightly slower in each case.

Manufacturers' distribution costs on branded packaged cereals ranged between 20–30% of manufacturers' sales revenue. The average is estimated as 25–27%, comprising advertising costs 13–16%, carriage and transport 3–5%, salesmen's salaries and expenses 3–5%, the remainder representing administrative selling costs. Manufacturers' distribution costs on unpackaged cereals were rarely above 5% of sales revenue.

The total distribution costs of all breakfast cereals are estimated at 41–45% of retail sales.

CHAPTER IX

MEAT, BACON AND FISH

1. MEAT

Consumers' expenditure and methods of distribution

Consumers' expenditure. Expenditure by domestic consumers on meat is estimated at approximately £180 millions in 1938. This figure represents purchases of carcase meat and edible offal. It excludes meat products such as sausages and pies, and also canned and potted meats, poultry, game, rabbits, bacon and ham. Consumption by producers and purchases by caterers and institutions have also been excluded. The above figure is, of course, lower than the aggregate turnover of butchers' shops, since butchers' total turnover included returns from the sale of meat products and to a certain extent from sales to caterers.

Slightly over one-half of the total expenditure was on home-killed and the balance on imported meat.

The methods of distribution: Home-killed meat. The principal channels of distribution and the approximate proportions passing through each expressed as percentages of total retail sales in 1938 are estimated as follows:

	%
Sales of dressed meat by wholesalers to retailers	36–40
Sales of dressed meat by wholesalers through commission agents to retailers	7–10
Sales of livestock by wholesalers to retailers on a dead weight value basis	10–12
Purchase by retailers of livestock on the hoof for conversion into dressed meat	40–45

These estimates refer for the most part to sales of dressed meat. No attempt is made to show the numerous possible channels through which livestock passed after leaving the producer and before being purchased by wholesalers or retailers and converted into meat.

In addition to the vertical channels of distribution shown above, wholesaler to wholesaler or accommodation sales were common in the trade, as particular wholesalers were not always in a position to match their suppliers of certain types or cuts to the demands of retailers at a particular time.

Features of the different channels of distribution. The purchase of dressed meat by retailers from wholesale meat salesmen in the meat markets of the cities was the usual method by which retailers in the urban areas obtained their supplies. The provincial, Scottish and some London wholesalers were in fact 'manufacturers' or 'processors' of meat. They acquired the great bulk of their supplies by outright purchases of livestock, selected to suit the requirements of their particular trade, accepting all risks including loss through disease. They usually arranged and paid for droving, grazing (where necessary), transport, and slaughter, and sold the dressed carcases or parts and the edible offals from their own premises or stalls in the wholesale market to retailers. In some cases wholesalers accepted consignments of meat or livestock for sale on a commission basis, but this represented a very small proportion of their total business.

The sale of dressed meat through commission agents was largely confined to Smithfield market. Practically all the home-killed meat at Smithfield, but not at the other smaller London markets, was sold to retailers by specialist commission salesmen who received consignments in the form of dressed meat from wholesalers (sometimes called dealer-slaughterers and mostly located in the producing areas) who had already performed the functions described above with the exception of distribution to the retailer. From 15–20% of all meat sold at Smithfield was home-killed, representing 7–8% of total home-killed meat supplies.

Some sales of livestock were made by wholesalers to retailers at prices based on the 'killing out' value of the animal, but this was not a very common method of sale The wholesaler selected and purchased the livestock, arranged transport and took all risks associated with possible condemnation, as described previously, but the retailer generally undertook or arranged for slaughter. This was the method by which a large proportion of the home-killed meat sold by retail co-operatives was obtained from the co-operative wholesale societies.

The purchase by retailers, usually from local dealers or farmers, of livestock on the hoof was largely confined to the rural districts or the fringes of urban areas. Retailers slaughtered or arranged for slaughter, either in public or in private slaughter-houses, and cut up the carcasc for sale in their own shops. There were 16,000 licensed slaughter-houses in Great Britain in 1938, but many were very little used, the bulk of slaughtering being carried out in, at the most, some 2,000 of them.

Multiple retailers selling home-killed meat obtained their supplies partly by the purchase of livestock which they slaughtered at public or private slaughterhouses, and partly in the form of dressed meat from wholesalers. One large multiple organization purchased 95% of its home-killed supplies on the hoof. The retail co-operatives obtained part of their supplies from the co-operative wholesale societies by the method described previously, and part from wholesalers.

The methods of distribution: Imported meat. The main channels of distribution and the estimated proportions passing through each expressed as percentages of total retail sales in 1938 were as follows:

	%
From importer direct to retailer or imported direct by multiple and co-operative organizations	85–95
Importer to wholesaler to retailer	5–15

The direct to retailer sales represent, for the most part, sales by some half-a-dozen companies controlling overseas processing and all stages of distribution right through to sales to retailer, and in one case to consumer, through the company's own shops. Also included in this channel are direct purchases by multiple and co-operative organizations from overseas or from importers.

The small proportion of imported meat shown above as passing through wholesalers reflects those methods of distribution where the importing and wholesaling functions were in separate hands. There were, for example, independent agents or importers who had no wholesaling organization of their own. These were more common in the trade in frozen meat from the Dominions than in the South American chilled trade. There were also a number of independent wholesalers who purchased their supplies from these agents and from other importers, including the companies referred to above, and who supplied retailers with quantities and cuts not always obtainable from other suppliers.

Imported meat was usually sold by importer/wholesalers and independent wholesalers through the wholesale meat markets or depots to retailers, the retailer in these cases arranging and paying for delivery. In the case of chilled beef particularly there had however been a development towards distribution direct from ship or store to retailer's depot or assembly point or even to retail shops. This was made possible by the grading of imported meat, which enabled the retail butcher to purchase by specification. It is estimated that some 15–20% of chilled beef was distributed in this way in 1938. The filling of such orders for selected quantities and types, however, made the use of markets and depots by these importer/wholesalers all the more necessary for the disposal of the remainder. The wholesale markets and depots supplied a centralized cutting service on which the smaller retailers were largely dependent and therefore remained the principal channels through which the bulk of imported meat was distributed to retailers.

Numbers of wholesalers and retailers. The number of wholesalers handling meat in 1938 is estimated at approximately 1,000–1,100. This includes wholesalers of home-killed meat, importer-wholesalers and the independent wholesalers referred to above. The number of retail butchers' shops in 1938 has been estimated at approximately 49,000, of which 5,000–5,200 were co-operative shops and 5,500–6,500 branches of multiple firms. Meat was also sold in stalls in retail markets and from barrows, but sales through these outlets represented a very small proportion of the total trade.

Sales by different types of retail outlet. The estimated proportions of the total sales of meat in 1938 undertaken by the different economic types of retail outlet are:

	%
Multiple shops	15–17
Co-operative shops	12–13
Unit retailers	70–73

The cost of distribution

The wholesalers' function both in the home-killed and imported trades was to provide a wide variety of cuts—carcases, sides, quarters and pieces—at different prices and of different qualities, from which the retailer could select those suited to his type of trade. Some retailers, if forced to buy carcases, for example, would not be able to dispose profitably of the better cuts and other retailers of the cheaper cuts. The retailer had tended to become more and more a purveyor of meat, much of the preparation and initial cutting up being undertaken by the wholesaler.

Wholesale margins on home-killed meat. As pointed out previously, the wholesaler of home-killed meat was not merely a distributor but also a 'manufacturer' of meat, and his margin had to cover his activities in this connection as well as those associated with the actual selling. At the same time it must be noted that his turnover included the sales of inedible offal as well as of dressed meat. To put on a comparable basis the expenses incurred where the wholesaler railed stock from long distances and where he bought in a nearby livestock market it has been decided to eliminate from the calculation of the average gross margin the cost of freight, usually paid by the wholesaler. Freight costs must however be considered in any estimate of the total spread between farmer and retailer. This leaves as expenses to be covered by the wholesaler's gross margin the costs of droving, lairage, slaughter, market tolls and general selling costs which, together with normal net profit, averaged approximately 5% on sales.

Commission agents, such as those operating at Smithfield, usually charged 3½–5% on sales, the charge varying from place to place and with the value of the product. This covered only the cost of selling, that is rental of stalls, the provision of credit facilities, labour costs and net profit, and was exclusive of slaughtering cost and of transport costs and market tolls, which were deducted from the return to the consignor.

Wholesale margins on imported meat. As the importers were, for the most part, the overseas packers and the wholesale distributors it is difficult to allocate costs as between the various stages of distribution of imported meat. The costs involved in distributing meat from its landing at the port to its sale to retailers are estimated at approximately 6–7% on sales of importer/distributors. Of this the distribution costs from the port to the market or depot, and market tolls, represented roughly one-half and selling expenses just over 40%. Freight, insurance, dock and landing charges and bank charges incurred in shipping and landing the meat are excluded.

The commission charged by the independent agents who sold largely in bulk to wholesalers was 2–2½% on sales. This excluded costs of freight, duty, insurance and cold store, only covering the expenses of premises, labour and net profit. The costs of distribution from the port to market, and tolls and storage charges which are included in the costs of importer/distributor companies given above, are not covered by this commission.

Retail margins on home-killed and imported meat. The gross margins earned by retail butchers varied considerably as between different types of retail business. By-and-large these differences reflected differences in operating costs. For example, a butcher doing mainly a cash trade could work on a lower percentage margin than another providing credit or delivery services, the latter service in some cases representing as much as 8% of retail sales. Multiple butchers with a large turnover could also work on a lower gross margin than the majority of unit shops, although there was in some cases a difference in the type of meat sold and the selection offered. The retailer's margin depended to a considerable extent on the demands of his customers for particular types or cuts of meat and on his skill in selection and cutting up to suit his particular trade. For some years the gap between the prices received for the better and the inferior cuts had tended to widen, and the gap between the on-cost or margin earned on the different cuts similarly widened. The retail butcher averaged his returns on various qualities of meat and over periods of time, averaging his costs in the same way.

The average gross margin of butchers in this sense is estimated to have ranged from 17–25% on sales in 1938 rising to 30% in certain types of business, with considerable variations for the reasons given above. The gross margins of the larger multiple organizations tended to range from 18–20% on sales, the margins of unit retailers varying mainly within the limits previously stated according to the type of business and the services provided.

Retailers bought from the importer/wholesalers on a weekly credit basis for approved accounts. Some independent wholesalers gave longer credit.

Stock turn. Retail butchers are estimated to have held 2½–3 days' stock.

Total distribution costs: Home-killed meat. Taking the margins quoted above and adding an estimate for cost of transport of livestock from farm to abattoir, and other handling costs incurred in the process, the average total distribution costs in the case of home-killed meat are estimated at 29–33% of retail sales. In the case of some multiple retailers buying livestock on the farm, the total spread is said to have represented 25% of retail sales, covering costs from farm to consumer and allowing for receipts from the sales of inedible offals and by-products. These estimates of spread do not, of course, represent the difference between the average price per lb. live weight received by the producer and the average price per lb. received by retailers. It has been estimated, for example, that the dressed weight of a carcase of beef (meat, fat and bones) after removal of offals is not much more than half the live weight.

Imported meat. The total spread between landed cost and returns from retail sales of imported meat, using a more or less arbitrary division of costs of distribution incurred in this country as distinct from those incurred prior to the landing of the meat, is estimated to have ranged from 25–29% on retail sales.

The total costs of distribution are estimated at 28–31% of retail sales.

2. BACON AND HAM

Consumers' expenditure and methods of distribution

Consumers' expenditure on bacon and ham other than canned products is estimated at approximately £70–71 millions in 1938, of which £5–6 millions was spent on ham. Purchases of bacon and ham by the catering trades and consumption on farms are excluded from this estimate.

Roughly two-thirds of the total bacon and ham supplies (including the estimated output of unregistered curers) was imported and the remainder home-produced.

The methods of distribution. The main channels of distribution and the proportions of goods passing through each channel expressed as percentages of retail sales in 1938 are estimated as follows:

	%
Imported:	
From importer direct to retailer	43–47
From importer to wholesaler to retailer	53–57
Home-produced:	
From curer direct to retailer	80–85
From curer to wholesaler to retailer	15–20

The sales from importer direct to retailer shown above consisted largely of sales by importers to multiple organizations and the co-operative wholesale societies. Some importers in the provinces distributed direct to unit retailers, combining the functions of importers and wholesale distributors.

Most unit retailers obtained their supplies through wholesalers who in turn purchased from importers. There was, in fact, an agreement in the trade in London by which importers distributed only to wholesalers and to certain multiple organizations and the co-operative wholesale societies.

The larger multiple firms supplemented their purchases from importers by the purchase of 'pieces' from wholesalers while the smaller multiple concerns relied on the wholesaler for most of their supplies.

A small proportion, possibly 10–15% of total sales, passed from the wholesaler to a smaller or secondary wholesaler before reaching the retailer.

Of home-produced bacon, about three-quarters represented the output of registered curers, the remainder being cured on farms and by small curers and retailers.

The larger curers sold practically entirely direct to retailers, mostly to high-class provision retailers and to multiple shops. The smaller curers used the wholesaler more extensively but also sold direct to local retailers. The co-operative wholesale societies had their own bacon factories.

Number of wholesalers and retailers. Wholesalers handling bacon were for the most part the general grocery and provision houses, which concentrated largely on imported bacon. Bacon was retailed by grocery and provision dealers and to some extent by butchers, the total number of shops selling this commodity being estimated at 140–160,000 in 1938.

Sales by different types of retail outlet. The approximate proportions of the national trade done by the different economic types of shops in 1938 have been estimated as follows:

	%
Multiple shops	22–24
Co-operative shops	19–21
Unit retailers	55–59

The cost of distribution

The margins obtained by the various distributors in 1938 can be summarized as follows:

Importers' margins were approximately 1½–2% on sales. Although importers did not physically handle the goods as did wholesalers, they arranged for transport from store to buyer, made inspections of consignments, carried risks of bad debts, and sometimes gave financial assistance to overseas curers.

Wholesalers aimed at a return of 5–7% on sales of bacon and ham. The gross return on sales to large buyers was generally 4–5% and to smaller buyers 9–10%. On the small proportion of home-cured bacon handled by wholesalers, the margin on sales was approximately 4–5%. Some wholesalers, particularly in the South, undertook the smoking of home-cured and imported bacon but the cost of this has not been allowed for in the margins quoted above. Wholesalers cut up sides of bacon, in this way enabling retailers to purchase only those cuts which suited their particular trade on grounds of quality or price.

Retailers' margins on sales of bacon varied to some extent with skill in cutting up. The price charged by the retailer varied with the cut, being higher in the case of prime cuts which comprised about half a side of bacon than for less popular cuts which he sold at a lower price. His overall margin on sales is estimated to have ranged from 14–20%, in cases rising to 25%, with an average of approximately 15%. The retailer's margin on cooked ham was in the region of 20% on sales although there were variations as between shops. Where the retailer purchased gammons for cooking himself his gross margin would of course be considerably higher to cover costs of labour involved and the loss of weight in the process.

Settlement discounts were usually 2d. in the £ for payment in a week, 1d. in the £ for payment in one month.

Stock turn. Wholesalers generally did not keep more than 3 days' stock of bacon and the average stock held by retailers was from 2–3 days.

Curers' distribution costs, including salesmen's salaries, wrappings, despatch and carriage, advertising, storage and general administrative selling costs are estimated to have averaged 5–7% on sales.

The total costs of distribution are estimated at 22–23% of retail sales.

3. POULTRY, GAME AND RABBITS

Consumers' expenditure and methods of distribution

Consumers' expenditure in 1938 on poultry, game and rabbits, other than canned products, is estimated at approximately £19 millions, of which roughly £10–11 millions was spent on poultry and game and £8–9 millions on rabbits. About three-quarters of the total represented expenditure on home-produced and the remainder on imported products. Consumption on farms and purchases by caterers and institutions are excluded from this estimate.

The methods of distribution. The main channels of distribution and the proportions of these goods passing through each expressed as percentages of retail sales in 1938 are estimated as follows:

	%
Home-produced:	
From producer direct to retailer	15–20
From producer to higgler to retailer	40–45
From producer or higgler to wholesaler or commission agent to retailer	38–42
Imported:	
From importer direct to retailer	30–35
From importer to wholesaler to retailer	65–70

In addition to sales through the channels shown above, a certain amount of accommodation or wholesaler to wholesaler sales took place.

Of the *home-produced* poultry and game a large proportion was bought in the first instance by higglers and dealers who collected from the farm or purchased at local auctions. Higglers and dealers distributed direct to retailers, particularly in the vicinity of the producing and fattening areas, and also consigned for sale by commission agents or wholesalers in the urban markets.

Producers and fatteners also consigned direct to wholesalers and commission agents in the urban markets, an estimated one-fifth to one-quarter of total sales being made in this way.

Some supplies were sent by producers and fatteners to packing stations, but this represented a very small proportion of the total trade.

Included above in sales from producer or fattener direct to retailer are purchases from producers by multiple and co-operative organizations for sale through their own retail outlets. Sales by producers direct to consumers have not been shown separately above, but are estimated at not more than 2–3% of total sales.

The distribution of rabbits followed much the same channels. Farmers, collectors and trappers sold to local dealers and also consigned for sale by wholesalers and commission agents in the city markets.

Imported poultry, game and rabbits were usually distributed to retailers by wholesalers who purchased from importers or who were in some cases importer/wholesalers.

Sales shown above as made direct from importer to retailer or imported direct by retailers include sales to the wholesale departments of multiple concerns, sales by wholesale co-operatives to retail societies and sales by importer/wholesalers. Amongst the importer/wholesalers were certain multiple organizations which supplied other retailers in addition to their own shops.

Approximately three-quarters of the total supplies of imported poultry are said to have passed through the London market, which was also the largest single market for home-produced supplies. Of the total supplies sold in Smithfield market approximately half were home-produced and half imported.

Number of retailers. Poultry, game and rabbits were sold retail by provision dealers, fishmongers, butchers and greengrocers. Butchers did a larger proportion of the rabbit than of the poultry trade and sales by hawkers were also an important feature of the former trade. The total number of shops regularly selling poultry and game is estimated at approximately 60,000, including about 5,000 multiple branches.

Sales by different types of retail outlet. The proportions of the total trade in poultry, game and rabbits done by the different economic types of retail outlet in 1938 are estimated as follows:

	%
Multiple shops	20–22
Co-operative shops	3–5
Unit retailers	73–77

The cost of distribution

The margins earned by the various distributors in 1938 can be summarized as follows:

Importers generally worked on a commission or margin of $2\frac{1}{2}$–5% on sales, the margin varying according to whether they merely arranged for sale or actually handled and stored the goods.

Higglers and dealers obtained margins ranging from $2\frac{1}{2}$–5%, earning the higher margin on their sales to retailers.

Wholesalers, who generally handled both home and imported poultry, game and rabbits, aimed at a gross margin of 5–7% on sales.

Commission agents when selling on behalf of producers or other principals usually returned to the seller a price which allowed the commission agent a margin of 6–7% on sales. The services provided by these agents were not confined to selling alone since producers and higglers rarely graded their poultry, and this was undertaken by the commission agent. The functions of the wholesaler and commission agents were very similar, the same firms often doing both types of business, acting as wholesalers where they bought and sold outright and as agents where they sold on behalf of a principal.

Retailers' margins on home-produced and imported poultry ranged from 15–25% on sales. The smaller retailer usually worked to a margin of 20–25% of sales, the larger multiple organizations to 15–20% of sales.

Retailers' margins on rabbits ranged from 15–17% of sales, including any return from the sale of the skin.

The retailer paid for delivery from the wholesale depot or the urban market.

Payment by retailers was usually on a strict weekly basis.

Transport costs from farm to wholesale market were paid by producers where the goods were consigned for sale on commission or by the purchaser when bought off the farm. On the basis of a rough average for the country as a whole transport costs are estimated to have represented an addition of less than 2% to the price paid at the farm or returned to the farmer.

The total costs of distribution are estimated at 26–28% of retail sales.

4. FISH

Consumers' expenditure and methods of distribution

Consumers' expenditure on fish in 1938 is estimated at £35–36 millions. This estimate relates to all fish other than canned but excludes the fish sold in fried fish shops and in catering establishments. Of the total expenditure it is estimated that approximately three-quarters was represented by the sale of 'white' fish, such as cod, haddock, hake, whiting, soles, and processed white fish such as haddock and codling. Just over one-tenth was represented by the sale of pelagic fish, such as herrings, mackerel and pilchards, and processed pelagic fish such as kippers and bloaters represented three-quarters of the sales of this group. Just under one-tenth was represented by the sale of salmon, trout, eels and smoked salmon, and the remainder by the sale of shell-fish such as crabs, lobsters, winkles, oysters and shrimps.

Methods of distribution. The proportions of the total sales of fish to the domestic consumer passing through the main channels of distribution in 1938 are estimated as follows:

	%
Port auction to port wholesaler to inland wholesaler to retailer	43–47
Port auction to port wholesaler to retailer	41–45
From processor to retailer	8–12
Port auction or fisherman to retailer	1–3

These estimates conceal some important variations in the methods of distribution between different types of fish. Practically all fish on landing was sold at port auctions with the exception of the landings —less than 5% of total landings—at small ports where no auctions were held. The five ports of Hull, Grimsby, Aberdeen, Milford Haven and Fleetwood handled about four-fifths by value of the British white fish landed. A very small proportion of white fish was purchased by retailers at the auctions, the proportion varying from port to port, but —excluding exports, sales to processors and to caterers, and sales of fishmeal—the bulk, over 90%, was purchased by port wholesalers. The port wholesalers sold to inland wholesalers, to retailers and to the catering trade including fish-fryers. The most important inland wholesale markets were those of Billingsgate, Glasgow, Manchester, Liverpool, Leeds, Sheffield and Birmingham. In some towns, for example Brighton, Plymouth and North Shields, the port wholesaler also acted as the inland wholesaler for fish railed to him. If the sales to the catering trades are excluded, then between 60 and 70% of the sales of port wholesalers of white fish were made to inland wholesalers who re-sold to retailers, the remainder being sold by port wholesalers direct to retailers. About two-thirds of the pelagic fish passed on landing direct to processors who in turn, excluding exports and sales to catering establishments, made three-quarters of their sales direct to retailers and the remainder through inland wholesalers who sold to retailers. The port wholesalers purchasing pelagic fish at auctions made about 60% of their sales, excluding purchases by caterers, direct to retailers, the remainder being sold to inland wholesalers who re-sold to retailers.

Salmon and shell-fish, both imported and home-caught, usually passed to an inland wholesaler and were then re-sold to retailers. The Billingsgate market was a particularly important centre for salmon and shell-fish.

A small proportion of the fish, estimated at about 5% of total retail sales, was handled by three or more wholesalers before reaching the retailer. Very often the third wholesaler was a wholesaler/retailer.

Retailers sold to the catering trades as well as to the public, but in the estimates given here these sales, representing approximately 10% of turnover, have been excluded.

Number of wholesalers and retailers. There were approximately 1,700–1,800 port wholesalers in 1938, 450–500 inland wholesalers, and 1,000 retailer-wholesalers. There were approximately 12,000 retail fishmongers who were principally engaged in selling fish. This estimate includes departments in co-operative shops and department stores selling fish. Of these shops 500–700 were branches of multiple organizations. There were a further 9–10,000 shops, engaged principally in other trades, which also sold fish. Fish was also retailed by hawkers, who numbered between 3–4,000. Of the national sales of fish, specialist fishmongers were responsible, it is thought, for 85–95% of the total turnover and shops selling fish as a subsidiary line, and hawkers, were responsible for the remainder.

Sales by different types of retail outlet. The proportions of total sales undertaken by the different economic types of shops are estimated as follows:

	%
Independent fishmongers	86–91
Multiple fishmongers	6–9
Co-operative stores	3–5

The sales by department stores, included in independent fishmongers' sales, were very small, being about 1% of total sales.

The cost of distribution

The port wholesaler when selling to the inland wholesaler worked to an on-cost ranging from 21–28% with an average of about 25%. The inland wholesaler selling to retailers worked to an on-cost of 15–25% with an average of about 19%. Retailers worked on widely varying on-costs ranging from 33⅓–50% and averaging about 40%. But losses due to deterioration, wastage and mark-downs were heavy and the realized margin of port wholesalers was approximately 17–18% on sales, of inland wholesalers 14–15% on sales and of retailers 23–26% on sales. The total realized margin of distributors of fish passing from port wholesaler to inland wholesaler to retailer was approximately 45–47% of the retail selling price.

These estimates have to be used with caution, as with a commodity such as fish prices varied widely owing to perishability and erratic supplies. And further there were some significant variations for different types of fish. On the more expensive fish the distribution costs averaged 45% and on the cheaper type of fish up to 60%. Where the fish went direct from the port wholesaler to the retailer it was usual for the port wholesaler's margin to increase proportionately. Higher transport costs were one factor here, and the retailer in some cases also obtained a higher gross margin by buying direct. Inland wholesalers usually purchased outright from port wholesalers, but in some cases the fish was sold by inland wholesalers on a commission basis. When they acted as commission salesmen their margin is estimated at 5%, but by debiting their customers with expenses the cost of this method of sale was approximately the same as when they bought the fish outright.

Distribution costs of fleet owners. The auctioneers operating at the fish port auctions were usually employed directly by the fishing fleet or boat owners. In some cases however they operated independently and received a commission of 5% on sales. The distribution costs incurred by the fleet owners, such as the payment of auctioneers and the provision of facilities, and by the processors of pelagic fish, such as transport to retailers and general selling costs, are estimated at 4–5% of the sales revenue of fleet owners and processors.

The total costs of distribution are estimated at 46–49% of retail sales.

CHAPTER X

DAIRY PRODUCTS AND FATS

I. MARGARINE

Consumers' expenditure and methods of distribution

Consumers' expenditure on margarine in 1938 is estimated at £11–12 millions. This estimate excludes the purchases of margarine by trade users, such as manufacturers and caterers.

The main channels of distribution of margarine and the proportions passing through them in 1938 expressed as percentages of retail sales are estimated as follows:

	%
From manufacturer direct to retailer	65–70
From manufacturer to wholesaler to retailer	30–35

Included in the sales from manufacturer direct to retailer are the sales by the co-operative wholesale societies to retail co-operative societies.

Number of wholesalers and retailers. The number of wholesalers handling margarine in 1938 was 1,500–2,000, and the number of selling points approximately 160–170,000. Between 70 and 80% of the sales were made in shops which were primarily grocers and provision dealers, and the remainder of the sales were made in general shops selling food, and dairies.

Sales by different types of retail outlet. The proportions of the total sales handled by the different economic types of outlet are estimated approximately as follows:

	%
Multiple grocers and dairies and variety chain stores	24–27
Co-operative stores	25–28
Unit retailers	45–51

The cost of distribution

Practically all margarine sold to the domestic consumer was branded and price maintained in 1938.

The margins earned by wholesalers and retailers in 1938 are estimated as follows:

Wholesalers' margins ranged between 8·5% and 10·5% on sales. Margins at the lower end of the range were usually earned on the medium-priced brands and the margins at the higher end on the lower-priced brands. Between one-half and two-thirds of the margarine was sold at medium price levels. These margins included 'wholesale distribution allowances', paid retrospectively if the manufacturer was satisfied that the policy regarding price maintenance and freshness had been followed by the particular wholesaler.

Retailers purchased from manufacturers and from wholesalers on the same terms. The retailer's margin on the sale of margarine ranged from 15–18·75% of the retail price. The lower margin was earned on the low-price brands and the higher margin on the medium-price brands.

Multiple organizations and co-operative societies purchasing direct from manufacturers received wholesale terms, although when split deliveries were made by manufacturers to multiple branches an extra sum was charged by manufacturers for this service.

Settlement discounts allowed to both wholesalers and retailers were 2d. in the £ for payment within 14 days, and 1d. in the £ for monthly payment.

Stock turn. The average stock turn of wholesalers in margarine was once every 1–2 weeks, and the average stock turn of retailers once a week.

Manufacturers' distribution costs varied according to the proportion of their sales made direct to retailers and the proportion made through wholesalers, and also with other aspects of sales policy such as advertising. Allowing for the proportions being sold through the different channels mentioned above, the average distribution costs of manufacturers, including carriage and transport, selling costs and advertising, are estimated at 17–18% of sales revenue, of which 3·5–4% was represented by carriage and transport, 7·5–8% by selling costs and 6–6·5% by advertising.

The total costs of distribution are estimated at 36–39% of retail sales.

2. BUTTER

Consumers' expenditure and methods of distribution

Consumers' expenditure on butter in 1938 is estimated at £64–65 millions of which approximately £61 millions was spent on imported and £3–4 millions on home-produced butter. Purchases by industrial users and caterers and consumption on farms are excluded from the above estimates.

The methods of distribution. The approximate proportions distributed through the various channels shown as percentages of total retail sales in 1938 are estimated as follows:

	%
Imported:	
From importer direct to retailer or imported by retailers	45–55
From importer to wholesaler or blender to retailer	45–55
Home-produced:	
From farmer or creamery direct to retailer	52–56
From farmer or creamery to higgler or wholesaler to retailer	44–48

In addition to sales through these channels there were also certain accommodation sales made by one wholesaler to another.

Purchases of *imported butter* by multiple organizations and the co-operative wholesale societies accounted for the bulk of the sales from importers to retailers and of the direct imports by retailers shown above. The importation of New Zealand butter, representing slightly over one-quarter of total imports, was under the control of the New Zealand Dairy Board, and was sold to wholesalers and large retailers in this country through agents acting on commission for the Board.

Home-produced butter, which represented a very small proportion of total butter sales, came from two sources, the farmhouse and the creamery. Farm butter—just under one-half of total sales of home-produced butter—was sold by farmers usually to local higglers and dealers. Approximately one quarter represented producer/retailer sales. Creamery butter was distributed largely direct to retailers, the co-operative wholesale societies and certain multiple dairies having their own creameries. Farm or creamery butter was not usually handled by city wholesalers.

Number of retail outlets. Butter was stocked regularly by most retail grocers and provision dealers including the provision departments of department stores and the retail co-operatives, and occasionally by fishmongers and butchers. The total number of shops selling butter in 1938 has been estimated at 150–170,000 of which approximately 16,000 were multiple branches.

Sales by different types of retail outlet. The estimated proportions of the total sales in 1938 undertaken by the different economic types of shop were:

	%
Multiple shops including multiple grocers and dairies	23–25
Co-operative shops	21–23
Unit retailers	52–56

The cost of distribution

The margins earned by the various distributors in 1938 can be summarized as follows:

Importers might be either principals or agents, a number of firms acting in both capacities. Their commission as agents was usually 2–2½%, being slightly higher where they acted as principals and undertook storage.

Wholesalers' margins on imported butter ranged from 4s.–7s. a cwt., sometimes rising to 10s. a cwt., and varying with the size of the sale. This margin was not usually reckoned as a percentage on selling price but in shillings per cwt. Roughly speaking, however, the wholesale margin can be said to have averaged 4–6% on sales. On a considerable percentage of the wholesalers' sales of pre-packaged, and, where they handled it, of home-produced butter, the margin was approximately 1d. a lb. or 9s. 4d. a cwt. Wholesalers drew supplies from cold store, held stocks and broke bulk where necessary. The packing and blending of butter was undertaken either by specialist firms acting on commission for importers or wholesalers, or by importers and wholesalers themselves.

Higglers or country dealers usually paid a flat rate for all farm butter, the margin obtained ranging from 3–5% on sales. They did not break bulk or carry large stocks.

Retailers' margins on butter averaged about 2d. per lb. In some instances it was lower than this when butter was sold at or near cost to attract other custom. Expressed as a percentage of sales retail margins ranged from 12–16%. The margins on pre-packaged butter were nearer the lower end of this range. Approximately 60% of butter was purchased by retailers in bulk and cut and weighed out on the premises and the remainder bought ready packaged.

Settlement discounts were 2d. in the £ for payment in one week, 1d. in the £ for payment in one month.

Stock turn. Wholesalers usually held 7–9 days' and retailers 3–7 days' stocks.

The total costs of distribution are estimated at 20–21% of retail sales.

3. FRESH MILK

Consumers' expenditure and methods of distribution

The domestic consumers' expenditure on fresh milk in 1938 is estimated at £86–87 millions. This represented 760–770 million gallons. The consumption of milk on farms and in schools and the purchases by the catering trade and institutions, totalling approximately 200–220 million gallons, are excluded from this figure.

The methods of distribution. The main channels of distribution of milk from farmer to consumer and estimates of the proportions of total sales of fresh milk passing through the different channels in 1938 are as follows:

	%
Sales by producer/retailers	19–20
From producer direct to retailer	40–45
From producer direct to town wholesaler and then to retailer	10–15
From producer to country depot and then to retailer	14–17
From producer to country depot to town wholesaler to retailer	8–12

A small proportion of the milk went through other channels, for example, from farmer to first wholesaler to second wholesaler to retailer, and from farmer to first depot to second depot to retailer, but these channels were only used in cases of emergency and when supplies were uneven.

The producer/retailers were important in rural areas and in some small towns. In 1938 there were approximately 70,000 producer/retailers in the United Kingdom, but many undertook only a very small retail trade in milk, the bulk of their production going to depots or to wholesalers and retailers. About 10% of the producer/retailers were responsible for over half of the total sales by this group.

Retailers and wholesalers purchasing direct from producers usually had contracts with the farmers for the regular supply of milk. In some instances retailers entered into contracts with farmers for 'level' delivery of milk, thus avoiding the problem of fluctuating supplies.

The very large urban centres—particularly marked in the case of London—drew their supplies from country depots. The farmer delivered to the depots situated in producing areas where the milk was bulked, brine-cooled, sometimes heat-treated and forwarded to wholesalers and retailers in the larger towns. Most of the depots—there were approximately 275—also undertook the manufacture of surplus milk into milk products. A number of these depots, 80–100, were controlled by large wholesale/retail concerns, including the co-operative wholesale societies.

Wholesalers, in the majority of instances, were also retailers and their retail sales accounted for the bulk of their turnover. Their wholesaling function was to supply retailers who for various reasons did not purchase all their supplies from the farmers or depots. Many retailers, usually small firms, were unable or unwilling to enter into contracts with farms or depots for the direct supply of milk, and purchased the whole of their supplies from wholesalers. Other retailers, without processing or bottling plants, found it convenient to purchase regularly a part of their supply, pasteurized and/or bottled, from wholesalers. And other retailers—this was the most usual practice—supplemented their ex-farm supplies by purchases from depots or wholesalers to maintain an even supply of milk to their customers.

Numbers of distributors. There were approximately 16–17,000 first-hand purchasers of milk, that is depots, wholesalers and retailers, and the total number of firms engaged in the retail distribution of milk, excluding the producer/retailers mentioned above, was approximately 30,000 in 1938. Many of these firms owned shops and the number of 'dairies', that is, retail shops, is estimated at 20–24,000. The sale of milk 'over the counter' in these shops represented only a small proportion of the total sales to the domestic consumer, the bulk of milk being delivered from distributing dairies by roundsmen. Few dairymen confined their sales to milk and milk products alone, the majority also selling some groceries, provisions and bread. This sale of goods other than milk was most marked in the case of firms possessing retail dairies, and it is estimated that of the total turnover of these firms, including sales on retail rounds as well as in the shops, the sales of groceries, provisions and bread averaged between 33–40%.

In addition to producer/retailers and dairies, milk was also sold retail by a large number of grocers, provision dealers and bakers, and the total number of regular selling points of milk in 1938 is estimated at 110–120,000. This total does not include the number of separate retail delivery vehicles.

The number of multiple dairies in 1938 is estimated at 2,000–2,500. (Dairies here are taken to refer to retail shops.) Most of the retail co-operative societies sold milk, although in the case of smaller societies the milk distribution was undertaken by a federal co-operative society. The number of societies distributing milk in 1938 was 632.

Sales by different types of outlet. The estimates of the number of multiple and co-operative retail dairies or shops do not throw any direct light on the proportion of total trade in milk undertaken by these organizations, as in some instances large organizations serving milk to the public possessed several distributing dairies but few retail dairies or shops. But taking multiple dairies as referring to distributing dairies as well as to retail shops, the proportions of the total trade undertaken by the different economic types of organization are as follows:

	%
Co-operative dairies	24–27
Multiple dairies	25–30
Producer/retailers	19–20
Other dairies and other retail outlets	25–30

While there were a large number of retail outlets for milk, distribution was, in fact, concentrated in the hands of relatively few firms. And it is estimated that 10–20% of the number of firms, including producer/retailers, engaged in the distribution of milk were responsible for 60–75% of the total sales of milk in 1938.

The cost of distribution

The distributive margins of the producer/retailer, wholesaler and retailer of milk in 1938 were determined to a large extent by the pool or wholesale price paid to farmers and the minimum wholesale and retail price laid down by the Milk Marketing Board in England and Wales, the three Scottish Milk Boards and the Northern Ireland scheme. Only a very small proportion of the total sales of milk to the private domestic consumer were made outside these marketing schemes.

The average gross margins earned by distributors in 1938 expressed as percentages of the retail price of milk were as follows:

	%
Producer/retailers	46–47
Retailers purchasing direct from farms	42–43
Retailers purchasing all milk from wholesalers	17–37

Producer-retailers. The gross margin earned by the producer/retailer on the distribution of milk is difficult to distinguish from the margin he earned on the production of milk. And while the producer/retailer in 1938 earned a higher margin than the retailer purchasing from the farmer, there is little doubt that a part of this margin related to production.

Wholesalers and retailers. The gross margin earned by the country depot or the wholesaler would vary according to the function performed. If milk was sold from the depot or by the wholesaler to the retailer already pasteurized, sterilized and bottled, then the margin of the wholesaler was 25–30% on sales while the margin of the retailer was near the lower limit of the range given above, 17–20% on sales. The average cost of bottling and pasteurizing, including container costs, was 11–12% of the retail price of milk. On the other hand, if the milk sold by the depot or wholesaler to the retailer was unpasteurized and unbottled, the premiums chargeable by the wholesaler to the retailer would be lower and his gross margin would range from 5–15% on sales while the retailer's margin would be near the upper limit of the range given above, 33–37% on sales. The average wholesale margin is estimated at 15–20% on sales and the average retail margin obtained when the purchases were made from wholesalers at 27–33% on sales.

In those instances where retailers purchasing direct from farms paid the farmer a premium for 'level' delivery, the average gross margin was approximately 2% below the figure 42–43% given above.

The farmer selling direct to wholesalers or retailers paid for transport of the milk from his farm to the buyer's dairy or if the milk was sold to depots the farmer paid the costs of transport both to the depot and —in England and Wales—was debited a Standard Freight Deduction for transport from the depot to the distributing dairy. Transport costs on milk from farm to town wholesaler or retailer are estimated to have averaged 5–6% of the retail price of milk. The costs of selling undertaken by the various marketing boards, that is advertising and publicity, are estimated to have ranged between 1·5 and 1% of the retail price of milk, but not all this cost was incurred in respect of fresh milk sold to domestic consumers.

The total costs of distribution are estimated at 46–49% of retail sales.

4. CANNED MILK

Consumers' expenditure and methods of distribution

Consumers' expenditure on canned milk, including full-cream and skimmed, sweetened and unsweetened, is estimated at approximately £7–8 millions in 1938. This estimate excludes purchases by manufacturers, the catering trades and institutions. Approximately 70% of the total was spent on home-produced and the balance on imported supplies. Nearly three-quarters of the expenditure on British canned milk was on whole-milk products while over three-quarters of the expenditure on foreign supplies represented purchases of skimmed condensed milk.

The methods of distribution. The estimated proportions of these goods distributed through the various channels, shown as percentages of total sales in 1938 were approximately:

	%
Home-produced:	
From manufacturer direct to retailer	45–50
From manufacturer to wholesaler to retailer	50–55
Imported:	
From importer direct to retailer	35–40
From importer to wholesaler to retailer	60–65

Home-produced canned milk was distributed by manufacturers direct to all retailers who could take a certain minimum quantity, the wholesaler supplying those wishing to buy in smaller quantities. Purchases by the wholesaling departments of multiple organizations, sales by the co-operative wholesale societies to retail societies and sales by manufacturers through their own retail outlets are included in sales direct to retailer.

Imported canned milk was distributed by importers to grocery and provision wholesalers who re-sold to retailers. The sales direct to retailer include sales by importers to multiple organizations and sales by the co-operative wholesale societies to retail societies.

Number of retail outlets and sales by different types of outlet. The principal outlets for canned milk were grocery and provision shops and retail dairies, numbering 150–160,000. The estimated proportions of total trade in 1938 undertaken by shops grouped by economic type were:

	%
Multiple shops including variety chain stores	19–23
Co-operative shops	15–20
Unit retailers	57–66

The cost of distribution

Practically all home-produced canned whole-milk and some imported products were sold at prices suggested by manufacturers or importers, representing 50–60% of total retail sales of canned milk.

Importers' margins were approximately 5% on sales.

Wholesalers' margins averaged 7–7½% on sales of whole milk products and 8½–9% on skimmed milk. Canned milk was sometimes sold by wholesalers on a lower margin to promote sales of other goods.

Retailers' margins varied with the brand and grade of milk ranging from 10–12½% on sales of skimmed to 16–17½% on whole-milk products.

Multiple organizations and variety chain stores and the wholesale co-operative societies usually bought on or near the same terms as did wholesalers.

Settlement discounts were not generally given on canned milk.

Stock turn. Wholesalers usually kept about a month's stock and retailers 3–4 weeks' stock.

Manufacturers' distribution costs on home-produced milk are estimated to have averaged 7–10% of sales revenue. Of these costs salesmen's salaries and expenses represented approximately one-quarter and advertising between one-quarter and one-third.

The total costs of distribution are estimated at 27–29% of retail sales.

5. CHEESE

Consumers' expenditure and methods of distribution

Consumers' expenditure. Purchases by domestic consumers, that is, excluding cheese bought by the catering trades and institutions and cheese consumed on farms, are estimated at approximately £19–20 millions in 1938. Of this, £13–14 was spent on imported cheese, £3 millions on processed cheese made in this country largely from imported varieties, and approximately £3 millions on British cheeses.

The methods of distribution. The main channels of distribution and the estimated proportions passing through each expressed as percentages of retail sales in 1938 were:

	%
Imported:	
From importer direct to retailer or imported direct by retailers	42–48
From importer to wholesaler to retailer	52–58
Home-produced:	
From farmer or manufacturer or processor direct to retailer	45–50
From farmer or manufacturer or processor to factor or wholesaler to retailer	50–55

Cheese was usually handled together with butter and the channels of distribution were similar.

Imported cheese was mostly sold by importers to wholesale distributors and to multiple organizations. The proportions sold to multiple organizations and to the co-operative wholesale societies by importers or imported direct by these bodies have been shown above in sales direct to retailers.

Of *home-produced* cheese, that made on farms represented approximately one-sixth, that made in creameries and factories about one-third, and processed cheese about one-half of total sales.

Farm cheese was distributed mainly from farmer to cheese factor to retailer, only about 10% going direct from farmer to retailer. The cheese factor was usually a specialist country dealer but a few city provision wholesalers also acted as cheese factors.

Of the factory and creamery cheese about two-thirds was distributed through cheese factors, occasionally going through a general wholesaler as well, and the remainder sold direct to retailers, including multiple organizations and the co-operative wholesale societies. The co-operative wholesale societies and the multiple dairy retailers had their own factories from which they drew part of their supplies.

Of the processed cheese approximately two-thirds was distributed by the makers direct to retailers, the remainder passing through the general grocery and provision wholesalers.

Number of, and sales by, different types of retail outlet. Retail outlets for cheese are estimated to have numbered from 100–120,000 in 1938, consisting mainly of grocers and provision merchants and retail dairies. The proportions sold by outlets grouped by organizational type are estimated as follows:

	%
Multiple shops and variety chain stores	20–22
Co-operative stores	22–24
Unit retailers	54–58

The estimate of total sales by multiple shops includes sales by multiple dairies as well as multiple grocers.

The cost of distribution

The margins earned by the various distributors in 1938 are summarized below:

Importers' margins ranged from 2–2½% when they acted as agents on a commission basis, as in the distribution of New Zealand cheese, and 2½–5% where they acted as principals and performed additional functions.

Wholesalers' margins on imported cheese averaged from 4s.–6s. a cwt. This margin was not usually reckoned as a percentage on selling price but was approximately equivalent to 6–8% on sales. On processed cheese the wholesaler obtained a margin of 10% on sales.

Factors' margins ranged from 4–6% on sales. Factors usually bought outright either at farm or factory, but occasionally acted on commission.

Retailers' margins on imported cheese ranged from 10–15% on sales and on English cheese 14–18%. On soft cheese margins tended to be higher, up to 20% in some cases, and on packaged processed cheese 10–15%.

Settlement discounts were usually 2d. in the £ for payment in one week or 14 days, 1d. in the £ in one month.

Stock turn. Wholesalers generally kept about 2 weeks' stock but on a fluctuating market or when buying cheese for maturing they might purchase 3 months' stock or more. Retailers usually stocked 1–2 weeks' supply, although some retailers also bought stock for maturing.

The distribution costs of manufacturers of processed cheese were of the order of 12–15% on sales. Approximately one-half of this was represented by expenditure on advertising. On farm cheese the cost of transport from farm to market was usually borne by the cheese factors. In the case of creamery cheese the costs of distribution including transport from creamery to factors and to retailers were between 3–5% of sales revenue of the producers.

The total costs of distribution are estimated at 21–23% of retail sales.

6. EGGS IN SHELL

Consumers' expenditure and methods of distribution

Consumers' expenditure in 1938 is estimated at approximately £40 millions, of which some two-thirds was spent on home-produced and one-third on imported eggs. This estimate relates to purchases by domestic consumers and attempts to exclude consumption by producers and purchases by manufacturers, the catering trades and institutions.

The methods of distribution. The estimated proportions distributed through the various channels shown as percentages of the total sales of eggs in 1938 were:

	%
Home-produced:	
From producer to higgler or packer to retailer	50–60
From producer, higgler or packer to wholesaler to retailer	20–25
Producer direct to retailer and direct to consumers	20–25
Imported:	
From importer direct to retailer or imported direct by retailers	43–47
From importer to wholesaler to retailer	53–57

Home-produced eggs entering the commercial market reached the consumer by a variety of different and sometimes devious channels, of which only the principal ones are listed above. Because of the multiplicity of channels, the seasonal variations in supplies, and the practice in certain areas of selling off the farm to local consumers, the estimates given above are only very approximate.

The greater part of home-produced supplies was bought by higglers or country dealers at farms or local markets and distributed largely to retailers and to a certain extent direct to consumers, the surplus being re-sold to wholesalers. The wholesaler, here defined as the general grocery wholesaler or specialist city egg wholesaler, did not handle a substantial proportion of home-produced eggs. In periods of glut however the surplus supplies passed to the country auction markets and to the wholesale markets of cities and large towns for sale on commission.

Of the supplies shown above passing from producer to higgler or packer to retailer approximately two-thirds were handled by higglers and the balance by packers.

An important development in the period between the wars was the growth of egg packing stations. The packer mostly collected from the farm, in this respect performing a similar function to the higgler's. At the packing stations the eggs were graded, the standards of grading varying amongst different packers, and the producer was generally paid on a grade basis instead of at the flat rate paid by higglers.

The packer sold largely direct to retailers including multiple organizations. It is estimated that some four-fifths of his sales were direct to retailers and the remainder to wholesalers. Certain multiple retailing organizations, the co-operative wholesale societies and the producers' organizations had their own packing stations.

With the object of introducing uniform standards of grading a voluntary scheme known as National Mark was set up in 1929. Certain packing stations adopting the standard grading system laid down were licensed as National Mark stations. Producers selling to these stations were paid on quality and weight revealed by testing. The National Mark packers sold largely to retailers, the surplus being distributed through Egg Central, a group of wholesalers who had agreed to sell National Mark eggs on a fixed commission basis mostly in London and the large cities. It is estimated that National Mark eggs represented approximately 10–15% of the total value of home-produced supplies.

Direct to retailer sales included a considerable trade done by producers with retailers and consumers in neighbouring districts and purchases from producers by multiple and co-operative organizations. Sales by producers' organizations to retailers through the formers' packing stations are included above in sales through packers.

Imported eggs were distributed in London by specialist egg importers mostly to wholesalers in the grocery and provision trade and to other large purchasers such as multiple organizations and the co-operative wholesale societies. In the provinces firms tended to combine the functions of importers and wholesalers. Sales by importers to multiple organizations and the co-operative wholesale societies and direct imports by these bodies have been included above in sales direct to retailers.

The city wholesaler tended to concentrate on imported eggs because of the regularity of supplies and the superior grading and packing. Importers and wholesalers had some knowledge of the quality and number of imported eggs they could expect on a particular day whereas supplies of home-produced eggs were less predictable. Imported eggs were distributed largely from the main ports to the populous urban areas.

Unit retailers who could not buy in the quantities quoted by the importers were supplied by the wholesalers. In some cases these eggs went through a smaller, secondary wholesaler before reaching the retailer.

Numbers of, and sales by, different types of retail outlet. Retailers selling eggs included grocery and provision dealers, milk vendors, greengrocers, and fishmongers, the total retail outlets for this commodity being estimated at 180–190,000. The estimated proportions of the total trade in 1938 undertaken by shops grouped by economic type were:

	%
Multiple shops	17–19
Co-operative shops	14–16
Unit retailers	65–69

The cost of distribution

Distributive margins expressed as percentages of selling price tended to vary greatly at different seasons with variations in supplies and prices. The average margins earned by the various distributors in 1938 are estimated as follows:

Higglers or dealers generally bought and sold at a flat rate by number. The margin earned would vary as between sales to wholesalers and to retailers. The range was from 10d. to 1s. 3d. per 120, that is a margin on sales in the region of 5–7%.

Packers' margins also varied considerably, but are estimated to have averaged from 7–10% on sales. This margin had to cover costs of collection, grading, packing, and transport to retailers and wholesalers. Packers tended to buy and sell at rates varying with the grade of egg rather than at a flat rate.

Importers aimed at a margin of 3% on returns, out of which they had to pay approximately $\frac{3}{4}$% to overseas agents.

Wholesalers' margins ranged from 5–10% on sales of imported eggs depending on the quantities in which they sold, with an average of 7–8%. On home-produced eggs the wholesale margin was usually 3–5% on sales. On National Mark eggs where the prices paid by wholesalers to packers and the re-sale price to retailers for varying grades were fixed by agreement, the wholesaler's margin averaged $3\frac{1}{2}$%.

Retail margins on home and imported eggs ranged from $12\frac{1}{2}$–16% on sales with an average of 14% after allowing for breakages and other losses. A number of retailers sold eggs at or about cost price at certain times to attract other custom. Retail prices generally did not rise or fall immediately after a change in wholesale prices, retailers preferring to sell at slowly changing prices over the year, thus evening out the profit and loss at certain seasons.

Settlement discounts. Terms were net.

Stock turn. Wholesalers usually held 2–3 days' and retailers 3–5 days' stock.

The total costs of distribution are estimated at 18–19% of retail sales.

CHAPTER XI

SUGAR, PRESERVES AND CONFECTIONERY

I. SUGAR

Consumers' expenditure and methods of distribution

Consumers' expenditure. Expenditure on sugar in 1938 by domestic consumers, that is excluding sugar purchased by manufacturers, caterers and institutions, is estimated at approximately £23 millions. This figure includes duty, which represented a little over a quarter of the total.

The methods of distribution. The main channels of distribution and the proportions distributed through each channel expressed as percentages of retail sales in 1938 have been estimated as follows:

	%
From refinery direct to retailer	44–46
From refinery to dealer or wholesaler to retailer	54–56

In addition to the usual channels shown above accommodation sales between wholesalers, dealers and brokers were usual in the trade. Sales shown above as passing from refinery direct to retailer consisted practically entirely of sales to the wholesale departments of multiple and co-operative organizations. The refiners had fixed terms for certain minimum tonnage orders and sold to all who could purchase in these quantities. In practice only dealers, wholesalers and multiple and co-operative organizations purchased from refiners. Unit retailers obtained their supplies from wholesalers or dealers.

The distinction between dealers and wholesalers was merely a nominal one, a dealer being defined as a member of a dealers' association. Some dealers undertook the actual distribution of sugar and some wholesalers performed exactly similar functions. Some dealers however offered no delivery, while some handled only sugar and others dealt in a wide range of commodities.

Number of wholesalers, dealers and retailers. Wholesalers handling sugar were mostly the general grocery wholesalers who together with dealers numbered approximately 2,000 in 1938. The number of retail outlets is estimated at 190–200,000 including grocers and provision dealers of all types and a number of small general shops.

Sales by different types of retail outlet. The proportions of total sales in

1938 undertaken by the different economic types of outlet are estimated as follows:

	%
Multiple shops	19–21
Co-operative shops	24–26
Unit retailers	53–57

The cost of distribution

Sugar was not price-maintained at the retail stage even in the case of the factory-packaged article. Approximately half the sugar sold retail was factory-packaged and customarily there was no difference in retail price between packaged and loose sugar.

The approximate margins and discounts obtained by the various distributors in 1938 were as follows:

The wholesale margin took the form of specific quantity rebates arranged on a sliding scale according to the size of the order plus a fixed discount. By agreement in the trade terms of re-sale were fixed, with the exception of the retail price, so that buyers received the same rebate off the list price for the stated quantities whether they bought from refinery, dealer or wholesaler. On sales of less than the minimum quantity the whole of the rebate was retained by the seller.

Buyers were entitled to rebates of 4½d. per cwt. on loose and 6d. per cwt. on packaged sugar on orders of 100 tons, 3d. and 4½d. per cwt. respectively on 50 tons, 1½d. and 3d. on 10 tons and 1½d. on packaged sugar on 5-ton orders. No rebate was obtained on loose sugar for quantities of 5 tons or less. The higher rebates were given on packaged sugar to encourage purchases in this form. The margins of particular distributors therefore varied according to the amounts sold—a dealer, for example, might buy 100 tons and re-sell to a wholesaler at the 50-ton rate, making 1½d. per cwt. The wholesaler might re-sell to a retailer in under-5-ton lots, making 3d. per cwt. A retailer prepared to buy in sufficient quantities would also qualify for the rebates.

As noted above all purchasers buying from the refinery in the listed quantities also received a settlement discount of 1½% for payment in 14 days. The average gross margin earned by wholesalers and dealers, derived from the quantity rebates and the cash discount, is estimated at slightly over 2% on sales, or approximately 2% of retail selling price. Wholesalers and dealers generally charged their customers for carriage on quantities and qualities not delivered by the refiners' services.

The retail margin obtained by grocers on granulated sugar was low. Sugar was frequently sold by retailers as a loss leader to attract other custom, often below the price which the retailer had paid for it. It has been estimated that a gross margin of 11% on sales was necessary to cover the retailer's cost of handling sugar and this margin was often only obtained by retailers buying on the most favourable terms. The margins obtained on cubes, caster and icing sugars was usually 15% on sales.

Delivery and stock turn. Wholesalers and dealers kept an average of 10–14 days' stock. They were not obliged to stock heavily as the refiners provided a service of direct delivery to wholesalers' and dealers' customers for orders of certain minimum quantities. These quantities and the delivery facilities provided differed according to whether the sugar was in bulk or packets and between one quality and another. Retailers usually kept 1–2 weeks' stock.

Refiners' distribution costs[1]. These varied as between one refiner and another and according to whether sugar was sold inclusive or exclusive of cost of delivery. It is estimated that approximately 40% of total deliveries to retailers were undertaken by the refiners, usually on behalf of wholesalers or dealers, the refinery paying delivery costs. Refiners' distribution costs averaged approximately 4–5% of sales revenue.

The total costs of distribution are estimated at 13–15% of retail sales.

2. JAM AND MARMALADE

Consumers' expenditure and methods of distribution

Consumers' expenditure on jam and marmalade in 1938 is estimated at £14–15 millions. This estimate excludes the purchases by catering establishments of jam and marmalade for sale as part of a meal and also excludes the purchases by institutions and the purchases by domestic consumers of fruit and sugar for jam making.

The methods of distribution. The proportions of total sales passing through the main channels of distribution in 1938 are estimated as follows:

	%
From manufacturer to wholesaler to retailer	35–40
From manufacturer direct to retailer	60–65

Included in the sales from manufacturer direct to retailer are the sales from manufacturers to multiple shops, whether delivered to multiple depots or by split delivery to multiple branches, and the sales by co-operative wholesale societies to retail co-operative societies.

[1] See p. 164.

In general it was the size of the order placed by retailers which determined whether manufacturers sold direct or through wholesalers and while some manufacturers were prepared to open direct accounts for orders of 6 dozen a month (very often those firms with a national sales organization) other manufacturers preferred to sell only in large lots and confined their direct sales to multiple organizations purchasing in quantity.

Number of wholesalers and retailers. Approximately 1,000–1,250 wholesalers handled preserves in 1938, although no wholesaler specialized exclusively in preserves, and there were an estimated 120–150,000 retail outlets.

Sales by different types of retail outlet. The proportions of total sales made by the different economic types of retail outlet in 1938 are estimated as follows:

	%
Co-operative shops	17–19
Multiple shops and variety chain stores	20–22
Unit retailers	59–63

The co-operative wholesale societies manufactured approximately 80–90% of the preserves sold by retail co-operative societies, and multiple firms which possessed manufacturing facilities produced 25–30% of the total sales of preserves in multiple shops.

The cost of distribution

The retail selling price of jam and marmalade was in the majority of instances suggested by the manufacturer and in general this price was adhered to by the retailer. But there was also an important sale of 'own label' jam by wholesalers and unit retailers. Multiple organizations also arranged for jams to be labelled in their name. Retail prices in these instances were fixed by the retailers.

The margins allowed to wholesalers and retailers by manufacturers varied according to the policy of the manufacturer and according to the type of jam and the extent to which the product was widely advertised and was a proprietary brand. The range of margins to wholesalers and retailers was as follows:

> *Wholesalers* received a discount of 6¼–7½% off the invoice price, and, in particular cases where the wholesaler purchased in very large quantities, the discount was increased to 10% or 12½%. The average discount on branded jams and marmalade was 7½%. In the case of unbranded jams, where the wholesaler affixed his own label, the margin earned was between 10% and 15% on sales.

Retailers earned a margin ranging from 16⅔–25% on the sale of various types of jams and marmalades. The average margin was 17½–18½%.

Multiple shops and co-operative stores purchasing from private manufacturers received, on large quantities, a discount off the invoice price of 5–6¼%. The average discount of this type was 5%. This was in addition to the usual retail margin.

Settlement terms. The retailer usually obtained the same terms from the wholesaler as he did from the manufacturers, but the manufacturers usually allowed the retailer a 2½% settlement discount for payment within the month. Wholesalers gave settlement discounts to retailers in relatively few instances, although when the wholesaler was competing directly with a manufacturer he would usually grant a discount. Wholesalers who made a practice of granting discounts of 2d. in the £ for payment in 7 days and 1d. in the £ for payment in 28 days on all purchases of groceries by retailers would include jams and marmalade in this discount.

Stock turn. The average stock turn of wholesalers is estimated at 20–25 times a year and that of retailers at 10–12 times a year.

Manufacturers' distribution costs varied widely between the different types of manufacturers. The costs, including carriage and packing, transport, selling expenses and advertising, of a national manufacturer selling the bulk of his product direct to retailers and having between 25–35,000 direct accounts amounted to 12–14% of sales revenue. Approximately one-third of this cost would be represented by advertising and one-quarter by transport and outward carriage costs. Smaller manufacturers with a local or regional rather than a national market and selling mainly through wholesalers had distribution costs amounting to 5–7% of sales revenue. The average manufacturers' distribution costs were between 9–11% of manufacturers' sales revenue.

The total costs of distribution are estimated at 31–33% of retail sales.

3. SYRUP AND TREACLE

Consumers' expenditure and methods of distribution

Consumers' expenditure on syrup and treacle in 1938 has been estimated at approximately £3·5 millions. This figure excludes purchases by manufacturers, the catering trades, and institutions.

The methods of distribution. The main channels of distribution and the estimated proportions passing through each shown as percentages of retail sales in 1938 were approximately:

	%
From manufacturer direct to retailer	40–45
From manufacturer to wholesaler to retailer	55–60

Sales to multiple organizations and sales by the co-operative wholesale societies to retail co-operatives are included above in sales direct to retailer.

Numbers of, and sales by, different types of retail outlet. Retail outlets for syrup and treacle are estimated at 150–170,000 in 1938. The estimated proportions sold by shops grouped by economic type were:

	%
Multiple shops and variety chain stores	16–18
Co-operative shops	23–25
Unit retailers	57–61

The cost of distribution

The principal brands, representing over three-quarters of total sales, were sold at retail prices determined by the manufacturers.

The margins obtained by the various distributors in 1938 are estimated as follows:

Wholesalers obtained a margin averaging 7% on sales.

Retailers were allowed margins on price-maintained brands of 16½% on sales of 2-lb. tins, representing about 70% of retailers' sales, and 18½% on 1-lb. sizes.

Settlement discounts were not generally given by manufacturers in the trade.

Manufacturers' distribution costs including salesmen's salaries, carriage and transport, warehousing and other selling costs are estimated to have represented from 5–7% of manufacturers' sales revenue.

Delivery and stock turn. Manufacturers generally undertook delivery to retailers acting as agents for the wholesaler. Deliveries were in minimum ½-cwt. lots on named days twice a week in the larger cities, less frequently in other areas. Wholesalers usually kept about 2–3 weeks' stock and the manufacturers directly discouraged stock-holding longer than 6-8 weeks. Retailers usually kept 1–2 weeks' stock.

The total costs of distribution are estimated at 26–29% of retail sales.

4. CHOCOLATE AND SWEETS

Consumers' expenditure and methods of distribution

Consumers' expenditure on chocolates and sweets in 1938 is estimated at £54–56 millions. Just over one-third was represented by expenditure on sweets and the balance by expenditure on chocolates.

The methods of distribution. The proportions of total sales passing through the main channels of distribution in 1938 are estimated as follows:

	Chocolate	*Sweets*	*Chocolate and sweets*
From manufacturer direct to retailer	38–42	28–32	32–38
From manufacturer to wholesaler to retailer	58–62	68–72	62–68

The larger firms sold a greater proportion of their output direct to retailers than did the smaller concerns, but with the exception of multiple retailers practically all retailers purchased some of their stock from wholesalers.

Number of wholesalers and retailers. There were about 4,000 wholesalers who handled chocolate and sweets in 1938 but 10% of them did more than half of the trade. Included in the 4,000 are some wholesaler/retailers, and a number of traders whose main business was in goods other than sugar confectionery. The number of selling points of chocolate and sweets is variously estimated at between 250–350,000. The number of regular sales points is thought to have been in the region of 280,000. Of these, specialist confectioners numbered 8–9,000, and confectioner/tobacconists and confectioner/newsagents 40–60,000.

Sales by different types of outlet. The proportions of the total trade undertaken by the different trade types of outlet in 1938 are estimated as follows:

	%
Specialist confectioners	16–20
Confectioner/tobacconists	43–49
Grocers, bakers, dairies, chemists, department stores, co-operative shops and general shops	25–30
Theatres, cinemas, canteens	7–10

The confectioner/tobacconists did most of their trade on the tobacco side.

The proportions of the total trade undertaken by the different economic types of retail outlet are estimated as follows:

	%
Multiple shops including variety chain stores	13–15
Co-operative shops	2–3
Unit retailers	82–85

There were also some 5,000 chemists with a very small trade in confectionery.

The outstanding feature of the retail trade was the small turnover of a large number of selling points. In 1938, the total retail trade could be roughly divided into four. One-quarter of the trade was undertaken by shops with a turnover in confectionery of less than £4 a week, and this included three-quarters of the total number of shops. Another quarter was undertaken by shops with a turnover of between £4 and £12 a week: these included nearly 20% of the shops. Another quarter was undertaken by shops with a turnover of between £12 and £35 a week, but only 5% of the number of shops were in this group. Finally there was a group containing no more than 1% or 2% of the total number of retail outlets each of which had a turnover of over £35 a week.

The cost of distribution

A large proportion of chocolates and a smaller proportion of sweets were branded and sold at retail prices fixed by the manufacturers.

On a large number of lines no wholesale prices as such were quoted by manufacturers but rebates were offered to both wholesalers and retailers according to the quantities purchased. The price lists were in many cases divided into various groups, and in each group reduced prices were quoted for increased quantities. The scale of rebates varied widely between manufacturers and also between the different products. The gross margin earned by the wholesaler would depend on the quantities he purchased and the size of the orders placed by his customers. The retailer's gross margin would vary similarly with the size of his order. Some manufacturers did not publish price lists but quoted special terms to large buyers.

The margins earned by wholesalers and retailers in 1938 were approximately as follows:

Wholesalers' margins on sweets and the cheaper chocolates ranged between 10–15% on sales, on the more expensive chocolates between 7–12%. The margins near the top of each range were more commonly earned by country wholesalers and those at the lower end by London and town wholesalers.

Retailers purchasing from wholesalers earned margins ranging from 20–40% on sales. Margins at the lower end of the scale were earned on small quantity purchases and on chocolates, and margins at the top end of the scale on large purchases and on sweets. The average margin on chocolates and sweets of retailers purchasing from wholesalers was about 33% on sales.

Retailers purchasing direct from manufacturers earned margins varying from 30–45% on sales. The margin on block chocolate was approximately 32%, on boxes of chocolates 33–35% and on chocolates that had to be weighed out by the retailer 35–40%. On sweets and toffees the margins were higher, between 36–48% on sales. On most of these lines the retailer had to weigh out. The average retail margin on purchases direct from manufacturers was 40% on sales.

Settlement discounts of 1¼% and sometimes up to 2½% were given for payment in the month. Practically all retailers obtained the 1¼% discount.

Special discounts of up to 5% were sometimes given to large distributors and extra discounts might also be given to subsidize the distributor's advertising of a particular brand. The number of such special discounts was, however, very small.

Stock turn. The average stock turn of wholesalers was 12–14 times a year. The stock turn of retailers varied very widely owing to the great variety of retail outlets for confectionery. In the case of specialist confectioners the stock turn ranged from 5–10 times a year. The stock turn of other retailers was sometimes as low as 3 times a year and sometimes as high as 24 times a year.

Manufacturers' distribution costs varied with sales policy. In some cases where unbranded goods were sold mainly to wholesalers the total costs rarely rose above 5% of sales revenue. In other cases where a firm was marketing a new product the costs were as high as 25% of sales revenue. For the trade as a whole, transport and warehousing costs were between 2% and 3% of retail value, advertising between 3% and 4%, and other selling costs and overheads brought the total of manufacturers' distribution costs up to between 7% and 10% of the retail value of chocolates and sweets.

The total costs of distribution are estimated at 48–51% of retail sales.

CHAPTER XII

FRESH FRUIT AND VEGETABLES

I. FRESH FRUIT AND VEGETABLES

Consumers' expenditure and methods of distribution

Consumers' expenditure on fresh fruit and vegetables, other than potatoes, in 1938 is estimated at £115–120 millions. Potatoes are excluded from this estimate as they are discussed in another study. Purchases by trade users and by the catering trades are also excluded from this figure. Just over one-half of this expenditure was on imported fruit and vegetables and the remainder on home-grown. The division between the products is somewhat similar in that just over one-half of the total expenditure was on fresh fruit and just under one-half on fresh vegetables. Approximately one-quarter of the sales of home-grown produce was represented by fruit and the remainder by vegetables, and just over one-quarter of the sales of imported produce by the sales of vegetables and the remainder by imported fruit.

Of the total sales of imported fruit oranges represented just over one-third and apples represented just under one-fifth. Of the home-grown crops, apples were the most important, representing just under one-half of the total sales of home-grown fruit. Tomatoes represented nearly two-thirds of the total sales of imported vegetables, and onions represented just under three-tenths of total sales. Expenditure on home-grown vegetables was evenly spread over a range of products of which the principal groups were cabbage and greens, broccoli and cauliflower, brussels sprouts, tomatoes and peas.

The methods of distribution of fruit and vegetables were extremely complex and a warning that the following discussion is somewhat over-simplified and the estimates very approximate is necessary.

Home-grown fruit and vegetables were distributed by individuals or firms performing the following functions:

- Growers who sold direct to consumers.
- Growers who sold direct to retailers, sometimes ex-farm, at a market, or ex-lorry.
- Producer-co-operatives which usually sold to retailers though sometimes to wholesalers.

Growers who sold to primary wholesale merchants or through commission salesmen.

Country merchants—sometimes known as local dealers—who usually bought outright from growers and then sold either outright to wholesalers or retailers or sent the produce to market for sale on commission. In some areas country merchants acted as commission salesmen to growers.

Commission salesmen who, when performing one function alone, did not take ownership of the produce but sold on commission for growers or merchants to wholesalers or retailers. In practice every commission salesman occasionally bought outright and many did so as a usual practice, thereby acting as wholesalers rather than as commission salesmen.

Wholesale merchants can be divided into primary and secondary wholesalers. The primary wholesaler either bought from a grower or, when acting as a commission salesman, sold for a grower. The secondary wholesaler bought from a primary wholesaler, that is either a primary wholesale merchant who owned the produce, or from a commission salesman.

Commission buyers acted for wholesalers and very occasionally for retailers and bought on commission from growers and from primary wholesalers or from commission salesmen. Occasionally they also acted as commission salesmen.

Retailers bought from any of the intermediaries listed above as well as from growers. Many retailers conducted joint wholesale-retail businesses.

Owing to the practice of many of these distributors of performing more than one function on different consignments and at different times of the year, the proportions of the total sales flowing through the different channels of distribution are extremely difficult to determine with accuracy. There were about a dozen different channels of distribution between grower and consumer regularly in use in 1938. These can be reduced to four if attention is focused on the number of intermediaries between the grower and the consumer, and estimates of the proportions of total sales of vegetables, excluding potatoes, and fruit passing through each channel in 1938 are as follows:

Method of distribution	*Vegetables*	*Fruit*	*Total sales of home grown produce*
From grower direct to consumer *or* grower direct to retailer	5–10	15–25	8–13

Method of distribution	*Vegetables*	*Fruit*	*Total sales of home grown produce*
From grower to commission salesman to retailer *or* from grower to wholesale merchant to retailer	45–55	30–40	42–51
From grower to commission salesman to wholesaler to retailer *or* from grower to first wholesaler to second wholesaler to retailer	30–35	27–33	29–35
From grower to three or more intermediaries such as grower to commission salesman to first wholesaler to second wholesaler to retailer	5–15	10–20	9–13

As the commission salesmen did not take financial possession of the fruit and vegetables that they handled whereas the wholesalers usually did, a further division of the methods of distribution distinguishing between the proportions handled by commission salesmen and by wholesalers is of interest. Of the total sales of home-produced fruit and vegetables approximately one-half is estimated to have been sold on commission, usually by a salesman acting on behalf of a grower. Slightly more fruit than vegetables was sold in this way. Nearly two-thirds of the total sales of fruit and vegetables are estimated to have passed through one or more wholesaler. Just under three-quarters of the vegetables and about one-half of the fruit were distributed in this way. The wholesalers, as shown above, purchased both from commission salesmen and from growers and re-sold to other wholesalers and to retailers. About a quarter of the total sales of fruit and vegetables passed through two or more wholesalers.

Again it must be stressed that these estimates are very approximate and are attempts to present a general picture of the methods of distribution. The estimates obscure the important variations in the methods of distribution used at different seasons of the year, for the different types of fruit and vegetables with differing degrees of perishability and from different producing areas.

Imported fruit and vegetables were distributed by individuals and firms performing the following functions:

Importers who held either an agency interest in the produce or a proprietary interest.

Commission salesmen who acted for importers and sold either by auction or by private treaty. In some cases the commission salesmen were themselves importers holding an agency interest in the produce. When selling by auction they were usually termed brokers.

Wholesale merchants who bought from importers holding a proprietary interest in the produce or from commission salesmen acting for importers or from commission salesmen who were importers. In certain instances wholesale merchants themselves imported. The wholesale merchants sold both to second wholesalers and to retailers.

Commission buyers who usually bought for wholesalers from importers or commission salesmen but who also sometimes bought for retailers.

Retailers usually bought imported produce from wholesale merchants but some of the larger concerns purchased directly from overseas agents or growers or from importers.

As in the case of home-grown produce there were a number of alternative methods of distribution in constant use and the proportions of total sales passing through the main channels can only be estimated approximately. These estimates are as follows:

Method of distribution	*Vegetables*	*Fruit*	*Total sales of home grown produce*
From importer direct to retailer *or* purchased by retailers abroad	Negligible	10–15	6–13
From importer to commission salesman (or broker) to retailer *or* importer to wholesale merchant to retailer	10–15	10–20	11–18
From importer to commission salesman (or broker) to wholesale merchant to retailer *or* from importer to first wholesaler to second wholesaler to retailer	65–75	60–70	62–70
From importer to three or more intermediaries such as importer to commission salesman (or broker) to first wholesaler to second wholesaler to retailer	15–20	5–10	8–12

As in the case of home-produced fruit and vegetables a further division of the methods of distribution to distinguish between commission salesmen or brokers and wholesalers can be attempted. Of the total sales of imported fruit and vegetables approximately 60–65% was handled by commission salesmen usually acting on behalf of importers. A higher proportion of imported vegetables was sold in this way than of imported fruit. Over four-fifths of the total sales of imported fruit and vegetables passed through one or more wholesalers who purchased as shown above either directly from importers or from commission salesmen and re-sold to other wholesalers or to retailers. About one-third of the total sales passed through two or more wholesalers.

Of the total sold by commission agents, about three-quarters was sold by brokers at auctions. The proportion handled by brokers was higher than this in the case of fruit, much higher for hard fruit, and very much lower for vegetables. Conversely private treaty sales on commission were most frequent in the case of vegetables and soft fruit. Outright sale to wholesalers was the general practice for bananas—though some were sold direct to retailers—and for some Canadian apples, most United States apples and citrus imports, and South American imports.

The number of wholesalers and retailers. The number of wholesalers of fruit and vegetables in 1938 is estimated at 5–6,000. Some of these were grower/wholesalers, some were wholesale merchants only, some were wholesaler/commission salesmen, some were wholesaler/retailers. The number of commission salesmen in 1938 is estimated at 2–3,000 but a large number of these are included in the total for wholesalers given above. There were about 300 commission buyers, and 4–5,000 growers sold regularly on retail terms to the public. The number of commission salesmen and brokers handling imported produce was approximately 200.

The number of retail outlets for fresh fruit and vegetables in 1938 is not known with any accuracy but is estimated at over 125,000. The number of specialist greengrocery outlets, including the greengrocery departments in co-operative and department stores, is estimated at 50–55,000. The remaining outlets were grocers, variety chain stores and general shops. The number of multiple greengrocery shops in 1938 is estimated at 800–1,200.

Sales by different types of retail outlet. The proportion of total sales undertaken by the different economic types of retail outlet in 1938 is estimated as follows:

	%
Multiple shops and variety chain stores	4–7
Co-operative shops	3–4
Unit retailers	89–93

The cost of distribution

The costs of distribution of fresh fruit and vegetables, which can be taken as the difference between the net price received by the grower or the landed price and that paid by the consumer, varied with the channels of distribution used, the type of fruit or vegetable, and according to the time of year. A division between home-grown and imported produce assists the discussion of the problem, but the estimates of the margins earned by distributors at various stages can only be approximate.

On home-grown produce the costs and margins in 1938 are estimated as follows:

The cost of transport to the primary market is estimated to have averaged about 10% on the grower's net price.

The primary wholesaler had to pay porterage and market tolls, and had to cover his overheads and usually the costs of providing containers to growers. His gross margin was usually in the form of a rate of commission of 7½% on sales plus a handling charge making an average total of 12½% on sales. The margins on sales made on commission only were nearer the 7½% figure.

The *secondary wholesaler's* margin had to cover the cost of buying the produce, sometimes through a commission buyer, the transport of the produce from the primary market or from another wholesaler where the two were not in the same market, market tolls and porterage, and delivery to retail customers if such was the local practice, in addition to the usual risk-bearing, overheads, credit to customers and net profit. The gross margins of secondary wholesalers varied between 9–16% on sales. In London they were near the lower limit, as larger quantities were handled and there were rarely any outward carriage costs. In the provinces the opposite was true and gross margins were nearer the top limit.

The retailers' margin had to cover losses on short weight and account, losses on overweight given and on wastage, the costs of re-grading and often of carriage inwards in addition to risks due to price fluctuations, general overheads, delivery costs, depending on the class of trade, and net profit. The margins varied between 33–60% on cost with an average of 50% on cost. The average realized margin of retailers after allowing for losses, wastage and mark-downs was 26–29% on sales.

On imported produce the costs and margins in 1938 are estimated as follows:

The spread between the landed price plus duty and the selling price to the secondary wholesaler averaged 15–18% on cost or

13–15% on sales. The margin had to cover handling, storage and transport costs up to the first point of sale and other importer's, agent's, broker's and primary wholesaler's expenses and profits. This gross margin would be split among the various distributors according to the various methods of handling imported produce discussed above.

Secondary wholesalers' gross margins varied over the same range as for home-grown produce but tended towards the lower level of 9% on sales as the quantities handled were usually considerable.

Retailers' gross margins on imported fruit were slightly lower than for home-grown fruit as there was little loss through short weight and, owing to better packing and grading, less loss through regrading. The average margin on imported fruit was 33–40% on cost and on imported vegetables 40–50% on cost. The average realized margin of retailers after allowing for losses and wastage was 25–28% on sales.

Stock turn. The rate of stock turn of different types of fruit and vegetables varies so widely that an average is of little meaning. For example while the duration of marketability of strawberries, raspberries and cherries must be measured in days, that of apples, savoys and turnips can be measured in weeks. On all fruit and vegetables, home and imported, the stock turn of the greengrocer averaged 80–100 times a year.

The total costs of distribution are estimated at 44–47% of retail sales.

2. POTATOES

Consumers' expenditure and methods of distribution

Consumers' expenditure on potatoes in 1938 is estimated at £23–24 millions. This estimate attempts to exclude the purchases of potatoes by fish-fryers and by the catering trades. About 5% of the sales to the domestic consumer were imported, mainly early potatoes. Home-grown early potatoes represented about 5% of total sales.

The methods of distribution. The three main types of potato supply, the main crop, home-produced early or new potatoes and imported potatoes, each followed somewhat different methods of distribution. These were as follows:

Growers sold the bulk of the main crop potatoes to two types of authorized potato merchants, the country collecting merchants and the town merchants. These firms were licensed by the Potato Marketing Board. The country collecting merchants sold partly direct to retailers but mainly to town wholesalers who re-sold to retailers. The town merchants, a few of whom purchased their supplies from country collecting merchants, re-sold to retailers.

Growers sometimes sold main-crop potatoes direct to a retailer and occasionally as grower/retailers to the consumer.

Home-produced early potatoes were sold partly through the channels of distribution described for home-grown vegetables and partly through potato merchants as in the case of main-crop potatoes. Authorization under Potato Marketing Board regulations was not required to buy early potatoes from growers and for this reason the trade was shared between these two categories.

Imported early potatoes were distributed, in the main, through the channels described for the distribution of imported vegetables.

The proportions of total sales of potatoes passing through the main channels of distribution in 1938 are estimated as follows:

	%
From grower to consumer *or* direct to retailer	5–10
From grower or importer to merchant *or* commission salesman to retailer	35–40
From grower or importer to merchant *or* commission salesman to wholesaler to retailer	50–55
From grower or importer to three or more intermediaries, for example grower to country merchant to town merchant to secondary wholesaler to retailer	0–5

Commission salesmen while completely unimportant in the main crop trade played some part in the home early trade and in the imported trade. Information would suggest that approximately four-fifths of the home earlies passed through commission salesmen. Imports from Jersey were almost always sold outright while most other imports were sold on commission. Private treaty sales of imported potatoes were more common than sales by auction.

Of the total sales, main crop, home earlies and imported, some four-fifths are estimated to have passed through one or more wholesaler. Nearly one-third passed through two or more wholesalers or merchants.

Number of wholesalers and retailers and sales by different types of retail outlet. The number of retailers handling potatoes in 1938 was approximately the same as that given for fruit and vegetables. A number of wholesalers handling fruit and vegetables would not however handle potatoes and many of the authorized potato merchants dealt practically exclusively in this product. The number of authorized potato merchants in 1938 was 3,400. This total would include some grower/wholesalers.

The proportions of total sales of potatoes undertaken by the different economic types of retail outlet were similar to those relating to fruit and vegetables, although the proportion of trade handled by multiple organizations was smaller as variety chain stores concentrated on fruit, rarely selling potatoes.

The cost of distribution

The cost of distribution, taken as the difference between the growers' net price and the price paid by the consumer, was made up of the following items:

Transport costs from the grower to the urban market were a large item in relation to the low unit cost of potatoes and are estimated at 10–15% on the growers' net price.

The country collecting merchant selling to wholesalers usually earned a gross margin of 5–10% on sales. The size of the margin was related directly to the function he undertook. When selling direct to retailers the country merchant's margin rose to 15–20% on sales.

The town merchant purchasing from the grower and selling direct to retailer usually obtained 15–20% on sales but when purchasing from a country merchant or when selling to a secondary wholesaler his margin was lower at 10–15% on sales. His margin also varied with the function performed in that when buying ex-farm the town wholesaler had to bear the cost of dressing and inspecting the crop whereas when buying 'free on rail' this charge was borne by the grower.

The average spread between the ex-farm price and the wholesale selling price on main crop potatoes was 33% on cost. This was split in several ways between the grower, country merchant, town merchant and wholesaler, depending on the functions they undertook. On imported early potatoes the spread between the landed price and wholesale selling price was slightly lower at 25–30% on cost.

The retailer worked to an on-cost of 45–75% when selling main crop potatoes and 40–50% when selling new potatoes. Main crop potatoes, however, involved heavy losses on wastage due to the inclusion of unsaleable tubers and dirt in the purchases and there was some loss due to over weight given and perishability. The losses on new potatoes arising from these factors were somewhat lower. The average realized margin of retailers on potatoes after allowing for losses was 27–30% on sales.

Stock turn. The rate of stock turn of retailers varied with the type of potato handled. The average, over the year and allowing for these variations, is estimated at between 60 and 80 times.

The total costs of distribution are estimated at 48–51% of retail sales.

CHAPTER XIII

CANNED FRUIT AND VEGETABLES, SAUCES, PICKLES AND CONDIMENTS

1. HOME-CANNED AND DRIED VEGETABLES AND CANNED AND BOTTLED FRUIT

Consumers' expenditure and methods of distribution

Consumers' expenditure on home-canned and dried vegetables and canned and bottled fruit in 1938 is estimated at £11–13 millions. Of this total, the expenditure on canned vegetables is estimated at £4·5–5 millions, on canned and bottled fruit at £4–5 millions, and on dried vegetables at £2·5–3 millions. Purchases by the catering trades and by institutions have been excluded, as far as possible, from these estimates.

The methods of distribution. The proportions of total sales of these goods passing through the main channels of distribution in 1938 are estimated as follows:

	%
From canner, bottler or processor to wholesaler to retailer	40–45
From canner, bottler or processor to retailer	55–60

Included in the sales direct to retailer are the sales by co-operative wholesale societies to retail co-operative societies and the sales by canners through their own retail outlets. The latter sales are estimated to have represented about 5% of the total sales.

Number of wholesalers and retailers. The number of wholesalers handling these goods in 1938 is estimated at 3–4,000. About one-third of these were greengrocery wholesalers and the remainder grocery and provision wholesalers. The number of retail outlets is estimated at 175–200,000. Approximately one-quarter of these outlets were shops that were primarily greengrocers and the remainder were grocers and provision dealers, general shops selling foods, variety chain stores and some butchers and fishmongers. The fresh fruit and vegetable trade was a more important outlet for canned vegetables than for canned fruit, which was distributed mainly through the grocery trade. But there were important variations in respect of individual canners. Certain firms, for example, being allied through their original approach to canning with the fruit and vegetables trade sold a far greater proportion of their products through that trade than did others who had had a different origin. This factor influenced the proportion of sales passing through the main channels of distribution, as the usual method of distribution in the fresh fruit and vegetable trade was through the wholesaler while direct trading with the retailer was far more common in the grocery trade.

Sales by different types of retail outlet. The proportions of total sales made by the different economic types of retail outlet in 1938 are estimated as follows:

	%
Multiple shops including multiple grocers, greengrocers and variety chain stores	21–25
Co-operative stores	17–19
Unit retailers	56–62

Greengrocers, including the greengrocery departments of co-operative shops, are estimated to have undertaken just under one-third of the total sales. The sales of variety chain stores are estimated to have represented about 5% of total sales.

The cost of distribution

Practically all these products were branded except dried vegetables, and of the branded goods it is estimated that just over one-half were resale price maintained by the canner.

The margins earned by wholesalers and retailers in 1938 are estimated as follows:

Wholesalers' margins varied between 7½–12½% on sales. The margins at the lower end of the range were usually taken by greengrocery wholesalers who expected a quick turnover in these goods. The average margin of wholesalers is estimated at 10% on sales.

Retailers' margins ranged from 17½–25% on sales. Where the retail grocer purchased from a wholesaler his margin was usually at the lower end of the scale but the greengrocer usually earned a margin near the top of the scale on his purchases from a wholesaler. The large buyers, that is multiples and variety chain stores, purchasing direct from canners usually bought at wholesale terms.

Settlement discounts of 1¼ or 2½% or sometimes of 1d. and 2d. in the £ were allowed in the grocery trade but not in the fruit and vegetables trade.

The average stock turn of wholesalers was 12 times a year, of retail greengrocers 12 times a year and of retail grocers 6–8 times a year.

Canners' distribution costs varied with the methods of distribution and sales policy adopted. The range was between 10–20% of sales revenue with an average for the whole trade of 10–12%. This was made up of selling costs 4–5%, carriage and transport 3–4%, advertising 1–2% and administrative selling costs 1–2%.

The total costs of distribution are estimated at 35–39% of retail sales.

2. IMPORTED CANNED FISH, FRUIT AND VEGETABLES AND DRIED FRUIT

Consumers' expenditure and methods of distribution

Consumers' expenditure on this group of foods in 1938 is estimated at £32–34 millions. Of this total, the expenditure on imported canned fruit is estimated at £12–14 millions, on imported canned fish at £10 millions, on imported canned vegetables at £4–6 millions and on dried fruit at £5 millions. Purchases of these products by the catering trade have been excluded from these estimates.

The methods of distribution. As was the case with most imported foodstuffs, the methods of distribution from the port to the consumer varied widely between one type of product and another and between one consignment of the same product and another. The channels of distribution are difficult to describe with close accuracy owing to the number of intermediaries each performing different functions. Importers, brokers, agents, distributing organizations of overseas canners, primary wholesalers, secondary wholesalers and the various types of retailers all took some part in the distribution of these goods and, to add to the complications, the functions each undertook varied to some extent between different types of product and different consignments. Sometimes an importer, for example, would act only as an importer and dispose of his consignment through a broker, at other times he would act as a distributor selling to wholesalers and sometimes selling direct to retailers. Similarly retailers would sometimes purchase from a secondary wholesaler and at other times direct from an importer or from the distributing organization of an overseas canner.

In an attempt to simplify the channels of distribution, three main methods have been distinguished, although the estimates of the proportions of total sales passing through each can only, owing to the absence of full information and to the variations in practice, be very approximate.

The three main channels were as follows:

From overseas canners, importers or brokers direct to retailers. By this method of distribution the wholesaling function, that is holding stocks, breaking bulk, arranging and paying for transport from the port, was undertaken by the retailers. Only large retail organizations purchased in this way. The co-operative wholesale societies, for example, are estimated to have purchased about one-half of their supplies of imported canned goods direct from overseas and one-half from importers. Multiple organizations also purchased from overseas but bought most of their supplies from importers or brokers and importer/distributors. Large independent retailers usually purchased from brokers or importers. The proportion of total sales passing through this channel is estimated at 35–45% of which just under one-half was purchased direct from overseas canners.

From overseas canners to importers who maintained depots throughout the country and then to retailers. These importer/distributors were sometimes representatives of overseas firms and sometimes independent distributors. They combined the functions of importers or brokers and of primary and sometimes of secondary wholesalers and sold both to wholesalers and to retailers. Here only their sales to retailers, that is sales for which they performed the wholesaling function, are considered. The proportion of total sales passing through this channel is estimated at 10–15%. (If the sales by these importer/distributors to wholesalers are considered as well, the proportion of total sales handled by these concerns would increase to 23–27%.)

From overseas canners to importers or brokers, to one or more wholesalers and then to retailers. Included in this channel of distribution are the sales made to wholesalers by the importer/distributors mentioned above and the sales by primary wholesalers to secondary wholesalers. The proportion of total sales passing through this channel is estimated at 45–50%. About one-quarter of these sales passed through two wholesalers on their way to the retailer.

The variations in the channels of distribution between the different commodities were approximately as follows. About 50% of the canned fish was imported direct by retailers or was distributed by importer/distributors direct to the retailer. The remainder went first to importers or brokers and then to wholesalers or retailers. About 20–25% of the canned and dried fruits was sold in the former way and about 30–35% of the canned vegetables. For the whole group just over one-half of the total sales was imported direct by retailers or sold by importing houses direct to the retailer while the remainder passed through importers, agents or brokers and then to wholesalers primary or secondary who re-sold to other wholesalers or to retailers.

Number of wholesalers and retailers. The number of wholesalers handling the goods is estimated at 3–4,000 and the number of retailers at 200–225,000. Over four-fifths of the trade was handled by grocers and provision dealers and general shops dealing in groceries, but the goods were also sold by most greengrocers and dairies, some variety chain stores, and some fishmongers.

Sales by different types of retail outlet. Estimates of the proportions of total sales undertaken by the different economic types of retail outlet in 1938 are as follows:

	%
Multiple shops including multiple grocers, dairies, greengrocers and variety chain stores	25–30
Co-operative stores	20–23
Unit retailers	47–55

Variety chain stores are estimated to have undertaken 5–6% of total retail sales.

The cost of distribution

Branding of these goods was usual except in the case of dried fruits, of which less than one-quarter was sold in packets. The branding took place at various stages of distribution. About four-fifths of the canned fish was branded by the importer and the remainder by either the packer, wholesaler or retailer. About one-half of the canned fruit and just over one-half of the canned vegetables was branded by the packer and the remainder by the importer, wholesaler or retailer. Re-sale price maintenance was only important in the case of importer-branded goods.

The margins earned by the various distributors are, as suggested above, difficult to estimate accurately owing to the varying functions performed by the distributors on different types of product and different consignments. The approximate margins earned were as follows:

Agents or brokers earned a commission ranging from 1–5% on sales with an average of 3–4%.

Importers selling goods ex-quay or ex-store at the ports and with carriage forward earned 5–6% on sales.

Importer/distributors who sold from depots, usually with carriage forward, earned 9–11% on sales. The margin on sales to large purchasers was somewhat lower.

Wholesalers purchasing from importers earned 5–12% on sales but the higher margins were only obtained on dried fruits and the top grades of advertised canned goods. On other canned goods the wholesalers' margins were between 6–7% on sales. Where the goods were sold by a wholesaler to a secondary wholesaler, the gross margin was slightly larger, 10–14%, and split between the two wholesalers.

Retailers' margins were 22–23% on sales of dried fruit and between 17–20% on sales of top-grade canned goods purchased direct from importing houses. Retailers who imported direct usually earned an average margin of 25–30% on sales. Retailers purchasing from wholesalers earned margins ranging from 12–18% on sales, with an average of 15%.

The estimated margins given above include the volume discounts which were allowed in some cases. One common system of volume discounts was linked with forward ordering whereby the purchaser obtained special terms from an importing house by agreeing to take fixed quantities of goods at three-monthly intervals.

Settlement discounts. In addition to these margins many wholesalers and most retailers could obtain the usual grocery trade settlement discounts of 2d. or 1d. in the £ for payment in 7 days or in the month.

The total costs of distribution are estimated at 28–30% of retail sales.

3. PICKLES, SAUCES, SALAD CREAM, SOUP, AND FISH AND MEAT PASTE

Consumers' expenditure and methods of distribution

Consumers' expenditure on this group of products in 1938 is estimated at £12–13 millions. Of this total, the expenditure on pickles, sauces and salad creams is estimated at £6–7 millions, on soups at about £4 millions and on fish and meat pastes £1·5–2 millions. Purchases by catering establishments have been excluded from these estimates. Expenditure on imported products represented approximately one-quarter of the total expenditure on this group.

The methods of distribution. The proportions of total sales passing through the main channels of distribution in 1938 are estimated as follows:

	%
From manufacturer or importer direct to retailer	50–60
From manufacturer or importer to wholesaler to retailer	40–50

Purchases by co-operative wholesale societies for re-sale to co-operative retail societies are classed as sales direct to retailers. These general averages conceal some important differences in the methods of distribution. Imported products, except those purchased by manufacturers, were almost always handled by wholesalers before reaching the retailers. Some large multiple organizations however imported direct, and the larger home manufacturers tended to sell a greater proportion, about two-thirds to three-quarters, of their output direct to retailers than did the smaller manufacturers.

Number of wholesalers and retailers. The number of wholesalers handling these goods is estimated at 2–3,000. For the most part they were general grocery and provision wholesalers. The number of retail outlets is estimated at 160–175,000. The retail outlets included grocers, provision dealers, dairies, greengrocers, fishmongers, general shops and a few chemists as well as co-operative and department stores and variety chain stores. Grocers and provision dealers including the grocery departments of co-operatives and department stores are estimated to have undertaken about four-fifths of the total sales.

Sales by different types of retail outlet. The proportions of total sales made by the different economic types of retail outlet in 1938 are estimated as follows:

	%
Multiple shops including multiple grocers, dairies, and variety chain stores	25–27
Co-operative shops	20–24
Unit retailers	49–55

Variety chain stores are estimated to have undertaken 5–7% of total retail sales.

The cost of distribution

Practically all these goods were branded. The producer usually branded, but the co-operatives, multiple organizations and variety chain stores also sold goods branded in their own names or under a brand name that was exclusive to them. Between one-half and three-quarters of the manufacturer-branded goods were re-sale price maintained.

The margins earned by wholesalers and retailers on these products in 1938 are estimated as follows:

Wholesalers earned a margin of 9–11% on sales. Settlement discounts of 1¼–2½% for payment in 7 days or one month were given by some manufacturers, usually when the margin was at the lower level.

Retailers buying from wholesalers obtained a margin averaging 16–17% on sales though on fish and meat paste the average was higher at 20–22%. Unit retailers purchasing direct from manufacturers earned margins ranging from 16⅔–20% on sales. These retailers were also usually entitled to a settlement discount of 1¼–2½% for payment in 7 days or in the month. Large retailers, such as multiple organizations, obtained an additional discount of 2½–5%, usually on imported goods, or in some cases purchased from manufacturers at wholesale terms.

The stock turn of wholesalers averaged 12–14 times a year and the stock turn of retailers between 8–10 times a year.

Manufacturers' distribution costs varied with the particular sales policy adopted. The distribution costs of manufacturers selling nationally advertised products direct to retailers were of the order of 16–22% of sales revenue, comprising selling expenses 5–6%, outward carriage costs 5–6% and advertising costs 6–10%. The distribution costs of manufacturers selling mainly through wholesalers were of the order of 5–8% of sales revenue, and in these instances the distributors' margins were usually at the higher end of the ranges given above.

The total costs of distribution are estimated at 32–36% of retail sales.

4. SALT

Consumers' expenditure and methods of distribution

Consumers' expenditure on salt in 1938 is estimated at approximately £2 millions. This estimate attempts to exclude the purchases of salt by industrial users and by the catering trades. About one-fifth of the salt was sold in tins and drums, three-fifths in packets and one-fifth in cut lumps.

The methods of distribution. The proportions of total sales passing through the main channels of distribution in 1938 are estimated as follows:

	%
From manufacturer to wholesaler to retailer	35–45
From manufacturer to retailer	55–65

The sales by co-operative wholesale societies to retail co-operative societies are classed as sales from manufacturers direct to retailers.

Number of and sales by different types of retail outlet. Almost all general grocery and provision wholesalers handled this product and the number of retail outlets is estimated at 150–175,000. The bulk of the sales was made by grocers, and general shops selling food.

The division of the total sales between the different economic types of retail outlet is estimated as follows:

	%
Multiple shops	18–22
Co-operative stores	20–24
Unit retailers	56–60.

The cost of distribution

Practically all domestic salt sold in containers and packets was price-maintained by the manufacturers in 1938 and in many instances cut lump salt was sold at prices recommended by the manufacturers.

The margins earned and allowed to wholesalers and retailers on the sale of salt in 1938 were as follows:

Wholesalers were not granted any special terms but usually purchased at the best possible quantity terms and re-sold to retailers in smaller quantities. The wholesalers' margin ranged from 5–8%

on sales of salt in tins and drums and from 8–12% on sales of packeted salt and cut lumps. The average wholesale margin was about 8% on sales.

Retailers purchasing from wholesalers obtained a margin ranging from 22–28% on sales. The average margin was 22–25% on sales. The retailer purchasing direct from manufacturers obtained a higher gross margin through purchasing on quantity terms and averaged 25–27% on sales. Multiple organizations usually purchased at or near wholesalers' terms, getting a gross margin of 28–31% on sales.

Settlement discounts. Both wholesalers and retailers were entitled to a settlement discount, usually 2½% for payment in 7 days.

The stock turn of wholesalers of salt is estimated to have averaged 15–20 times a year and the stock turn of retailers about 10 times a year.

Manufacturers' distribution costs including carriage and transport, selling costs, administrative expenses and advertising, averaged 25–30% of sales revenue. Of this advertising costs represented about one-sixth.

The total costs of distribution are estimated at 47–51% of retail sales.

CHAPTER XIV

BEVERAGES

I. TEA

Consumers' expenditure and methods of distribution

Consumers' expenditure. Expenditure by domestic consumers in 1938 is estimated at approximately £45 millions including duty. This figure excludes tea served in cafés and restaurants and purchases by institutions.

The methods of distribution. Expressed as percentages of total sales the proportions distributed through the main channels in 1938 are estimated as follows:

	%
From packer or dealer direct to retailer	75–80
From packer or dealer to wholesaler to retailer	20–25

The bulk of the tea on reaching this country was auctioned by brokers at weekly sales held in London. Some two-thirds of these supplies passed to five large packer-distributors, sometimes referred to as primary wholesalers. There were also a number of smaller packers and specialist dealers. The large firms blended, packaged and distributed largely direct to retailer. Two of these concerns, one of which was the English and Scottish Joint Co-operative Wholesale Society, distributed exclusively to their own retailing organizations, a third supplying both its own shops and independent retailers. In addition these packer-distributors also branded teas for particular wholesalers and large retailers and sold a small proportion of bulk tea to wholesalers and retailers who did their own blending and packaging. The small proportion of bulk tea purchased by unit retailers was usually obtained from dealers or secondary wholesalers. It is estimated that 85–90% of tea sold retail reached the retailer in pre-packaged form.

Number of wholesalers and retailers. There were about 80 packer-distributors or primary wholesalers and 1,500–2,000 secondary wholesalers who were mostly general grocery wholesalers handling other goods as well. Retail outlets are estimated at over 200,000 in 1938, including grocery and provision shops of all types, shops specializing in tea, branches of catering firms selling packaged teas, small general shops, department stores and variety chain stores.

Sales by different types of retail outlet. The estimated proportions of total sales in 1938 undertaken by shops grouped by economic type were:

	%
Multiple shops and variety chain stores	25–27
Co-operative shops	23–25
Unit retailers	48–52

The cost of distribution

It is estimated that approximately 65% of tea was branded and sold at retail prices determined by the packer-distributors. This estimate excludes teas branded and packed by multiple organizations and by the co-operative wholesale society for sale exclusively through their own retail outlets. The retail price of tea was kept relatively stable, since the effects of fluctuations in the auction price were cushioned by the holding of large stocks by packers.

The margins obtained by the various distributors in 1938 were approximately as follows:

Selling brokers operating at the tea auctions worked on a commission of 1%, buying brokers on ½%.

Wholesalers', i.e. secondary wholesalers' margins ranged from 6–10% on sales of packaged teas varying with the brand, the average being approximately 7½%. Wholesalers' margins on bulk teas ranged from 9–12% on sales.

Retailers' margins on pre-packaged teas ranged from 8½–16% on retail selling price. On the cheaper and the more highly advertised brands the retail margin averaged 9–10% while on the more expensive teas, for example China tea, a margin of 16% was obtained. Taking the trade as a whole, the average retail margin was in the region of 10–13% on sales.

Multiple retailers buying price-maintained proprietary teas received an extra 1½% in the form of an annual bonus from some packers and from others up to 5% discount off wholesale price, sometimes given in the form of a settlement discount. A number of the larger multiple concerns sold their own brands of tea.

Settlement discounts. Some packers gave 1¼% for settlement, others gave what were in effect quantity discounts, and some packers gave no settlement discounts at all.

Stock turn. Wholesalers held an average of 2–3 weeks' and retailers 10–14 days' stock. Packer-distributors tended to discourage the holding of large stocks and in most of the large cities undertook weekly deliveries to retailers.

Packers' distribution costs. The difference between the cost of tea purchased by packer-distributors and their returns from sales ranged from 13–20% on turnover, the estimated average being 14–16%. This spread included the pre-distributive or processing costs of blending and costs of packaging as well as the costs of distribution. The distributive costs, that is, salesmen's salaries, carriage and transport, advertising, warehousing and general administrative selling costs are estimated to have averaged 8–10% of packers' sales revenue for the trade as a whole. Sales revenue in each case is based on a selling price which includes duty.

The total costs of distribution are estimated at 19–21% of retail sales.

2. COFFEE

Consumers' expenditure and methods of distribution

Consumers' expenditure on coffee in 1938 was approximately £2–2·5 millions. This estimate excludes coffee purchased by manufacturers and by the catering trades and institutions. Coffee essences and extracts are also excluded.

The methods of distribution. The proportions distributed through the various channels expressed as percentages of total retail sales in 1938 are estimated as follows:

	%
From dealer or packer to retailer	60–65
From dealer or packer to secondary wholesaler to retailer	35–40

Coffee was imported practically entirely in the form of raw beans. The greater proportion was roasted, ground and blended by the large dealers who sold loose, pre-packed and green coffees direct to retailers and to secondary wholesalers. Some of the latter did their own roasting and blending and packed under their own proprietary names. It is estimated that 70–80% of retailers' purchases of coffee were in 'loose' form, the remainder representing purchases of pre-packaged proprietary lines, including packs put up by the multiple organizations and the co-operative wholesale societies for sale in their own shops. Sales to the wholesale departments of multiple organizations and sales by the co-operative wholesale societies to retail societies are included above in the proportions shown going direct from dealer to retailer.

Numbers of and sales by different types of retail outlet. Coffee was sold by grocery and provision shops, specialist tea and coffee retailers, including certain multiple cafés, variety chain stores, the retail co-operatives and the department stores. The total number of outlets is estimated at 100–120,000. The proportions of the total trade undertaken in 1938 by shops grouped by economic type are estimated as follows:

	%
Multiple shops and variety chain stores	15–20
Co-operative shops	10–15
Unit retailers	65–75

The cost of distribution

Proprietary coffees sold at retail prices fixed or suggested by the packer, excluding brands packed by the multiple and co-operative organizations which were sold exclusively in their own shops, are estimated to have represented about 15–20% of retail sales of coffee in 1938.

The margins earned by wholesalers and retailers in 1938 were approximately as follows:

Secondary wholesalers' margins on loose and on pre-packed proprietary coffees averaged about 10% on sales.

Retailers' margins on loose coffees ranged from 20–25% on sales, and in some cases were slightly higher. On nationally advertised proprietary coffees retailers' margins tended to be lower, ranging from 17–20% on sales.

Multiple organizations purchasing proprietary blends obtained terms similar to those allowed to wholesalers.

Stock turn. Retailers usually kept 1–3 weeks' stock of coffee and wholesalers 4–6 weeks' stock.

Dealers' and packers' distribution costs varied greatly depending on whether they distributed largely in bulk to wholesalers and multiple concerns or sold direct to small retailers, and on the amount of advertising undertaken. For the trade as a whole distribution costs, including the costs of blending and packaging, incurred by dealers and packers are estimated at approximately 6–8% of sales revenue.

The total costs of distribution are estimated at 31–33% of retail sales.

3. COCOA

Consumers' expenditure and methods of distribution

Consumers' expenditure on cocoa in 1938 is estimated at £2·5–3 millions. This estimate attempts to exclude the purchases of cocoa by the catering trades and institutions.

The methods of distribution. The proportions of total sales of cocoa passing through the main channels of distribution in 1938 are estimated as follows:

	%
From manufacturer to wholesaler to retailer	25–30
From manufacturer direct to retailer	70–75

Included in the sales direct to retailer are the sales by the co-operative wholesale societies to co-operative retail societies.

Number of wholesalers and retailers. Almost all grocery and provision wholesalers handled cocoa and it was also stocked by a small number of confectionery wholesalers. The number of wholesalers handling cocoa is estimated at approximately 1,500. The number of retail outlets in 1938 is estimated at 150–165,000. The grocery shops did the bulk of the trade.

Sales by different types of retail outlet. The proportions of total sales undertaken by the different economic types of retail outlet in 1938 are estimated as follows:

	%
Multiple shops, including variety chain stores	27–30
Co-operative stores	25–27
Unit retailers	43–48

Variety chain stores are estimated to have undertaken 2–4% of total sales.

The cost of distribution

Almost all the cocoa was branded, mainly by manufacturers but occasionally by wholesalers and large retailers, and about three-quarters of the output was re-sale price maintained. *The margins* earned by wholesalers and retailers in 1938 were approximately as follows:

Wholesalers. No special terms were given, as a general rule, to wholesalers but they usually bought in large quantities, thereby securing a reduction in price, and re-sold to retailers in small consignments. Wholesalers' margins ranged from 5–10% on sales. The average margin was 7–9% on sales.

Retailers purchasing from wholesalers obtained a margin of 15–16% on sales and when purchasing direct from manufacturers 16–23% on sales. Only the large retailers would earn margins at the top end of the range, the average margin being about 20% on sales.

The settlement discounts granted were usually 2½% for payment in the month.

The stock turn of wholesalers was approximately 10–12 times a year and the average for retailers 4–6 times a year. Some retailers would only turn over their cocoa stocks about once a year, however, while others, larger retailers, might turn it over almost every month.

Manufacturers' distribution costs averaged 20–25% on sales revenue. Transport and warehousing costs were in the region of 4%, salesmen's salaries and administrative selling costs 3–4% and advertising 14–16% of sales revenue.

The total costs of distribution are estimated at 38–42% of retail sales.

4. HEALTH FOOD BEVERAGES

Consumers' expenditure and methods of distribution

Consumers' expenditure on health food beverages with cereal and milk base is estimated at £1·75–2 millions in 1938. This estimate excludes the purchases of these goods by catering establishments, hospitals and institutions.

The methods of distribution. The proportions of total sales of health food beverages to the private consumer passing through the main channels of distribution in 1938 are estimated as follows:

	%
From manufacturer to wholesaler to retailer	65–70
From manufacturer direct to retailer	30–35

Sales to the co-operative wholesale societies and then to retail societies are included in the sales from manufacturer direct to retailer.

Number of wholesalers and retailers. The number of wholesalers handling these goods in 1938 is estimated at 1,000–1,500 and these wholesalers were mainly grocers' and chemists' wholesalers or sundriesmen. The total number of retailers regularly stocking these goods is estimated at 40–50,000.

Sales by different types of retail outlet. The proportions of the total sales made by different trade types of retail outlet are estimated as follows:

	%
Chemists' shops	17–23
Grocers' shops	70–80
Other shops including department stores	4–6

The proportion of total sales made by the different economic types of outlet, in 1938, are estimated as follows:

	%
Multiple shops and variety chain stores	15–17
Co-operative stores	15–20
Unit retailers	63–70

Sales in grocers' and chemists' multiple branches are both included in the estimate of the proportion of sales made by multiple shops.

The cost of distribution

Practically all these products in 1938 were re-sale price maintained by the manufacturers.

The price at which the goods were sold by manufacturers to wholesalers or retailers varied with the quantity purchased. There were no special terms to buyers according to their trade, that is wholesaler, retailer or multiple organization, but all were entitled to buy at the same price.

The discounts allowed off the retail selling price ranged from 19–20% in the case of the smallest quantities purchased, to 30–32% in the case of the largest quantities purchased.

The margins earned by the various distributors were as follows:

Wholesalers, multiple organizations, variety chain stores, large independent chemists and grocers and co-operative societies would usually purchase at a discount off the retail price of 27–32%. This discount includes cash settlements, which varied between 1¼–2½% for payment in 7 days. The average discount earned on large purchases was about 30%.

Small retailers and retailers purchasing through wholesalers usually obtained a discount of 19–20% off the retail selling price, again including settlements for cash payment or payment within the month.

Wholesalers usually purchased at a discount of 30–32% off the retail price and sold to retailers at 19–20% off the retail price, giving the wholesaler a margin of 13–15% on returns.

The stock turn of wholesalers is estimated at 10–12 times a year and the stock turn of retailers 3–4 times a year.

Manufacturers' distribution costs are estimated at between 40–45% of manufacturers' sales revenue. Advertising represented 35–40% of these costs and delivery, carriage, warehousing and administrative selling costs the remainder.

The total costs of distribution are estimated at 57–63% of retail sales.

CHAPTER XV

ALCOHOLIC BEVERAGES AND TOBACCO

1. BEER, WINES AND SPIRITS SOLD BY ON-LICENCES

Consumers' expenditure and methods of distribution

Consumers' expenditure on beer, wines and spirits sold through on-licences in 1938 is estimated at £237–238 millions (including duty). Of this it is estimated that approximately four-fifths was represented by the sale of home-produced and imported draught and bottled beer, ale, stout, porter and cider, just over one-tenth by the sale of spirits and just under one-tenth by the sale of wines. Imports represented approximately 10% of the total sales of spirits and 90% of the total sales of wine.

The methods of distribution. The proportions of the total on-licence sales of beer, spirits and wines passing through the different channels of distribution in 1938 are estimated for each of the main product groups as follows:

Beer. All draught beer went direct from the brewer to the retail outlet; and 75–80% of bottled beer went direct to retailer, the remainder going from brewer to wholesale bottler and then to retailer. A small proportion of imported beer, about 3% by quantity of the total beer consumed, was distributed through wholesale bottlers and then to retailer.

Beer, draught and bottled, sold in on-licences was distributed approximately as follows:

	%
From brewer direct to retail outlet	94–98
From brewer to wholesaler to retailer	2–6

Home-produced spirits were distributed approximately as follows:

	%
From bottlers to wholesalers to retailers	75–85
From bottlers direct to retailers	15–25

The bottlers and blenders were usually the brand owners and well-known branded lines accounted for a very high proportion of the total sales of home-produced spirits.

In estimating the proportions passing through the two channels, the spirits passing from bottlers and blenders to brewers for sale in retail outlets tied to the brewer have been classed as sales to wholesalers.

A similar definition has been used in the discussion of imported spirits and imported and British wines.

Imported spirits were distributed approximately as follows:

	%
From foreign distillers or bottlers or their agents or brokers to wholesalers and then to retailers	75–85
From foreign distillers or bottlers to wholesalers, then to second wholesalers, then to retailers	13–17
From foreign distillers or bottlers or their agents or brokers to retailers	4–6

It is estimated that four-fifths of imported spirits was shipped by agents or brokers and the remainder by wholesalers. The combination of the agent/wholesaler was very frequent.

Imported wines were distributed approximately as follows:

	%
From foreign growers or their agents to wholesalers to retailers	55–65
From foreign growers to wholesalers to second wholesalers to retailers	27–33
From foreign growers or their agents to retailers	8–12

It is estimated that about one-tenth of imported wines were shipped by agents and the remainder by wholesalers.

British wines. The channels of distribution were approximately as follows:

	%
From producers to wholesalers to retailers	75–85
From producers direct to retailers	15–25

Total sales of liquor. The proportions of total sales of all liquor sold in on-licences in 1938 passing through the main channels of distribution are estimated as follows:

	%
From producers, home or overseas, or the agents of overseas producers, direct to retailers	75–85
From producers, home or overseas, or their agents to wholesalers and then to retailers	16–20
From overseas producers or their agents to wholesalers to second wholesalers to retailers	2

Number of wholesalers and retailers. The number of brokers or agents for imported spirits was approximately 250, and the number of wholesalers who imported and acted as agents for overseas wines was approximately 500. There were some 300 beer bottlers and wholesalers, some of whom were controlled by breweries, and about 2,500–3,000 wholesalers of spirits and wines.

The number of on-licence retail outlets in 1938 was approximately as follows:

Public-houses, railway refreshment rooms and cars	81,000
Hotels, restaurants and theatres	3,250
Registered clubs	18,250

While practically all the hotels, restaurants and clubs were licensed to sell beer, wines and spirits, some 20% of the public-houses were licensed for the sale of beer only.

In addition to these regular on-licence outlets, 'occasional licences' were also granted and these numbered some 36,000 in 1938. These licences were, however, only granted for special occasions and the sales made under them were negligible compared with total on-licence sales.

Tied houses. It is estimated that approximately 90–95% of the public-houses and railway refreshment rooms and cars in England and Wales in 1938 were 'tied'; that is, they were houses owned by brewers and either leased to tenants or run by managers. In both cases there were agreements to buy all or the greater part of their beer from the brewers owning the house. The remaining houses were 'free houses' and were able to purchase beer from whom they pleased. In Scotland, on the other hand, the houses and railway refreshment rooms, numbering some 7,000, were free houses. In all, approximately 67,000 houses in the United Kingdom were tied and the sales of beer by these houses represented approximately 85% of the total retail sales of beer in public-houses. Just under three-quarters of these tied houses it is thought were run by tenants and the remainder by managers. There was a tendency for the larger houses to be run by managers on behalf of a particular brewer. Approximately one-quarter of the hotel, restaurant and theatre group of outlets was tied to brewers. Houses were also tied to brewers for the purchase of spirits and wines, and it is estimated that in the case of spirits the number of outlets which were tied to brewers was 40–41,000, and in the case of wines, 25–30,000.

Of the total sales of beer, spirits and wines, it is estimated that the proportions sold by tied houses were respectively 80%, 55% and 25–30%. Approximately 70–75% of total liquor sales through on-licences were made by tied outlets.

Sales by different types of retail outlet. The proportions of the total sales of liquor in on-licences in 1938 undertaken by the different types of outlet are estimated as follows:

	%
Public-houses, railway refreshment rooms and cars	86–90
Hotels, restaurants and theatres	3–4
Registered clubs	7–10

The sales of beer are estimated to have represented approximately four-fifths of the total turnover of the public-house group, spirits just over 10% and wines under 10%. Beer sales represented about 45% of the total sales of the hotel group, spirits just over 20% and wines about one-third. Beer sales are estimated to have represented just under four-fifths of the total sales of registered clubs, spirits 15–20% and wines about 5%.

The cost of distribution

Retailers' margins on the sale of beer, spirits and wines varied widely according to the type of on-licence. The division of on-licences into the three main categories given above enables the main variations to be allowed for when estimating an average for the trade as a whole. It will be appreciated, however, that within each category there was quite a wide variation in margins, such as the sales in public bars as compared with saloon bars of public-houses, the sales in houses in working-class districts compared with the sales, say, in the West End of London, and the many variations between the different types of registered clubs. An attempt has been made to strike an average within these ranges, but the figures are only approximate.

The margins earned by retailers in on-licences will be considered separately for beer, spirits and wines.

Margins and costs: Beer. On the sale of beer, the margins earned by the different types of retail outlet and the distribution costs incurred by brewers are estimated as follows:

Public-houses. Brewers selling their beer through tied houses usually suggested selling prices for the public in the different bars. These were usually adhered to, and free houses in fixing their prices followed the suggested prices fairly closely.

On draught beer, the retailers' margins in public bars ranged from 16–20%, with an average of 18%. In saloon bars the margins ranged from 25–33% with an average of 28%. The variations in the margins earned by different retailers depended partly on the different proportions of the types of beer sold, the turnover in saloon compared with other bars, and the allowance which had to be made for wastage per barrel. On an estimate that 65–70% of the sales were made in public bars, and that the retailer obtained on an average 284 pints to the barrel, the average margin of public-houses on draught beer was 21–22%.

On bottled beer the margins in public bars ranged from 23–30% with an average of 26%, and in saloon and other bars from 32–35% with an average of 33%. Taking the same proportion of public and other bar sales as in the case of draught beer, the average margin of public-houses on bottled beer was 27–28%. Using an estimate of the sales, by value, of draught and bottled beer at 4 : 1 the average margin earned by the public-house on the sale of beer was 22–23%. It should be noted that houses licensed only for beer usually sold all beer at public-bar prices and that their average was nearer 19%.

Hotels, restaurants and theatres. The margins earned in these outlets were roughly the same as those earned in the saloon bars of public-houses, that is an average of 28% on draught and 33% on bottled. With sales estimated at slightly over one-half on draught and the remainder on bottled beer, the average margin was between 30% and 31%.

Registered clubs. There were very wide variations in the margins earned on the sale of beer in this type of retail outlet. The majority of clubs were working men's clubs, and the usual range of margins in these outlets was 17–22% on the sale of beer with an average of 20%.

Allowing for the varying proportions sold in the different types of outlets, the average retail margin on beer, draught and bottled, was 22–23%.

Brewers' distribution costs varied widely. As a percentage of brewers' turnover, selling costs varied from less than 1–2%, delivery costs from $1\frac{1}{2}$–3%, advertising from less than 1–3%. Brewers' total distribution costs might be taken as 4–5% of their turnover. Where beer went through a wholesaler-bottler the margins earned by the bottler were 8–9% on sales.

Margins and costs: Spirits. On the sales of spirits the margins earned by wholesalers and by the different types of retail outlet and the blenders' and brokers' distribution costs are estimated as follows:

Wholesalers' margins ranged from 3–4% on sales on home-produced spirits to 8% on sales on imported spirits.

Public-houses. The usual range of margins on the sale of spirits 'per nip' was 40–45%. The margin in public bars was sometimes below this figure but it is estimated that 75–80% of sales were in bars other than the public bar, and that the average margin was 42–43%.

Hotels, restaurants and clubs. The margins earned on the sale of spirits in hotels and restaurants and theatres were usually 45–50% and in registered clubs, while there were wide variations, the average margin is estimated to have been 33–40%.

Weighting the margins earned and the sales made in the different types of retail outlet, the average retail margin on the sale of spirits was 42–43%.

Blenders' and bottlers' distribution costs on home-produced spirits are estimated to have ranged from 3–9% on their turnover, with an average of 6%. These costs include transport, selling and advertising. Agents' commissions for imported spirits were about 5% on sales.

Margins and costs: Wines. On the sale of wines, the margins earned by agents and wholesalers and by different types of retail outlet in 1938 are estimated as follows:

Agents and wholesalers. Agents' commission on imported wines ranged from 5–8% on sales and wholesalers' margins from 10–15% on sales. Second wholesalers obtained 4–5% on sales. On British wine the wholesalers' margins were usually 15% on sales.

Retail sales of wine. Publicans' margins varied from 33–45% with an average of 40%. Hotels, restaurants and theatres had a wider range from 33–50% with an average of 45%. The margins on the sale of wine in clubs ranged from 25–40% with an average of 33%.

On the total sales of wines by the different types of retail outlet, the average retail margin was 39–40%.

The wine-makers' distribution costs including advertising, catalogues and other selling costs are estimated at 5–6% of sales revenue. There is considerable difficulty, of course, in making an estimate of the costs incurred on sales to on-licences as distinct from total distribution costs on sales to both on- and off-licences.

The total costs of distribution are estimated at 30–32% of retail sales.

2. BEER, WINES, SPIRITS AND CIDER SOLD BY OFF-LICENCES

Consumers' expenditure and methods of distribution

Consumers' expenditure on beer, wines and spirits sold for consumption off the premises in 1938 is estimated at £59–60 millions. Of the total, it is estimated that beer represented 15–20%, spirits 55–60%, wines 23–27% and cider less than 1%.

Of the spirits, approximately 90% was home-produced, of which one-fifth, by value, was gin and the remainder whisky. Imported spirits were mainly rum and brandy, with some liqueurs and Dutch gin. Just over four-fifths of the wine, by value, was imported, from the Empire (20%) and from other countries.

The methods of distribution. The approximate proportions of the total sales of beer, spirits and wines made through off-licences passing through the different channels of distribution in 1938 are estimated for each main product group as follows:

Beer and cider. About 10% of the beer sold for consumption off the premises was sold through the jug-and-bottle department of on-licences.

Of the remainder, about three-quarters went direct from the brewer to the retail off-licence, either in bottles or barrels, and the balance went from the brewer to wholesale bottler and then to retailer. Some retailers, mainly multiples, bought in barrels and did their own bottling.

About four-fifths, by value, of the cider went from the cider-maker direct to retailers and one-fifth to wholesalers and then to retailers.

Home-produced spirits. Whisky and gin were bottled and blended at various stages of the distributive chain. The approximate proportions and channels of distribution are as follows:

About 65% went from blenders and bottlers of whisky or distillers of gin, who were proprietary brand owners, to wholesalers and then to retailers.

About 15% went from blenders and bottlers of whisky and distillers of gin, who were proprietary brand owners, direct to retailers.

About 5% went from distillers to wholesalers who blended, bottled and branded under their 'own name' brands and sold to retailers.

About 15% went from distillers to retailers, mainly multiple concerns, wine merchants and department stores, who blended, bottled and sold under 'own name' brands.

There was a slight variation between whisky and gin, in that there was less wholesale and retail blending, bottling and branding of gin than of whisky. In this discussion of the channels of distribution the purchases of spirits by tied off-licences from the controlling brewery have been classed as sales passing through wholesalers. A similar classification has been used in the discussion of imported spirits and of wines.

Imported spirits. About 30% was bought by retailers from agents or brokers of overseas distillers or from the distillers direct. It was usual for spirits purchased in this way to be bought in bulk f.o.b. at a foreign port, matured, blended and bottled by retailers, and about one-half of the brandy purchased direct from overseas by retailers was bought in this way. Other spirits were bought in bottle ex-bond in the United Kingdom.

About 60% was bought by retailers from wholesalers who bought in the same way as described above, except that very often wholesalers were also agents for overseas distillers.

About 10% was bought by retailers from wholesalers, who bought from other wholesalers. This occurred mainly with brandy and rum, which were bought in bulk by the first wholesaler, matured, blended, bottled and branded by him and re-sold to a second wholesaler who re-sold to a retailer.

Imported wine. About 40% was bought by retailers from foreign growers or their agents, including importer/wholesalers acting as agents. Empire wines were usually bought from growers, and other overseas wines through agents. All Empire wine and most foreign wine—champagne and château wines being the exceptions—were shipped in bulk and bottled and sometimes matured in the United Kingdom.

About 50% was bought by retailers from wholesalers who bought in the same way as described above for retailers buying direct.

About 10% was bought from wholesalers who bought from other wholesalers.

British wine. Approximately 80% of the sales of British wines in off-licences passed in bulk from the wine-maker to the wholesaler, who usually bottled before re-selling to the retailer. About 20% passed direct from the wine-maker to the retailer.

Total sales of liquor. Of the total sales of all beer, wines, spirits and cider made by off-licences the proportions passing through the main channels of distribution in 1938 are estimated as follows:

	%
From brewer or home or overseas distiller or blender or grower or wine-maker to retailer	37–43
From brewer or home or overseas distiller or grower to wholesaler to retailer	55–60
From overseas distiller or grower to wholesaler to second wholesaler to retailer	2–3

Number of distributors. In 1938 there were approximately 250 brokers or agents for imported spirits, 500 agents, or wholesalers who sometimes acted as agents, for imported wines and 2–2,500 wine and spirit wholesalers who supplied both on- and off-licences. There were approximately 300 wholesale beer bottlers, many of whom were controlled by brewers.

All on-licences were able to sell for consumption off the premises, but it is estimated that sales of this type represented only about 5% of the total off-licence sales.

There were approximately 27,000 licences issued in the United Kingdom for sales off the premises, of which 25,000 were magistrates' licences and 2,000 'dealer' licences. Retailers holding 'dealer' licences could sell to the public only in certain minimum quantities and a number of them were taken out only for the period preceding Christmas. It is thought that they accounted for less than 1% of total sales.

Of the 25,000 magistrates' licences, about 22,000 were in England and Wales, 2,500 in Scotland and 400 in Northern Ireland. Approximately 7–8,000 of these licences were held by retailers selling mainly, and in many cases only, beer, wines and spirits. The remaining licences were held by retailers who sold other goods besides liquor and the most important retailers of this type were the grocers and provision dealers. All off-licences in Scotland were of the latter type.

Of the 7–8,000 retail shops selling mainly, or only, beer, wines and spirits, approximately 1,500–2,000 were multiple wine and spirit dealers and 200–300 were retail wine merchants who had 'offices' rather than shops and 'clients' rather than customers. The 7–8,000 shops are estimated to have undertaken 70–75% of total sales.

The number of 'tied' off-licences is not known with any accuracy. It is thought to be in the region of 750–1,000. Such tied off-licences tended to purchase all their beer from the controlling brewery, but, as in the case of tied on-licences, a smaller proportion of their wines and spirits.

Sales by different types of outlet. The proportion of sales made by different economic type of retail outlet is estimated as follows:

	%
Multiple off-licences	15–20
Department stores and co-operative stores	2–3
Unit retailers	77–83

Included in the sales by multiple shops are a small number of multiple grocers holding licences to sell beer, wines and spirits, but the sales of off-licences owned by breweries are not included.

The cost of distribution

Almost all beer was branded by the brewers, but little was price-maintained. Approximately four-fifths of the home-produced spirits was branded by blenders and bottlers and re-sale prices were fixed. The remainder was branded, but usually was not price-maintained. Imported wines and spirits were all branded, but price maintenance was mostly confined to a small proportion of imported spirits. Some four-fifths of the British wine was branded and price-maintained by the wine-makers.

Margins and costs of distribution. The margins earned by wholesalers, importers and retailers on the sale of beer, spirits and wines in off-licences and the distribution costs incurred by brewers, distillers and wine-makers are estimated for each of the main products in 1938 as follows:

Beer and cider. The retailers' margins on the sale of beer ranged between 25% and 35% on sales, with an average of 30%. The retailers' margins on the sale of cider were between 33–40% with an average of 35%. The margins of wholesale bottlers were approximately 8–9% on sales. Brewers' distribution costs were approximately 4–5% on sales revenue.

Home-produced spirits. On proprietary brands the wholesalers' margins were 3–5% on sales and retailers' margins ranged from 9–12½% on sales, although some multiple retailers might obtain up to 14%. The margins earned by wholesalers and retailers on non-proprietary brands were usually higher than those given above. The combined average wholesalers' and retailers' margins were 14–15% of the retail price. Blenders' and bottlers' distribution costs, including advertising, were approximately 6% on sales revenue.

Imported spirits. Agents' commissions were 3–5% on sales and wholesalers' margins 8–10% on sales. Where there were two wholesalers, the margin split between them was 10–12%. Retailers usually earned a margin of 15% on sales, though in some cases the margin rose to 20% on sales.

Imported wines. On Empire wines wholesalers' margins were 12–15% on sales. Retailers' margins on wines branded by growers, agents or wholesalers ranged between 30–38%. On wines imported and branded by the retailers, their margins ranged between 40% and 50%. The combined margins of wholesalers and retailers of Empire wines averaged 43% of retail selling price.

For other imported wines, agents' commissions were 4–6% on sales and wholesalers' margins 10–15% on sales. Where the higher margin was earned by wholesalers, this was usually split between two wholesalers. On champagne, agents' commissions were 2–3% on sales and wholesalers' margins ranged from 5–10% on sales. Retailers' margins ranged from 25–40%, the latter margin being earned when they imported directly. The retailers' margins on champagne were 15% on well-known branded lines and 20% or more on other lines.

For all imported wines, agents', wholesalers' and retailers' margins, weighted according to the proportions going through different channels and the types of wine sold, were 39–40% of the retail price.

British wines. Wholesalers' margins ranged from 15–20% on sales. Retailers buying from wholesalers earned 20–33% on sales, with an average of 25%. Retailers buying direct from producers earned from 35–50% on sales. The higher margin was earned on the sale of their own brands. The combined margin earned by wholesalers and retailers on British wines was approximately 38% of the retail selling price. Wine-makers' distribution costs on sales to off-licences are estimated at 5–7% of sales revenue.

Stock turn. Wholesalers had an average stock turn on branded spirits of 6 times per year and their stock turn on wine was ½–1 times a year. Retailers' stock turn for beer was weekly or fortnightly and on home-produced spirits monthly. The retailer's stock turn of imported spirits and wines varied according to whether he was also the importer or whether he bought from agents or wholesalers. In the former case he would hold up to 6 months' stock and in the latter case between 1 and 2 months' stock.

The total costs of distribution are estimated at 28–29% of retail sales.

3. TOBACCO AND CIGARETTES

Consumers' expenditure and methods of distribution

Consumers' expenditure on tobacco, cigarettes, cigars and snuff in 1938 is estimated at £177 millions, of which £90 millions represented duty. Cigarettes accounted for £144 millions, tobacco for about £30 millions, and cigars and snuff for less than £3 millions. Practically all the tobacco goods sold were manufactured in the United Kingdom.

The methods of distribution. The proportions of total sales passing through the main channels of distribution in 1938 are estimated as follows:

	%
From manufacturer to wholesaler to retailer	50–55
From manufacturer to retailer	45–50

Included in the sales direct to retailer are the sales by the co-operative wholesale societies to retail co-operative societies, and also the sales by the retail side of mixed wholesale and retail businesses.

Number of wholesalers and retailers. There were approximately 3–4,000 wholesalers of tobacco goods in 1938, that is firms selling tobacco on wholesale terms only, but in addition there were a further 10–12,000 firms who sold both by wholesale and by retail. For probably the greater part of these traders the retail side of their business was the principal one. Both groups include wholesalers who dealt in goods other than tobacco, and the number of specialist tobacco wholesalers was small.

The number of retail outlets for tobacco can be roughly gauged by the number of Tobacco Dealers' Licences issued in 1938—545,000. This figure included the wholesale firms mentioned above, and automatic machines not on premises already licensed, but excludes occasional licences. The retail outlets can be grouped into two broad divisions: those purchasing some or all of their supplies direct from manufacturers and those usually purchasing through wholesalers. The first group, numbering approximately 110–140,000, included most of the wholesaler/retailers mentioned above, specialist tobacconists dealing solely in tobacco goods and tobacconists' sundries, 10–15,000, the larger mixed confectioner/tobacconists, newsagent/tobacconists and hairdresser/tobacconists, 50–60,000, multiple shops in other trades such as grocery and provisions, department stores and other retail outlets which had a fairly large turnover in tobacco goods. Many of these retailers also purchased from wholesalers. The second group, numbering approximately 400–420,000, consisted mainly of the smaller mixed confectioner/tobacconists, newsagent/tobacconists and hairdresser/tobacconists, 50–60,000, licensed premises including on- and off-licences, hotels and clubs, 80–90,000, and grocers, 50–60,000, and the remaining 210–220,000 were general shops, garages, cinemas, canteens, unlicensed restaurants, chemists and automatic machines.

Sales by different types of outlet. The proportions of the total trade in tobacco goods represented by the different trade types of retail outlets are estimated as follows:

	%
Specialist tobacconist shops	12–13
Mixed tobacco and confectionery, newsagents' and hairdressers' shops	28–32
Grocery shops and general shops including co-operatives and department stores	23–27
Licensed premises—on- and off-licences, clubs and hotels	9–13
Other outlets—garages, cinemas, canteens, cafés, restaurants, automatic machines	19–24

The proportions of the total sales made by the different economic types of retail outlet are estimated as follows:

	%
Multiple shops including multiple tobacconists, multiple grocers, multiple tobacconist-confectioners and multiple off-licences	5–7
Co-operative stores	7–9
Unit retailers	84–88

Tied on-licences are not included in the sales by multiple shops. The number of specialist tobacconist multiples is estimated at 1,750–2,250 and they are thought to have done 2–3% of the total trade. Between a fifth and a quarter of the sales of tobacco goods by retail co-operative stores were the products of co-operative manufacturing establishments.

The cost of distribution

Practically all the tobacco goods sold to the private consumer in 1938 were price-maintained by the manufacturer. The exceptions were some cigars and snuff, a small proportion of retailer-manufactured cigarettes and tobacco, some loose tobacco and some imported brands. These represented about 5% of total sales.

The margins earned and allowed to wholesalers and retailers on these goods in 1938 were as follows:

Wholesalers' margins on tobacco goods ranged from 2½–12½% but the average margin on cigarettes was 4% on sales and on tobacco 2½% on sales.

Retailers purchasing from wholesalers earned an average of 17% on sales of cigarettes and 12–14% on sales of tobacco. Retailers purchasing direct from manufacturers earned an average of 20% on sales of cigarettes and 14–15% on sales of tobacco.

The wholesale and retail margins on cigars and snuff were higher than those on tobacco and cigarettes, ranging from 5–10% for wholesalers and 20–30% for retailers.

Bonus and discounts. The estimated average margins on tobacco and cigarettes include the allowances given for prompt settlement, but in addition a number of manufacturers operated bonus or deferred discount schemes under which payments were made, usually half-yearly, to participating firms on the basis of their purchases over a certain period. Almost all the wholesalers took part in these schemes which, on average, represented an addition of ½–1½% to their gross margin. Retailers were also eligible and the bonus earned by those participating, usually the retailers who purchased direct from manufacturers, represented an average addition of 1% to their gross margin.

Stock turn. The average stock turn of wholesalers on cigarettes and tobacco is estimated at between 15–30 times a year or 10 to 20 days, and that of retailers 17–26 times a year.

Manufacturers' distribution costs varied widely between manufacturers. Almost all manufacturers maintained their own sales organization, employed travellers, advertised widely and paid carriage and transport on most of the goods despatched. For the whole trade, manufacturers' distribution costs including administrative selling costs, salesmen's salaries, carriage and packing and advertising, are estimated at 5–7% of manufacturers' sales revenue, of which advertising represented 3–4%.

The total costs of distribution are estimated at 24–26% of retail sales.

CHAPTER XVI

COAL AND HOUSEHOLD STORES

I. COAL

Consumers' expenditure and methods of distribution

Consumers' expenditure. The expenditure by domestic consumers in 1938 on household coal, anthracite and boiler fuel is estimated at £97–98 millions, the quantity bought being approximately 43 million tons. This estimate excludes miners' coal.

Types of distributor. There were four main types of private trader engaged in the distribution of domestic coal in 1938, that is, collieries, factors, large merchants, and small merchants, dealers or traders.

Collieries usually sold direct to factors or merchants at the pithead, but in some instances, for example the Lancashire Associated Collieries and the South Staffordshire Associated Collieries, retail selling networks were maintained by the colliery. Factors or wholesalers acted as intermediaries between the colliery and the small merchant, dealer or casual trader. The smaller retailers had not the finance, the turnover or in many cases the knowledge, to purchase direct from collieries, and by purchasing from factors they could obtain the necessary range of different grades of coal. In some instances factors acted, in effect, as selling agencies for particular collieries. Large merchants usually bought direct from collieries and maintained order offices and railhead depots. A number of large merchants undertook some wholesaling, that is, re-sale to smaller merchants and dealers, although their primary concern was with retail sales direct to the public. The smaller merchant, dealer or casual trader usually obtained his supplies, as suggested above, from factors or large merchants, but in the producing areas, up to a radius of approximately 30 miles round the pithead, the small dealers and others found it economical to purchase direct at the pithead in lorry-loads. The Scottish Co-operative Wholesale Society and the Co-operative Wholesale Society purchased direct from collieries, and the latter also sold from their own pits. The retail societies purchased most of their coal through the wholesale societies, although a certain proportion was also purchased either direct from collieries or through private factors.

The methods of distribution. The proportions of the total sales of domestic coal passing through the different channels of distribution in 1938 are estimated as follows:

	%
From colliery land-sale depots to merchants or dealers and then to consumer or by colliery selling organizations direct to consumer	6–8
From colliery by sea to wholesaler (factor or large merchant) and then to small merchant or direct to consumer	6–8
From colliery by rail to wholesaler (factor or large merchant) and then to small merchant or direct to consumer	84–88

Approximately half of the sales from colliery land-sale depots were distributed through a colliery selling organization and the remainder by merchants.

By weight, 38–39 million tons are estimated to have passed from collieries by rail and sea to factors or large merchants, and just over one-half, or 19–21 million tons, was re-sold to other retail distributors. The remainder was sold by merchants direct to the consumer.

Of the estimated 19–21 million tons passing through wholesalers $4\frac{1}{2}$–5 million tons were sold by the co-operative wholesale societies to retail co-operative societies, and the remainder, 15–16 million tons, was sold by factors or large merchants to small retailers. It is estimated that 'pure' factors, that is factors who only sold full truck-loads to merchants and dealers and did not undertake retail sales to the consumer, handled 6–8 million tons of the 15–16 million tons sold by factors or large merchants to retailers, and the remainder, 8–9 million tons, was sold by large merchants to retailers.

Of the 18–19 million tons sold direct by collieries to retail merchants, omitting the sales by colliery land-sale depots, approximately 17 million tons went from colliery to large merchants and $1\frac{1}{2}$–2 million tons was sold by collieries to retail co-operative societies. A small proportion of these purchases by retail co-operative societies was made through factors.

The proportions of total sales of household coal passing through the main channels of distribution in 1938 can therefore be estimated approximately as follows:

	%
From colliery to wholesaler to retailer	34–40
From colliery direct to retailer and colliery direct to consumer	60–66

In terms of tonnage a slightly higher proportion of total output passed through the second main channel of distribution. The sales by collieries to co-operative wholesale societies, 4½–5 million tons, have been included as sales direct to retailer.

Number of wholesalers and retailers. The number of retailers of household coal in 1938 is not known with any accuracy, but is estimated at between 25–30,000. This total includes 740 retail co-operative societies engaged in the coal trade. Some 8–10,000 of these retailers were merchants, in the sense of usually operating from depots, being regularly engaged in the coal trade and in most, though not all, cases purchasing in full truck-loads direct from collieries, and the remainder were dealers and casual traders, that is retailers who usually bought in lorry-loads from factors, merchants or wholesale depots, undertook only small sales of domestic coal, or were engaged intermittently in the trade. There were approximately 300–400 factors of domestic coal, and probably as many as 5,000 merchants undertook some wholesaling of coal. In many cases this was not a regular feature of their business.

Sales by different types of outlet. The proportions of the total sales of coal undertaken by the different types of retail outlet are estimated for 1938 as follows:

	%
Dealers or casual traders	23–27
Merchants	56–63
Co-operative societies	13–14
Colliery land-sale depots and colliery retail networks	1–3

In addition to these outlets there was a small sale of coal, coke and anthracite in paper cartons by grocery and hardware shops. About 15% of the total sales are estimated to have been made by organizations, including collieries, possessing a number of branches, order offices and depots for retail sale. These may be classed as multiple organizations.

The cost of distribution

The cost of distribution of household coal in the country as a whole in 1938 is difficult to estimate with any accuracy, owing to the wide variations of both the pit-head price and the retail price of household coal in different areas. For example, the average retail price of coal varied from 36s. in the Northern colliery area to 57–58s. in South-Eastern England, and the pit-head price varied from 20s. to 27s. per ton at different collieries. The large number of different grades of coal and variations in the prices charged by different types of retailers add to the complications. The following estimates of distributive costs on household coal in 1938 are attempts to give a general picture of the margins earned as far as the available information allows.

The wholesaler, the factor or the large merchant acting as a factor earned a margin varying from 6d. to 3s. a ton. The margin would vary according to the particular services rendered by the factor to the retail dealer and according to the price of the coal. The average margin is thought to have ranged between 1s. 6d. to 1s. 9d. per ton.

The merchant buying direct from the colliery and selling to the domestic consumer obtained a margin ranging widely from 10–20s. per ton. The average is estimated to be 14–15s.

The dealers or casual traders purchasing their coal from factors or large merchants again earned widely varying margins. Sometimes it was as low as 5–6s. a ton and in others 15–17s. a ton. The average is estimated at between 11s. 6d. and 13s. 6d. per ton.

The cost of transport of coal from the pit-head to the merchant depot clearly varied with the region served, and for the country as a whole the average transport costs on domestic coal, including wagon hire, are estimated at 8–9s. a ton. This charge was paid by the factor and by large merchants, though in some instances coal was bought at a price inclusive of delivery to the merchant's depot.

The average pit-head price of domestic coal in 1938 is estimated at 22–24s. per ton and the average retail price at 45–47s. per ton. Transport costs on domestic coal it is estimated averaged 17–18% of the retail selling price, and merchants' margins, when buying direct from the colliery and selling to the domestic consumer, 30–33%. The margin of the factors, or large merchants acting as factors, averaged 5% on sales or 3–4% of the retail selling price, and the margin of the dealer or casual trader purchasing coal from the wholesaler averaged 26–29% of the retail selling price. These estimates relate to national averages and would not, of course, for the reasons given above, necessarily apply to the position in particular areas.

The colliery selling costs on household coal are difficult to distinguish from the total selling costs of the colliery including those incurred on sales of industrial coal. It is estimated that—apart from collieries which maintained a retail selling network—the distribution costs of household coal incurred by the collieries, that is administrative selling costs and salesmen's salaries, were rarely higher than 2% of the sales revenue on household coal. In some instances, as suggested above, factors undertook the rôle of selling agents for the colliery.

The total costs of distribution are estimated at 48–51% of retail sales.

2. KEROSENE (PARAFFIN)

Consumers' expenditure and methods of distribution

Consumers' expenditure on kerosene in 1938 is estimated at £4·8 millions, representing about 115 million gallons. This estimate excludes the purchase of approximately 40 million gallons by railways and other industrial users, and of a further 47 million gallons of vaporizing oil for power purposes. Of the 115 million gallons sold for domestic use, approximately 25 million gallons were of premier grade.

The methods of distribution. The large distributors delivered in bulk by road tank wagon to retailers, mainly general stores, ironmongers and hawkers. Some garages also retailed kerosene. Distribution was combined as far as possible with the distribution of petrol and lubricating oil. A very small proportion, probably less than 5%, was sold to wholesalers who redistributed to retailers.

The cost of distribution

There were no fixed retail prices to the public in 1938, although the large distributors fixed wholesale prices for different zones throughout the country. There were differences in price between the zones of up to 1½d. a gallon for bulk delivery through hose. The average price paid by the consumer in 1938 for ordinary grades was 9½d. a gallon and on premier grades 1d. or 2d. more.

Purchase terms to dealers. The average wholesale spot price of the ordinary grade of kerosene for delivery in bulk (minimum quantity a 20-gallon lot) was 7¼d. per gallon, and when it was delivered from the hose in 200-gallon lots or more an additional rebate of ¾d. a gallon was given. Large retailers were granted contract rebates for their total requirements at the rate of ½d. per gallon on 15,000 gallons per annum and over, and ¾d. a gallon on 50,000 gallons per annum and over. About 20% of the sales were made on contract terms. The premier grade of kerosene was marketed by most of the large distributors at a differential of 1d. per gallon.

The wholesalers purchasing from distributing companies and re-selling to retailers would usually earn near-maximum rebates and re-sell at the spot price given above. This gave them a margin on sales of 10–15%.

The retailers' margin ranged from 23–35% and averaged 25–27% of the retail price.

Retailers kept only small stocks of kerosene and the average stock turn is estimated at 20–26 times a year.

The distribution cost incurred by the distributing companies is estimated at approximately 20% of the retail price.

The total costs of distribution are estimated at 44–48% of retail sales.

3. MATCHES

Consumers' expenditure and methods of distribution

Consumers' expenditure on matches in 1938 is estimated at between £10–11 millions. Some 45% of the matches sold in the United Kingdom in that year were imported, and the remainder home-manufactured. The duty on home-manufactured matches in 1938 was 4s. 2d. per gross and on imported matches 4s. 4d. per gross; that is, between 33% and 40% of consumers' expenditure on matches in 1938 was represented by duty.

The methods of distribution. The proportions of total sales passing through the main channels of distribution in 1938 are estimated as follows:

	%
From manufacturer or importer to wholesaler and then to retailer	66–70
From manufacturer or importer direct to retailer	30–34

Included in the sales direct to retailer are the sales to depots of multiple organizations, as well as split deliveries to branches, and the sales to the co-operative wholesale societies.

Number of wholesalers and retailers. There were probably more retail outlets for matches than for any other consumer good except tobacco. Grocers and tobacconists were, of course, the main outlets for the sales of these goods, but they were also sold in a large number of shops handling ironmongery, hardware and general goods. It is thought that there were in the region of 500,000 retail outlets for matches. The sales in grocers' and tobacconists' shops were about equal. The wholesalers handling matches numbered 6–8,000 and were, for the most part, either wholesale grocers, wholesale tobacconists, wholesale/retail tobacconists or wholesale tobacconist/confectioners.

Sales by different types of retail outlet. The proportions of total sales made by different economic types of retail outlet in 1938 are estimated as follows:

	%
Multiple shops including tobacconists, grocers and variety chain stores	14–16
Co-operative shops	9–11
Unit retailers	73–77

The cost of distribution

Most of the matches sold in 1938 were sold at a uniform retail price and in many instances the retail price was fixed or suggested by the manufacturer or importer. A proportion of the sales, however, were made at prices below the general retail price, particularly where retail sales in large quantities were made.

The margins earned by wholesalers and retailers were as follows:

The wholesaler earned a margin of 8% on his cost price.

The retailer purchasing either from wholesalers or direct from manufacturer or importer earned a margin of 25% on his cost price. No special terms were given for bulk purchases from manufacturers.

The settlement discounts usually allowed were 2½% for payment within a fortnight, and all wholesalers and the majority of retailers earned this cash discount. Allowance has been made for this cash discount in the above margins.

The distribution costs of manufacturers and importers, including warehousing, carriage and packing, advertising, selling and office costs amounted to just over 5% of sales revenue. Of this total, advertising represented just over one-quarter.

The total costs of distribution are estimated at 27–28% of retail sales.

4. SOAP

Consumers' expenditure and methods of distribution

Consumers' expenditure on soap in 1938 is estimated at £27–28 millions. This estimate excludes the purchase of soap and soap flakes by commercial and industrial users. Approximately one-third by value was hard soap, one-third soap powders, just under one-sixth toilet soap, just over one-tenth soap flakes, and the remainder scourers and shaving soap.

The methods of distribution. The proportions of total sales of soap, soap powder, and soap flakes passing through the main channels of distribution in 1938 are estimated as follows:

	%
From manufacturer to retailer	75–80
From manufacturer to wholesaler to retailer	20–25

Included in the sales direct to retailers are the sales by the co-operative wholesale societies to retail co-operative societies.

Number of wholesalers and retailers. There were approximately 2,000–2,500 wholesalers who regularly handled soap in 1938, and the number of retail outlets is estimated at 200–250,000. This estimate excludes sales of soap by barrow-men.

Direct sales from manufacturer to retailer covered some 125,000 outlets, the remaining outlets being supplied by wholesalers, though some retailers would purchase both from manufacturers and from wholesalers. Soap was normally a subsidiary to other lines and this is illustrated by the size-grouping of direct accounts of one leading company in 1938. Of 58,000 direct accounts, in the case of 42,000, or 70%, the yearly purchases of soap from the manufacturer were under £20. A further 10,000 accounts made yearly purchases between £20 and £40, and a further 5,000 accounts yearly purchases between £40 and £100.

Sales by different types of outlet. The proportion of total sales made by the different trade types of outlet are estimated as follows:

	%
Grocers and provision dealers	75–80
Chemists	8–10
Other shops, including variety chain stores, department stores, ironmongers, hardware dealers, oilmen and chandlers and hairdressers	12–15

The grocers sold mainly hard soap, soap powders and soap flakes and under half of the toilet soap. Chemists confined their sales almost exclusively to toilet and shaving soap and were responsible for approximately half of the total sales of these goods.

The proportions of the total sales of soap made by different economic types of outlet in 1938 are estimated as follows:

	%
Multiple shops, including variety chain stores	23–26
Co-operative stores	17–20
Department stores	1–3
Unit retailers	51–59

Of the soap sold by co-operative societies, 60–70% was represented by the production of wholesale societies, the remainder being purchased from outside manufacturers.

The cost of distribution

Approximately two-thirds of the hard soap and between 80–90% of the soap powders, flakes and toilet soap were branded by manufacturers or wholesalers in 1938 and almost all these products carried a 'suggested' retail price. This price was usually accepted by the retailer, although in some areas selling under the 'suggested' price was common. The extent of 'cutting' also varied according to the type of soap. Hard soaps were generally cut more frequently than other kinds, and toilet soaps least of all. The small proportion of soap sold under retailers' and wholesalers' 'own name' brands was mostly hard soap.

The wholesale margins varied as between the grocer's and the chemist's trade. The grocery wholesalers usually obtained a margin of 2½–9% on sales, and the chemists' wholesalers 10–12½% on sales. These margins include allowances for cash discounts and bonus payments or volume rebates where given. In practice the different terms applied to different types of soap, the grocery wholesalers' margin applying to hard soap, soap flakes and powders, and the chemists' wholesalers' applying to toilet soap. The wide range of margins in the case of grocery wholesalers is a reflection of the existence of wholesalers who cut prices and also of the variations in the different discounts allowed. The average margin of grocery wholesalers was approximately 4–6%.

The retail margins. Grocers and general retailers purchasing from wholesalers earned margins ranging from 14–17% on sales, the lower margins being earned on hard soap and powders and the higher margins on toilet soap. Chemists purchasing toilet soap from wholesalers obtained margins varying widely from 10–42% on sales, the usual margin being round about 25% on sales. The actual terms given by wholesalers to retailers tended to vary according to the size of the order placed.

Retailers purchasing direct from manufacturers usually received a discount graduated according to the size of order, although this was sometimes replaced by a deferred bonus based on total purchases over a period. In addition, a cash discount was usual, ranging from 2½–7½% for payment in 28 days. These variations in volume discounts and cash discounts tended to be balanced by corresponding differences in the starting list price and there was broad agreement between manufacturers as to the net selling prices and margins allowed to retailers. These margins, including rebates, bonus payments and discounts were as follows:

On hard soap, soap powders and soap flakes, retailers' margins ranged from 16–30% of retail price. The highest margins were earned on unbranded soaps. The average retail margin was approximately 20% on sales.

On toilet and shaving soap, the margins earned by grocers and general retailers ranged from 21–36% with an average of 23–25% of retail price.

The retail margins earned by chemists varied widely from 21–42% on sales, but the average was 25–28% on sales.

The highest margins in this group were earned on some soaps listed by the Proprietary Articles Trade Association. In addition to a basic margin of 25–33% some manufacturers of these soaps allowed discounts of 7½–17½% for bulk purchases or window display and up to 5% for cash settlement.

Stock turn. The average stock turn of soap of retail chemists and grocers was 7–8 times a year.

Manufacturers' distribution costs varied with the sales policy of particular manufacturers and with the type of soap. In the case of manufacturers producing unadvertised goods and selling to a local market, their distribution costs, including selling and transport, were rarely over 10–15%, and the greater part of this would be represented by selling costs as these tended to be high on the unbranded and unadvertised soap. But in the case of manufacturers selling mainly direct to retailers and selling a heavily advertised line such as toilet soap, distribution costs, including advertising, gift coupons, free samples, selling and transport, would amount to 40–45% of sales revenue. These cases were exceptional and the costs of distribution of most types of soap ranged from 15–35% of sales revenue with an average for the trade as a whole of 24–25%. The main factor accounting for these differences in manufacturers' distribution costs was advertising, which ranged from 10–30% of sales revenue, while selling and transport costs showed smaller variations of from 5–7½% in the former case and from 2½–4% in the latter.

The total distribution costs are estimated at 39–41% of retail sales.

5. CANDLES AND NIGHTLIGHTS

Consumers' expenditure and methods of distribution

Consumers' expenditure on candles and nightlights in 1938 is estimated at £900,000, of which just over three-quarters was represented by the purchase of candles.

The methods of distribution. The proportions of the total sales passing through the main channels of distribution are estimated as follows:

	%
From manufacturer to wholesaler to retailer	37–43
From manufacturer direct to retailer	57–63

Included in the sales direct to retailer are the sales to multiple organizations, whether to head office or by split deliveries, and sales by the co-operative wholesale societies to retail societies.

Number of wholesalers and retailers. The number of wholesalers handling candles and nightlights is estimated at 1,500–2,000, of which the majority were grocery and hardware wholesalers and factors. Some chemist's wholesalers also handled nightlights. The number of retail outlets is estimated at approximately 100,000, of which just over two-thirds were grocers' shops. Other shops selling these goods were hardware stores, chemists' (mainly selling nightlights), and variety chain stores.

Sales by different types of retail outlet. The proportions of the total trade undertaken by the different economic types of retail outlet in 1938 are estimated as follows:

	%
Multiple shops, including multiple grocers, chemists, hardware shops and variety chain stores	18–22
Co-operative stores	10–15
Unit retailers	63–72

The cost of distribution

Candles and nightlights were not price-maintained in 1938. Occasionally candles were sold at or about cost price in order to encourage the sale of other goods.

The margins earned by wholesalers and retailers in 1938 are estimated as follows:

Wholesalers earned a margin of 4½–6% on sales.

Unit retailers, whether purchasing direct from manufacturers or from wholesalers, usually worked to an on-cost of 20% or 16–17% on sales. The margins earned by chemists on the sale of nightlights were usually higher, ranging from 25–30% on sales.

Multiple organizations and co-operative wholesale societies usually purchased on wholesale terms.

Settlement discounts. Wholesalers and retailers purchasing direct from manufacturers were usually entitled to a settlement discount of 2½% for payment in the month.

Manufacturers' distribution costs. There was a wide difference between the distribution costs incurred by manufacturers producing for the national market and those producing for local sale. For the whole trade, manufacturers' distribution costs, including carriage, packing and transport, sales promotion, administrative expenses and advertising, are estimated to have averaged 20–24% of sales revenue. Of this total, nearly two-thirds was represented by carriage, packing and transport, and under one-tenth by advertising.

The total costs of distribution are estimated at 40–42% of retail sales.

6. HOUSEHOLD POLISHES AND STORES

Consumers' expenditure and methods of distribution

The main constituents of this commodity group are boot, floor, furniture and metal polishes, black lead, starch and blues.

Consumers' expenditure on this group of goods cannot be calculated with any close degree of accuracy, but it is suggested that in 1938 it was of the order of £6–9 millions.

The methods of distribution. The proportions of total sales passing through the main channels of distribution in 1938 are estimated as follows:

	%
From manufacturer to wholesaler to retailer	60–70
From manufacturer direct to retailer	30–40

Included in the sales direct to retailer are the sales to multiple shops whether delivered to a central depot or by split deliveries to branches, and sales by co-operative wholesale societies to retail societies.

There were important variations in the methods of distribution between different manufacturers and between the different commodities in this group. For example, in the case of boot and shoe polish, approximately 75–80% was sold through wholesalers, whereas in the case of furniture polish, blues and starch, only about half was sold through wholesalers.

Number of wholesalers and retailers. The number of wholesalers handling these commodities is estimated at 3–4,000. Almost all grocery, boot and shoe and hardware wholesalers and factors carried some stock of these products. The number of retail outlets for these goods in 1938 is estimated at 75–100,000. These included grocers, hardware shops, boot and shoe shops, boot and shoe repairers, multiple chemists and variety chain stores. Grocers were the most important outlet, being responsible for 60–70% of the total sales of these goods.

Multiple shops, including multiple grocers, boot and shoe shops and variety chain stores, are estimated to have undertaken 15–19% of the total sales, and co-operative stores 10–15%.

The cost of distribution

The majority of these goods were price-maintained and branded and, in many instances, nationally advertised with the price. Selling under the fixed retail price was, however, quite common.

The margins earned by the various distributors in 1938 are estimated as follows:

Wholesalers. The make-up of the margin earned by wholesalers varied with the policy of the different manufacturers. In some instances, for example metal polishes, a straight discount of 10–12½% on wholesale selling price was given without any volume rebates, and a cash discount of 2½% for payment in the month. In other cases, particularly on boot and shoe and floor polishes, wholesalers' margins were determined by the quantity purchased. These volume rebates ranged from 10% on an order of £3 value to 17½% for an order of £10 or £12 and upwards. The average margin for wholesalers purchasing under volume rebate terms was 15–17½% on sales. The majority of wholesalers earned the maximum rebate terms.

Retailers purchasing through wholesalers earned margins averaging 25–30% on sales. In a few instances they were under 25% and in some cases rose to 33⅓%.

Volume rebates were paid on a number of lines, particularly in the case of boot and shoe, floor and furniture polishes, and retailers were entitled to rebates ranging from 2½–12½%. The average volume discount earned was 5–6%. Occasionally these volume rebates could be earned on purchases through wholesalers, but generally they were earned only by retailers purchasing direct from manufacturers.

The average gross margin earned by unit retailers purchasing direct from manufacturers, including volume rebates but not settlement discounts, was just over 31% on sales. Settlement discounts to retailers were the same as those to wholesalers, 2½% for payment in the month.

Multiple organizations. The margins earned by multiple organizations varied according to the policy of the manufacturer. In some instances they bought at wholesale terms and were entitled to wholesale volume rebates where given, in others they bought at retail terms, plus the full volume discount for quantity purchases. The average gross margin earned by multiple organizations was in the region of 40% of the retail selling price.

The stock turn of wholesalers was between 8–12 times a year and that of retailers 3–5 times a year.

Manufacturers' distribution costs on these goods varied between different manufacturers, but taking the trade as a whole they are estimated at between 15–20% of sales revenue. Of this, carriage and transport averaged between 3–5%, selling costs, mainly salesmen's salaries and administrative costs, 6–7%, and advertising between 4% and 12%.

The total distribution costs are estimated at 47–51% of retail sales.

CHAPTER XVII

FURNITURE AND FURNISHINGS

I. FURNITURE

Consumers' expenditure and methods of distribution

Consumers' expenditure on household furniture in 1938 is estimated at £63–64 millions. Included in this total are bedroom and dining-room furniture, chairs, upholstered furniture, occasional furniture, and hearth, wicker, and kitchen furniture. Excluded from this estimate are purchases by hotels and commercial firms and consumers' expenditure on soft furnishings, floor coverings and office furniture.

The methods of distribution. The main channels of distribution of household furniture in 1938 and the proportions of total sales passing through them are estimated as follows:

	%
From manufacturer to retailer	73–82
From manufacturer to wholesaler to retailer	10–15
Through manufacturers' wholesale departments to retailer	4–6
From manufacturer direct to consumer	3–7

Included in the sales from manufacturer direct to retailer are sales by the co-operative wholesale societies to retail co-operative societies and sales to retailers through independent agents. Such agents generally acted for a number of small manufacturers who did not maintain travelling staffs.

The trade handled by the independent wholesalers was, to a considerable extent, made up of imported furniture and items of occasional furniture. There was a substantial demand for the latter, but production was largely in the hands of small manufacturers whose turnover did not justify direct-to-retailer sales. Some wholesalers provided showrooms for the display of furniture produced by the smaller manufacturers.

Some manufacturers bought special lines from other manufacturers to give variety to their showrooms and catalogues. In some instances large manufacturers performed some final manufacturing processes on these goods.

The sales from manufacturer direct to the consumer include the producer/retailer sales of cabinet-makers and carpenters, the sales made by manufacturers' mail order departments and the sales made by manufacturers to the public through the retailer acting as an agent. The last named were known as 'intro' sales; the retailers' customer made his selection in the manufacturers' showrooms and the goods were usually sent direct to the private address, but the contractual arrangements were between the private customer and the retailer on the one hand and the retailer and the manufacturer on the other. This type of selling arrangement was also used between retailers and wholesalers.

Number of wholesalers and retailers. The number of furniture wholesalers in 1938 is estimated at 100, but there may have been up to double that number handling some furniture. The number of retailers regularly selling and stocking furniture is estimated at 10–12,000. This includes department stores and co-operative retail stores selling furniture. In addition, a proportion of kitchen furniture was sold through ironmongers.

Sales by different types of retail outlet. Of the total sales of furniture, excluding the sales direct to the consumer, the proportions handled by the different economic types of outlet in 1938 are estimated as follows:

	%
Multiple furniture shops	28–32
Department stores	13–17
Co-operative stores	6–8
Unit retailers	43–53

The cost of distribution

In very few instances did the manufacturer fix or suggest the retail selling price of the goods, and wholesalers and retailers usually worked to an on-cost depending on the type of furniture and the state of the market.

The margins earned by the various distributors of furniture in 1938 are estimated as follows:

Wholesalers usually bought from manufacturers at a discount of 5–12½% off the normal price charged by manufacturers to retailers. The average discount was 10%. But there were many instances in which the manufacturers who sold to wholesalers did not normally sell to retailers, and the wholesaler in these cases re-sold to retailers at an on-cost varying from 15–33⅓%. The usual on-cost was in the region of 20–25%, giving the wholesaler 17–20% on returns.

Retailers worked to an on-cost of 50–75%. In a few instances an on-cost of 100% was charged, but the average was between 50–60%. These margins applied generally whether the goods were purchased direct from manufacturers, wholesalers or agents but the average conceals wide variation, as it was a normal practice for retailers to vary on-costs in order to attract purchasers.

Agents. The commission earned by independent agents who acted for small manufacturers and sold direct to retailers was usually 2½–3% on sales. The retailer selling goods by the 'introduction' of his customer to the manufacturer or wholesaler, and who did not physically handle the furniture, received the normal retail margin less 10–15%.

Volume discounts on a sliding scale based on turnover were a common practice in some sections of the trade. In some instances the discount was 10% at the top of the scale.

Settlement discounts. In addition to these basic margins, manufacturers usually allowed settlement discounts which ranged from 2½–3¾% for payment of the account within the month. Larger purchasers, for example multiple organizations, obtained a discount of 5%, and, for payment in 7 days, sometimes an extra 1¼%.

The stock turn of specialist retailers averaged 2½–3 times a year. Multiple shops had a higher average stock turn, 4–5 times a year.

Manufacturers' distribution costs. The manufacturers usually paid transport costs from the factory to the wholesaler or the retailers. These costs varied according to the extent to which a national or a regional market was covered and, for the trade as a whole, are estimated to have averaged 5–6% of sales revenue. Most of the direct advertising of furniture was undertaken by the retailer, although there were a few lines, such as arm-chairs and mattresses, which were branded and advertised by manufacturers. The main selling costs of manufacturers were represented by charges for the annual trade fairs, the upkeep of permanent showrooms and warehouses, salesmen's salaries, and catalogues. Manufacturers also found it necessary to give retailers extended credit, owing to the importance of hire purchase in this trade, and the cost of this service, with allowance for bad debts, was considerable.

Total manufacturers' costs of distribution, including transport, sales promotion, stockholding and the provision of credit facilities, is estimated at 17–20% of sales revenue.

Hire purchase. It is estimated that at least 60% of furniture was sold on hire-purchase terms in 1938, while multiple furniture shops made about 90% of their sales in this way. On hire-purchase sales the retailer generally added 100–125% to the wholesale price.

The total costs of distribution are estimated at 49–51% of retail sales.

2. FURNISHING FABRICS

Consumers' expenditure and methods of distribution

Consumers' expenditure on furnishing fabrics in 1938 was approximately

£10 millions. Purchases of furnishing fabrics by manufacturers and by large users such as hotels and institutions and shipping and railway companies have been excluded from the estimate given above, which refers only to furnishing fabrics purchased by domestic consumers.

The methods of distribution. The proportions of these goods passing direct to retailers and through wholesalers shown as percentages of total retail sales in 1938 are estimated as follows:

	%
From manufacturer (merchant converter or merchant producer) direct to retailer	35–40
From manufacturer to wholesaler to retailer	60–65

No very clear-cut distinction can be drawn between manufacturers and wholesalers in this trade. Some manufacturers wholesaled goods purchased from other manufacturers, while a number of wholesalers took an active part in the production of lines made to their own specifications and designs.

Furnishing fabrics fall into two broad groups. Approximately three-quarters of total sales represented furnishing drapery, standardized lines which were mainly distributed by merchant converters to wholesalers. Some of the larger retailers however bought direct from merchant converters, and some did their own converting. The remaining quarter comprised the more exclusive lines produced by the specialist manufacturers and merchant producers which were sold largely direct to retailers, mainly to the department stores and specialist furnishing shops.

Number of retailers. Furnishing drapery was sold by department stores, speciality furnishing shops and by some general drapers. The sale of the more exclusive lines was restricted, for the most part, to the larger department stores and the specialist retailers. The number of shops selling furnishing fabrics in 1938 is estimated at 12–14,000, of which approximately 1,500 were multiple shops.

Sales by different types of retail outlet. The estimated proportions of the total sales in 1938 undertaken by shops grouped by economic type were:

	%
Multiple shops	16–20
Department stores	25–30
Co-operative shops	3–5
Unit retailers	45–56

The cost of distribution

Re-sale price maintenance in this trade was negligible.

The margins earned by wholesalers and retailers in 1938 have been estimated as follows:

Wholesalers' margins ranged from 12% on sales of the cheapest fabrics to 20% on the most exclusive lines; the average margin for the trade as a whole being in the region of 15–17%.

Retailers usually worked to a mark-up of 50% on cost on the higher-priced lines and from 33–50% on cost on furnishing drapery. The average realized margin obtained was approximately 30% on sales.

Settlement discounts were usually 3–3¾% for payment in 7 days, 2½% in a month.

Stock turn. The larger retailers, including certain multiple shops and department stores, turned over their stock 5–6 times a year, the smaller retailers 3–4 times.

Manufacturers' or converters' distribution costs. These costs, covering salesmen's salaries, pattern books, packaging and transport, advertising, and general administrative selling costs, varied according to whether a particular manufacturer sold largely direct to retailers or distributed through wholesalers. In the former case the costs are estimated to have averaged 14–16% of manufacturers' sales revenue and in the latter 3–5%.

The total costs of distribution are estimated at 44–46% of retail sales.

3. HOUSEHOLD TEXTILES AND SOFT FURNISHINGS

Consumers' expenditure and methods of distribution

Consumers' expenditure on household textiles and soft furnishings in 1938 is estimated at £24–25 millions, approximately £11 millions of which represented purchases of sheets, pillow-cases and towels, £6 millions blankets and the balance household linens, cushions, mattress ticking, curtains and blinds.

An attempt has been made to exclude purchases by hospitals, institutions and hotels from this estimate.

The methods of distribution. The main channels of distribution and the proportion passing through each in 1938 expressed as percentages of retail sales are estimated as follows:

	%
From manufacturer or converter direct to retailer	40–45
From manufacturer or converter to wholesaler to retailer	55–60

Sales to the central depots or warehouses of multiple organizations and sales by the wholesale co-operative societies to retail societies are included above in sales direct to retailers. The sales of goods through mail order houses have been classed as sales direct to retailer, as these houses usually purchased direct from manufacturers or converters and in effect acted as retailing organizations.

The large department stores, the buying groups for smaller stores and the multiple organizations bought substantial quantities of household textiles, particularly sheets and towels, direct from manufacturers.

Sales to smaller retailers were made mainly through wholesalers but a number of manufacturers of well-known brands of sheets, towels and blankets also distributed direct to small retailers.

Number of and sales by different types of retail outlet. Household textiles and soft furnishings were sold by 15–20,000 shops including drapers, department stores, retail co-operatives, and retailers specializing in the sale of furnishings. Variety chain stores usually sold only the smaller textiles such as tea-towels.

The estimated proportions of the total sales in 1938 undertaken by shops grouped by economic type were:

	%
Multiple shops and variety chain stores	10–15
Co-operative shops	3–6
Department stores	25–30
Unit retailers	52–59

The cost of distribution

Although branding was common in the case of sheets, towels and blankets, retail price maintenance was negligible.

The margins earned by wholesalers and retailers in 1938 can be summarized as follows:

Wholesalers' margins ranged from 13–17% on sales, the average realized margin being near 15%.

Retailers obtained margins ranging from $27\frac{1}{2}$–36% on returns, the average realized margin for the trade being estimated at 30%.

Settlement discounts were usually $3\frac{3}{4}$% for payment in 7 days, $2\frac{1}{2}$% in the month.

Stock turn. Retail stock turn averaged 3–4 times a year. In the larger department stores it tended to be nearer to 4–6 times.

Manufacturers' distribution costs. The distribution costs of manufacturers were relatively small where the manufacturer depended on the wholesaler for the marketing of his goods. Where he maintained a distribution organization of his own, and sold direct to retailers, his costs, including salesmen's salaries, carriage and transport, advertising, warehousing and general selling costs are estimated to have averaged 10–15% and up to 20% in the case of manufacturers who advertised their goods extensively.

The total costs of distribution are estimated at 42–44% of retail sales.

4. CARPETS

Consumers' expenditure and methods of distribution

Consumers' expenditure on carpets in 1938 is estimated at £16–17 millions. Of this £13–14 millions was represented by home-produced carpets and the remainder by imported carpets. Approximately half the imported carpets were of the 'Oriental' type, i.e. Indian, Persian, Chinese, and the remainder were imported from Europe.

This estimate of consumers' expenditure attempts to exclude sales to hotels, business houses and institutions.

The methods of distribution. The main channels of distribution and the proportions of total retail sales passing through them in 1938 are estimated as follows:

	%
From manufacturer or importer direct to retailer	45–50
From manufacturer or importer to wholesaler to retailer	50–55

Included in the sales from manufacturer direct to retailer are the sales by the co-operative wholesale societies to retail co-operative societies and the sales by manufacturers direct to the public or to mail order houses who sold direct to the public.

There was some variation in the methods of sale used for home-manufactured carpets according to different localities. The firms in Scotland, for example, which were very much larger than those in the rest of the country, sold a higher proportion of their output direct to retailers than did firms in the Kidderminster area and in other parts of England.

Of the imported carpets, some of the Indian carpets were imported by firms who maintained technical control of the manufacture in India and a large proportion of these carpets were distributed by the importers from their warehouses direct to the retailers. Indian carpets were also consigned to importers and then sold in bulk by brokers to wholesalers who distributed to retailers. Other Oriental carpets imported for sale in Britain were usually higher in price than Indian carpets and were sold for the most part direct by importers to large or specialist retailers. Imported carpets from the Continent were usually sold by importers or brokers to wholesalers and then to retailers.

A slightly lower proportion of home-manufactured carpets was sold to wholesalers than was the case with imported carpets.

Number of and sales by different types of outlet. In 1938 there were approximately 50 importers of carpets and 200–250 wholesalers. Most furniture retailers sold carpets and in addition there were a number of shops specializing in the sale of this product. The number of regular retail outlets for carpets in 1938 is estimated at 9–10,000. The proportion of total sales undertaken by the various economic types of outlet is estimated as follows:

	%
Multiple shops	18–22
Co-operative stores	3–5
Department stores	20–25
Unit retailers	48–59

There was a small sale direct from manufacturer or importer to consumer by mail order.

The cost of distribution

The margins and mark-ups of distributors of imported and home-manufactured carpets in 1938 were as follows:

Imported carpets: margins of importers and wholesalers. Importers of carpets worked to a mark-up ranging from 10–50% on landed cost. In the case of the sales of Indian and European carpets to wholesalers, the importer's mark-up ranged from 10–12½%, and the wholesaler's mark-up from 10–12½%. In the case of sales of Indian and European carpets direct to retailers, the importer's mark-up ranged from 20–25%. In the case of Oriental carpets, other than Indian, the importer's mark-up on the higher-class goods ranged from 25–50% on landed cost.

Retailers sold at a mark-up of 40–75% on cost. The average on cost was approximately 50%.

Settlement discounts. The usual terms for settlement on imported carpets were 3% for cash and 2½% for payment within the month.

Home-manufactured carpets: margins. There was no re-sale price maintenance on home-manufactured carpets but there was a measure of agreement between manufacturers as to prices to the trade. About one-tenth, by value, of the output was however sold as 'job lots' and on these no range of prices or discounts was agreed.

Wholesalers of home-manufactured carpets purchase at the list price (that is, wholesale price) less 12½%. They re-sold to retailers at the list price. Manufacturers sold direct to retailers at list price. On job lots the wholesaler earned widely varying margins from 10% up to 20% on sales.

Volume rebates up to 5% were given by manufacturers to wholesalers, while rebates averaging 7½% off the list price were given to large retailers who purchased direct from manufacturers. Such rebates were not universal, being given by about one-half of the trade.

Retailers sold at a mark-up of 33⅓–50% on the list price. The average retail mark-up was nearer 50%.

Settlement discounts on home-manufactured carpets were 2½% for payment within the month and 3½–3¾% for payment within 10 days.

The stock turn of retailers was 2–3 times a year, although in the case of the more expensive imported carpets stock turn was very much lower.

Manufacturers' distribution costs. The manufacturers maintained showrooms at their factories and showrooms and warehouses in the larger towns. Advertising by manufacturers was limited but patterns and catalogues were used on an extensive scale. Manufacturers' distribution costs, including the above items and packing and transport, may be put at 7–8% of turnover.

The total costs of distribution are estimated at 46–49% of retail sales.

5. LINOLEUM

Consumers' expenditure and methods of distribution

Consumers' expenditure on linoleum, cork carpet, felt base and floor cloth in 1938 is estimated at £7·5–8 millions, of which linoleum constituted about three-quarters and felt base about one-fifth. This figure excludes the sales, estimated at 7–10% of total production, to hotels, business houses and Government departments.

The methods of distribution. The proportions of total sales of linoleum, excluding sales to industrial and commercial users, passing through the main channels of distribution are estimated as follows:

	%
From manufacturer direct to retailer	75–85
From manufacturer to wholesaler to retailer	15–25

Number of wholesalers and retailers. There were about 300 wholesalers in 1938 who handled linoleum. The number of retail outlets is estimated at 7–8,000. A large number of furniture retailers regularly sold linoleum and felt base, and in addition there were a number of retailers, 100–150, who specialized in the sale of this product.

Sales by different types of outlet. The proportions of total sales undertaken by the different economic types of outlet are estimated as follows:

	%
Multiple shops	20–24
Co-operative stores	4–6
Department stores	16–20
Unit retailers	50–60

The cost of distribution

Linoleum was not retail price maintained in 1938 but most manufacturers by agreement fixed prices to the trade. *The margins* earned were as follows:

Wholesalers purchased at list price (wholesale price) less 10% trade discount and less 10% wholesale discount. Wholesalers generally re-sold to retailers at list price less 10% discount but in some cases at the list price. The average wholesale margin in 1938 is estimated at 11–12% on wholesale price.

Retailers who bought direct from manufacturers purchased at list price less 10% trade discount. In addition they obtained settlement discounts from manufacturers and generally from wholesalers of 4½% for cash and 3¾% for payment in the month.

Retailers normally sold at list price plus 33⅓–50%. The usual range was 45–50% on cost.

The stock turn of retailers of linoleum was approximately 5–6 times a year.

Manufacturers' distribution costs, including costs of patterns and catalogues, administrative selling costs, and packing and transport and stock holding costs, averaged 9–11% of manufacturers' sales revenue.

The total costs of distribution are estimated at 44–47% of retail sales.

CHAPTER XVIII

POTTERY AND GLASSWARE, HOLLOW WARE AND DOMESTIC IRONMONGERY

I. POTTERY AND GLASSWARE

Consumers' expenditure and methods of distribution

Consumers' expenditure on pottery and glassware in 1938 was between £14–15 millions. Under the heading 'pottery and glassware' are included china, earthenware, domestic and fancy glassware and glass mirrors. Tiles, sanitary earthenware, electrical ware, glass bottles and containers and sheet- and plate-glass have been excluded from this estimate. The purchases by commercial and industrial users, for example catering establishments, hotels and institutions, of pottery and glassware, estimated at 15–20% of total production, have been excluded from this estimate of consumers' expenditure. Imports of china and earthenware were relatively small in relation to home production and sales of these goods, but retained imports of domestic and fancy glassware represented one-third of home sales of glassware.

The methods of distribution. The proportions of total sales of pottery and glassware to the private consumer passing through the main channels of distribution in 1938 are estimated as follows:

	%
From manufacturer direct to retailer	70–75
From manufacturer or importer to wholesaler to retailer	25–30

Included in the sales from manufacturer direct to retailer are the sales through the co-operative wholesale societies to retail co-operative societies and the sales by importer/wholesalers to retailers. Excluded from the sales through wholesalers is that proportion of the wholesalers' sales which was made to industrial and commercial users. It is estimated that some 20% of the wholesalers' turnover was represented by sales such purchasers.

There were some important variations between the channels of distribution of particular commodities. For example, in the case of home-produced domestic and fancy glassware, it is estimated that 90% passed direct from manufacturer to retailer, whereas a large proportion of imported glassware went from importer to wholesaler and then to retailer. Similarly, in the case of earthenware and china, the higher class of goods tended almost invariably to go direct to retailer, whereas 'seconds', i.e. faulty china or earthenware, representing 5–10% of output, tended usually to go through wholesalers, except in the case of purchases by variety chain stores.

In addition to the channels listed above, there was a small sale by manufacturers and by wholesalers to private users. Also wholesalers sometimes arranged for goods to pass direct from manufacturer to retailer, although the goods were invoiced through the wholesaler. It is thought that 2–3% of the sales were made in these ways.

Number of wholesalers and retailers. There were between 200–250 wholesalers in the pottery and glass trade in 1938 and a further 100 wholesalers who handled a small quantity of pottery and glass. A number of these wholesalers could be classed as agents receiving commission rather than as wholesalers who held stock, broke bulk and re-sold in small quantities to retailers. Also included in this figure are some wholesalers who specialized almost exclusively in sales to industrial commercial users.

The number of specialist pottery and glass retailers, that is retailers whose main turnover was in these goods, is estimated at between 750–1,000, of which 75–100 were multiple shops. The total number of shops regularly selling some pottery and glassware is estimated at 15–20,000. This number includes a large variety of trade types, such as ironmongers, general shops, antique dealers, variety chain stores, department stores, co-operative shops, as well as specialist pottery and glass dealers.

Sales by different types of retail outlet. Estimates of the proportions of the total sales made by different economic types of outlet are as follows:

	%
Specialist pottery and glassware shops	15–20
Variety chain stores	15–20
Department stores	13–17
Co-operative stores	5–7
Other shops and outlets	39–49

Branches of multiple organizations, including variety chain stores, are estimated to have been responsible for about one-fifth of the total sales of pottery and glassware.

The cost of distribution

A very small proportion of domestic pottery and glassware on sale in 1938 was price-maintained by the manufacturers. It is estimated that not more than 5% of total sales came within this category.

The margins earned by distributors on the sale of pottery and glassware in 1938 were approximately as follows:

Wholesalers. The main range of wholesalers' on-cost was 25–50% on buying price. In some instances a much higher on-cost was usual. But there were important differences in the methods of calculating the buying price. Some wholesalers used the ex-works price and worked out their on-cost on this figure; others added the carriage costs from factory to wholesaler—which were paid by the wholesaler in most instances—to the ex-factory price and then calculated the on-cost; others added carriage cost but deducted trade discounts before calculating on-costs. The variation in the methods of calculating the buying price accounts in part for the wide range of on-cost in that the firms using the ex-factory price would add a higher on-cost than the firms using the delivered price: the former 40–50%, the latter 25–33%. The type of pottery and glassware under consideration also influenced on-cost. Trade discounts to wholesalers, which were granted on about three-quarters of the purchases, averaged between 5–7½%. The gross margin of wholesalers, including trade discounts, averaged 33–35% on sales. Out of this margin they had to meet the cost of transport and carriage both from the factory and to the retailer as well as the usual wholesalers' expenses.

Importers or importing agents of domestic and fancy glassware worked to a margin of 15–33% on cost. This margin had to cover the cost of carriage and transport to the wholesaler or retailer. If these costs were borne by the purchaser, the importer's margin was 5–10% on cost.

Retailers' mark-ups varied with the source of purchase, with the type of pottery and with the shop. When purchasing direct from manufacturers the most common range of mark-ups was 50–66⅔% on the ex-factory price, but mark-ups were in some cases as low as 40% and as high as 120%. Retailers purchasing direct usually had to pay carriage and there was, as in the case of wholesalers, a variation in the mark-up depending on whether carriage and transport costs were added to the ex-factory price or borne out of the margin. Retailers sometimes obtained a trade discount of up to 5% on direct purchases but this was not very usual. On purchases from wholesalers the retailers' mark-ups were 40–50% on buying price. In these cases the wholesalers usually paid transport and carriage costs. The settlement discounts to retailers were usually 2½% for payment in the month.

The differences between the types of shop were approximately as follows: specialist retailers and department stores tended to work to an on-cost of 60–70% on ex-factory price; variety chain stores 45–60% on ex-factory price; and general shops and ironmongers, usually purchasing through wholesalers, 40–50% on cost.

The average gross margin earned by retailers is estimated at 35–38% on returns.

The stock turn of wholesalers averaged between 3–4 times a year and the stock turn of retailers between 2–3 times a year. The stock turn of department stores and variety chain stores was slightly higher than this average, while that of general shops was very much lower.

Manufacturers' distribution costs, including carriage and packing, salesmen's salaries, administrative selling costs and advertising, were between 15–18% of manufacturers' sales revenue. Carriage and packing represented 5–8% of these costs, although in most cases, as suggested above, these charges were paid as a separate item by the wholesaler or retailer. Also included in this estimate of manufacturers' distribution costs are losses due to breakages and damaged goods.

The total costs of distribution are estimated at 46–49% of retail sales.

2. DOMESTIC HOLLOW-WARE, HARDWARE AND APPLIANCES, AND TOOLS AND APPLIANCES

Consumers' expenditure and methods of distribution

This group of commodities covers four main divisions: domestic hollow-ware such as pots, pans, buckets, baths, galvanized iron, enamel or aluminium ware and other domestic utensils; non-electric domestic appliances and hardware such as mangles, wringers, portable stoves, washing- and cooking-boilers, cork products, lamps, lanterns and mantles; garden accessories and tools such as lawn-mowers, garden rollers, wheelbarrows, spades, forks, shovels, horticultural woodware and wire netting; engineers' and carpenters' tools and accessories such as hammers, screw-drivers, saws, planes, nuts, bolts, screws, nails, locks, keys and miscellaneous pressings and stampings of iron, steel and brass such as hinges and brackets.

Consumers' expenditure on these groups of commodities in 1938 is estimated at £22–23 millions. Owing to the fact that these goods are purchased by industrial users, for example the catering trades, builders, carpenters and industrial concerns, as well as by the domestic consumer, estimates of the expenditure by the latter on these goods can only be approximate. But an attempt has been made to exclude industrial and commercial sales from this total.

The methods of distribution. The main channels of distribution and the proportions of total sales passing through them in 1938 are estimated as follows:

	%
From manufacturer to retailer	55–65
From manufacturer to wholesaler or factor to retailer	27–37
From manufacturer direct to consumer (including mail order)	6–10

Included in the sales of manufacturer direct to retailer are the sales by the co-operative wholesale societies to retail co-operative societies.

There were variations in the channels of distribution between the different commodities or commodity groups. For example the mail order trade was significant in the case of commodities with a relatively high unit value such as lawn-mowers and specialist engineers' and carpenters' tools. This type of commodity, when not passing through mail order channels, usually went direct from manufacturer to retailer. The smaller type of tools, particularly accessories, and the smaller domestic appliances such as nuts, bolts, screws, mouse-traps and clothes-pegs, tended on the other hand to pass mainly from manufacturers to wholesalers and then to retailers. In the case of domestic hollow-ware, that is pots, pans, buckets and kettles, the channels of distribution varied with the policy of the particular manufacturer and with the character of the article. For example, aluminium and galvanized hollow-ware tended to go direct from manufacturer to retailer, whereas enamelled hollow-ware went mainly from manufacturer to wholesaler and then to retailer. There was a further variation in channels according to the location of the sales. Wholesalers, for example, were used by manufacturers to a much greater extent when selling in the South of England and in Scotland than when selling in the Midlands and the North of England. The location of the main production areas in the Midlands influenced this tendency.

Number of wholesalers and retailers. The number of wholesalers or hardware factors handling this group of goods in 1938 is estimated at between 300 and 400. Many of these, however, did not deal in these goods as their chief trade, and the number of wholesalers dealing mainly in hollow-ware, hardware, tools and general ironmongery is estimated at 100–150. The number of retail outlets of these commodities in 1938 is estimated at 10–11,000. The majority of these outlets can be classified as ironmongers' and hardware shops, but there was also an important sale for these goods in department stores, co-operative shops and variety chain stores.

Sales by different types of outlet. The proportion of sales made by the different types of trade outlet are estimated as follows:

	%
Ironmongers' and hardware shops	55–60
Department stores and co-operatives	15–20
Variety chain stores	8–12
Other shops, mainly general shops	13–17

The relative importance of different economic types of retail outlet for these goods in 1938 is estimated as follows:

	%
Multiple shops (multiple hardware stores) and variety chain stores	18–23
Department stores	10–15
Co-operative stores	4–5
Unit retailers	57–68

There were important variations in the type of turnover of ironmongers' and hardware shops according to the location of these shops. For example, ironmongers' and hardware shops situated in rural towns and country districts did a different type of trade, for example a bigger sale of agricultural implements, to that of the ironmongers situated in industrial towns, where sales of engineers' and carpenters' tools would be prominent. Again, ironmongers situated in suburban areas sold a higher proportion of domestic hollow-ware and appliances. Further, some ironmongers tended to specialize in particular branches of the trade. The department stores, co-operatives and variety chain stores sold relatively few of the specialized articles and concentrated on domestic hollow-ware, hardware and the simple type of gardening and engineers' tools and accessories.

The cost of distribution

A very small proportion, less than 10%, of these goods were re-sale price maintained in 1938, although for certain types of hollow-ware and tools a rather higher proportion was branded or trade-marked by the manufacturers.

The margins earned by wholesalers and retailers are estimated as follows:

Wholesalers' or factors' margins varied between 12½–30% on sales. The mark-up on hollow-ware ranged between 33–40% on cost, on domestic appliances was about 33% on cost, on tools 27–33% on cost, and on garden equipment 25–33% on cost. The average margin of wholesalers on sales is estimated at 22–24%. Wholesalers and factors in some cases did not directly handle the goods but took orders from retailers and secured direct delivery by the manufacturer to the retailers and in these instances the factoring margin averaged 15% on sales.

Retailers' margins varied widely owing to the large number of manufacturers and the large number of different items handled, each of which had a slightly varying rate of stock turn. The wide range in the unit price of the goods also influenced the range of margins in that the higher-priced articles such as wringers or lawn-mowers carried a lower percentage margin than many low-priced goods. The retailers usually worked to an on-cost of 33–60%, and the average on-cost on this group of goods as a whole is estimated at between 40–50%, or 28–33% on sales.

Multiple organizations, variety chain stores and department stores usually purchased from manufacturers at wholesale terms or sometimes at a special discount of 10% off the retail buying price.

Quantity rebates or discounts were not common although in the case of small items, particularly nuts, bolts, nails and screws, prices to wholesalers and retailers varied inversely with the quantities purchased.

The settlement discounts for both wholesalers or factors and retailers were usually 3½% for settlement in 7 days and 2½% for payment within the month.

The stock turn of wholesalers varied widely with the different types of goods handled but overall is estimated at between 6 and 7 times a year. The average stock turn for retailers is estimated at 3–4 times a year.

Manufacturers' distribution costs, including administrative selling costs, warehouse costs, salesmen's salaries, advertising (which usually took the form of catalogues) and carriage, packing and transport, varied widely. For some manufacturers, who sold unbranded and unadvertised products almost entirely through wholesalers, the costs rarely exceeded 5% of sales revenue. Other manufacturers, selling direct to retailers, employing a large sales force and holding stocks against orders, spent up to 25% of sales revenue on sales promotion, warehousing and transport. The average for the whole trade, allowing for the different methods and practices of distribution, is estimated at 8–12% of manufacturers' sales revenue. Advertising expenditure represented approximately one-fifth of these costs.

The total costs of distribution are estimated at 47–49% of retail sales.

3. HOUSEHOLD BROOMS AND BRUSHES

Consumers' expenditure and methods of distribution

Consumers' expenditure on household brooms, mops and brushes (including non-electric carpet-sweepers) is estimated at £2–2½ millions. This estimate attempts to exclude the purchases of brushes by industrial users.

The methods of distribution. Of the total sales of household brooms and brushes the proportions passing through the main channels of distribution in 1938 are estimated as follows:

	%
From manufacturer direct to retailer	55–65
From manufacturer or importer to wholesaler or factor to retailer	30–35
From manufacturer direct to consumer	5–10

The wholesalers or factors tended to specialize in imported brushes. Many of the smaller manufacturers sold their entire output to local retailers.

Number of retailers. The number of outlets for household brooms and brushes in 1938 is estimated at 10–15,000. Ironmongers were the most important outlet, but brushes were also sold by department stores, co-operative stores, furniture dealers, variety chain stores and grocers.

Sales by different types of retail outlet. Estimates of the proportions of total sales made by the different economic types of retail outlet are as follows:

	%
Department stores	15–20
Multiple shops and variety chain stores	10–15
Co-operative stores	6–7
Unit retailers (mainly ironmongers and grocers)	58–69

The cost of distribution

Very few of these goods in 1938 were price-maintained by manufacturers, though a large proportion were branded.

The margins earned by wholesalers and retailers in 1938 were as follows:

Wholesalers' margins ranged between $17\frac{1}{2}$–33% on sales. The average margin for wholesalers was 20–25% on returns.

Retailers usually worked to a mark-up of 50% on cost, although in the case of the few nationally advertised products the margin was sometimes lower. Department stores and variety chain stores usually purchased near wholesalers' terms. Some manufacturers and wholesalers gave retailers additional discounts for volume purchases, which would range from $2\frac{1}{2}$% on a purchase of 3 dozen to 10% on a purchase of 12 dozen.

Settlement discounts were usually $2\frac{1}{2}$–$3\frac{3}{4}$% for payment in the month, although some manufacturers gave $3\frac{3}{4}$–5%.

The stock turn of wholesalers is estimated at 5–6 times a year, and the stock turn of retailers 3–4 times a year.

Manufacturers' distribution costs varied widely according to the particular policy pursued. One or two manufacturers engaged in door-to-door sales to the consumer, and in these instances manufacturers' distribution costs, including salesmen's salaries or commission, advertising, administrative selling costs and carriage and transport, were in the region of 35–40% of sales revenue. This type of sale, however, represented only a small proportion of the total trade and the average distribution costs of manufacturers are estimated at between 6–8% of sales revenue.

The total costs of distribution are estimated at 48–51% of retail sales.

4. PAINTS, DISTEMPER AND WALLPAPER

Consumers' expenditure and methods of distribution

Consumers' expenditure on this group of goods is estimated at £4–5 millions. The expenditure on paint, varnishes, enamel and distemper is estimated at £2·5–3 millions and on wallpaper at £1·5–2 millions. An attempt has been made to exclude from these estimates of consumers' expenditure the sales by merchants and retailers to trade users and the joint purchases of services and commodities, for example wallpaper and the labour to paper the walls, by private consumers.

The methods of distribution: Paints and distemper. The proportions of total sales of paints, varnishes, enamel and distemper in 1938 passing through the main channels of distribution are estimated as follows:

	%
From manufacturer to wholesaler or factor to retailer	30–40
From manufacturer direct to retailer	60–70

These estimates refer only to the goods which were sold 'over the counter' to the private domestic consumer. For the paint trade as a whole, including the paint sold to industrial and trade users which represented the bulk of the sales of paint, the proportion sold through merchants or factors is very much higher.

The methods of distribution: Wallpaper. The proportions of total sales of wallpaper passing through the main channels of distribution in 1938 are estimated as follows:

	%
From manufacturer to factor or builders' merchant to retailer	20–25
From manufacturer direct to retailer	75–80

Again, these estimates refer only to the wallpaper sold to the private domestic consumer.

Number of outlets. Most retail ironmongery and hardware shops sold paint, and a smaller number sold wallpaper. In addition there were a number of specialist retailers concentrating on the sale of wallpaper and/or paint. Paint was also sold in relatively small quantities in variety chain stores and department stores. The number of retail outlets for paint in 1938 is estimated at 10–12,000 and the number of retail outlets of wallpaper at 3–4,000. The number of branches of multiple organizations specializing in the sale of paints, distemper and wallpaper is estimated at 500–1,000. At the wholesale stage these goods were handled by most hardware factors and builders' and decorators' merchants, and by wallpaper pattern-book merchants.

Multiple shops, including variety chain stores, are estimated to have undertaken 10–15% of the total sales of these goods, and co-operative and department stores together approximately 5%.

The cost of distribution

The cost of distribution: Paints and distemper. A high proportion of the paints, varnishes and distemper sold to the domestic consumer in 1938 was branded and price-maintained. Wholesalers and multiple organizations also sold their 'own name' brands.

The margins allowed at the various stages were approximately as follows:

> *Wholesalers, factors or merchants* bought at the retail price less 25% less 15% wholesale discount, or less 33⅓% less 10% wholesale discount. In addition wholesalers or factors very often were entitled to a quantity rebate and in some cases an over-riding discount. These would represent an additional discount of 7–10%. Where the goods were not price-maintained by the manufacturers and where wholesalers sold 'own name' brands, the mark-up was 20–25%. The average wholesaler's or factor's margin, including rebates, was 20% on sales.
>
> *Retailers'* discount off the retail selling price ranged from 25–33⅓%. The average was nearer 30–33%. Large retailers, purchasing direct from manufacturers, received in a number of cases quantity rebates or an over-riding discount on annual purchases. Multiple organizations usually received the basic retail margin and a discount of 10–15%.

Settlement discounts for wholesalers or factors and retailers were up to 5% for payment in the month following delivery and 2½% for payment at 3–6 months from the date of invoices, usually on quarterly accounts.

The cost of distribution: Wallpaper. With a few exceptions the manufacturer had no control over the price charged for wallpaper by the retailer and the gross margins earned by the latter varied with the size of the undertaking and the quality of paper handled.

The margins earned by wholesalers and retailers in 1938 were approximately as follows:

Wholesale builders' merchants and wallpaper pattern-book merchants stock-selling to retailers worked to 10–20% on cost. The average margin on sales was about 12½%.

Retailers purchasing from wholesalers worked to an on-cost of 50–100% with an average nearer the 50% on-cost or 33⅓% on sales. Retailers purchasing in large quantities direct from manufacturers worked to an on-cost ranging from 66–125% with an average of 100% on cost or 50% on sales. This includes the extra discount earned for quantity purchases. Smaller retailers purchasing direct would not normally earn a quantity discount and their mark-up was lower, 50–75%.

In most cases the on-cost at the top end of the range applied to the more expensive paper and the lower on-cost to the cheaper paper.

Settlement discounts were usually 3¾ and 2½% for payment in the quarter.

Manufacturers' distribution costs. Owing to the fact that in the case both of paint and of wallpaper the great proportion of the sales by manufacturers were to trade users and not to the private domestic consumer, estimates of manufacturers' distribution costs on this proportion of their trade are difficult to make with any measure of accuracy. It is suggested, however, that distribution costs of manufacturers of paint, distemper and wallpaper averaged between 17–20% of sales revenue. In the case of paints, advertising represented between one-third and one-half of these costs.

The total costs of distribution of paints are estimated at 53–56% of retail sales and the total distribution costs of wallpaper at 53–57% of retail sales.

5. CUTLERY

Consumers' expenditure and methods of distribution

Consumers' expenditure on cutlery, table, dessert and tea knives, pen and pocket knives and scissors in 1938 is estimated at £1·2–1·5 millions. This estimate attempts to exclude the purchases of cutlery by industrial and commercial users, such as the catering trade, shipping companies and business houses.

The methods of distribution. The proportions of total sales of cutlery to the domestic consumer passing through the main channels of distribution in 1938 are estimated as follows:

	%
From manufacturer to retailer	60–65
From manufacturer to wholesaler to retailer	35–40

A small proportion was sold by manufacturers on mail order direct to consumers. Included in the sales from manufacturer direct to retailer are the sales by co-operative wholesale societies to retail co-operative societies. The sales to trade users—manufacturers, wholesalers and some retailers all sold to some extent to trade users—have been excluded as far as possible from these estimates of the proportions passing through the main channels of distribution.

Number of wholesalers and retailers. There were approximately 150–200 wholesalers who regularly handled cutlery in 1938, although almost all hardware wholesalers and most jewellery wholesalers handled a certain amount of cutlery. The number of retail outlets is estimated at 12–15,000. Most ironmongers', hardware and jewellers' shops sold some cutlery.

Sales by different types of retail outlet. The proportions of total sales of cutlery to the domestic consumer made by the different types of retail outlet are estimated as follows:

	%
Hardware shops, including sales in the hardware departments of department stores and co-operative shops	70–80
Jewellers, including sales in the jewellery departments of co-operative and department stores	15–20
Other shops, general shops and variety chain stores	5–10

The division of the retail sales by economic type of retail outlet is estimated as follows:

	%
Multiple and variety chain stores	13–17
Department stores	15–20
Co-operative stores	4–6
Unit retailers	57–68

The cost of distribution

While the great majority of cutlery was branded in 1938, that is manufacturers sold their goods under a trade-mark, not more than 10% of the goods were re-sale price maintained.

The margins earned by wholesalers and retailers in 1938 are estimated as follows:

The wholesaler's margin ranged from 10–20% on sales, that is he received a discount of 10–20% off the trade or list price, although in many instances the manufacturers gave wholesalers no discount off the trade price and sold to retailers and wholesalers at the same price. The average margin of wholesalers is estimated at 10–12% on sales.

The retailer usually put 45–50% on cost. Multiple organizations usually purchased at or near wholesale terms, that is, list price less wholesalers' discount.

Settlement discounts given to both wholesalers and retailers were usually $2\frac{1}{2}$% for payment within the month. Some firms gave a higher discount of $3\frac{3}{4}$% for payment in 7 days, although a number of firms did not allow any cash discount.

The stock turn of retailers is estimated at 3–4 times a year and of wholesalers 6–7 times a year.

Manufacturers' distribution costs, including administrative selling costs, advertising, catalogues, carriage and packing, are estimated at between 9–15% of sales revenue. About one-half of these costs were represented by selling costs and about one-third by carriage and packing costs.

The total costs of distribution are estimated at 45–47% of retail sales.

CHAPTER XIX
ELECTRICAL GOODS

I. ELECTRIC FIRES, IRONS, KETTLES, TOASTERS AND OTHER HOUSEHOLD APPLIANCES

Consumers' expenditure and methods of distribution

Consumers' expenditure in 1938 on portable electric fires, irons, kettles, toasters and other household appliances is estimated at between £5–6 millions. This estimate excludes the small purchases made by industrial and commercial users.

The methods of distribution. The main channels of distribution and the proportions of total sales estimated to have passed through them in 1938 are as follows:

	%
From manufacturer to supply undertakings	10–15
From manufacturer to wholesaler or factor to retailer	25–30
From manufacturer to retailer or electrical contractor	55–65

The wholesalers or factors re-sold these goods mainly to retailers, but a small proportion of their trade, 10–20% of their turnover, was with trade users. Such sales have been excluded in the above estimates. The sales of manufacturers to multiple organizations—whether to head offices, depots or by split deliveries to branches and to co-operative wholesale societies—are included in the manufacturer direct to retailer group.

Number of wholesalers and retailers. There were approximately 600–800 wholesalers in 1938 who did some trade in electrical domestic appliances, but the bulk of the turnover was handled by 300.

There were 4–5,000 retail shops specializing in the sale of electrical goods, though there were some 10,000 other shops which did some trade in these appliances. Included in this group are the electrical sections of department stores and co-operative retail stores, multiple radio and cycle equipment shops and other radio shops, ironmongers' and general shops. Electrical appliances were also purchased from electrical contractors who sometimes did not possess a shop or showroom.

Sales by different types of retail outlet. The specialist electrical retailers are considered to have undertaken about 60% of the retail turnover in this group of appliances, department stores 5–10%, multiple radio and electrical shops 8–12%, and co-operative stores 1–3%, and the remainder was sold in shops handling, but not specializing in, electrical equipment, of which variety chain stores and ironmongers were the most important types. The electrical goods handled by supply authorities—estimated at about 15% of the total—were not usually sold outright to consumers but sold on hire purchase or put out on straight hire.

The cost of distribution

Practically all these appliances in 1938 were sold at retail prices suggested by the manufacturer or in some cases by the wholesaler. Selling below the suggested price was not very frequent. The margins and discounts allowed in the course of distribution of these goods were, in general, laid down by the Electrical Fair Trading Council, a body representative of manufacturers', wholesalers' and retailers' trade associations. *The margins* earned by wholesalers and by retailers are estimated as follows:

Wholesalers or factors usually received a discount of 25% off the retail price less 10–20%. Occasionally the margin would be higher, up to 25% when wholesalers earned a quantity rebate, but in many cases part of this would be passed on, in one form or another, to the retailer or supply authority. The average margin earned by wholesalers and factors was 15–17½% on sales.

Supply authorities received a basic discount of 25% off the retail price. In addition they were entitled on bulk purchases to a quantity rebate ranging from 10–15%. A group of supply authorities in 1938 combined to form the Bulk Purchasing Committee which made direct contracts with manufacturers for the production of a range of these appliances to specification. On these purchases the margin earned by supply authorities, apart from hiring or hire-purchase arrangements, averaged 30–35% on sales.

Electrical retailers and contractors and other retailers selling electrical equipment obtained a margin of 25% on sales whether purchasing direct from manufacturers or through wholesalers. The larger retailers, department stores, and multiple and variety chain stores on their direct purchases would usually qualify for an additional quantity rebate ranging from 10–15%.

Settlement discounts. In addition to these discounts all purchasers were usually entitled to settlement discounts ranging from 3¾%, and sometimes 5%, for payment in 7 days to 2½% for payment in the month. Wholesalers, large retailers and supply authorities usually earned the terms for payment in 7 days, the specialist electrical contractor or retailer the 2½% discount, but many general shops did not qualify for a discount.

Stock turn. The average stock turn of wholesalers is estimated at 5–6 times a year and the average stock turn of retailers at 6–8 times a year.

Manufacturers' distribution costs on these appliances are difficult to calculate owing to the wide variety of goods produced by the manufacturers of this equipment and the diverse methods of distribution employed. Some firms, for example, advertised a trade-mark applying to a range of products sold to both domestic and industrial users rather than to a particular appliance. Others distributed almost entirely through wholesalers and supply undertakings while a few sold only direct to the retailer. Estimates of manufacturers' distribution costs including transport, salesmen's salaries, administrative selling costs and advertising can therefore be somewhat misleading, but what evidence there is suggests that on this group of appliances they were of the order of 12–15% of manufacturers' sales revenue. Advertising represented between a quarter and a third of these costs.

The total costs of distribution are estimated at 43–45% of retail sales.

2. GENERAL SERVICE ELECTRIC LAMPS

Consumers' expenditure and methods of distribution

Consumers' expenditure on general service electric lamps in 1938 is estimated at between £1·5–2 millions. This estimate attempts to exclude all lamps purchased by industrial and commercial undertakings and Government departments and refers only to those lamps purchased by the private consumer. This represents a sale of between 30–35 million lamps, of which roughly 40% were 60-watt and 30% 40-watt. Owing to the multiplicity of voltages prevailing in the country, the lamps were manufactured in more than 15 different voltages, of which 230 volts (one-third of the total) was the most common.

The proportions of total sales of general service electric lamps passing through the main channels of distribution are estimated as follows:

	%
From manufacturer to wholesaler or factor and then to retailer	27–33
From manufacturer direct to retailer	55–65
From manufacturer direct to supply authority	8–12

Number of wholesalers and retailers and sales by different types of outlet. The number of wholesalers is estimated at 400–500 and the number of retail outlets at between 35–40,000. The proportions of total sales made by the different types of retail outlet are estimated as follows:

	%
Electrical retailers and contractors	41–47
Variety chain stores	30–33
Electricity supply authorities	10–15
Other outlets, including ironmongers, department stores and co-operative stores	10–14

The sales in multiple shops, including multiple electrical retailers', multiple ironmongers' and variety chain stores, are estimated to have represented 35–38% of total sales. The proportion of total sales undertaken by co-operative stores is estimated at 2–4%.

The cost of distribution

Some two-thirds of the general service electric lamps sold to the private consumer in 1938 were sold at retail prices fixed by the manufacturers. Approximately one-third of the lamps were sold by wholesalers, factors and retailers under terms fixed by the Electric Lamp Manufacturers' Association.

The margins allowed in the trade were as follows:

Wholesalers and factors. Wholesale distributors and factors, listed by E.L.M.A., received discounts, in the former case of 35% off the retail price, and in the latter case of 30% off the retail price, and a rebate according to annual purchases. The combined discount and rebate earned by factors and wholesalers averaged 34% and 39% respectively off the retail price.

Wholesalers received from non-E.L.M.A. firms a discount of 33⅓% off the retail price plus a rebate of 10–20% according to size of purchase. The average discount and rebate earned was 43–44% off the retail price.

Retailers. Any retailer of electrical goods purchasing lamps from E.L.M.A. member firms or E.L.M.A. lamps from wholesalers received a discount of 21% off the retail price, plus a rebate according to turnover ranging up to 14%, although in no case did the rebate actually reach this figure.

Retailers who elected to sell only lamps manufactured by members of E.L.M.A. received an additional 6%, making a total discount of 27%, plus a rebate according to turnover. Retailers purchasing from wholesalers or factors were entitled to the same discounts and rebates as retailers purchasing direct from manufacturers. The combined discount and rebate of such retailers averaged 30% off the retail price. The combined discount and rebate to supply authorities averaged slightly higher at 33%.

Retailers selling non-E.L.M.A. lamps received a discount of 33⅓% and a rebate according to turnover. The combined discount and rebate for these retailers averaged 35% and, in the case of supply authorities, slightly higher, 37%.

The average wholesale margin on both E.L.M.A. and non-E.L.M.A. lamps was 15% on sales. The average retailer margin on both types of lamps was 33% on sales.

The general service electric lamps sold in variety chain stores were rarely price-maintained by the manufacturers and these outlets were an important avenue of sale for the cheaper lamp. The gross margins earned on the sale of these lamps in variety chain stores varied with the price policy of the particular firm and ranged from 30–50% on sales.

The settlement discount allowed by E.L.M.A. firms was 2½% and by other firms was 3¾% for payment in 7 days and 2½% for payment in the month. Wholesalers and retailers in 1938 usually earned 2½% discount.

Stock turn. The multiplicity of voltages referred to above—to which is added the multiplicity of lamp types and finishes—presents the wholesaler in particular, and the retailer, with complicated stockholding problems. Efforts have been and are being made to reduce both types of multiplicity, but most distributors were expected to hold stocks of all types of lamps, whether obsolete by current standards or no. This had a bearing on stock turn which, in the case of wholesalers, averaged 3–5 times a year and for retailers 5–6 times a year. Stockholding was encouraged by most manufacturers, in that wholesalers and retailers were required to hold minimum stocks expressed as a percentage of purchases.

Manufacturers' distribution costs. As in the case of other electrical appliances, the costs incurred in the distribution of this particular product, general service electric lamps, are difficult to distinguish from the costs of distributing other electrical equipment and, further, the sale of lamps to the domestic consumer comprised less than one-third of the total market for lamps in 1938. Bearing this in mind, estimates of manufacturers' distribution costs on domestic lamps are subject to many qualifications. The evidence suggests that these costs, administrative selling costs, salesmen's salaries, carriage and transport and advertising, ranged from 5–15% of manufacturers' sales revenue in 1938. In some instances transport and advertising costs together totalled 5–7% and the other costs were small, but in other cases advertising alone amounted to 10–12% of sales revenue.

The total costs of distribution are estimated at 44–46% of retail sales.

3. VACUUM CLEANERS

Consumers' expenditure and methods of distribution

Consumers' expenditure on vacuum cleaners in 1938 is estimated at £5–5·5 millions. Excluded from this total are the purchases of vacuum cleaners by institutions and business houses.

The methods of distribution. The main channels of distribution and the proportions of total sales passing through them in 1938 are estimated as follows:

	%
From manufacturer to wholesaler to retailer	25–30
From manufacturer direct to retailer	60–70
From manufacturer direct to consumer	5–10

Included in the sales direct to retailers are the sales to supply undertakings, sales made by the co-operative wholesale societies to retail co-operative societies and also the sales through retail outlets which were effected by door-to-door salesmen. About two-thirds of the sales direct to retailers were promoted by retail salesmen employed by the manufacturers, who obtained orders and passed them to the local retail shop which stocked the particular model for fulfilment. The retailers meeting orders placed in this way usually carried their stock on a sale or return basis.

Number of outlets and sales by different types of outlet. The number of outlets of vacuum cleaners in 1938 is estimated at 8–10,000, but the bulk of the trade was handled by about 2,000 outlets. The number of door-to-door salesmen employed by manufacturers is estimated at 6–7,000 in 1938. The sales by branches of multiple organizations represented some 3–5% of total sales, the sales of department stores about 5%, the sales by co-operative stores about 1%, the sales by supply undertakings about 15%, and the remaining sales were undertaken by unit retailers.

The cost of distribution

Practically all vacuum cleaners in 1938 carried retail prices fixed by the manufacturers.

The margins earned by wholesalers or factors and retailers on the sale of these goods are estimated as follows:

The wholesaler or factor obtained a discount of 25–33% off the retail price and a further trade discount of 10–20%. On two-thirds of the total sales the wholesale discount ranged between 10–12½% on sales and, in the remaining cases, between 15–20% on sales.

The retailer purchasing either from the wholesaler or direct from the manufacturer obtained a margin of 25–33% on sales. In approximately two-thirds of the cases the margin was 25% and in the remaining cases 33%.

The retailer selling on orders obtained by salesmen employed by the manufacturers obtained a discount ranging from 12½–20% on sales. The average margin earned by retailers on these sales was near the lower limit of this range.

Supply undertakings usually obtained a discount of 25% off the retail price and in a number of instances were entitled to a further discount of 10–15%.

Settlement discounts were not usual in the trade. Where they were given, on possibly one-third of the total sales, they were at the rate of 3¾% for payment in 7 days, 2½% for payment in the month.

The stock turn of retailers of vacuum cleaners is estimated to average 7–9 times a year. The retailers selling against orders obtained by door-to-door salesmen usually had a higher rate of stock turn than this, while the stock turn of other outlets was very much lower.

Manufacturers' distribution costs varied widely with the method of sale. The costs of distribution of manufacturers who did not employ retail salesmen and sold a large proportion of their products through wholesalers are estimated to have averaged 12–15% of sales revenue. These costs include packing and carriage, travellers' salaries, administrative selling costs and advertising. The costs of distribution of manufacturers employing retail salesmen who undertook sales to the public, or, more frequently, passed orders to local dealers for fulfilment, are estimated to have averaged 30–35% of manufacturers' sales revenue. This figure excludes the discount allowed to retailers. The costs, in addition to those given above, include the commission and salaries paid to salesmen and supervisors and the cost of their training.

For the trade as a whole there was not a great deal of difference between total distribution costs incurred by manufacturers selling to wholesalers who re-sold to retailers, that is manufacturers' distribution costs plus wholesalers' and retailers' margins, and the costs incurred by manufacturers who employed retail salesmen.

Hire purchase. Approximately three-quarters of the vacuum cleaners sold in 1938 are estimated to have been sold on hire-purchase terms. Practically all the cleaners sold by supply undertakings were on these terms.

The total costs of distribution are estimated at 44–47% of retail sales.

4. RADIO RECEIVERS AND RADIOGRAMS

Consumers' expenditure and methods of distribution

Consumers' expenditure on these goods in 1938 is estimated at £15·5–16 millions.

The methods of distribution. The proportions of total sales passing through the main channels of distribution in 1938 are estimated as follows:

	%
From manufacturer to retailer	75–80
From manufacturer to wholesaler or factor and then to retailer	20–25

Included in the sales direct to retailer are sales by the co-operative wholesale societies to retail co-operative societies. Many manufacturers confined the bulk of their sales to retailers acting as their agents, though very few retailers handled one make of radio alone.

Number of wholesalers and retailers. There were between 400–450 wholesalers who handled radio sets in 1938 and 25–28,000 retail outlets. These figures include wholesalers and retailers who only occasionally dealt in radio sets and the number of those engaged substantially in the trade is estimated at 80–100 wholesalers with possibly a further 75–100 branches or depots and 9–10,000 retailers.

Sales by different types of retail outlet. The importance of the various economic types of retail outlets for radio sets in 1938 is estimated as follows:

	%
Multiple shops dealing mainly in electrical goods	10–15
Department and co-operative stores	2–5
Unit retailers	80–88

The cost of distribution

The great majority of radio receivers and radiograms in 1938 were sold at retail prices fixed by the manufacturers. The exception was the purchase of sets by large retailers to sell under their own brand name.

The margins allowed to wholesalers, factors and retailers in 1938 are estimated as follows:

Wholesalers or factors received a discount off the retail price of from 30–33⅓% less a further discount of 12½% to 30–33⅓% less 40%. The smaller discounts tended to be given by firms who had an established reputation in the trade and dealt with a relatively small number of wholesalers. The larger discounts, particularly those of 33⅓% less 40% or sometimes less 50%, were exceptional and tended to be given either by firms trying to establish connections in the trade, or by firms that had over-produced. The average terms on which wholesalers and factors purchased were 30–33⅓% off the retail price less a further discount of 15–17½%.

Retailers' margins ranged between 30–33⅓%. Appointed agents for particular manufacturers would, however, in some instances get

30–33⅓% less 5–10%. The average margin of non-multiple retailers was estimated at just under 33⅓%. Multiple organizations obtained special terms from manufacturers in a number of cases ranging from 30–33⅓% less 10% to less 12½% and less 15%. Multiple shops and department stores also purchased sets in bulk and sold these under their own brand name and, in these instances, would earn a margin of 40–45% off the retail price.

Volume rebates, except in the form mentioned above for special purchases by multiple organizations or department stores, were infrequent in the trade.

Settlement discounts allowed to retailers and wholesalers were usually 3¾% for payment in 7 days and 2½% for monthly settlement. In some cases discounts for prompt settlement, both by wholesalers and retailers, were increased to 5–7%, and in one case no settlement discounts were given at all. Relatively few retailers earned more than 2½% discount in 1938.

The stock turn of wholesalers and factors of radio sets averaged 6–7 times a year and that of retailers 5–6 times a year. The trade was very seasonal, heavy sales occurring in the early winter months and relatively few sales in the spring and summer. This factor complicated both production methods and stockholding by distributors.

Manufacturers' distribution costs, including administrative selling costs, carriage and packing, salesmen's salaries and advertising, varied between manufacturers according to sales policy. In the case of sales through wholesalers, these costs are estimated at between 10–15% of manufacturers' sales revenue in 1938 and in the case of sales direct to retailers 20–25%, the average for the trade as a whole being 20% of manufacturers' sales revenue. Advertising represented 9–10% of these costs, carriage and transport and packing 3–4%, salesmen's salaries and similar selling costs 3–4%.

Hire-purchase trading was common in this industry, and it is estimated that about 75% of the sets sold in 1938 were sold on hire-purchase terms.

The total costs of distribution are estimated at 50-52% of retail sales.

CHAPTER XX

FOOTWEAR

I. LEATHER BOOTS AND SHOES

Consumers' expenditure and methods of distribution

Consumers' expenditure on boots and shoes and other footwear in 1938 is estimated at £63 millions; the expenditure on men's shoes represented one-third of the total, on women's just over a half, and the remainder was on juvenile footwear. This total excludes the sale of rubber boots and shoes, the sale of footwear accessories such as soles, heels and shoelaces, and the sales to Government departments and industrial undertakings.

The methods of distribution. The proportions of the total sales passing through the main channels of distribution in 1938 are estimated as follows:

	%
From manufacturer to wholesaler to retailer	27–33
From manufacturer direct to retailer	67–73

Included in the sales direct to retailer are the sales by co-operative wholesale societies to retail societies and the sales by manufacturers to the central depots or by split deliveries to branches of multiple footwear organizations.

Within the general framework suggested above, special methods of distribution were employed by manufacturers of particular grades and types of footwear. For example, in the medium and higher priced ranges of footwear the 'in-stock' system was common. This was an arrangement whereby manufacturers made agreements with retail dealers for the latter to act as special agents for particular brands and types of footwear and the manufacturers carried a wide range of stock on which retailers were able to draw at 24 or 48 hours' notice. Such retailers were often given in their immediate neighbourhood a 'protected area' of sales by the manufacturer for whom they were acting as an agent. This in-stock system did not apply to more than 5–7% of the total sales of boots and shoes.

A second feature was the existence of a large number of retail outlets which had direct links with manufacturing units. In a few cases the retail units were controlled by manufacturers, but far more usual was the retail firm controlling a manufacturing concern. These retail groups were in almost every case multiple trading units.

Number of wholesalers and retailers. There were between 300–350 wholesalers or factors of boots and shoes in 1938 and some 20–22,000 retail outlets regularly selling footwear. This estimate includes the boot and shoe departments in co-operative stores and department stores and also the outlets for these goods in variety chain stores. Of this total number of outlets, between 13,500–15,500 were specialist boot and shoe retailers and shops in co-operative and department stores, and these shops were responsible for over four-fifths of the total trade.

Sales by different types of retail outlet. The division of the sales of footwear between the different economic types of retail outlet in 1938 is estimated as follows:

	%
Co-operative shops	9–11
Multiple shops (including sales in variety chain stores)	45–47
Department stores	6–7
Unit retailers	36–39

The sales of footwear by variety chain stores are estimated at 4–5% of total sales. There were approximately 1,000 retail co-operative shops regularly selling footwear in 1938, and the production by co-operative wholesale societies and productive societies represented between 50–60% of the total sales of footwear by the retail societies. There were approximately 4,500–5,000 multiple footwear shops in 1938 and approximately 2,000–2,250 of these were linked with important manufacturing units. Of the sales by the multiple retail firms linked with important production units, it is estimated that between a quarter and a third were represented by their own production. More women's shoes than men's were bought outside by these firms.

The cost of distribution

Re-sale price maintenance of footwear was not very common in 1938, representing not more than 5% of the total sales (the sale of footwear in retail shops linked with manufacturers is not considered as re-sale price maintenance).

The margins earned by the various distributors of footwear in 1938 are estimated as follows:

Wholesalers' margins varied considerably between types of footwear handled. These margins normally ranged from 12½–17% on sales, the margins in the latter case being earned on the sale of women's fashion shoes. The average after allowing for mark-downs was between 12–13%.

Retailers' margins ranged widely from 18–45%. The margins at the lower end of this range were sometimes earned by multiple retailers having a rapid stock turn in the medium and lower price groups of men's wear. The margins at the top end of the range were sometimes earned in the highest class of trade by retailers giving multiple fitting service and carrying large stocks of women's fashion footwear. This is only a part of the picture, however, as the footwear trade, particularly the women's trade, was subject to heavy mark-down due to changes in taste, and to this problem was added the need to stock a wide range of fittings. A high margin on some sales would be offset by the later sale of the same type of footwear near or at purchase price to clear stock.

The average retail margin for the trade, allowing for mark-downs, is estimated at 26% on sales of both men's and women's footwear. On the low priced footwear, 12s. 9d. per pair and below, which represented nearly two-thirds of total sales, the realized margin averaged 20–25%, and on the high priced footwear, representing just over one-tenth of total sales, the realized margin averaged 30–35%.

Settlement discounts. The usual purchase discounts allowed to wholesalers, in addition to the margins discussed above, varied from 2½–5% and a further 1¼% for prompt payment, thus making the discounts 3¾% or 6¼%. In cases where large orders were placed it was possible to obtain a discount in excess of the 3¾% or 6¼%. Retailers were also entitled to cash discounts ranging from 2½–6¼%. Some retailers, usually multiple concerns, earned 6¼% but the discounts normally earned were between 2½ and 3¾%. Again on large orders retailers might receive slightly more favourable terms.

Stock turn. The average stock turn of wholesalers, excluding the firms who performed only a factoring function of buying and selling and not stocking, was between 5 and 6 times a year. The stock turn of retailers varied considerably according to their type of trade and between the different types of footwear stocked, and even shops doing the same type of trade but in different areas showed varying rates of stock turn between men's and women's and staple and fashion lines. Allowing as far as is possible for these variations, the average independent specialist retailers' stock turn in the medium and high grade trade is estimated to have been twice a year and the average multiple retailer's stock turn in the low and medium grades 3½–4½ times a year in 1938.

Manufacturers' distribution costs reflected the different methods of distribution used. In the case of manufacturers linked with a chain of retail shops the distribution costs incurred on the manufacturing side cannot be distinguished with any degree of accuracy from the costs of performing the wholesale and retail functions. In the case of manufacturers producing high grade branded footwear the distribution costs including administrative costs, salesmen's salaries, packing and transport and advertising ranged between 10–15% of sales revenue. In the case of manufacturers selling direct to multiple firms or to wholesalers, distribution costs averaged 3–5% of sales revenue.

The total costs of distribution are estimated at 36–37% of retail sales.

2. RUBBER FOOTWEAR

Consumers' expenditure and methods of distribution

Consumers' expenditure on rubber footwear, including canvas shoes with rubber soles, in 1938 is estimated at £5–5·5 millions. This estimate excludes purchases by industrial users and Government departments. Just over one-third, by value, of the rubber footwear sold to the domestic consumer in 1938 was imported, and goods from Canada represented about one-half of the value of imports.

The methods of distribution. The proportions of total sales of rubber footwear passing through the main channels of distribution in 1938 are estimated as follows:

	%
From manufacturer or importer to wholesaler or factor to retailer	36–41
From manufacturer or importer to retailer	59–64

Included in the sales direct to retailer are the sales by co-operative wholesale societies to retail co-operative societies and purchases by multiple organizations, whether delivered to central warehouse or to individual shops. Also included in the sales direct to retailer are those goods which passed from manufacturers to mail order houses and then to the consumer. This type of sale is thought to have amounted to 3% of total sales.

The importers of rubber footwear, other than Canadian, were usually agents who arranged for the goods to be sent directly from the ports to the warehouses of wholesalers or central depots of multiple and co-operative organizations. In a few cases large-scale retailing organizations themselves imported directly. The importers of Canadian rubber footwear, on the other hand, took full possession of the goods, maintained warehouses, employed salemen and sometimes advertised. These importers sold both to wholesalers and direct to the central depots of large retailing organizations.

Number of wholesalers and retailers. The number of wholesalers or factors of rubber footwear in 1938 is estimated at 450–500. This total includes almost all wholesalers of leather footwear and, in addition, a number of wholesalers in other trades, for example sports goods, often carried rubber footwear. The number of retail outlets is estimated at 22–25,000. The majority of these, 12–14,000, were specialist shoe shops but, in addition, 3–5,000 drapers and outfitters, 1–1,500 sports goods shops, and variety chain stores and general shops also sold rubber footwear.

Sales by different types of retail outlet. The proportion of the total sales to the domestic consumer of rubber footwear undertaken by the different economic types of retail outlet is estimated as follows:

	%
Multiple shoe shops, including variety chain stores	42–48
Department stores	3–5
Co-operative retail stores	6–8
Unit retailers, including sports outfitters	39–43
Mail order houses	2–4

Sales by variety chain stores are estimated at 7–10% of total sales.

The cost of distribution

A considerable quantity of home-manufactured rubber footwear and some imported rubber footwear was sold at retail prices suggested by manufacturers or wholesalers.

The margins earned or allowed by the various distributors were as follows:

Importers' margins on Canadian footwear ranged from 13–18% on sales. Excluding ocean freight clearance charges and discounts allowed to purchasers, the average margin was 14% on sales. Agents importing other footwear earned a commission ranging from 1½–5% on sales.

Wholesale margins ranged between 12½–20% on sales. The margin on home-manufactured footwear and on Canadian imports was usually 12½%, but on other imported goods it was 15–17½%, and sometimes 20%. On certain rubber footwear specialities such as sheepskin overshoes and knee-length Wellingtons, the wholesale margin was 15–17½% on sales. This type of goods, however, represented a very small proportion of total turnover.

Retailers' margins on home-manufactured and imported Canadian rubber footwear averaged 25% on returns. The margin on other imported footwear fluctuated more widely, from 20–30%, but the average was nearer 25%. Multiple organizations usually purchased at wholesale terms.

Settlement discounts in the trade were 3¾% for payment in 7 days and 2½% for payment within the month.

The stock turn of wholesalers and factors on rubber footwear is estimated at 5–6 times a year and the stock turn of retailers 4–5 times a year.

Manufacturers' distribution costs on home-produced rubber footwear, including administrative selling costs, salesmen's salaries, carriage, packing and advertising, are estimated at 8–10% of manufacturers' sales revenue.

The total costs of distribution are estimated at 39–42% of retail sales.

CHAPTER XXI

MEN'S AND BOYS' CLOTHING

I. INTRODUCTION

Consumers' expenditure and methods of distribution

Consvmers' expenditure on men's and boys' clothing in 1938 is estimated at £123 millions. This trade has been discussed in the following chapter in five main groups:

Group	*Consumers' expenditure* £ million
Outerwear	68–69
Shirts, collars and pyjamas	13–14
Hosiery	24–25
Hats and caps	5–6
Other men's and boys' wear	8–10

The expenditure by consumers on retail bespoke tailoring has been excluded from the total and group estimates.

As many features of distribution were common to more than one group, some purpose is served by a general discussion here of the chief characteristics of the men's and boys' wear trade and of the definitions used in the studies.

The methods of distribution in each instance refer only to the methods by which the goods in a finished state were distributed to the consumer, and do not refer to the passage of materials and semi-finished goods to makers-up and manufacturers.

The proportion of the total sales classed as sales from manufacturers direct to retailer includes the goods sold by manufacturers in their own retail outlets, the goods passing from manufacturers to the central depots and warehouses of multiple, variety chain store and department store organizations as well as the deliveries to the branches of such organizations, and the goods either manufactured by or purchased by the co-operative wholesale societies and re-sold by them to retail societies.

In some of the groups a combination of the functions of manufacturing and of wholesaling was a common feature. Some manufacturers in the shirt and collar, hosiery and hat and cap trades, for example, both made goods themselves and also purchased from other manufacturers for distribution through their own selling organization. An attempt has been made, though the estimates can only be very approximate, to class the goods bought by one manufacturer from another in this way as sales through wholesale channels. Further, the wholesalers in these trades were often specialists who had interests in manufacture or who had special lines made for them by manufacturers which they sold under their own brand names. The general wholesale clothing and textile houses did not handle a very large proportion of men's wear. The small proportion of total sales passing through two wholesalers before reaching the retailer have not been separately identified and are included in the sales through wholesalers.

Of the total retail sales of men's and boys' clothing it is estimated that some 60% was represented by distribution direct from manufacturer to retailer and the balance was distributed through wholesalers.

Wholesalers and retail outlets. The number of wholesalers handling some or a complete range of men's and boys' clothing in 1938 is estimated as 300–350. Retail outlets for men's and boys' wear can be divided into two main classes: retailers whose sales of these goods represented the major part of their turnover, and retailers selling men's and boys' wear as a subsidiary to some other trade, usually women's and girls' wear. The number of outlets in the first class is estimated at 11–13,000 and the number in the second at approximately 35–40,000. The number of branches of multiple organizations selling mainly men's and boys' wear is estimated at 3–4,000. Most of the variety chain stores, certain department stores and some 2,300 co-operative shops sold a small range of men's and boys' clothing.

The manufacturing multiple firms sold tailored ready-to-wear clothing and also engaged in wholesale bespoke tailoring, while the multiple outfitters and hosiers concentrated largely on shirts, pyjamas, underwear and sportswear. The sales made in variety chain stores were mainly of goods with a relatively rapid stock turn such as underwear and other hosiery goods and certain lines of boys' wear.

The estimated proportions of the total sales of men's and boys' clothing in 1938 undertaken by the various economic types of outlet were:

	%
Multiple shops, including variety chain stores	28–30
Department stores	7–9
Co-operative shops	6–7
Unit retailers	54–59

The range of margins earned by wholesalers and retailers on the various groups of men's and boys' wear is discussed in the respective case studies, and where possible estimates have been given of the average margin obtained on a particular group of goods. Excluding clothing sold by manufacturers through their own outlets, the proportions of men's and boys' wear sold at retail prices determined by manufacturers or wholesalers was very small, and wholesalers and retailers were largely free to fix their own mark-ups on cost. These varied mainly with the class of goods sold and in some instances with the type of retail outlet. Markdowns were not a very common feature of the men's and boys' wear trade.

The average rates of stock turn given in the case studies are necessarily approximations since there were often marked differences between the number of times a year a small outfitter would turn over his stock of a particular group of goods, for example underwear, and the stock turn of these goods in the variety chain stores or the large men's-wear shops.

2. OUTERWEAR

Consumers' expenditure and methods of distribution

Consumers' expenditure on men's, youths' and boys' factory-made outer-clothing including suits, sportswear, jackets, trousers, overcoats, dressing-gowns, overalls and rainwear is estimated at approximately £68–69 millions. Roughly two-thirds of the total represented wholesale tailoring, and the remainder wholesale bespoke tailoring, rainwear and overalls. The estimate of consumers' expenditure excludes sales of retail bespoke tailored wear and all sales of uniforms and overalls to business and industrial users.

The methods of distribution. The proportion of men's and boys' outerwear passing through the principal channels of distribution, expressed as percentages of retail sales in 1938, are estimated as follows:

	%
From manufacturer direct to retailer	75–80
From manufacturer to wholesaler to retailer	20–25

The sales by multiple shops of clothing produced in their own manufacturing establishments and sales by the co-operative wholesale societies to retail co-operatives are included in sales direct to retailer. It is estimated that approximately one-third of the sales direct to retailer were undertaken by the manufacturing multiple concerns. Department stores and unit retailers obtained a large proportion of their supplies direct from manufacturers.

Wholesalers, who supplied mostly the smaller shops, often those selling drapery and other clothing, tended to concentrate on the cheaper lines of men's clothing and on boys' wear. Slightly over half of the rainwear and overalls was distributed through wholesalers.

Sales by different types of retail outlet. The estimated proportions of total sales in 1938 undertaken by shops grouped by economic type were:

	%
Multiple shops, including manufacturing multiple branches	33–37
Department stores	6–8
Co-operative shops	4–5
Unit retailers	50–57

There were several different types of multiple concern selling men's and boys' outerwear. Most important were the large manufacturing multiple firms which produced all the goods sold in their own shops with the exception of a few lines such as rainwear. These firms were responsible for nearly three-quarters of the total sales in multiple shops. The remainder of the sales made in multiple shops were undertaken by those multiple tailors and outfitters who manufactured some of the goods sold in their shops and also purchased from other manufacturers, and by other multiple concerns whose functions were purely distributive.

The cost of distribution

Excluding the goods sold by manufacturing multiple firms, approximately 15% of men's and boys' heavy clothing was sold at retail prices suggested or recommended by manufacturers.

The margins earned by wholesalers and retailers in 1938 were as follows:

Wholesalers' mark-ups were usually in the region of 20% on cost, yielding 16–17% on sales.

Retailers, whether buying from manufacturers or wholesalers, usually worked to a mark-up of 50% on cost, giving $33\frac{1}{3}$% on sales. The usual margin earned on lines which were price-maintained was $33\frac{1}{3}$% on sales, while a slightly lower margin, 31–32%, was obtained on certain nationally advertised lines of slacks and sportswear.

The retail margin of the manufacturing multiple firms cannot easily be distinguished from the costs incurred in manufacturing and distributing these goods to their retail shops. The prices at which other large retailers bought were usually a matter of negotiation.

Volume discounts were not usual in the trade. Sometimes an additional 2–4% might be given for large orders of a particular line.

Settlement discounts were usually $3\frac{3}{4}$% for payment by the 10th of the next month, $2\frac{1}{2}$% for settlement by the following month.

Stock turn averaged 3–4 times a year in the small shops, but in the case of some of the larger stores was slightly higher, 5–6 times a year.

Manufacturers' distribution costs are taken to include salesmen's salaries and expenses, carriage and transport, advertising, warehousing and general administrative selling costs. In the case of manufacturers who distributed through wholesalers, and who were in fact often makers-up for wholesalers, or who sold a large proportion of their output to multiple retailers, these costs were very small, some 3% of sales revenue. Where manufacturers' sales were largely direct to unit retailers their distribution costs are estimated at approximately 10–12% of sales revenue. Of this, salesmen's salaries, patterns, and associated selling costs represented nearly one-half, warehousing approximately one-third, despatch and carriage and advertising (where undertaken) the remainder.

The distribution costs incurred by the manufacturing multiple firms covered the whole process of distribution from factory to consumer. No effective division can be made between the manufacturers' distribution costs in the sense referred to above and the costs of wholesaling and retailing by these concerns. The total spread between factory cost and retail selling price in these cases, however, is estimated to have ranged from 30–40% of the latter, varying with the circumstances and the organization of the firms concerned.

The total costs of distribution are estimated at 41–43% of retail sales.

3. SHIRTS, COLLARS AND PYJAMAS

Consumers' expenditure and methods of distribution

Consumers' expenditure in 1938 on men's and boys' shirts, collars and pyjamas is estimated at £13–14 millions.

The methods of distribution. The main channels of distribution and the proportions passing through each expressed as percentages of retail sales in 1938 are estimated as follows:

	%
From manufacturer direct to retailer	60–64
From manufacturer to wholesaler to retailer	36–40

Included in the sales direct to retailers are sales by co-operative wholesale societies to retail co-operatives. These sales along with direct sales to department stores and multiple organizations accounted for approximately two-thirds of the total sales made direct to retailer.

A number of multiple organizations and the variety chain stores bought from manufacturers who made practically exclusively for them; other large retailers manufactured some of the goods they sold and also bought outside.

Some manufacturers who distributed direct to retailers purchased part of their supplies from other manufacturers, to this extent performing the function of wholesalers. The general wholesale houses tended to concentrate on the cheaper lines and to supply mostly the smaller outfitters and shops selling men's and women's clothing.

Sales by different types of retail outlet. Retailers selling these goods included the specialist men's and boys' outfitters, some department stores, retail co-operatives, variety chain stores and some general drapers. The estimated proportions of the total trade in 1938 undertaken by retail outlets grouped by economic type were:

	%
Multiple shops and variety chain stores	20–22
Department stores	8–10
Co-operative shops	10–12
Unit retailers	56–62

The cost of distribution

It is estimated that less than 5% of these goods were price-maintained.

The margins earned by various distributors in 1938 were approximately as follows:

Wholesalers' margins ranged from 15–17½% on returns.

Retailers usually worked to a mark-up of 50% on cost to give 33⅓% on returns. A similar margin was usually allowed on price-maintained lines. On the cheaper lines a 33⅓% mark-up was common, yielding 25% on sales. Department stores' margins on this group of goods ranged from 30–37% on sales.

Multiple concerns and some department stores purchased unbranded goods on terms similar to those given to wholesalers, or more often had lines made to their own specifications. On purchases from manufacturers who branded and advertised their goods, large retailers in some instances received terms similar to those given to unit retailers and in others received a small price concession.

Settlement discounts varied from 2½–3¾% for payment in a month. In some cases a discount was given for payment in 2 months.

Stock turn of unit retailers averaged 2–3 times per year. Some multiple shops and variety chain stores had a stock turn of 5–7 times a year.

Manufacturers' distribution costs varied depending on whether manufacturers sold mainly to wholesalers and the wholesale departments of multiple concerns, or mainly to unit retailers. In the former case their distribution costs are estimated to have amounted to 3–5% of sales revenue, in the latter 12–16%, although in the case of highly advertised branded goods they sometimes rose to 20%. Of these costs salesmen's salaries represented approximately two-fifths, carriage and transport rather over one-tenth and administrative selling costs one-quarter. Advertising ranged from one-fifth to two-fifths of total costs.

The total costs of distribution are estimated at 42–44% of retail sales.

4. HOSIERY

Consumers' expenditure and methods of distribution

Consumers' expenditure in 1938 is estimated at £12–13 millions on men's and boys' underwear, £6–7 millions on men's and boys' socks, and £5–6 millions on men's and boys' fancy hosiery, including pullovers, scarves and other knitwear.

The methods of distribution. Taking the group as a whole, the estimated proportions distributed direct to retailers and through wholesalers to retailers, expressed as percentages of retail sales in 1938, were:

	%
From manufacturer direct to retailer	30–35
From manufacturer to wholesaler to retailer	65–70

Included in the direct sales are sales to the wholesale departments of multiple concerns and variety chain stores, and sales by co-operative wholesale societies to retail co-operatives.

Multiple outfitters and variety chain stores purchased most of their supplies direct from manufacturers, and in addition a few manufacturers of branded price-maintained wear distributed direct to unit retailers. A greater proportion of hosiery goods, however, was distributed through wholesalers than was the case with most other types of men's clothing. A mixture of the functions of wholesaling and manufacture was fairly common in the trade, certain firms both manufacturing and purchasing from other manufacturers for distribution to the retailer. An allowance for purchases from other manufacturers in this way has been included in the sales from manufacturers to wholesalers.

Sales by different types of retail outlet. Shops selling these goods included the men's and boys' specialist outfitters, department stores, retail co-operatives, the variety chain stores and some general drapers selling both men's and women's wear.

The approximate proportions of the total trade in 1938 undertaken by shops grouped by economic type were:

	%
Multiple shops and variety chain stores	20–22
Department stores	8–10
Co-operative shops	10–12
Unit retailers	56–62

The cost of distribution

Although 80–90% of hosiery goods in this group were branded, only a small proportion were price-maintained.

Wholesalers' margins ranged from 8% on sales of the very low-priced lines of underwear and socks, to 25% on exclusive ranges of underwear and fancy hosiery. The usual wholesale margin earned on underwear and socks is estimated at between 13–15%. On fancy hosiery the usual range was from 15–20%.

Agents buying for large retailing organizations received a commission of 5%. Agents, however, did not perform the normal wholesale function of stockholding, but merely passed on orders to manufacturers.

Retailers worked to mark-ups which would give 25–35% on returns, varying with the price of the line and the type of retailing organization: 25% on returns was common on the cheaper types of underwear, 30–33⅓% a more usual margin on the better-class lines and on knitted outerwear. The margin allowed on price-maintained branded hosiery was usually 33⅓%.

Multiple concerns and variety chain stores usually received terms similar to those given to wholesalers, and in some cases where very large orders were placed for delivery to a central warehouse, an additional 5%. Branded price-maintained lines, where sold by multiple shops, were in some instances bought on the same terms as those given to unit retailers, but multiple shops and chain stores as a rule did not stock many of these lines.

Settlement discounts were normally 3½% and in some cases up to 5% for payment in 14 days, 2½% in the month. Some manufacturers gave 3½% for payment in the month.

The stock turn of these goods ranged from 3–4 times per year in the smaller shops. In some multiple shops, the variety chain stores and certain department stores, stock turn was from 5–6 times a year and in some cases even higher.

Manufacturers' distribution costs. The distribution costs of manufacturers selling mainly to wholesalers or to the wholesale departments of multiple organizations are estimated to have averaged approximately 3% of sales; the costs of manufacturers selling direct to independent retailers ranged from 12–20% of sales, the variations being largely due to the relative amounts spent on advertising.

The total costs of distribution are estimated at 42–44% of retail sales.

5. HATS AND CAPS

Consumers' expenditure and methods of distribution

Consumers' expenditure on men's and boys' hats and caps in 1938 is estimated at £5–6 millions. This estimate attempts to exclude purchases by trade users and Government departments.

The methods of distribution. The main channels of distribution of hats and caps in the finished state and the proportions passing through each of these channels in 1938 are estimated as follows:

	%
From manufacturer direct to retailer	30–40
From manufacturer to wholesaler to retailer	60–70

Sales by the co-operative wholesale societies to retail co-operatives are included in sales direct to retailer.

Multiple outfitters and hosiers, some of whom specialized in the sale of hats, frequently contracted with manufacturers to have lines made to their own specifications and sold under their own brand names. A few had their own factories.

Wholesalers were usually specialist houses, mostly distributing under their own brand names, and in some cases having interests in manufacture. The general wholesale clothing houses handled a relatively small proportion of the trade in men's and boys' hats, but were more prominent in the cloth-cap trade.

Sales by different types of retail outlet. The principal retail outlets for men's and boys' hats and caps were the specialist hatters, outfitters and hosiers, but these goods were also sold by certain department stores and by some retail co-operatives. Caps were also sold by the variety chain stores and by some drapers and general stores.

The approximate proportions of total sales in 1938 undertaken by shops grouped by economic type were:

	%
Multiple shops, including variety chain stores	22–24
Department stores	6–7
Co-operative shops	4–6
Unit retailers	63–68

The cost of distribution

Although branding was common in the trade, the proportion of total sales represented by goods sold at prices recommended by manufacturers was very small.

The margins obtained by wholesalers and retailers in 1938 are estimated as follows:

Wholesalers' margins ranged from 20–25% on sales, the usual margin being nearer 25%. This margin had to cover heavy warehousing costs due to the bulky nature of the goods and the special packing required.

Retailers usually worked to a mark-up of 50% on cost, giving an average realized margin of 30–33% on sales. The margin varied to some extent with the class of goods sold. For example, on some of the cheaper lines of caps the margin was near 30% on sales while 35% was often obtained on sales of the more exclusive ranges of men's hats.

Multiple organizations purchased from manufacturers at prices determined by negotiation where they placed orders for large quantities, usually receiving terms similar to or in some cases better than those given to wholesalers.

Settlement discounts were generally $3\frac{3}{4}$% for payment in a month, $2\frac{1}{2}$% in 2 months.

Stock turn ranged from 3–4 times a year in the smaller shops, from 5–6 times in some of the larger stores.

Manufacturers' distribution costs are estimated at 2–5% on sales revenue, where sales were made largely to wholesalers and the wholesale departments of multiple concerns. The costs incurred by the few manufacturers trading direct with retailers throughout the country were similar to the gross margin earned by the specialist wholesaler, that is 25% on sales revenue.

The total costs of distribution are estimated at 48–51% of retail sales.

6. MEN'S AND BOYS' HANDKERCHIEFS, TIES, BRACES

Consumers' expenditure and methods of distribution

Consumers' expenditure on this group of goods in 1938 is estimated at approximately £8–10 millions, slightly under half of which represented expenditure on ties.

The method of distribution was usually through wholesale houses. In the case of men's braces, for example, it is estimated that some 80% of the trade passed through wholesalers. There were a few large manufacturers of ties and handkerchiefs who sold under proprietary brand names direct to retailers throughout the country, but such sales represented only a small proportion of the total trade. The variety chain stores and the multiple outfitters purchased largely direct from manufacturers, some of whom made practically exclusively for these firms.

Slightly under two-thirds of the sales of these goods were made by unit retailers, about one-fifth in multiple shops, and the remainder in department stores and retail co-operatives.

The margins obtained by wholesalers generally ranged from 15–17½% on sales. Retailers usually worked to mark-ups which gave a return of 27½–33⅓% on sales, although on certain higher priced lines sold by some of the larger stores a margin of up to 40% was obtained. For the trade as a whole the average retail margin, after allowing for mark-downs, is estimated at approximately 30% on sales.

Stock turn on handkerchiefs and ties was approximately 5–6 times a year in the larger department stores and men's outfitters, and 3–4 times in the smaller shops. It is estimated that over three-quarters of the sales of handkerchiefs were made in the three months prior to Christmas, and this was also the peak period for the sale of ties, although sales of these goods were spread more evenly over the year.

Manufacturers' distribution costs, where goods were sold largely to wholesalers or the wholesale departments of multiple organizations, are estimated at 2–4% of sales revenue. Only a small proportion of the sales in this group were made direct to unit retailers. The distribution costs incurred by manufacturers whose sales were mostly of this type, while difficult in some cases to separate from the costs of selling a number of other goods, are estimated to have ranged from 10–15% on sales. Variations were due largely to the amount of advertising undertaken.

The total costs of distribution are estimated at 42–44% of retail sales.

CHAPTER XXII

WOMEN'S, GIRLS' AND CHILDREN'S WEAR

I. INTRODUCTION

Consumers' expenditure in 1938 on women's, girls' and children's wear and general drapery is estimated at approximately £238 millions. The goods belonging to this trade are discussed in the following chapter in nine main groups.

Group	*Consumers' expenditure* £ million
Outerwear	83–86
Underwear and nightwear	19–20
Stockings and socks	34–35
Corsets and brassières	9–10
Fur clothing	9–11
Millinery	18–20
Gloves	6–7
Dress materials	14–16
Haberdashery and other drapers' goods	38–40

These estimates exclude sales of retail bespoke tailoring and clothing made by private dressmakers, and sales to businesses and industrial users.

A number of features of the distribution of clothing common to several of these groups, and the definitions used in the case studies, are discussed briefly below.

The methods of distribution relate in all instances to the distribution of goods when in the finished state and not to the flow of materials and semi-finished goods to manufacturers and makers-up.

Included throughout in sales by manufacturers direct to retailers are goods distributed by manufacturers to the wholesale depots of multiple stores or to wholesale houses controlled by retail groups, goods manufactured by firms with their own retail outlets, and goods manufactured or purchased by the wholesale co-operative societies and re-sold to the retail societies.

The department stores and the multiple concerns purchased the bulk of their outerwear and fashion goods direct from manufacturers, using the wholesale houses to fill in on certain lines such as haberdashery, sundries, underclothing and other so-called 'bread-and-butter' lines on which prices were fairly standardized and volume discounts obtainable. Wholesalers were also used in those cases where they acted as sole distributors for certain manufacturers. The variety chain stores, which concentrated on sales of the more standardized lines of clothing, particularly of hosiery goods and the cheaper ranges of outerwear, bought practically entirely direct from manufacturers. Some had their own materials made up on a commission basis by manufacturers. Small drapers, who generally did not stock a large proportion of fashion-wear, obtained most of their supplies through wholesalers.

Some of the specialist wholesalers in the trade had interests in manufacture, and a number of them distributed under their own proprietary brand names.

Numbers of wholesalers and of retail outlets. The number of wholesalers can only be estimated very approximately. There were a large number of very small wholesalers whose turnover was in effect lower than that of many retail businesses. Some 300–350 wholesalers, including the general houses and a number of specialists, were members of the Wholesale Textile Association, which prescribed a certain minimum size of turnover and premises as a condition of membership. Some wholesale houses were closely associated with retail groups and were, in effect, the central warehousing and buying organizations for these groups.

The number of shops whose main trade was in women's and children's wear is estimated at 20–25,000. Other retail shops selling some of these goods are estimated to have numbered 60–65,000 in 1938. The principal outlets were the department stores, numbering 450, which were particularly important in this trade, the variety chain stores, general drapers who usually sold certain lines of women's and children's wear, haberdashery, baby linen and knitting wool, and the specialist outlets such as the modistes, tailors, furriers, hosiers and milliners. The number of multiple shops, including multiple department stores, selling mainly women's and children's wear and drapers' goods, is estimated at 1,500–2,000.

Sales by different types of retail outlet. The estimated proportions of total sales of all women's and children's wear and drapers' goods in 1938 undertaken by shops grouped by economic type were:

	%
Multiple shops, including variety chain stores	14–16
Department stores	25–30
Co-operative shops	6–8
Unit retailers	46–55

The range of wholesale and retail margins and estimates of the average realized margins earned on particular goods are given in the case studies. Wholesalers and retailers were generally free to fix mark-ups on cost, since only a small proportion of these goods were sold at retail prices determined or suggested by manufacturers or wholesalers. As retailers usually marked up their goods in certain popular price steps, for example, 4s. 11d., 5s. 11d., manufacturers and wholesalers frequently had to sell at prices which would fit in with these steps and allow retailers their traditional margin.

Stock losses and wastage were incurred by wholesalers and retailers in the form of pilferage and of returned, damaged and shop-soiled goods, and, in the case of dress materials, of remnants left over after cutting. End-of-season mark-downs are traditional in the drapery trade, which is the only trade to feature regular half-yearly sales. The incidence of mark-downs was greater in some groups of clothing than in others, particularly in fashion goods, for example millinery. Mark-downs on these goods, however, were usually allowed for by high initial mark-ups at the beginning of the season. The extent to which mark-downs were adopted depended also on the attitude of particular wholesalers and retailers towards stock turn. Some large stores marked down all slow-moving stock and pursued a policy of drastic price reductions on fashion wear at the end of six months. For the drapery trade as a whole the average mark-down has been estimated at 3–4% and the average realized margin at approximately 30% on sales. Most of the larger department stores aimed at an average overall realized margin of 33⅓% on sales of clothing, while in those stores which concentrated on goods with a rapid stock turn the average realized margin was between 25–30% on sales.

Settlement discounts varied considerably depending on the policy of particular manufacturers and wholesalers. This discount was frequently used as a competitive device and in some cases forward dating of invoices was practised to allow longer credit. Some wholesalers gave 4 and up to 5 months' credit, allowing the settlement discount of 2½%. The settlement discount was also used in some instances as a form of volume discount to large buyers.

The average stock turn rates quoted in the case studies, based on sales divided by stock at selling price, are very approximate as stock turn varied greatly with type of goods and the size and type of retail outlet. The rate ranged from 2–3 times a year in the smallest drapery shops to 10 times on certain fashion wear of the type sold in department stores. For the trade as a whole an overall stock turn of 4–5 times a year on clothing and drapery was considered good.

Manufacturers' distribution costs showed marked differences depending on the type of sales policy pursued. In most of the case studies an attempt has been made to give separate estimates of these costs where manufacturers distributed largely to wholesalers and the wholesale depots of large retail organizations, and where goods were sold largely direct to unit retailers. Where an average figure is given for the trade as a whole, this, of course, takes into account the proportions of the goods passing direct to retailers and through wholesalers.

Mail order and credit trading have not been discussed separately in the case studies, as in the former case most of the sales were made by retail organizations and are included in their total sales, while in the latter the provision of credit had little direct effect on methods of distribution or realized margins.

2. OUTERWEAR

Consumers' expenditure and methods of distribution

Consumers' expenditure on women's and children's outerwear in 1938 is estimated at £83–86 millions. The estimate excludes sales of fur clothing, retail bespoke tailoring, and clothing made up by private dressmakers. The principal groups included are tailored wear, that is coats, suits, slacks and other wear associated with the heavy clothing trade; proofed wear; dresses, unlined suits, skirts, blouses, overalls and dressing-gowns associated with the light clothing trade; and knitted outerwear and children's outerwear.

The methods of distribution. The main channels of distribution and the proportions distributed through each expressed as percentages of total retail sales in 1938 are estimated as follows:

	%
From manufacturer direct to retailer	62–68
From manufacturer to wholesaler to retailer	32–38

These figures conceal certain differences in the methods of distribution of the various groups of clothing included under the general heading of outerwear. It is estimated that 65–70% of tailored outerwear and 60–65% of dresses, blouses and overalls passed direct from manufacturers to retailers. About 50% of proofed wear, over 80% of infants' wear and a large proportion of knitted outerwear was distributed through wholesalers. The wholesalers' trade tended to be largely in those groups of outerwear which were relatively less subject to fashion changes and were in the lower- and medium-price ranges.

Included in sales direct to retailer are sales to department stores through linked wholesale houses, sales to multiple organizations including the variety chain stores and to mail order houses, and sales by wholesale co-operative societies to retail co-operatives.

The larger retailers often arranged with manufacturers to have lines made to their own specifications, some having their own materials made up on a commission basis. The manufacturing multiple organization prominent in the men's outerwear trade, however, was not an important feature of the trade in women's outerwear.

Some manufacturers sold direct to retailers of all types. Other manufacturers selling the more exclusive lines distributed only to high-class specialist dress shops and to the model departments of large stores, while a few manufacturers of branded high fashion wear sold on a more restricted basis to selected retailers in particular areas, who acted as their exclusive agents.

Numbers of retail outlets and sales by different types of outlet. The total number of outlets for these goods in 1938 is discussed in the introduction to this chapter. The proportions of the total sales in 1938 undertaken by shops grouped by economic type are estimated as follows:

	%
Multiple shops and variety chain stores	14–16
Department stores	29–33
Co-operative shops	6–7
Unit retailers	44–51

The cost of distribution

It is estimated that less than 5% of women's outerwear was price-maintained. This estimate excludes the sales of goods by retail outlets linked with manufacturers.

The margins earned by wholesalers and retailers in 1938 can be summarized as follows:

Wholesalers' margins varied with the price group of the goods, the higher-priced ranges generally bearing higher percentage mark-ups. On tailored wear and the exclusive lines of women's dresses wholesale margins ranged from 16–20% on sales, averaging 17% after allowing for mark-downs and stock losses. On the cheaper and more standardized ranges of blouses, dresses, household overalls and knitted outerwear wholesalers' margins averaged approximately 15% on sales. On the very low-priced lines of this type of clothing the wholesale margin earned was nearer 12%.

Retailers usually worked to mark-ups which, after allowing for end-of-season mark-downs and stock losses, would give a return of 30–33⅓% on sales. There were, of course, variations in the mark-ups and margins obtained on goods of different price ranges and as between goods sold by different types of retail outlet. Certain department stores and some specialist shops, for example, obtained margins of 40% and in some cases of 50% on sales of the more exclusive lines of women's outerwear, while on the cheaper types of household overalls, blouses and knitted outerwear sold in variety chain stores retail margins averaged 25–30% on sales. On some ranges these stores worked to a margin of nearer 20%.

Settlement discounts varied to some extent with the relative strengths of buyers and sellers and were in effect in some instances a form of volume discount to large buyers. Discounts ranged from $3\frac{3}{4}$–5% in some cases for payment in 7 days, and from $2\frac{1}{2}$–$3\frac{3}{4}$% for settlement in a month, or in many cases in a considerably longer period.

Stock turn. There were marked differences in rates of stock turn on different classes of outerwear, depending on whether the goods were subject to fashion changes, on their price group and on the type and size of shop in which the goods were sold. The stock turn in the smaller shops of the type not selling high fashion outerwear is estimated at some 4–5 times a year. The larger department stores had stock turns of 7–8 times a year on women's fashion wear and children's wear, and 10 times and in some instances higher on certain quick-selling lines such as blouses.

Manufacturers' distribution costs varied greatly depending on whether sales were largely to wholesalers and the central depots of multiple concerns, or direct to unit retailers. There were considerable differences between the costs of individual manufacturers shown as a percentage of sales, owing to such factors as the amount of advertising undertaken, the size of turnover in relation to overhead costs, and the type of goods sold, that is fashion goods or the more standardized lines. Where sales were largely to wholesalers, manufacturers' distribution costs, including salesmen's salaries, despatch and carriage, advertising, and warehousing and administrative selling costs are estimated at 3–5% of sales revenue. The costs incurred by manufacturers selling direct to retailers ranged from 10% on the less advertised and more standardized lines to 15–20% and in some instances higher where manufacturers sold only to exclusive outlets on a restricted sales basis. For the trade as a whole manufacturers' distribution costs are estimated to have averaged between 7–9% of sales revenue. Of these costs salesmen's salaries and expenses represented approximately one-third, despatch and carriage one-fifth, and warehousing and general selling costs, including advertising, the remainder.

The total costs of distribution are estimated at 43–45% of retail sales.

3. UNDERWEAR AND NIGHTWEAR

Consumers' expenditure and methods of distribution

Consumers' expenditure on women's and children's underwear and nightwear in 1938 is estimated at £19–20 millions.

The methods of distribution. The main channels of distribution of this group of goods and the proportions passing through each expressed as percentages of total retail sales in 1938 are estimated as follows:

	%
From manufacturer direct to retailer	33–37
From manufacturer to wholesaler to retailer	63–67

Sales of these goods direct to retailers comprised for the most part sales to the wholesale departments of variety chain stores, multiple concerns and certain department stores and sales by wholesale co-operative societies to retail co-operatives. The larger retailing organizations in some instances made these purchases through buying agents acting on their behalf. The department stores, which normally obtained most of their supplies of clothing direct from manufacturers, relied to a greater extent on the wholesaler for the more standardized lines such as underwear on which volume discounts were obtainable on large orders. A number of the specialist wholesale distributors of underwear and other hosiery wear manufactured some of these goods themselves and also bought from other manufacturers for sale under their own brand names. Of the few manufacturers of branded price-maintained underwear and nightwear some sold mainly direct to retailers and others largely to wholesalers.

Sales by different types of retail outlet. Shops selling underwear and nightwear included a large number of general drapers, women's and children's outfitters, specialist hosiery shops, department stores, the variety chain stores and the retail co-operatives. There were some mail order sales, mostly of goods in the cheaper ranges, but sales of this type represented a small proportion of total sales of these goods. The variety chain stores sold large quantities, in limited ranges of style and colour, of the less expensive types of underwear. The estimated proportions of the total sales in 1938 made by shops grouped by economic type were:

	%
Department stores	19–21
Multiple shops, including variety chain stores	20–23
Co-operative shops	5–10
Unit retailers	46–56

Sales in variety chain stores represented between two-thirds and three-quarters of the sales by multiple shops.

The cost of distribution

Most of the goods in this group were branded but only a small proportion, under 5%, was sold at retail prices suggested by manufacturers or wholesalers,

The margins earned by wholesalers and retailers in 1938 can be summarized as follows:

> *Wholesalers'* margins ranged from 12% on the cheapest lines to 20% on exclusive brands. On women's vests and knickers, for example, 12–15% was usually earned on the cheaper ranges and 17½–19½% on the better quality goods and on outsize fittings. For the group as a whole the average margin earned by wholesalers after allowing for mark-downs and stock losses was approximately 15% on sales. Agents buying on behalf of large retailing interests usually received a commission of 5%.
>
> *Retailers* worked to mark-ups giving a return of 25–36% on sales depending on the class of goods sold and on the type of shop. On many of the lines sold by variety chain stores a margin of 25–30% was obtained and on the very cheapest lines 20%, while certain department stores expected a return of 36% or higher on certain of their more exclusive lines. The average margin earned on this group of goods, after allowing for stock losses and mark-downs, is estimated at approximately 30% on sales. Mark-downs on underwear were generally less significant than on outerwear, which was more subject to fashion change.
>
> *Multiple* concerns and variety chain stores purchasing direct from manufacturers bought on terms similar to those given to wholesalers. In many instances their orders were larger than those of wholesalers and they received better terms, sometimes an additional 5%. Some of these large retailing organizations had lines made to their own specifications, often by manufacturers who made more or less exclusively for them, the price at which they purchased in such cases being a matter of negotiation between buyer and seller.

Settlement discounts varied considerably. A large retailer might obtain 5% for payment in 7 days, but 3¾% was more usual. For settlement in the month, and in many cases up to several months, 2½% was usual but in some instances 3¾% was allowed.

Stock turn of these goods in the smaller drapers' shops is estimated to have averaged between 3–4 times a year, in department stores between 5–6 times.

Manufacturers' distribution costs, where goods were distributed mainly to wholesalers and the wholesale depots of large retail concerns, were of the order of 3–4% on sales revenue, covering salesmen's salaries, despatch and carriage, warehousing and general selling costs including any advertising costs. The costs incurred by manufacturers when selling direct to unit retailers averaged 8–10% on sales revenue, rising to

15% in the case of a few highly advertised lines. These costs varied as between manufacturers, as shown above, but were generally not so heavy as the costs involved in selling outerwear, where advertising was heavier and specialized travellers necessary.

The total costs of distribution are estimated at 42–44% of retail sales.

4. STOCKINGS AND SOCKS

Consumers' expenditure and methods of distribution

Consumers' expenditure on women's and maids' stockings in 1938 is estimated at approximately £30–32 millions, and on women's, girls' and children's socks at £3–4 millions.

The methods of distribution. The proportions of women's and maids' stockings passing through each of the main channels of distribution expressed as percentages of total retail sales in 1938 are estimated as follows:

	%
From manufacturer direct to retailer	45–50
From manufacturer to wholesaler to retailer	50–55

A rather greater proportion of women's, girls' and children's socks was distributed through wholesalers.

Just over one-half of the sales made direct to retailers were sales by manufacturers to the wholesale departments of multiple organizations and variety chain stores, and sales by the co-operative wholesale societies to retail societies. Most of the manufacturers of the well-known branded stockings had their own wholesaling organizations through which they sold to unit retailers, multiple concerns and department stores and in some instances to the wholesale co-operatives. The variety chain stores and to a lesser extent the multiple concerns and department stores purchased unbranded lines direct from manufacturers, often through buying agents. The variety chain stores placed orders with manufacturers for large quantities in limited ranges of colour and quality. A number of wholesalers had close links with manufacturers, and marketed goods under their own brand names, while some manufacturers with their own wholesaling organizations bought a certain amount of goods from other manufacturers and also handled imported stockings.

Sales by different types of retail outlet. Women's stockings and children's socks were sold by most drapers and department stores including the drapery departments of co-operative shops, by specialist hosiery shops and by variety chain stores. A few lines were sold by retailers of footwear and by small general shops, and in some instances by modistes and hairdressers. The estimated proportions of the total sales in 1938 undertaken by shops grouped by economic type were:

	%
Multiple shops, including variety chain stores	15–17
Department stores	15–20
Co-operative shops	10–15
Unit retailers	50–58

The cost of distribution

It is estimated that approximately 40% of the total sales of women's stockings represented goods which carried a retail selling price suggested by manufacturers or wholesalers. All the manufacturers of well-known brands had recommended selling prices, although in practice strict price-maintenance was not always enforceable.

The margins earned by wholesalers and retailers in 1938 were approximately as follows:

Wholesalers' margins ranged from 15–25% on sales, varying with the class of goods. On the highly advertised branded lines, where these were handled by wholesalers, margins tended to be nearer the lower end of this range. The average margin obtained by wholesalers after allowing for mark-downs and stock losses is estimated at approximately 16% on sales.

Agents buying on behalf of large retailers earned a commission of approximately 5%.

Retailers earned margins ranging from 20% or under on the very cheapest lines of seamless stockings to 40% on the most exclusive lines. It is estimated that approximately half of the total sales of stockings were of goods retailing at 2s. a pair or under and that the retail average margin earned after allowing for mark-downs and stock losses was between 25–29% on sales.

Multiple organizations and variety chain stores in many cases bought unbranded goods from manufacturers at prices determined by negotiation, the price depending on whether deliveries were made to a central warehouse or to retail shops. Large department stores and multiple concerns obtained price concessions on some branded goods purchased from manufacturers, while in other instances they bought on terms similar to those obtained by unit retailers, but often received additional support in the way of advertising and display facilities provided by manufacturers.

Stock turn is estimated to have averaged between 5–7 times a year. Some large department stores and the variety chain stores turned over their stock 10–12 times in a year. Owing to marked seasonal variations in consumer demand the amount of stock held by retailers varied considerably at different times of the year.

Settlement discounts ranged from 2½–3¾% for payment in the month. Sometimes larger discounts were given to large purchasers. Some wholesalers gave 2½% for settlement in 2 months, and 1¾% in 3 months.

Manufacturers' distribution costs showed marked variations depending on whether goods were distributed to retailers throughout the country or mainly to wholesalers and the wholesale depots of multiple stores. For the trade as a whole manufacturers' distribution costs are estimated to have averaged between 6–9% on sales revenue, of which salesmen's salaries and expenses represented approximately one-quarter, advertising approximately one-third, and despatch and carriage, warehousing and other selling costs the remainder.

The total costs of distribution are estimated at 41–43% of retail sales.

5. CORSETS AND BRASSIÈRES

Consumers' expenditure and methods of distribution

Consumers' expenditure in 1938 on corsetry, including corsets, brassières, suspender belts and similar goods, is estimated at £9–10 millions.

The methods of distribution. The proportions of these goods passing through each of the main channels of distribution, expressed as percentages of total retail sales in 1938, are estimated as follows:

	%
From manufacturer direct to retailer	35–40
From manufacturer to wholesaler to retailer	50–55
From manufacturer to his agent to consumer	9–11

Corsets and brassières may be divided into three main groups each with its characteristic method of distribution. The mass-produced lines were largely distributed through wholesalers, although multiple organizations and variety chain stores tended to purchase this type of goods direct from manufacturers; the medium and higher priced lines were for the most part sold direct to retailers, particularly to department stores which often provided fitting services; made-to-measure corsets were, in effect, sold direct to consumers through corsetières who were agents of the manufacturer. Some of these agents owned drapers' shops but the majority did not.

Sales by different types of retail outlet. The estimated proportions sold by retail outlets in 1938, grouped by economic type, were:

Multiple shops and variety	%
chain stores	8–10
Department stores	15–20
Co-operative shops	10–15
Manufacturers' agents	9–11
Unit retailers	48–54

The cost of distribution

Some 60% of these goods were sold at retail prices fixed or recommended by manufacturers or wholesalers.

The margins earned by wholesalers and retailers in 1938 were approximately as follows:

Wholesale margins ranged from 15% on returns on the cheapest lines with a retail price of 5s. or less, to 25% on exclusive lines. The average realized wholesale margin earned is estimated at approximately 17% on sales.

Retailers earned margins ranging from 19% on returns on the very low priced lines of corsets and brassières to 33⅓% on medium and higher priced goods. Some retailers, particularly the larger stores which had lines specially made for them, worked on a margin of 35% on returns, and sometimes higher. In these cases special fitting services were usually provided by the retailer. The manufacturers' agents referred to above were allowed a margin of 33⅓% on sales. The average realized margin earned by retailers is estimated at approximately 33% on sales of corsets and 25% on brassières.

Volume discounts were not usually given on price-maintained goods. Multiple and variety chain stores bought on terms arrived at by negotiation, usually receiving terms at least as favourable as those given to wholesalers.

Settlement discounts were around 3¾% for payment in the month, 2½% in 2 months, but there were variations in terms given by different manufacturers and wholesalers.

Stock turn ranged from 6–8 times per year in the larger department stores and variety chain stores, 4–5 times a year in the smaller drapers' shops.

Manufacturers' distribution costs varied quite widely. In some cases where the goods were sold direct to retailers and the product was nationally advertised, the distribution costs amounted to 12–15% of sales revenue. Other manufacturers selling mainly to wholesalers had distribution costs of 4–6% of sales revenue. The average for the trade is estimated at 8–10% of sales revenue, of which advertising represented between one-quarter and one-third.

The total costs of distribution are estimated at 45–47% of retail sales.

6. FURS AND FUR GARMENTS

Consumers' expenditure and methods of distribution

Consumers' expenditure on this group of goods, comprising fur coats, capes, furs and fur accessories other than fur gloves, was approximately £10 millions in 1938.

The methods of distribution. The estimated proportions of the total sales of fur goods in the finished state passing through each of the various channels in 1938 were approximately:

	%
From manufacturer direct to retailer	68–72
From manufacturer to wholesaler to retailer	20–25
From manufacturer or wholesaler to consumer	5–10

Manufacturers are defined as the makers-up of the finished goods. The sales direct to retailer include sales by manufacturers through their own shops and to the wholesale depots of multiple organizations and department stores, and sales by the co-operative wholesale societies to retail societies. Manufacturing multiple organizations in the trade made both for their own shops and for sale to other retailers. Wholesalers supplied mostly the smaller drapers selling certain lines of fur goods. Sales direct to consumers comprised goods made up by wholesalers and manufacturers to private customers' orders.

Sales by different types of retail outlet. Furs and fur goods were sold by some 1,250 specialist furriers' shops of which approximately 100–150 were branches of multiple concerns, and by department stores, gown shops and some general drapers. Excluding sales direct to consumers, the estimated proportions of total sales in 1938 undertaken by the different economic types of retail outlet were:

	%
Multiple shops	10–13
Department stores	53–56
Co-operative shops	1–2
Unit retailers	29–36

The cost of distribution

There was no retail price maintenance in this trade.

The margins earned by wholesalers and retailers in 1938 were approximately as follows:

Wholesalers' margins ranged from 19–25% on sales, the average realized margin earned being near 20%.

Retailers tended to work to high initial mark-ups to allow for heavy mark-downs at the end of the season. Realized margins ranged from 30–40% on sales, averaging approximately 33⅓%.

Settlement discounts allowed by manufacturers were usually 3¾% for payment in 1 month, 2½% in 2 months.

Stock turn. The larger department stores turned over their stock 3–4 times a year but for the trade as a whole average retail stock turn is estimated at around 2½ times a year.

Manufacturers' distribution costs, excluding the costs incurred and margins earned by manufacturing multiple concerns, are estimated to have ranged from 9–12% on sales revenue.

The total costs of distribution are estimated at 45–47% of retail sales.

7. MILLINERY

Consumers' expenditure and methods of distribution

Consumers' expenditure on millinery, including all women's and children's headwear, is estimated at approximately £18–20 millions in 1938. Purchases by businesses and institutions are excluded from this estimate.

The methods of distribution. The proportions passing from manufacturers direct to retailers and through wholesalers expressed as percentages of total retail sales in 1938 are estimated as follows:

	%
From manufacturer direct to retailer	20–25
From manufacturer to wholesaler to retailer	75–80

By agreement in the trade these goods were largely distributed through wholesale houses and to the wholesale departments of multiple and co-operative organizations. Millinery wholesalers tended to be specialists and a number of them took an active interest in manufacture. Some of these wholesalers had their own factories or work-rooms or had certain lines and designs made exclusively for them. The sales direct from manufacturers to retailers comprised sales by the few manufacturers who sold direct to large and small shops and sales by the speciality retailers who did a certain amount of making up in their own workrooms, together with sales by manufacturers to the wholesale departments of large retailing organizations.

Sales by different types of retail outlet. The principal retail outlets for millinery were the specialist milliners and the department stores. Some lines of millinery, particularly children's wear, were also sold by general drapers, including co-operative shops with drapery departments, and the cheaper ranges were stocked by some variety chain stores. The approximate proportions of the total sales in 1938 undertaken by retail outlets grouped by economic type were:

	%
Multiple shops and variety chain stores	4–6
Department stores	18–22
Co-operative shops	4–6
Unit retailers	66–74

The cost of distribution

Only a very small proportion of millinery was sold at prices fixed or recommended by manufacturers, wholesalers and retailers working to mark-ups on cost. Initial mark-ups were often high as millinery was particularly subject to fashion changes and heavy end-of-season mark-downs were common in the trade.

The margins earned by wholesalers and retailers in 1938 were approximately as follows:

Wholesalers' margins ranged from 20–25% on sales, the average realized margin earned being nearer to 20%. Mark-ups on particular lines and at the beginning of the season were in some instances up to 40% on cost to allow for mark-downs at a later date or on other stock.

Retailers' mark-ups varied greatly as between goods in different price ranges and with the type of retail outlet. The usual margins aimed at by department stores, for example, were from 40–46% on returns. On so-called 'bread-and-butter' lines, however, a retail margin of 25% on sales was common in many shops. The average realized margin earned by retailers is estimated at between $33\frac{1}{3}$–35% on sales.

Settlement discounts were $2\frac{1}{2}$–$3\frac{3}{4}$% for payment in the month, and sometimes $2\frac{1}{2}$% for settlement in 2 months.

Stock turn tended to be rapid owing to the necessity, due to changes in fashion, to clear stock frequently by end-of-season mark-downs. The larger department stores turned over their stock 15–17 times in a year; in the smaller shops, however, stock turn was nearer 5–7 times a year.

Manufacturers' distribution costs, including salesmen's salaries and carriage and packing and other selling costs, on sales to wholesalers and to the wholesale departments of multiple and co-operative organizations were of the order of 3–5% on sales revenue.

The total costs of distribution are estimated at 48–51% of retail sales.

8. DRESS MATERIALS

Consumers' expenditure and methods of distribution

Consumers' expenditure on dress materials is estimated at approximately £15 millions in 1938. This figure excludes sales of cloth to makers-up and to bespoke tailors.

The methods of distribution. Of the sales of dress materials to private consumers the proportions passing through each of the main channels expressed as percentages of total retail sales in 1938 are estimated as follows:

	%
From manufacturer direct to retailer	55–60
From manufacturer to wholesaler to retailer	40–45

'Manufacturer' is here taken to include merchant-converters. Sales by co-operative wholesale societies to retail societies and sales by manufacturers to retail buying groups are included in sales direct to retailers. Most of the department stores, which did a fairly substantial proportion of the total trade, purchased the bulk of their materials direct from manufacturers or converters.

The wholesaler did not handle a large proportion of the 'counter trade' in dress materials. Sales by wholesalers to makers-up are excluded from the estimates given.

Sales by different types of retail outlet. Retail shops selling these goods included the department stores, some drapers and retail co-operatives and a few shops specializing in the sale of dress materials. The smaller draper tended to concentrate more on the sale of made-up goods. Practically no dress materials were sold by multiple shops other than the multiple department stores, and none by the variety chain stores. The estimated proportions of the national trade done by shops grouped by economic type in 1938 were:

	%
Department stores	61–66
Co-operative stores	6–8
Unit retailers	26–33

The cost of distribution

A very small proportion of dress materials was price-maintained by manufacturers, this practice being limited to two or three firms.

The margins earned by wholesalers and retailers in 1938 were approximately as follows:

Wholesalers earned margins from 13–17½% on sales, varying with the price range of the goods. The average realized margin was approximately 15% on sales.

Retailers' margins generally ranged from 27½–36% on sales, although on the very cheapest lines the margins obtained by some retailers were near 22%. The average margin earned after allowing for stock losses, mark-downs and remnants is estimated at between 30–33⅓% on sales. A margin of 33⅓% was usually allowed by those few manufacturers who fixed the retail selling price of their materials.

Settlement discounts were 3¾% for payment in 7–10 days, 2½% in one month. In many instances longer periods of credit were given. Large buyers sometimes received up to 5% for prompt settlement.

Stock turn in the smaller shops averaged 3–4 times a year, rising to 5 times a year in the larger department stores.

Manufacturers' or converters' distribution costs, including salesmen's salaries, pattern books, carriage and packing, warehousing and general selling costs, are estimated to have averaged from 6–8% of sales revenue.

The total costs of distribution are estimated at 42–44% of retail sales.

9. GLOVES

Consumers' expenditure and methods of distribution

Consumers' expenditure on men's, women's and children's gloves of all kinds, other than industrial and protective gloves, is estimated at approximately £8 millions. Imports represented 20–25% of the value of retail sales.

The methods of distribution. The proportions of goods passing direct to retailers and through wholesalers respectively, expressed as percentages of total retail sales in 1938 are estimated as follows:

	%
From manufacturer direct to retailer	25–30
From manufacturer to wholesaler to retailer	70–75

The sales direct to retailers comprised mostly sales by manufacturers to large purchasers such as department stores and multiple and variety chain store organizations and by the co-operative wholesale societies to retail societies. These large retailers, however, also purchased through wholesalers, while the independent retailer relied mostly on the wholesaler for his supplies. A few large distributors were both manufacturers and wholesalers in that they bought supplies from other firms for distribution to the retailer and also produced the goods themselves.

Imported gloves were mainly distributed through wholesalers. Some of the larger retail organizations, however, purchased direct from foreign manufacturers.

Sales by different types of retail outlet. Gloves were sold by a large number of shops, including drapers, outfitters, men's and women's hosiers, variety chain stores and department stores, and the retail co-operatives. The proportions of the total sales undertaken by outlets grouped by economic type in 1938 are estimated as follows:

	%
Multiple shops and variety chain stores	10–14
Department stores	20–25
Co-operative stores	6–8
Unit retailers	53–64

The cost of distribution

There was no price-maintenance in this trade, wholesalers and retailers being free to determine their own mark-ups.

The margins earned by wholesalers and retailers in 1938 were approximately as follows:

Wholesalers' margins varied with the price range of the line from 14–20% on sales, the average realized margin earned being approximately 16% on sales.

Retailers' margins averaged near 30% on sales after allowing for stock losses and mark-downs. The larger retailers, for example the department stores, worked to margins of 30–35% on sales, the margin of shops doing a cheaper trade being nearer to $27\frac{1}{2}$%.

Multiple shops and variety chain stores bought large quantities of particular lines by arrangement with manufacturers, buying in some cases on terms somewhat similar to those on which wholesalers purchased, and in others receiving more favourable terms.

Settlement discounts were $3\frac{3}{4}$% for payment in 7 days, or in some instances in the month; $2\frac{1}{2}$% for settlement in a month, or sometimes in 2 months.

The stock turn of retailers is estimated to have averaged 3–4 times per year.

Manufacturers' distribution costs, including costs of salesmen's salaries, carriage and packing and general selling costs, were approximately 3–4% of sales revenue for the trade as a whole.

The total costs of distribution are estimated at 42–44% of retail sales.

10. OTHER DRAPERS' GOODS

Consumers' expenditure and methods of distribution

Consumers' expenditure on drapers' sundries, including haberdashery of all kinds, i.e. pins, needles, buttons, lace, trimmings and embroideries, sewing thread, knitting wools, miscellaneous goods such as handkerchiefs, scarves and certain fancy goods, and baby linen, is estimated very approximately at £38–40 millions.

The methods of distribution. Haberdashery and drapers' sundries were largely distributed through wholesalers, some of whom, the sundries, art goods and haberdashery wholesalers, specialized in the sale of these goods. The larger department stores and other large retail buyers who tended to go direct to manufacturers for their supplies of fashion wear and textiles relied to a greater extent on the wholesaler for haberdashery and similar standardized goods of this type.

Some branded products in this group were, however, distributed largely direct by manufacturers to both large and small retailers. A prominent example is sewing thread, on which the private consumer spent £1·25–£1·5 millions in 1938. Of the total sales of sewing thread it is estimated that not more than 25–30% at the most was distributed through wholesalers.

Allowing for the marked variations in the methods of distribution of different products in this general group of goods, the proportion of total sales passing through wholesalers is estimated at between two-thirds and three-quarters. This estimate is only very approximate.

Sales by different types of retail outlet. These goods were sold by a large number of shops, including general drapers, department stores, variety chain stores, co-operative stores with drapery departments, and small general shops, the total number of retail outlets being estimated at 60–70,000. The estimated proportions of total sales in 1938 undertaken by the different economic types of retail outlet were as follows:

	%
Multiple shops and variety chain stores	18–22
Department stores	18–22
Co-operative stores	7–9
Unit retailers	47–57

The cost of distribution

The margins obtained by wholesalers and retailers in 1938 were approximately as follows:

Wholesalers' margins ranged from 15–17½% on sales. On sewing thread, which was largely price-maintained, the wholesalers received 10% off the wholesale price and a volume discount ranging from 1–6%.

Retailers' margins ranged from 28–35% on sales. On sewing thread the retailer was allowed 25–33⅓% on sales, varying with the length of the reel, the average being 27½% on sewing thread and 33⅓% on embroidery thread. On knitting wools, which were also largely proprietary products, retailers were allowed 30% on sales, and on proprietary handkerchiefs 33⅓% on sales.

Settlement discounts were 3¾% for cash and 2½% for payment within one month, although there were considerable variations in the terms given.

Stock turn of department stores on haberdashery was 5–7 times a year and on knitting wools 8–10 times. The average stock turn of the smaller draper, however, is estimated at 3–4 times a year.

The total costs of distribution are estimated at 41–45% of retail sales.

CHAPTER XXIII

BOOKS, NEWSPAPERS, MAGAZINES AND STATIONERY

I. BOOKS

Consumers' expenditure and methods of distribution

Consumers' expenditure on books in 1938 is estimated at £7–8 millions. Purchases by schools, libraries and other institutions of both educational and non-educational books are excluded from this estimate.

The methods of distribution. The proportions of total sales of books to the private consumer passing through the main channels of distribution in 1938 are estimated as follows:

	%
From publisher to retail bookseller	65–75
From publisher to wholesaler to retail bookseller	23–27
From publisher direct to consumer	3–7

Included in the sales from publisher direct to consumer are sales through book clubs and sales made by door-to-door canvassing.

Number of wholesalers and retailers. The number of wholesalers dealing mainly in books was less than a dozen in 1938. The number of retail booksellers is estimated at about 5,000. This figure refers to those shops whose main turnover was in books, but in addition there was a larger number of shops which sold particular types of books or a limited range of books. Some 700–800 of the main retail outlets for books were multiple booksellers and newsagents.

Sales by different types of retail outlet. The proportions of the total sales of books made by different types of economic outlets in 1938 are estimated as follows:

	%
Multiple shops	10–12
Department stores and co-operative shops	2–3
Unit retailers	85–88

The cost of distribution

Practically all books, other than educational and second-hand books, were sold under the Net Book Agreement by which the publisher fixed the price at which the retailer had to sell to the public. But there was no uniformity in the terms given by publishers to wholesalers, by publishers to retailers and by wholesalers to retailers. There were, however, certain ranges in the discounts for particular types of order which were coming to be fairly generally recognized in the trade. The terms on which wholesalers and retailers purchased were sometimes quoted as a straight discount off the retail price, but more usually in two parts, a discount off the retail price plus a further trade discount of 5%, 7½% or 10% off the invoice price.

Wholesalers purchased from publishers at a discount off the retail price ranging from 25% off the retail price and 5% off the invoice to 33⅓% and 10%. The more general range was 25% and 7½% to 33⅓% and 5%. The actual discount earned depended partly on whether the wholesaler bought on 'subscription' terms or on day-to-day orders or after subscription. Here 'on subscription' refers to orders given prior to actual publication. The higher discounts were usually given for on subscription purchases and it is estimated that three-quarters of the purchases by wholesalers were made on these terms. The average discount off the retail price earned by wholesalers was 33⅓%, representing an average gross margin on sales of 11%.

Retailers when buying direct from the publisher received discount off the retail price ranging from 16⅔% off the retail price and 5% off the invoice to 33⅓% and 5%. The more usual range was 25% and 5% to 33⅓%. The actual discount earned by retailers also depended partly on their method of purchase, that is whether on subscription terms or not, and partly on the character of the book. The higher discounts were given for purchases on subscription, and it is estimated that one-half of the purchases by retailers were on subscription. The discounts at the lower end of the range, 16⅔–25%, were allowed on technical, scientific and higher educational books. Only a small proportion of these were sold to the private buyer, the majority going to educational institutions and libraries. Retailers purchasing from wholesalers usually bought on the after subscription or on the day-to-day basis and, excluding specialists' books, usually received a discount of 25% off the retail price.

In exceptional cases the discount given to a retail bookseller might be as low as 10% where the bookseller obtained orders for a book which he did not carry in stock and passed the order to the publisher. The average discount earned by retailers on their purchases both direct from publishers and through wholesalers and after allowing for mark-downs and losses was approximately 25%.

Stock turn. The average stock turn of retailers is estimated at 1½–2 times per year.

Publishers' distribution costs varied widely between firms, but in the larger houses advertising was the biggest single cost. This ranged between 7–15% of publishers' sales revenue, and the average for the trade was approximately 12% of sales revenue. In addition, most publishers employed salesmen, and the total selling costs including advertising, review copies, exhibitions, salesmen's salaries, administrative selling costs and stockholding averaged 15–18% of publishers' sales revenue.

The total costs of distribution are estimated at 39–42% of retail sales.

2. NEWSPAPERS

Consumers' expenditure and methods of distribution

Consumers' expenditure on daily and Sunday newspapers in 1938 is estimated at approximately £33 millions. Some 42% of this expenditure was represented by the sale of London morning newspapers, 30% by the sale of provincial morning and evening newspapers, 20% by the sale of London and provincial Sunday newspapers and 8% by the sale of London evening papers.

The methods of distribution. The channels of distribution varied with the type of newspapers and the area in which the newspapers were sold. The variations in the proportions of sales of the different newspapers passing through the main channels of distribution in 1938 are estimated as follows:

Type of newspaper	*Publisher direct to retailer*	*Publisher to wholesaler to retailer*
London morning newspapers	Negligible	100
London evening newspapers	70–80	20–30
Provincial morning and evening newspapers	75–85	15–25
Sunday newspapers	Negligible	100

If the newspapers passing through the wholesale branches of multiple retailing organizations are classed as sales from publishers direct to retailers, the proportions of total sales of all newspapers passing through the main channels of distribution in 1938 are estimated as follows:

	%
From publisher to wholesaler to retailer	54–59
From publisher to retailer	41–46

A very small proportion, less than 1%, went direct from newspaper office to the reader.

Number of wholesalers and retailers. The number of wholesalers of newspapers in 1938 is estimated at 300–400. The number of retailers selling a fair range of newspapers is estimated at 35–40,000. Sunday newspapers were not generally handled by the same wholesalers as daily newspapers and there were approximately 5,000 agents for or wholesalers of Sunday newspapers. Some 2–3,000 of the retail newsagents were branches of multiple organizations and they were responsible for 12–15% of total sales.

The cost of distribution

The margins or discounts allowed to wholesalers and retailers on the sale of newspapers varied with the type of paper and the method of distribution. Estimates have been made as follows:

London morning newspapers. Just over one-third of the sales of these newspapers were made in the London area, and the wholesalers collected direct from the newspaper offices and sorted, packed and delivered to retailers. Some half a dozen London wholesalers did three-quarters of this trade. The wholesalers paid 1s. 6d. for 27 copies (on 1d. newspapers and *pro rata* for 2d. newspapers) less 10% less $1\frac{1}{4}$%. The wholesalers in 1938 also received a weight allowance varying with the number of pages which averaged $\frac{1}{2}$d. per quire. The wholesaler re-sold to the retailer at 1s. 6d. per 26 copies (on 1d. newspapers and *pro rata* for 2d. newspapers). The difference in the number of copies sold represented an additional $3\frac{3}{4}$% discount to the wholesaler. The retailer sold to the public at 2s. 2d. per 26 copies or 4s. 4d. on 2d. newspapers.

The average gross margin of the wholesaler was 17–18% on sales and of the retailer 30–31% on sales.

Just under 3% of the sales of these newspapers was in towns which printed provincial or Northern editions of the London newspapers. In these towns the wholesalers collected newspapers from the newspaper offices and bought at 1s. 6d. per 27 copies less 7·5%, and re-sold to retailers at 1s. 6d. per 26 copies. The wholesaler's margin averaged 10–11% on sales and the retailer's margin 30–31% on sales.

The remainder of the sales of London morning newspapers, just under two-thirds, was in the provinces, and the newspapers were despatched by the newspaper owners to wholesalers in the towns and villages where they were to be sold. This was mainly done by rail, the newspaper trains, which were train services subsidized by the Newspaper Proprietors' Association. Not all the newspapers were collected at stations by wholesalers—in the small towns and villages wholesaler/retailers were common, and just over 10% of the total sales of London morning newspapers are estimated to have passed through wholesaler/retailers. The wholesalers who undertook no retail sales in the provinces paid 1s. 6d. for 27 copies less 6% (*pro rata* for 2d. newspapers) and re-sold at 1s. 6d. for 26 copies. No weight allowance was paid to provincial wholesalers.

The average margin of wholesalers was 9–10% on sales, and of retailers 30–31% on sales.

The wholesaler/retailers handling London morning newspapers received varying terms. Some direct retail agents received net terms, that is 1s. 6d. for 27 copies, wholesaler/retailers 1s. 6d. for 27 copies less 2·5% and others 1s. 6d. for 27 copies less 5%. In each case they got the odd copy as they re-sold to other retailers at 1s. 6d. for 26 copies. The wholesaler/retailer's margin ranged from 3·5% to 8·5% on sales and the retailer's margin averaged 30–31% on sales.

London evening newspapers. Approximately three-quarters of the London evening newspapers went direct from the newspaper offices to retailers or street vendors. The newspaper owners provided the labour for sorting, packing and transport. On these sales the retailer or street vendor received a margin of 30–31% on sales.

The remainder of the London evening newspapers went to country agents and to wholesalers. Delivery to these agents and wholesalers was made by the newspaper proprietors. The agents or wholesalers bought at 1s. 6d. for 26 copies less 5–10%, usually nearer 10%. The agent's or wholesaler's margin was therefore between 5–9% on sales and the retailer's margin 30–31% on sales.

Provincial morning and evening newspapers. Approximately three-quarters of the sales of provincial newspapers were represented by evening editions and a quarter by morning newspapers. The evening newspapers were usually delivered direct to retailers by the newspaper owners, who provided the labour for sorting, packing and transport. The morning newspapers usually went through wholesalers or agents, who in some cases collected the newspapers from the newspaper office, and in others, where the circulation covered a wide area, collected from the station, carriage paid by the newspaper owners.

There were no standard terms for either wholesalers or retailers of provincial evening and morning newspapers. Nor were there any general terms as to the unit of sale, i.e. 12 or 13 copies, 25, 26 or 27 copies. It would appear, however, that there were three main groups of terms to retailers, and in each group the wholesaler received a discount of between 5–10% or an average of 7–7·5% on sales. The wholesalers, it is estimated, handled 20% of the sales, the remainder going direct from newspaper offices to the retailers. The margins earned by retailers in the three groups averaged 33·3%, 30·7% and 25%

respectively, and the proportion of total sales represented by each group was about equal.

London and provincial Sunday newspapers. About three-quarters of the sales of Sunday newspapers were made outside the towns in which the newspapers were printed. In these cases newspaper owners provided the labour for packing and sorting and also the transport, which was usually by rail, and the wholesalers collected from stations or depots. In those towns where the newspapers were published the wholesalers collected from the newspaper offices.

The wholesalers or agents of Sunday newspapers paid 2s. 9d. for 26 copies (2d. newspapers). They re-sold to the retailer at 3s. 3d. per 26 copies. These terms applied whether the wholesaler or agent collected from the newspaper offices or from local depots or stations. In addition to this margin the wholesaler or agent in many cases also received a weight allowance. On all Sunday newspapers the average weight allowance was ¼d. per quire. The average margin of the wholesaler was 16% on sales and the average margin of the retailer was 25% on sales.

The costs of distribution incurred by the newspaper owners varied widely with the type of newspaper as follows:

On London morning newspapers the total cost of distribution including carriage, salesmen's salaries, packing, advertising and publicity averaged 45–50% of the net sales revenue of the newspaper owners. Of this approximately half was represented by carriage, packing and salesmen's salaries.

On London evening newspapers the distribution costs as listed above and including delivery van costs averaged 50–55% of net sales revenue. Of this salesmen's salaries, packing and carriage amounted to approximately three-quarters and delivery van costs including drivers' wages and running and upkeep costs one-fifth.

On provincial morning and evening newspapers distribution costs averaged 27–33% of net sales revenue. Of this just under two-thirds was represented by carriage, packing and transport costs.

On Sunday newspapers, distribution costs averaged 40–45% of net sales revenue, of which approximately half was represented by carriage, packing and transport costs.

In considering these costs of distribution expressed as a percentage of net sales revenue, it must be remembered that the newspaper owners also obtained revenue from advertisements. The gross revenue from advertisements earned by London and provincial morning, evening and Sunday newspapers in 1938 is estimated at £25·6 millions.

The newspaper owners also made a full refund at trade prices to wholesalers on unsold copies. Returns of unsold copies in 1938 are estimated to have averaged 10% for London morning newspapers,

18% for London evening newspapers, 12% for provincial morning and evening newspapers and 15% for Sunday newspapers. The newspaper owners paid carriage costs on returns. The wholesaler in most cases paid the retailer full trade prices on returns but in some areas, for example the London area, he charged the retailer 1d. per quire on returns to cover the cost of collecting, and in parts of the provinces the charge was as high as 2d. per quire.

The total costs of distribution of all newspapers are estimated at 60–65% of retail sales.

3. MAGAZINES AND PERIODICALS

Consumers' expenditure and methods of distribution

Consumers' expenditure on magazines and periodicals of general interest in 1938 is estimated at £15 millions. These magazines, weekly, monthly and quarterly, were published by commercial firms and circulated among the general public. Excluded from this estimate are special interest magazines, published by organizations such as churches, schools and societies, and technical and trade journals. Just under four-fifths of the estimated total expenditure was on weekly periodicals.

The methods of distribution. Practically all magazines passed from publisher to wholesaler and then to retailer. A very small proportion, probably less than 1%, was sent direct to subscribers by the publishers. Sometimes a large wholesaler would sell to a small provincial wholesaler, who then re-sold to the retailer, but a very small proportion of magazines was handled by three distributors.

Number of wholesalers and retailers. In 1938 there were approximately 750 wholesalers and approximately 35,000 retailers of magazines and periodicals. Some 2–3,000 of these were branches of multiple organizations and these outlets were responsible for 10–14% of total sales.

The cost of distribution

The margins allowed to wholesalers and retailers varied considerably between one publisher and another, but some averages for the trade as a whole can be estimated.

Wholesalers in London received a higher margin than those in the provinces, but the London wholesaler generally had his own vans and collected the magazines from the publishers' premises. The provincial wholesaler, on the other hand, collected his parcel from the local railway station, the publisher paying the cost of transport to the provinces.

The usual terms were as follows (a weekly magazine selling at 2d. is taken as the example):

Wholesalers bought 13 copies for 16d. The London wholesaler received a discount of 4–5%.

Retailers bought 13 copies from the wholesaler for 18d. If the retailer bought less than 13 copies he paid 1½d. each for them. The retailer sold at 2d.

Some publishers sold 12 copies to the dozen instead of 13 and did not give the special London discount. This practice was more general in the case of magazines costing 1s. and upwards and periodicals with small circulation.

The margins earned by wholesalers and retailers in 1938 were as follows:

> *The wholesaler's* margin ranged in London between 11·1–22% and in the provinces between 11·1–17·9% depending on the terms allowed by the publishers and the methods of purchase of the retailers. The average margin of the London wholesaler on weeklies was 17·5% and on monthlies was 15% on sales. The average margin of the provincial wholesaler on weeklies was 14% and on monthlies was 12·5% on sales.
>
> The average wholesaler's margin for the country, weighting sales of weeklies and monthlies according to the figures above and taking the sales through London wholesalers as one-quarter of the total, was 14–15% on sales.
>
> *The retailer's* margin varied between 25–33%, although the latter margin was earned in relatively few cases. The average retail margin is estimated at about 27·5%.

On return copies, which averaged 5–10% of total retail sales, the retailer usually received 16d. for 13 copies (retail price 2d.), so that the wholesaler charged him 2d. a dozen to cover the expenses involved. The publishers usually took back all returns at cost price though some publishers restricted returns to 4 copies in 26.

Publishers' distribution costs, including transport charges to wholesalers, free gifts, the cost of maintaining a department for direct subscribers, and advertising, averaged 18–22% of net sales revenue. Of this total, transport costs represented about 4–6%, advertising and publicity 8–10%, and other selling costs, packing, and salesmen's salaries 5–7%.

The total costs of distribution are estimated at 49–52% of retail sales.

4. STATIONERY

Consumers' expenditure and methods of distribution

Consumers' expenditure on stationery in 1938 is estimated at £17–18 millions. An attempt has been made to exclude from this estimate sales of stationery to commercial users. The main product divisions of the goods considered are:

Paper and cardboard products, of which the main items were domestic writing materials, greeting cards, table stationery, calendars and diaries, and playing-cards.

Pens and pencils, including fountain pens and propelling pencils.

Writing inks and accessories, including marking and drawing inks and ink-stands and ink-wells.

Consumers' expenditure on the first group represented approximately 70% of total sales, the remainder being split between the other two groups.

The methods of distribution. The proportions of total sales of stationery to the domestic consumer passing through the main channels of distribution in 1938 are estimated as follows:

	%
From manufacturer or importer to retailer	62–68
From manufacturer or importer to wholesaler to retailer	32–38

The proportion of paper products passing through wholesalers was slightly higher than the average for the whole trade given above, and the proportion of fountain pens and propelling pencils and writing inks passing through wholesalers was lower than the average. Importers were not significant in this trade, except in the case of fountain pens and propelling pencils, where they handled approximately 15% of the total home trade.

Number of wholesalers and retailers. There were approximately 300–500 wholesalers of stationery products in 1938. The number of retailers whose main trade was in stationery is estimated at 4–5,000. In addition, there were a number of other shops who did some trade in stationery, but this trade was subsidiary to another trade, such as the sale of newspapers, books or chemists' goods. The number of these shops is estimated at 16–17,000. It is estimated that the 4–5,000 specialist stationers were responsible for some three-quarters of the total trade.

Sales by different types of outlet. The proportions of the total sales undertaken by different economic types of retail shop in 1938 were approximately as follows:

	%
Multiple stationers and other multiple shops	14–18
Variety chain stores	12–16
Department and co-operative stores	5–7
Unit retailers	61–70

The sales by co-operative stores are estimated at less than 2% of total sales.

The cost of distribution

Most stationery products were branded by either the manufacturer, the wholesaler or the retailer. In some sections of the trade, notably pens, pencils and inks, all the products were branded. Nationally advertised goods were usually price-maintained to the consumer, but by no means all branded products were price-maintained.

The margins and discounts allowed to wholesalers and retailers varied slightly with the different product groups and in 1938 were estimated as follows:

> *Paper products.* The retailer purchasing from the wholesaler usually obtained a discount of 33⅓% off the retail price and in many cases a settlement discount of 2½% for payment in the month. The wholesaler received a discount ranging from 12½–25% plus 5% off the wholesale selling price. The usual discounts were 20–25%. The retailer purchasing direct from the manufacturer earned a margin ranging from 33⅓–50% of the retail selling price. The retailer was also entitled to a settlement discount of from 2½–5% and usually earned 2½%. In some sections of this trade an additional volume discount was given of 5–10%. Where a volume discount was given the starting margin of retailers was usually 33⅓%.

The average margin including volume and settlement discounts earned by retailers purchasing from wholesalers was 34% on sales, by wholesalers 25–27% of wholesale selling price and by retailers purchasing direct from manufacturers 43–44% on sales.

> *Fountain pens and propelling pencils.* The retailer purchasing from a wholesaler earned a margin ranging from 33⅓–40%. In addition the retailer was in many cases entitled to a cash settlement of 2½%. In those cases where the retail margin was 33⅓% the wholesaler's margin was usually 10% on the wholesale selling price plus a settlement discount of 2½%. In those cases where the retail margin was 40%, the wholesaler's margin was sometimes 20–25% on sales. In addition the wholesaler could earn 3¾% cash settlement terms. The retailer purchasing direct from manufacturer or importer earned a basic margin of 33–35% and was entitled in many cases to a volume discount ranging from 5–10%. The terms ranged from 5% on orders of £100 up to 10% on orders of £1,000. Where a settlement discount of 2½% was paid the basic margin

was usually $33\frac{1}{3}\%$, and where there was no settlement discount the basic margin was correspondingly higher at 35%.

The average margin earned by retailers purchasing from wholesalers was 35–36% and the average margin earned by wholesalers was 18–20% of wholesale selling price. The average margin earned by retailers purchasing direct from manufacturers was 40% of the retail selling price.

Writing inks and accessories. The retailer purchasing ink from wholesalers in large quantities usually earned a margin of 50% of the retail price, but where he bought in small quantities this margin would be nearer $33\frac{1}{3}\%$. The wholesaler selling in large quantities to retailers earned a margin of 15% on wholesale selling price plus $2\frac{1}{2}\%$ settlement discount, but where the retailer purchased in small quantities the wholesaler's margin was nearer 30–33% on sales. The retailer purchasing ink direct from manufacturer received a basic margin of 50% plus a volume discount ranging from nil to 15%. In addition a settlement discount of $2\frac{1}{2}\%$ was given in many cases.

The average margin of wholesalers was 25% on sales and the average margin of retailers purchasing from wholesalers was just over 35% on sales. The average margin of retailers purchasing direct from manufacturers was 55–56%.

Wholesale and retail margins on accessories were slightly lower than those on inks as smaller quantity purchases were made. The retailer's margin on goods purchased from wholesalers averaged 34% on sales, the wholesale margin 20% on sales and the margin of retailers purchasing direct from manufacturers 40–45% on sales.

The stock turn of wholesalers of stationery goods is estimated at 6–8 times a year and the stock turn of retailers at 4–6 times a year.

Manufacturers' distribution costs. There were wide variations in manufacturers' distribution costs between different types of firm, and estimates of the costs relating to the sales of non-commercial stationery are very difficult to distinguish from the costs of total sales including commercial and non-commercial. There are also wide variations depending on the channel of distribution used by manufacturers and the extent to which the goods were branded and advertised.

In some instances, where the goods were neither branded nor advertised and were sold mainly through wholesalers, the total distribution costs of manufacturers were approximately 3–4% of sales revenue. Most of these were carriage and packing costs. In other instances, where a firm was selling a well-known branded product direct to retailers, total distribution costs were in the region of 40% of sales revenue, of which carriage and packing accounted for 2–3%, selling costs 17–18% and advertising 20%.

The total costs of distribution are estimated at 50–54% of retail sales.

CHAPTER XXIV

MOTOR CARS, ACCESSORIES, TYRES, PETROL AND OIL

I. MOTOR CARS

Consumers' expenditure and methods of distribution

Consumers' expenditure on new private motor cars in 1938 is estimated at £51–52 millions. An attempt has been made to exclude from this total the purchases of cars by trade users and Government departments. The imports of cars in 1938 were insignificant as a proportion of total sales.

The methods of distribution. There were four types of distributor engaged in selling private motor cars in 1938, and before any discussion of the proportions of the total trade handled by each, a note on the different functions performed by them is necessary. The use made of the different distributors and the functions undertaken by each varied according to the particular policy of the manufacturer of the car being sold, but taking the trade as a whole the distinctions between the four types of distributors, that is distributors or main dealers, dealers, retail dealers and casual traders, can be described as follows:

The distributors or main dealers were appointed by each manufacturer for a given territory of the country. The distributor was limited to this area for his trade sales, that is, sales to dealers, retail dealers or casual traders. The size of the territory of each distributor varied according to the population in the area, the type of car being sold, and the policy of the manufacturer by whom the distributor was appointed. Distributors took a quota of new cars and vehicles each year from the manufacturer and were under an obligation to maintain showrooms, demonstration cars and workshops with skilled mechanics and to carry a stock of new cars and spare parts. In addition, the distributor had the task of the business management of the area to which he was appointed, acting as a wholesaler distributing cars and spare parts to dealers, retail dealers and casual traders in his territory. Practically all cars passed from manufacturers to distributors and distributors made sales direct to the consumer, to dealers, to retail dealers and to casual traders.

The dealers were appointed to cover a territory within the territory of the distributor from whom they received cars and spare parts. Again the size of the area and the volume of trade done by the dealer would vary with the type of car handled and the policy of the distributor. The dealer took a quota of new cars and spare parts each year and was required to have showrooms, a workshop with skilled mechanics and demonstration cars. Dealers purchased all their cars from distributors and sold direct to the consumer, to retail dealers and to casual traders.

The retail dealers obtained their cars from dealers or distributors and were under an obligation to stock new cars and spare parts, and to provide service facilities. They could not, however sell at trade terms to other dealers, but could only sell retail to the consumer.

The casual traders purchased their cars from dealers or distributors, but were not under any obligation to stock new cars, though the normally provided some service facilities. They sold only to the consumer.

The main channels of distribution of new private cars in 1938 and the proportions of total sales passing through them are estimated as follows. Practically all cars were sold by manufacturers to distributors in the first instance.

	%
From distributor direct to consumer	30–35
From distributor to dealer to consumer	40–45
From distributor to retail dealer and casual trader to consumer	10–15
From distributor to dealer to retail dealer and casual trader to consumer	10–15

Of the sales by distributors approximately one-third were made to consumers while the remainder were made at trade terms to dealers, retail dealers and casual traders: and of the sales by dealers approximately three-quarters were made to the consumer, while the remainder were made at trade terms to the retail dealer or casual trader. Of the purchases by the consumer distributors were responsible for about one-third, retail dealers and casual traders for about one-quarter, and the remainder of the sales were made by dealers. Casual traders as distinct from retail dealers are estimated to have been responsible for 5–8% of total sales.

Number of distributors and dealers. In 1938 there were between 900–1,000 distributors or main dealers; approximately 2,500 dealers; 3,500 retail dealers; and 6,000 casual traders. All these types of distributors and dealers sold cars on retail terms, and the number of retail selling points totalled some 13,000 in 1938.

The cost of distribution

Margins earned by distributors, dealers and traders on the main makes of private cars did not vary very much between the different makes. There were, however, variations in margins allowed to different distributors in the case of specialized cars with a relatively small sale, and on imported cars. Practically all private cars in 1938 were price-maintained by the manufacturers. The manufacturers fixed the ex-factory or retail price and transport to the consumer was an additional charge to the purchaser.

The distributor or main dealer received a discount of 17½–20% off the ex-factory price. In the majority of cases the percentage was 20%, in a few cases it rose to 22½%. In addition, the distributor received a volume rebate on all cars purchased. The actual scale varied with each manufacturer and ranged from ¼% on net purchases of £500 to 5½% on net purchases of £100,000. The average volume rebate earned by distributors was between 2½–3% on their wholesale turnover.

Margins of distributors. The margins and volume rebates earned by the distributor varied with the channels of re-sale as follows:

The distributor, on his sales direct to the consumer, earned the full margin of 17½–20% plus volume rebate of 2½–3% on his net purchases, or together 21–23% on sales.

The distributor, on his sales to dealers, allowed the dealers a discount of 17½–20% off the ex-factory price. In the majority of cases this discount was 17½%, although in a few cases a 20% discount was paid. In addition, the distributor paid the dealer a volume discount on all cars purchased through him and this again ranged between ¼%–5%, but with an average of between 1½–2% on the net purchases. This left the distributor an average margin of 3¼–4% on sales.

The distributor, on his sales to retail dealers and casual traders, allowed the latter a discount off the ex-factory price of 10–18½%. The retail dealer, in most cases, received a discount of 17½% off the ex-factory price and, in addition, the distributor paid him a volume discount which averaged between 1–1½% on net purchases. This gave the distributor an average margin of 4–5% on sales. The casual trader received a discount from the distributor of 10–17% off the ex-factory price, although in most cases it was between 10–15%. The casual trader did not receive a volume discount. These sales gave the distributor an average margin of 10–12% on sales.

Margins of dealers, retail dealers and casual traders. The margins and rebates earned by the other dealers similarly varied with the channels of re-sale as follows:

The dealer on his sales direct to the consumer earned the margin suggested above of 17½–20%, plus a volume rebate on net purchases of 1½–2%; together yielding an average of 18–20% on sales. The dealer on his sales to retail dealers allowed the retail dealer a discount of 15–18½% (usually 17½%) off the ex-factory price, plus a volume rebate averaging ½–1% on purchases. This gave the dealer an average margin of 2–3% on sales. The dealer allowed the casual trader a discount of between 10–17%, usually between 10–15%. The casual trader did not obtain a volume discount. These sales gave the dealer an average margin of 7–7½% on sales. The retail dealer earned an average margin of 17½% on sales and the casual trader an average margin of 12½% on sales.

The stock turn of distributors averaged 6 times a year and the stock turn of dealers and retail dealers 3–4 times a year.

Manufacturers' distribution costs on private motor cars are difficult in most cases to distinguish from the costs incurred in the distribution of commercial vehicles and spare parts. There were also variations between manufacturers as to advertising policy. Making allowances for these factors as far as possible, manufacturers' distribution costs on private cars, including administrative selling costs, warranty and policy, and advertising, averaged 7–8% of sales revenue. Of this advertising represented just under one-half.

The total costs of distribution are estimated at 28–30% of retail sales.

2. MOTOR CAR SPARE PARTS AND ACCESSORIES

Consumers' expenditure and methods of distribution

Consumers' expenditure on motor car spare parts and accessories in 1938 is estimated at about £10 millions. This estimate attempts to exclude the sale of parts and accessories to manufacturers for installation on private cars before their sale to consumers and also the sale of spare parts and accessories to the owners of commercial vehicles, but such exclusions can only be made approximately.

Three main groups of products can, for convenience of discussion, be distinguished:

Mechanical component parts, such as piston rings, crown wheels and pinions, valves, silencers, gaskets, springs, clutches and clutch-plates, brake shoes and linings, and chains.

Accessories, such as mirrors, muffs, jacks, mats, fog-lamps, head-, side- and tail-lamps, wrenches, and radiator heaters.

Ignition and electrical equipment spare parts and batteries, such as moulded ignition parts, armatures, wipers, brushers, fuses and batteries.

Consumers' expenditure on mechanical component parts is estimated at about £4 millions, on accessories at about £2 millions and on ignition and electrical equipment spare parts and batteries at about £4 millions.

The methods of distribution. The proportions of total sales passing through the main channels of distribution in 1938 for each of the three groups are estimated as follows:

Mechanical component parts:

	%
From manufacturer to distributor or main dealer or retailer and then to consumer	30–40
From manufacturer to distributor or main dealer, and then to retail dealer or casual trader, and from manufacturer to wholesaler or factor and then to retailer	60–70

A small proportion of these sales passed through three intermediaries before reaching the consumer, for example a distributor sold to a dealer who re-sold to a retail dealer who sold to the consumer.

Accessories:

	%
From manufacturer to service agent or to retailer and then to consumer	33–40
From manufacturer to wholesaler, factor or service agent and then to retailer	60–67

The service agents acted as wholesalers but a small proportion of their sales were direct to the consumer. Many firms in this trade sold the whole of their output to wholesalers or factors who re-sold to retailers but other firms had a substantial direct to retailer trade. A very small proportion of these goods were sold by mail order by the manufacturers.

Ignition and electrical equipment spare parts and batteries:

	%
From manufacturer to manufacturer's service depots or to service agent or to retailer and then to consumer	20–25
From manufacturer to service agent or to wholesaler or factor and then to retailer	75–80

Taking the three groups together and allowing for the variations in consumers' expenditure, the proportions of total sales passing through the main channels of distribution in 1938 are estimated as follows:

	%
From manufacturer direct to retailer	25–35
From manufacturer to an intermediary to retailer	65–75

Number of wholesalers and retailers. The number of factors of these three groups of goods is estimated at 150, the number of service agents at about 2,500. All motor car distributors and dealers handled a range of spare parts and accessories and the number of retailers of motor car spare parts, accessories and batteries is estimated at 30–40,000.

The cost of distribution

The margins earned by the various distributors in each of the three main groups of goods in 1938 were as follows:

Mechanical component parts. The discounts to distributors and main dealers and to wholesalers on mechanical component parts ranged from 30–40% off the retail selling price. In most cases this represented a straight discount, in others it was made up of a discount plus an extra 5% bonus on a monthly stock order over a certain amount. Distributors and dealers obtained an average discount of 33–36% but wholesalers or factors usually obtained 40%. The retailer's margin was usually 25% on sales. The margins of distributors and wholesalers when selling to retail dealers ranged between 12–20% on sales with an average of 17½%.

Accessories. The discounts off the retail selling price obtained by wholesalers and service agents ranged from 40–50%. The actual discount earned would vary with the quantity purchased. Retailers purchasing from wholesalers or service agents or from manufacturers usually earned 25–33% on sales. The higher margin was obtained on large purchases. The wholesaler's or service agent's margin therefore ranged from 20–25% on sales. Some large retailers purchasing direct from manufacturers could earn a volume discount on their purchases yielding a retail margin of 25% plus 25% or 44% on sales.

Ignition and electrical equipment spare parts and batteries. The discounts off the list, or retail, price obtained by wholesalers and service agents on ignition and equipment spare parts averaged 42½%. On batteries, wholesalers and service agents purchased at the list, or retail, price less 25% less 20%. The retailers received a discount of 25% off the retail price on ignition and equipment spares and on batteries, giving the wholesaler or service agent a margin of 20–23% on returns. The retailers of batteries on about one-half of their total sales received in addition from manufacturers a quarterly rebate of 10% on the net invoice value of goods. This rebate was paid by the manufacturer when the goods were purchased through a wholesaler or service agent.

Settlement discounts of 3¾% for payment in 7 days and 2½% for payment in the month were allowed on most products to wholesalers, factors, agents and retailers.

Manufacturers' distribution costs on these goods varied widely. They were higher on some products than on others owing to the different methods of distribution undertaken and the great differences in advertising expenditure. For the whole group, manufacturers' distribution costs including administrative selling costs, salesmen's salaries, advertising and carriage and packing costs averaged 14–18% of manufacturers' sales revenue.

The total costs of distribution of motor car ignition parts, batteries and accessories are estimated at 50–54% and of motor car spare parts and mechanical components 45–48% of retail sales.

3. MOTOR CAR, MOTOR CYCLE AND CYCLE TYRES AND TUBES

Consumers' expenditure and methods of distribution

Consumers' expenditure on tyres and tubes in 1938 is estimated at £6–7 millions. Tyres sold for fitment to new vehicles or cycles are not included in this figure, neither are sales of car and giant tyres for use on commercial vehicles. Of the total, the sales of motor car tyres and tubes are estimated at £5–6 millions, of motor cycle tyres and tubes at £200,000, and of cycle tyres and tubes at £650,000.

The methods of distribution: Motor car tyres and tubes. The proportions of total sales of motor car tyres and tubes passing through the main channels of distribution in 1938 are estimated as follows:

	%
From manufacturer to tyre house or dealer	55–65
From manufacturer to tyre factor or wholesaler to retail dealer	35–45

The tyre houses and dealers sold retail direct to the consumer. Tyre houses dealt almost exclusively in tyres. The term dealer embraces distributors such as garages and motor agents who also handled components and parts relative to the motor trade. It is suggested that of the estimated 60% being sold to tyre houses and dealers, 10–20% were sales to dealers and the remainder sales to tyre houses, but the dividing line between these two types of retail outlet is in many instances difficult to determine.

Tyre factors and wholesalers normally re-sold to retail dealers, though occasionally they re-sold to tyre houses. In some instances factors and wholesalers sold direct to the public, but this practice was not generally recognized in the trade. Tyre factors and wholesalers normally handled a variety of automobile and electrical products, but there were a few who confined their activities mainly to the motor trade.

Number of outlets. There were about 300 tyre factors or wholesalers in 1938, and the number of retail outlets, including tyre dealers and garages which regularly stocked and sold tyres, was about 25,000.

The cost of distribution. All tyre manufacturers published a retail price list in 1938 and the majority of products were price-maintained at all stages. The number of instances of tyres being sold below or above the fixed retail price was relatively few in proportion to the total sales of motor car tyres and tubes. Where lower prices were charged, these often took the form of special discounts on quantity purchases by the consumer.

The margins allowed or earned by factors and dealers varied between the different makes of tyres and according to the policy of the manufacturer.

The margins allowed in 1938 are estimated as follows:

Factors or wholesalers were invoiced at trade list price—that is the retail selling price less 20–25%—less 3¾–5%, and their purchases were subject to volume rebates which varied according to the policy of the manufacturer, ranging from 5–25%. The average wholesaler's or factor's volume rebate was 12½–15%.

Retail dealers obtained a margin of 20–25% off the retail price. In addition, dealers were allowed volume rebates on the same scale as wholesalers and factors, and they averaged between 10–13%. Factors or wholesalers when selling to tyre houses or dealers offered the same volume rebates as the tyre manufacturers, although as the purchases by dealers through factors were smaller the rebates earned were smaller. There existed no financial incentive for dealers to purchase direct from manufacturers, but in the case of the larger tyre houses and dealers this method of purchase was found to be more convenient.

Settlement discounts allowed to factors or wholesalers and to retail dealers were 3¾% and occasionally 5% for payment within 7 days and 2½% for monthly account.

The factors or wholesalers earned an average gross margin of 10–12% on sales to dealers: the dealers and tyre houses earned a gross margin of 30–40% on sales, depending on whether they purchased through factors or direct, and the average was 35–37%.

Motor car tubes were subject to the same discount and volume rebates as for covers. There were, however, special discounts for bulk purchases of tubes, ranging from 10% on orders of 2 dozen to 15% on orders of 100 or more.

Stock turn. A very large stock of tyres had to be maintained by the tyre dealers and tyre houses owing to the great variety of sizes in demand; the stock turn of tyre factors averaged 3–4 times a year and that of tyre houses 1½–2½ times a year.

The methods of distribution: Motor cycle and cycle tyres and tubes. The main channels of distribution of motor cycle and cycle tyres and tubes in

1938 and the proportions of total sales passing through them are estimated as follows:

	%
From manufacturer to dealer	45–55
From manufacturer to factor or wholesaler to retail dealer	45–55

Included in the sales direct from manufacturer to retail dealer are the sales by manufacturers to the central depots or warehouses of multiple organizations.

Number of wholesalers and retailers. The majority of factors or wholesalers handled all classes of tyres, although there were several who handled motor cycle and cycle tyres only. Approximately half the dealers, including tyre houses, handling motor car tyres handled motor cycle and cycle tyres as well and, in addition, there were about 9,000 motor cycle and cycle dealers handling tyres in these two classes only. Multiple cycle and cycle accessory dealers are thought to have been responsible for 8–10% of the total turnover.

The cost of distribution. Practically all motor cycle and cycle tyres and tubes were branded and price-maintained by the manufacturers in 1938.

The margins allowed to the various distributors in 1938 are estimated as follows:

Factors or wholesalers were invoiced for motor cycle tyres and tubes at trade list prices—that is the retail price less 25%—less 20%, and their purchases were subject to a volume rebate ranging from 1–10%. Factors or wholesalers were invoiced for cycle tyres at trade list price—that is the retail price less $33\frac{1}{3}$%—less 15%, and their total purchases were subject to a volume rebate ranging from 1–10%.

Retailers of motor cycle tyres were allowed a discount of 25% plus a volume rebate ranging from 5–15%. Retailers of cycle tyres obtained a discount of $33\frac{1}{3}$% plus a volume rebate ranging from 5–15%.

Settlement discounts to factors and retailers were $3\frac{3}{4}$% and occasionally 5% for payment in 7 days and $2\frac{1}{2}$% for monthly settlement. Most of the factors and large retailers earned the higher discount.

Multiple organizations purchasing cycle tyres and tubes would usually receive factors' or wholesalers' terms. As in the case of motor car tyres, factors were allowed to sell to dealers on level terms with tyre manufacturers, although the smaller purchases of retailers who bought through factors meant that they did not earn a very high volume rebate.

During the winter season some manufacturers introduced special terms for stock orders which usually carried an extra 5% discount.

There were qualifications as to the minimum quantity to be taken and a time limit during which the order was to be placed.

Special discounts were given on bulk purchases of motor cycle tubes on the same basis as for motor car tubes. There were no special discounts for bulk purchases of cycle tubes, although some tubes were sold at special prices according to the quantity ordered; but in these instances the purchases did not qualify for volume rebate.

The stock turn of factors and wholesalers of motor cycle and cycle tyres and tubes was 4–5 times a year and the stock turn of retail dealers 3–4 times a year.

Manufacturers' distribution costs of motor and cycle tyres and tubes. Most, if not all, manufacturers of motor car tyres and tubes also manufactured motor cycle and cycle tyres and tubes and it is difficult to distinguish manufacturers' distribution costs on the different products. Taking the sales of motor car, motor cycle and cycle tyres and tubes together, manufacturers' distribution costs, including carriage and packing, administrative selling costs, salesmen's salaries, and advertising, averaged 14–16% of manufacturers' sales revenue. Advertising expenditure represented between one-half and two-thirds of these distribution costs.

The total costs of distribution of motor car tyres and tubes are estimated at 50–54% and of cycle and motor cycle tyres and tubes at 50–54% of retail sales.

4. PETROL

Consumers' expenditure and methods of distribution

Consumers' expenditure. Expenditure by the private motorist on petrol in 1938 is estimated at approximately £37 millions (including duty). This estimate excludes purchases by commercial travellers and other business users. The sales were divided between 270 million gallons approximately of premier grade and 230 million gallons of commercial grade spirit, valued at £21 millions and £16 millions respectively. A small proportion, some 8% of total sales, was home-produced from various sources such as benzole and hydrogenation.

The methods of distribution. Practically all petrol was imported and distributed by importing/distributing companies direct to the retailers. These companies transferred petrol from tankers to ocean storage depots from which it was distributed direct to retailers in the regions round the depots and, in more distant regions, to the companies' inland depots and then to retailers. A small proportion of the petrol was distributed by companies who purchased their supplies through brokers.

Number of outlets. In 1938 there were approximately 35,000 retail outlets ranging from the hotel with one pump to the large filling station with as many as a dozen. The total number of pumps was approximately 100,000, but the annual sales per pump varied widely and, in general, increased with the size of the station. Sales in cans were practically restricted to central London. A few organizations controlling five or more garages or petrol stations existed in 1938 but they handled a very small proportion of the total trade.

The cost of distribution

The importing/distributing companies fixed the price of all petrol sold retail. These companies paid the import duty on the petrol and it was included in the retail price. There was no duty on home-produced spirit.

Prices and margins. In 1938 the retail price throughout England, Wales and Southern Scotland was 1s. 7d. a gallon for premier grade and 1s. 5d. for commercial grade. The import duty for both grades was equivalent to 9d. a gallon. The retailer received a discount of 1d. on both grades, and, in most cases, an exclusive buying rebate of 1¾d. on premier grade and 1¼d. on commercial grade spirit. These rebates were paid to all retailers who restricted their sales either to the petrol of the 'national' companies on the one hand or to the petrol of the 'independent' companies on the other. The 'national' companies, three in number, handled some 80% of the petrol distributed. There were approximately 100 'independent' companies.

As a percentage of the retail price, the retailers' total margin averaged approximately 14% on premier grade spirit and 13% on commercial grade.

Importers' distribution costs. Importer/distributors bore the cost of transport from depot to retailer and most of the cost of storage, as retailers' stocks averaged only about 10 days' supply. The importer/distributors maintained 10–14 days' supplies at their inland storage depots and 2–3 months' supplies at the ocean storage depots. Total importer/distributors' costs, including inland transport (but not shipping costs), storage, depreciation, advertising, selling costs and other overheads, were approximately 2d. a gallon. These costs incurred on the sales to both the private motorist and the commercial user represented 11–12% of total retail sales.

The total costs of distribution of petrol are estimated at 25–26% of retail sales.

5. MOTOR OIL

Consumers' expenditure and methods of distribution

Consumers' expenditure. The private motorists' expenditure on motor oil in 1938 is estimated at £4·5 millions, representing some 15 million gallons. This figure includes the duty of £70,000. The purchases of oil by commercial users are excluded.

About 60% of the oil used by the private motorist and motor cyclist was of standard grades, that is branded first-grade oils sold at a fixed price and comprising generally a light, medium, heavy and extra-heavy grade, and the remainder was of non-standard grades which were used largely by commercial vehicles.

The methods of distribution. A large proportion, between two-thirds and three-quarters, of the motor oil sold to private motorists in 1938 was distributed by 10 importing/distributing companies to retailers. The remaining oil was sold by importers to some 600 small distributors who then re-sold to retailers.

There were approximately 35,000 retailers of motor oil in 1938.

The cost of distribution

The retail prices of the standard grades were generally fixed by the importer/distributors, but the margins earned by retailers were variable. In the case of non-standard grades there was no retail price-fixing. The price of standard grades in 1938 averaged about 7s. a gallon in bulk with an addition of 8d. a gallon for delivery in cans. Non-standard grades were retailed usually at 3s. 6d. a gallon, but in some cases at up to 5s. a gallon.

Purchase terms to retailers. All garages and dealers taking regular deliveries on annual contracts obtained rebates as follows: spot buyers received a sliding-scale deferred rebate on standard grades only, starting at 2d. for the first 50 gallons with an additional ½d. for every succeeding 50 gallons up to 500 gallons. This meant that the tenth 50 gallons was rebated by 6½d. per gallon, giving an average rebate over the whole 500 gallons of 4¼d. per gallon. Contract buyers received a minimum allowance of 4d. per gallon below spot prices. In addition, there were deferred rebates payable at the end of 12 months on the quantities taken, ranging from 1d. per gallon for a 500-gallon contract to 4d. per gallon for a contract of 4,000 gallons and over. These deferred rebates relate to purchases of standard grades. On non-standard grades the rebates ranged from 1d. a gallon for a contract of 300 gallons to 5d. a gallon for a contract of 3,000 gallons.

The retailer's margin varied according to the quantity sold and the method of delivery, and ranged between 33⅓–50% of the retail price. The average margin earned on sales to the private motorist is estimated at 45%.

The stock turn of motor oil varied considerably with the grade and the brand. The average retail stock turn is estimated at 8–10 times a year.

Distribution costs of importer/distributors on all grades of oil in 1938, including cost of transport (other than shipping), storage, selling costs, advertising, and other overheads, averaged 1s. 6d. a gallon, or 25% of the retail price. Advertising represented between 3–4% of these costs.

The total costs of distribution are estimated at 65–69% of retail sales.

6. MOTOR CYCLES AND MOTOR CYCLE ACCESSORIES

Consumers' expenditure and methods of distribution

Consumers' expenditure on motor cycles and motor cycle accessories in 1938 is estimated at £4·5–5·5 millions. Of this £3–3·5 millions was represented by the sale of motor cycles and £1·5–2 millions by the sale of motor cycle accessories.

The methods of distribution. The proportions of total sales of motor cycles and motor cycle accessories passing through the main channels of distribution in 1938 are estimated as follows:

	%
Motor cycles	
From manufacturer to main dealers	75–85
From manufacturer to main dealer to sub-dealer	15–25
Motor cycle accessories	
From manufacturer to factor or main dealer or service agent to retail dealer or subdealer	55–65
From manufacturer to main dealer or retail dealer	35–45

Number of retailers. The number of dealers regularly selling motor cycles in 1938 is estimated at 2,000. In addition to this there were a number of retailers or dealers who sold motor cycles occasionally. The number of dealers or retailers selling motor cycle accessories, the whole range or a few lines, numbered approximately 5–7,000. This figure includes garages and similar types of retail outlet.

The cost of distribution

Almost all motor cycles and a slightly smaller proportion of motor cycle accessories were sold in 1938 at retail prices fixed by manufacturers.

The margins allowed in 1938 were approximately as follows:

Motor cycles

Main dealers received a discount off the retail price varying from 17½–25% plus a volume rebate ranging from 1–5%.

Sub-dealers' discounts ranged from 12½–20%.

The average margin on sales of the main dealer, including volume rebates, was 25% and the average margin of sub-dealers was about 15%. The main dealer obtained a margin of approximately 12% on sales when selling to sub-dealers.

Manufacturers delivered the machines to dealers carriage paid and the terms were strictly cash.

Motor cycle accessories

Factors and main dealers received a discount off the retail price of 20–45% plus 10–20% trade discount.

Retailers and sub-dealers received a discount of 20–45%.

The average retail margin was 33⅓%. The average margin earned by factors and main dealers on their sales to retailers was 17–20% on returns.

In a few cases the volume rebate on accessories was also given by the manufacturer, and in the majority of cases cash discounts were allowed at the rate of 3¾% for cash payment and 2½% for monthly settlement.

Manufacturers' distribution costs on motor cycles and motor cycle accessories are estimated to have averaged 10–15% of sales revenue. These costs include the charges of carriage and transport, selling expenses and advertising. Advertising is estimated to have represented between one-quarter and one-third of these costs.

The total costs of distribution of motor cycles are estimated at 33–34% and of motor cycle accessories at 48–52% of retail sales.

CHAPTER XXV

JEWELLERY, TOYS, AND SPORTS AND LEATHER GOODS

I. JEWELLERY AND SILVER AND ELECTRO-PLATE

Consumers' expenditure and methods of distribution

Consumers' expenditure on this group of goods in 1938 is estimated at £15–17 millions. This estimate attempts to exclude purchases by business houses, clubs and institutions. The commodities considered can be grouped under three main headings:

Real jewellery (i.e. containing precious metals) on which consumers' expenditure was £4·5–5·5 millions.

Silver and electro-plate, including plated cutlery, on which consumers' expenditure was £7–8 millions.

Fancy or imitation jewellery, on which consumers' expenditure was £3–4 millions.

Imports of finished jewellery were significant only in relation to fancy and imitation jewellery, of which nearly half came from overseas.

The methods of distribution. The proportions of total sales passing through the main channels of distribution in 1938 are estimated as follows:

	%
From manufacturer or importer to retailer	70–75
From manufacturer or importer to wholesaler to retailer	23–27
From manufacturer or wholesaler direct to the public	1–4

The channels of distribution varied in each of the three groups mentioned above.

Real jewellery, consisting mainly of high priced articles, generally passed direct from manufacturer to retailer; although in the cheaper grades of real jewellery, possibly representing one-quarter of total sales, some of the goods were sold through wholesalers.

Silver and electro-plate, including plated cutlery, similarly generally passed direct from manufacturer direct to retailer. Again at the cheaper end of the trade a proportion of the goods was sold through wholesalers.

Fancy and imitation jewellery was, with few exceptions, sold in bulk by manufacturers or importers to wholesalers, who broke bulk, classified and re-sold to retailers. The exceptions are sales by manufacturers or importers to multiple shops, to variety chain stores and to some department stores. Variety chain stores often bought the entire output of a fancy jewellery manufacturer.

Number of wholesalers and retailers. In 1938 there were approximately 550–600 wholesalers in this trade, although not all of them specialized exclusively in jewellery. A number carried a wide range of fancy goods. The number of retail shops dealing in jewellery as a main trade is estimated at 4,500–5,500, although the number of selling points was very much higher, particularly of fancy jewellery and electro-plate, which were sold in a wide range of shops, including hardware and ironmongers', chemists', fancy goods shops, drapers' and variety chain stores. The number of first-class jewellers dealing solely in jewellery and covering the whole range of goods in 1938 is estimated at 2,700–3,000.

Sales by different types of outlet. The proportions of the total trade undertaken by the various economic types of retail outlet are estimated as follows:

	%
Multiple jewellers or multiple watch and clock repairers	10–15
Variety chain stores	5–10
Department stores	5–10
Specialist jewellery shops	60–70
Other outlets (ironmongers, fancy goods shops, drapers, chemists)	5–10

The cost of distribution

The margins earned by wholesalers and retailers in 1938 are estimated as follows:

Wholesalers worked to an on-cost ranging from 25–50% or 20–33⅓% on returns. The actual margins depended on the type of goods handled. In the case of fashion goods, particularly in the fancy trade, the on-cost was near the 50% mark, though the realized margin was lower owing to loss on obsolete stock; on non-fashion articles, real jewellery and some electro-plate the on-cost was nearer 25–33%. Importers of fancy jewellery who sold to wholesalers worked to an on-cost of 5–10%.

Retailers worked to an on-cost of 50–100%. Again the actual on-cost within this range would depend on the type of goods. With fashion goods and fancy jewellery, the mark-up of 100% was common; on real jewellery the mark-up was usually 60–90% and on silver and electro-plate 40–70%.

Multiple retailers and department stores usually purchased on the same terms as the wholesaler and their on-cost varied widely from 50–150%.

Settlement discounts to wholesalers and retailers ranged from 2½–5% for payment within the month. In a number of cases, mainly in respect of large purchases, discounts on the invoice up to 10% were given and these discounts represented partly settlement discounts and partly rebates for volume purchases. In practice, however, the usual credit period granted by manufacturers and wholesalers to retail jewellers was 3 months and 6–12 months was not uncommon. Few small retailers, therefore, qualified for the settlement discounts.

Stockholding. Manufacturers of the better quality real jewellery tended to produce to order for particular retailers and almost all stock of finished real jewellery was held by retailers. Owing to the granting of extended credit, however, the manufacturers tended to finance this stockholding by retailers. Stocks of fancy jewellery were usually held by manufacturers and wholesalers rather than by retailers owing to the seasonal and 'fashion' nature of the trade.

The stock turn of wholesalers averaged twice a year. The variations for the particular groups of commodities were: real jewellery and silver and electro-plate 1–1½ times a year, fancy jewellery 2½–3 times a year and wedding rings, signet rings, silver cigarette cases, etc. 2½–3 times a year.

The stock turn of the average retail jeweller was approximately once in 12–15 months, for fancy jewellery it was about once in 6–9 months, and for real jewellery and silver and electro-plate once in 12–15 months.

Manufacturers' distribution costs. Manufacturers of jewellery and silver-plate maintained their own sales organizations, usually with a small travelling staff, and sometimes showrooms were maintained. Delivery costs in the trade were small, the parcel post being used extensively, and advertising by manufacturers was insignificant. Distribution costs, including administrative selling costs, salesmen's salaries, carriage and costs of showrooms are estimated at 3–4% of manufacturers' sales revenue.

The total costs of distribution are estimated at 48–52% of retail sales.

2. WATCHES AND CLOCKS

Consumers' expenditure and methods of distribution

Consumers' expenditure on watches and clocks in 1938 was approximately £8–9 millions. The bulk of these goods was imported and there was a further sale of imported movements which were assembled in the

United Kingdom into cases made in this country. There was also, particularly in regard to the more expensive type of watch, an export of gold and silver cases from this country to be assembled abroad and re-imported as complete watches. Just under one-third of the total sales was represented by clocks, including electric clocks, and the remainder by watches. Nearly nine-tenths of the watches were imported and just over one-half of the clocks.

The methods of distribution of watches and clocks depended on whether the goods were imported complete or whether they were assembled or manufactured in the United Kingdom.

Of the watches and clocks which were imported, the proportions of total sales passing through the main channels of distribution are estimated as follows:

	%
From importer/wholesaler to retailer	60–70
From importer to wholesaler to retailer	15–25
Imported direct or through agent by retailer	5–10
From importer/wholesaler direct to public	5–10

The main channels of distribution of watches and clocks assembled or manufactured in the United Kingdom and the proportions of total sales passing through each were as follows:

	%
From manufacturer or assembler to wholesaler to retailer	65–75
From manufacturer or assembler to retailer	15–25
Assembled or manufactured by retailer	8–12

As approximately three-quarters, by value, of the watches and clocks sold were imported complete, and the remainder assembled or manufactured in the United Kingdom, the estimation of the channels of distribution of imported and home-manufactured goods is as follows:

	%
From manufacturer or importer/wholesaler to retailer	50–58
From manufacturer or importer to wholesaler to retailer	30–34
From manufacturer or importer/wholesaler direct to public	5–6
Imported by retailer or assembled or manufactured by retailer	7–10

In a few instances overseas manufacturers had their own retail outlets in this country, but these would not account for more than 1–2% of total sales. The purchases by retailers direct from importers or in some cases from overseas manufacturers were usually made by multiple concerns and large stores.

Number of wholesalers and retailers. The number of wholesalers and importer/wholesalers of watches and clocks in 1938 was between 300 and 350, although the number specializing in these goods was smaller. The number of retail outlets for watches and clocks in 1938 is estimated at 10–12,000. This includes variety chain stores, department stores with a jewellery department, and electrical goods retailers who sold electric clocks. Variety chain stores selling the cheaper imported watches are thought to have been responsible for 5–10% of the total turnover in 1938. Specialist multiple branches in the watch and clock and jewellery trades were responsible for a further 10–16%. Of the remaining sales, multiple shops in other trades, for example chemists, are estimated to have undertaken 2–4% of sales, department stores about 5%, co-operative stores 2–3% and unit retailers 64–74%.

The cost of distribution

Branding and advertising of particular types of watches in 1938 was not very common and only approximately 10% of the total watches sold carried a suggested retail price. The proportion was rather higher in the case of clocks, being particularly marked in the case of electric clocks.

The margins obtained by wholesalers and importers on the sale of watches and clocks in 1938 were approximately as follows:

	% *on-cost*
The importer/wholesaler usually worked to	30–60
The wholesaler usually worked to	20–30
The importer or agent performing that function alone usually worked to	5–10

The margins of the wholesaler and importer varied not only according to the function they performed, i.e. as importer only or importer/wholesaler, but also according to the type of watches handled. The wholesaler and importer would usually put a greater on-cost on the more expensive watches than on the cheaper ones; and in those cases where the importer or wholesaler was the sole agent of a particular type or make of watch his on-cost would be greater, as he would have to carry larger stocks than the normal wholesaler or importer. On electric clocks the wholesaler averaged 20% on returns.

The margins earned by retailers on the sale of watches and clocks in 1938 were approximately as follows:

Retailers purchasing watches from wholesalers or importers worked to 50–100% on cost.

Retailers purchasing direct from overseas or through agents, or from manufacturers, worked to 80–120% on cost.

The average retail margin on all watches sold was 40–50% on sales.

Retailers selling imported clocks worked to 40–65% on cost.

Retailers selling home-manufactured clocks, including electric clocks, worked to 50% on cost. In the case of the cheaper electric clocks the margin on sales was 30%.

The average retail margin on all clocks was 33–38% on sales.

Settlement discounts. In addition to these margins the wholesalers and retailers were usually entitled to a 2½% cash discount for payment within the month. While wholesalers and multiple shops usually earned this discount, other retailers obtained extended credit from wholesalers and manufacturers.

The retailer's margin on watches and clocks varied considerably within these ranges. In general, the cheaper the watch, the smaller the on-cost and vice versa. The main reason for the high on-cost, 100–120% on the expensive watches, was the cost of providing, free of charge to the consumer, before- and after-sales service on these watches. Such service was not usually given on the cheaper types of watches. A second element which affected the on-cost structure was the existence of various price steps and ranges of retail prices. For example, the movements of imported watches which were sold at retail prices ranging from 10s. to 2 guineas would very often be identical, the only difference between the watches being in the cases and faces. The differential in the cost of making the different types of cases in this range was very small. The consumer would expect a series of price steps between 10s. and 2 guineas, but would be unable to distinguish the movements of one watch from another, and the retailer would provide the watches for sale at the expected different price steps. The on-cost put on by the retailer within this range of watches would clearly vary very widely. A third factor influencing overall on-cost practice was the policy of multiple shops, particularly in the lower price ranges, of relying on low on-cost and high turnover.

The stock turn of wholesalers of watches and clocks averaged 3–4 times a year, and the stock turn of retailers 1½–2 times a year.

Manufacturers' distribution costs. As the bulk of these goods were imported, manufacturers' distribution costs were incurred on only a small proportion of the total sales. In these cases manufacturers' distribution costs, including selling costs, advertising, carriage and packing, amounted to 8–10% of manufacturers' sales. The distribution costs of manufacturers of electric clocks were rather higher, averaging 10–14% on sales revenue. Of this advertising expenditure represented 5–6%.

The total costs of distribution are estimated at 52–56% of retail sales.

3. SPORTS GOODS

Consumers' expenditure and methods of distribution

Consumers' expenditure on sports goods in 1938 is estimated at £7·5–8·5 millions. Excluded from this total are sales to schools, clubs and institutions. Sportswear and indoor parlour games are considered elsewhere in the studies on clothing and toys. Of the total expenditure golf clubs and golf balls represented 15–20%, racquets of various descriptions 20–25%, and tennis balls 5–10%.

The methods of distribution. The proportions of total sales passing through the main channels of distribution in 1938 are estimated as follows:

	%
From manufacturer to retailer	77–83
From manufacturer to wholesaler to retailer	10–12
From manufacturer to professional golfer	8–10

Included in the third group are sales by manufacturers to the Professional Golfers' Co-operative Alliance as well as the sales by manufacturers direct to professionals. Approximately 60% of the purchases by professional golfers were made through the P.G.C.A.

Numbers of wholesalers and retailers. In 1938 there were fewer than 25 wholesalers who regularly handled a wide range of sports goods. There were approximately 1,500 specialist sports goods retailers including the sports shops in department stores. Multiple specialist sports goods shops were few, numbering less than 25, and undertook less than 3% of total sales.

In addition to the specialists there were approximately a further 1–1,500 shops which sold a medium range of sports goods and a further 2–2,500 shops selling a very limited range of these goods. Such shops tended to buy from wholesalers or factors and sports goods would be a subsidiary sale. For example, some boot and shoe shops sold footballs, and during the summer at seaside resorts a mixed group of shops—confectioners, stationers, chemists—offered some sports equipment for sale. There were approximately 1,200 golf professionals in 1938 selling golfing equipment, and in some cases, where tennis clubs were attached to the golf clubs, tennis balls and racquets.

Sales by different types of retail outlet. The proportions of total sales undertaken by the different types of retail outlets in 1938 were approximately as follows:

	%
Specialist retail sports shops	60–70
Golf and tennis professionals	8–12
Other outlets	22–28

The sales by department stores, included in specialist shops above, are estimated to have represented some 10% of the total sales, and the sales by co-operative societies, included in other shops above, less than 2% of the total.

The cost of distribution

Approximately 40% of the leather goods and 60% of the tennis and golf equipment were price-maintained by manufacturers in 1938.

The margins allowed or earned by the different types of distributor were as follows:

Wholesalers' or factors' margins varied widely. Some wholesalers bought from manufacturers on the same terms as specialist retailers, others obtained the retailers' discount plus 10%, and on some goods, for example certain indoor sports goods, the wholesalers might obtain the retailers' margin plus 20%. The average discount of wholesalers was in the region of 33⅓% off the retail price and 10% wholesale discount.

Retailers' margin also varied. In the case of tennis and golf balls the margin ranged from 25–27½% on tennis balls and 25–29% on golf balls. On other price-maintained goods such as tennis racquets the retailer's margin was usually 33⅓% on sales. In the case of non-price-maintained goods the retailers usually worked to an on-cost of 50%, that is, 33⅓% on returns. In the few cases where goods were branded by the retailer, he sometimes put 75–100% on cost. The Professional Golfers' Co-operative Alliance received the same terms as the retailer on price-maintained goods, plus a 10% discount. The professional golfer buying through the P.G.C.A. obtained the retailer's margin plus 6¼%. In the case of non-price-maintained goods the professional golfer on re-sale worked to an on-cost of 50–100%. The latter margin would be earned in those cases where the goods were specially selected and branded. The professional golfer purchasing direct from the manufacturer, the usual course in the case of golf balls, received the retailer's trade discount, that is 25–29% on sales.

Settlement discounts in the trade ranged from 3¾–5% for payment in 7 days to 2½% for payment within the month. These terms applied to wholesalers, retailers and the P.G.C.A. The large retailers, the P.G.C.A. and some wholesalers usually earned the higher cash discount, while the smaller specialist retailers and professionals buying direct from manufacturers usually earned the monthly settlement discount.

The stock turn of the specialist sports goods retailer averaged 2–3 times a year.

Manufacturers' distribution costs[1] varied widely, according to the selling and advertising policy of the firm. In addition to press advertising, many manufacturers promoted tournaments, exhibition matches and similar forms of publicity. These costs included transport and delivery, salesmen's salaries, administrative selling costs and the various forms of sales promotion, and are estimated to have averaged 10–12% of manufacturers' sales revenue in 1938; of this transport costs represented between one-quarter and one-third.

Sales to clubs and schools, which are excluded from the estimates in this study, were an important feature of the trade and represented some 10% of total sales. Manufacturers sold some equipment direct to clubs and schools, particularly goods such as gymnasium equipment, but the bulk of the sales to clubs was undertaken by specialist retailers and 10–15% of the turnover of specialists represented this type of sale. The clubs and schools purchasing direct from manufacturers usually obtained a $33\frac{1}{3}$% discount off the retail price and in a few cases $33\frac{1}{3}$% plus 10%. Retailers selling to clubs and schools would allow a discount of 5–10% off the retail selling price.

The total costs of distribution are estimated at 42–44% of retail sales.

4. TOYS

Consumers' expenditure and methods of distribution

Consumers' expenditure on toys of all sorts including parlour games is estimated at £8–9 millions in 1938. Imported goods represented just under one-third of this total.

The methods of distribution. The proportions distributed through the various channels expressed as percentages of retail sales in 1938 have been estimated as follows:

	%
Home-manufactured	
From manufacturer direct to retailer	60–70
From manufacturer to factor or wholesaler to retailer	30–40
Imported	
From importer/wholesaler to retailer	70–80
Imported direct or through agent by retailer	15–20
From importer to wholesaler to retailer	5–10

Home-manufactured toys. Some of the larger manufacturers sold entirely direct to retailers, others sold partly direct and partly through wholesalers. The small manufacturers tended to sell more extensively through factors and wholesalers. The factor, as distinct from the wholesaler,

[1] See page 164.

took an active interest in manufacture, frequently financing small manufacturers and giving large orders for lines made to the factor's specifications, or in some cases taking the whole of a manufacturer's output. Factors sold largely to retailers but also distributed to wholesalers. Wholesalers generally supplied the smaller retailers and stocked mostly the cheaper ranges of toys. They usually handled other goods as well, for example fancy goods, stationery, sports goods.

Imported toys were, for the most part, bought outright by speciality toy importers who distributed to retailers, and who often combined the importation of foreign toys with the factoring of home-produced goods. Some imported toys were sold on commission by agents acting for foreign firms or purchased direct by the larger retailers from overseas manufacturers.

Numbers of wholesalers and numbers of retail outlets. It is estimated that there were approximately 400 wholesalers who regularly stocked toys. Some 750–1,000 shops specialized in the sale of toys, and toys were also stocked regularly by a wide range of shops including department stores, variety chain stores and stationers. The bulk of the sales by shops such as department stores were made in the Christmas period. A large number of smaller shops stocked toys as a sideline during the Christmas season. The estimated proportions of total sales in 1938 undertaken by shops grouped by economic type were approximately:

	%
Multiple shops and variety chain stores	23–27
Department stores	28–32
Co-operative shops	3–5
Unit retailers	36–46

The cost of distribution

The large manufacturers usually branded their toys but strict price maintenance was not an important feature of this trade.

The margins earned by importers, wholesalers and retailers in 1938 were approximately as follows:

Wholesalers' margins on home-produced and imported toys usually ranged from 20–25 % on sales, varying with the price of the goods. Owing to mark-downs and stock losses the average realized margin was near the lower limit. Where the goods were sold to a second wholesaler, the margin was split between them.

Agents usually received a commission of 7–10 % on sales of imported toys.

Retailers usually worked to a mark-up of 50 % on cost on home and imported toys, giving $33\frac{1}{3}$ % on sales. Again mark-downs and losses tended to give the retailer a slightly lower realized margin on sales. Some manufacturers and factors gave large retail buyers an additional 10% off wholesale price.

Settlement discounts given by manufacturers were usually 2½% for payment in 7 days, or in some instances in one month. Wholesalers usually gave longer credit.

Stock turn. Wholesalers usually carried stocks of the cheaper lines only, stocks of the more bulky high priced goods being largely held by manufacturers, factors and importers. Retailers other than the specialist toy shops generally stocked a large range of toys only in the 3–4 months prior to Christmas, their average stock turn being 1½–2 times a year. It is estimated that over half the total retail sales were made during the Christmas season.

Manufacturers' distribution costs showed marked differences depending on whether they sold largely to factors and wholesalers or undertook distribution to retailers. In the former case manufacturers' distribution costs were relatively small. Manufacturers and factors with their own distributive organizations who carried large stocks in preparation for the Christmas season, and whose delivery costs, in the case of bulky goods such as toys, were high, had distribution costs averaging 30–33% on sales, and from 15–20% where distribution was partly through wholesalers and partly direct to retailer.

The total costs of distribution are estimated at 53–57% of retail sales.

5. LEATHER GOODS

Consumers' expenditure and methods of distribution

Consumers' expenditure in 1938 on leather goods, including travel goods, ladies' handbags and other receptacles of leather or material resembling leather, fancy goods such as leather booklets and writing cases, and miscellaneous leather goods, is estimated at £9–11 millions. Imported leather goods accounted for approximately 5–10% of total expenditure.

Between one-quarter and one-third of the total represented expenditure on travel goods, just under one-half expenditure on ladies' handbags and just under a quarter expenditure on other fancy goods. Leather footwear, gloves and other leather clothing and sports goods are excluded from this estimate.

The methods of distribution. The proportions of these goods distributed through the principal channels, expressed as percentages of retail sales in 1938 are estimated as follows:

	%
From manufacturer to wholesaler to retailer	25–33
From manufacturer direct to retailer	67–75

Travel goods and ladies' handbags were distributed largely direct to retailer, only the cheaper lines being handled by wholesalers. A much larger proportion, 50–60%, of the leather toilet and fancy goods were distributed by wholesalers.

Imported leather goods were usually purchased by wholesalers direct from foreign manufacturers, but some of the cheaper varieties were purchased by wholesalers through importers or agents.

Sales by different types of retail outlet. Leather goods were sold by department stores, drapers, stationers, leather goods specialists, saddlers, chemists, tobacconists, variety chain stores and the retail co-operatives. The proportions of sales made by the different outlets classified according to economic type are estimated as:

	%
Multiple shops and variety chain stores	13–16
Co-operative stores	1–3
Department stores	20–25
Unit retailers	56–66

Multiple shops selling leather goods include specialist leather goods retailers, chemists, stationers and the variety chain stores.

The cost of distribution

Very few of these goods were price-maintained. Manufacturers tended to produce largely for traditional retail price ranges.

The margins earned by wholesalers and retailers on the sale of leather goods in 1938 are estimated as follows:

> *The wholesaler's* mark-up on cost ranged from 10–33⅓% depending on the price of the line. It tended to be higher on fancy leather goods than on travel goods and handbags. The wholesaler's average mark-up was approximately 25% on cost, giving 20% on sales.
>
> *The retailer's* mark-up ranged from 33⅓–60% on cost, varying with the price of the line and the type of outlet. The on-cost on toilet articles and fancy goods was usually higher than that on travel goods and handbags.
>
> Taking the trade as a whole the average retail mark-up was from 50–60% on cost, giving 33⅓–40% on returns. Mark-downs were common and the realized gross margin in the trade was 33–35%.

Settlement discounts of 3¾% for payment in 7 days, 2½% in 30 days were usual in the trade.

Stock turn for leather goods was markedly seasonal, one-half of the total sales of handbags, for example, occurring in the Christmas period, October-December, and of travel goods in the period May-August. The average retailer kept from 3–4 months' stock, variety chain stores 1–1½ months' stock. The wholesaler usually held 4–6 months' stock.

Manufacturers' distribution costs are estimated to have averaged from 8–10% on sales.

The total costs of distribution are estimated at 47–49% of retail sales.

CHAPTER XXVI

TOILET PREPARATIONS AND REQUISITES, MEDICINES AND DRUGS AND PHOTOGRAPHIC GOODS

I. BEAUTY PREPARATIONS

Consumers' expenditure and methods of distribution

Consumers' expenditure on beauty preparations in 1938 is estimated at £6–7 millions. Included in this group of products are all cosmetics, nail varnishes, hand creams and face lotions.

The methods of distribution and the cost of distribution of these products varied between particular subdivisions of the trade and in a marked way between different price ranges. In discussing these problems it is convenient to subdivide the trade into four main groups. These groups and the proportion of total sales estimated to have been represented by each in 1938 are as follows:

	%
High price trade	5–10
Medium price trade	25–30
Popular price trade	55–60
Low price trade	5–10

The low price beauty preparations were usually unadvertised.

The methods of distribution. The proportions of total sales passing through the main channels of distribution in 1938 are estimated as follows:

	%
From manufacturer to retailer	70–75
From manufacturer to wholesaler to retailer	25–30

A small proportion of these products was made up by retailers and sold under their 'own name' brands. There were important variations in the channels of distribution in each of the four price groups. The high price trade was practically entirely direct from manufacturer to retailer. Four-fifths of the medium price trade was distributed in the same way. Just under three-quarters of the popular price trade was distributed direct from manufacturer to retailer, but less than a third of the low price trade, the remainder in this group going through wholesalers.

Number of wholesalers and retailers. The wholesalers handling these products were mostly chemists' and hairdressers' wholesalers and sundriesmen. The total number of wholesalers dealing in these goods in 1938 was in the region of 400, but about a quarter of that number were responsible for the bulk of the trade. The number of retail outlets of these products is estimated at between 32–36,000. Of these, chemists and drug stores numbered between 17–18,000, women's hairdressers and beauty salons about 14–15,000. Variety chain stores and department stores made up the remainder. Some of the products, though not the complete range, were sold through other outlets such as grocers and general stores.

Sales by different types of retail outlet. The proportion of the total sales handled by the different trade types of retail outlet in 1938 is estimated as follows:

	%
Chemists and druggists	59–63
Ladies' hairdressers and beauty salons	14–16
Variety chain stores	12–13
Department stores	9–10
Other outlets	1–3

There were variations in the proportions of sales made by the different types of outlet according to the different retail price groups. The following estimates have been made. About half of the total sales of the high price goods were made by department stores, about 30% by chemists and drug stores, and one-fifth by ladies' hairdressers and beauty salons. Nearly two-thirds of the sales of medium price goods were made by chemists and drug stores, one-fifth by ladies' hairdressers and beauty salons, and about 15% by department stores. The popular and low price trade was handled almost entirely by chemists and drug stores, representing two-thirds of total sales, and by variety chain stores, one-fifth of total sales. Ladies' hairdressers undertook about one-tenth of the total sales of this group. The remaining sales were made by department stores and other outlets.

Multiple shops including variety chain stores are estimated to have undertaken 30–33% of the total trade, department stores 9–10%, and co-operative stores, usually the chemist's department of co-operative stores, 3–4%. The remaining sales were made by unit retailers.

Firms specializing in the high price trade would have of the order of 1–3,000 retail accounts, and these retailers were often district concessionaires for the firm's products. In the medium price trade direct retail accounts of manufacturers numbered between 3–6,000, and in the popular price trade up to 20,000.

The cost of distribution

A very high proportion of beauty preparations in 1938 was re-sale price maintained by the manufacturer.

The margins earned by and allowed to wholesalers and retailers were as follows:

> *Wholesalers* in the medium price trade earned between 10–15% on returns plus a settlement discount ranging up to 5% for payment in 7 days. The wholesaler in the popular price trade received a margin ranging from 10–20% on sales with a settlement discount ranging up to 5% for payment in 7 days. The wholesaler in the low price trade received a margin of 15–25% on sales plus settlement discounts ranging up to 5% for payment in 7 days.
>
> *Retailers* purchasing from wholesalers in the medium price trade received a margin of 25–33% on sales plus a settlement discount of up to 2½% for payment in the month. Retailers buying from wholesalers in the popular price trade received a margin of 20–33% on sales plus a settlement discount ranging up to 2½% for payment in the month. Retailers purchasing from wholesalers in the low price trade received a margin of 33% on sales.
>
> Retailers purchasing direct from manufacturers in the high price trade received a basic margin of 33% and were entitled to additional discounts dependent sometimes on the volume of purchase, sometimes on window display, sometimes on quarterly or annual turnover; or in some cases to a bonus in the form of 13 to the dozen or 25 to the two dozen. The discounts ranged up to 10% on invoice price. The settlement discounts were up to 2½% for payment in the month. The retailer purchasing direct from manufacturers in the medium price trade received a basic discount of 25–33% on sales plus an additional volume discount or bonus ranging up to 15% and a settlement discount ranging up to 5% for payment in 7 days. The retailer purchasing direct from manufacturers in the popular and low price trade received a basic margin varying from 20–33⅓% on sales plus a bonus ranging up to 17½% and a settlement discount ranging up to 5% for payment in 7 days.

The combined wholesale and retail margins expressed as a percentage of the retail price averaged 41% in the medium price trade, 40% in the popular price trade and 48% in the low price trade. The margin of the retailer purchasing direct from the manufacturer averaged 36% of the retail price in the high price trade, 37–38% in the medium price, 35% in the popular price and 42–43% in the low price trade.

The stock turn of retailers in these goods varied considerably according to the price range handled and the type of shop. Variety chain stores turned over their stocks on the average every 2 weeks. Multiple chemists turned over their stock every 1–2 months, the independent chemists every 3–5 months and the hairdresser and beauty salons once a month.

Manufacturers' distribution costs varied with the type of goods sold and the methods of distribution. In the high price trade it is estimated that advertising represented 20–25% of manufacturers' sales revenue, carriage and transport 3–5% and salesmen's salaries and administrative selling costs 8–12%, making a total of 35–38% of sales revenue. In the medium price trade some firms selling branded goods advertised widely, and allowed distributors margins at the lower end of the scale suggested above. Other firms did relatively little advertising but allowed distributors' margins near the upper limits suggested above. But the former firms predominated. Average distribution costs of manufacturers in this group are estimated as follows: advertising costs 14–18%, carriage and transport 2–3%, other selling costs 7–10%, making a total of 25–30% in sales revenue. In the popular price trade there was greater divergence between the distribution costs of different manufacturers. Some firms selling well-known branded products had advertising costs of 35–40%, carriage and transport 1–2% and other selling costs 10–12%, making a total of about 50% on sales. Other firms had distribution costs as low as 10% of turnover. The average manufacturer's distribution cost in the popular trade is estimated at 30–33% on sales revenue. The average distribution costs of manufacturers of the low priced products, which were not usually widely advertised, are estimated at 10% of manufacturers' sales revenue.

Manufacturers' distribution costs on all beauty preparations are estimated at about 30% of manufacturers' sales revenue.

The total costs of distribution are estimated at 54–57% of retail sales.

2. PERFUMES AND TOILET WATERS

Consumers' expenditure and methods of distribution

Consumers' expenditure on perfumes and toilet waters in 1938 is estimated at approximately £2 millions.

This trade is somewhat similar to that of beauty preparations in that there were differences in the methods of distribution and the costs of distribution in various price groups. These groups and the proportions of sales represented by each in 1938 are estimated as follows:

	%
High price trade	8–12
Medium price trade	43–47
Popular price trade	35–40
Low price trade	5–10

The high price perfumes were practically all imported, and the low price perfumes were usually unadvertised lines.

The methods of distribution. The proportions of total sales of perfumes and toilet waters passing through the main channels of distribution in 1938 are estimated as follows:

	%
From manufacturer or importer to retailer	65–70
From manufacturer or importer to wholesaler to retailer	30–35

Nearly all the goods in the high price trade went direct from manufacturer or importer to retailer, four-fifths of the medium price trade followed the same channel, and three-fifths of the popular price trade went direct to retailer. Just under one-third of the goods in the low price trade, on the other hand, went direct to retailer, the remainder passing through wholesalers. A small proportion of these goods was made up by retailers and sold under their 'own name' brand.

Sales by different types of retail outlet. The number of wholesalers and of retail outlets in this trade is almost identical with that in the beauty preparations trade discussed above. The proportions of total sales undertaken by the different trade types of retail outlet in 1938 are estimated as follows:

	%
Chemists and drug stores	62–65
Ladies' hairdressers and beauty salons	10–14
Variety chain stores	11–13
Department stores	7–9
Other outlets, including general shops	4–5

There were important variations in the type of trade done by the different retail outlets. Chemists and drug stores, ladies' hairdressers and beauty salons, and department stores are each estimated to have undertaken one-third of the total sales of the high price perfumes and toilet waters. Chemists and drug stores are estimated to have undertaken just under three-quarters of the total sales of medium price perfumes and toilet waters, ladies' hairdressers and beauty salons one-tenth, and department stores just under one-tenth. Of the popular and low price perfumes and toilet waters, chemists and drug stores are estimated to have undertaken three-fifths of the total sales, variety chain stores just under one-third, and the remaining sales were made by ladies' hairdressers and beauty salons and general shops.

Multiple shops including variety chain stores are estimated to have undertaken 26–28% of total sales of perfumes and toilet waters, department stores 8%, and co-operative stores 3–4%. The remaining sales were undertaken by unit retailers.

The cost of distribution

A large proportion of the perfumes and toilet waters were sold at prices fixed or suggested by the manufacturers.

The margins earned or allowed to wholesalers and retailers of perfumes and toilet waters in 1938 are estimated as follows:

Wholesalers in the medium price trade earned a margin ranging from 5–20% on sales plus a settlement discount of up to 2½% for payment in the month. Wholesalers in the popular and low price trade received a margin ranging from 10–20% on sales and a similar settlement discount of up to 2½% for payment in the month.

Retailers purchasing from wholesalers in the medium price trade received a margin ranging from 25–33% on sales plus a settlement discount of up to 2½% for payment in 7 days. The retailer buying from wholesalers in the popular and low price trade received a margin of 30–33% off the retail price plus a settlement discount of up to 2½% for payment in the month.

Retailers purchasing direct from manufacturers in the high price trade received a basic margin of 33⅓% on sales and were entitled to other discounts for volume purchases, window display or turnover of up to 10% plus a settlement discount of 2½% for payment in the month. The retailer in the medium price trade received a margin of 25–33⅓% on sales and could earn a further discount of up to 10% plus a further discount of up to 2½% for payment in the month. The retailer in the popular and low price trade purchasing direct from manufacturers received a basic margin of 25–33⅓% and could earn an additional discount ranging up to 15% plus a settlement discount of up to 2½% for payment in the month.

The combined wholesale and retail margins expressed as a percentage of the retail price in the medium price trade averaged 43% and in the popular and low price trades 44%. The average margins earned by retailers purchasing direct from manufacturers in the high price trade was 36%, in the medium price trade 38% and in the popular and low price trade 40%.

The stock turn of wholesalers of perfumes and toilet waters averaged about once every 2–3 months. The stock turn of retailers averaged once every 4–6 months, though in the case of variety chain stores and multiple retailers the stock turn was slightly higher, once every 2–3 months.

Manufacturers' distribution costs on perfumes and toilet waters were very similar to those on beauty preparations and, in general, showed the same variation between the different price groups in the trade. The average distribution costs of manufacturers including administrative selling costs, salesmen's salaries, carriage and packing and advertising were about 30% of manufacturers' sales revenue.

The total costs of distribution are estimated at 56–59% of retail sales.

3. SANITARY TOWELS

Consumers' expenditure and methods of distribution

Consumers' expenditure on sanitary towels in 1938 is estimated at £2–3 millions.

The methods of distribution. The proportions of the total sales passing through the various channels of distribution in 1938 are estimated as follows:

	%
From manufacturer to wholesaler to retailer	65–70
From manufacturer direct to retailer	30–35

Sales to multiple shops, whether by split delivery to individual branches or to the wholesale department of the organization, and sales to co-operative wholesale societies for re-sale to retail co-operatives are included in sales direct to retailer.

Number of retail outlets. The number of retail outlets for these goods in 1938 is estimated at 75–100,000 and the proportions of total sales made by the different trade types of outlet are estimated as follows:

	%
Drapers', baby linen or wool shops	55–60
Chemists' shops	25–30
Other outlets, including hairdressers, variety chain stores and general stores	10–20

The variety chain stores are estimated to have undertaken 5–10% of total sales.

Sales by different types of outlet. The proportions of sales made by the different economic types of outlet are estimated as follows:

	%
Multiple shops including variety chain stores	17–23
Co-operative stores	8–12
Unit retailers	65–75

The cost of distribution

Most of the lines were price-maintained in 1938, although some manufacturers produced both branded and unbranded lines.

The margins earned by wholesalers and retailers were approximately as follows:

Wholesalers' margins ranged between 15–18½% on returns. The standard branded lines usually earned a margin near the lower end of this range.

Retailers usually obtained 25% on returns. On one or two lines the margin rose to 29–30% on sales. Some manufacturers allowed a volume discount ranging from 2½% on an order of £1 10s. to 7½% on an order of £6.

Retailers purchasing in small quantities direct from manufacturers usually obtained the same terms as when purchasing from wholesalers, but multiple organizations and variety chain stores would generally receive wholesale terms.

Settlement discounts for wholesalers were 2½% for payment in the month. For retailers the discounts varied from 2½–3¾% for payment in 60 days.

Stock turn. Wholesalers in 1938 received very frequent deliveries from manufacturers and never held towel stocks for any length of time. A proportion of the stock was in their possession for less than 24 hours, and the average stock turn of wholesalers was in the region of once a week. The stock turn of retailers averaged between 6–12 times a year.

Manufacturers' distribution costs varied widely according to the different policies pursued by manufacturers. Taking these costs to include transport costs, advertising, salesmen's salaries and administrative selling costs, the average ranged between 10–12% of sales revenue. Of these costs transport charges were approximately 2–4%, advertising 3–5%, and salesmen's salaries and administrative selling costs 3–5%.

The total costs of distribution are estimated at 45–48% of retail sales.

4. RAZORS AND RAZOR BLADES

Consumers' expenditure and methods of distribution

Consumers' expenditure on razors and razor blades in 1938 is estimated at £2·5–3 millions. Sales of razor blades represented the greater part of this expenditure.

The methods of distribution. The proportions of total sales passing through the main channels of distribution in 1938 are estimated as follows:

	%
From manufacturer to wholesaler to retailer	65–70
From manufacturer to retailer	30–35

Number of wholesalers and retailers. The number of wholesalers handling razors and blades is estimated at 3–3,500. About one-third of the trade was handled by chemists' wholesalers and sundriesmen and a further one-third by hairdressers' wholesalers. The remaining wholesalers handling these goods were in the hardware, grocery, tobacco and newsagent's trades. The total number of retail outlets for razor blades is estimated at 150–200,000.

Sales by different types of retail outlet. The division of the total sales according to the trade type of outlet was approximately as follows:

	%
Chemists	30–40
Hairdressers	20–25
Variety chain stores	10–15
Hardware shops, newsagents, grocers, tobacconists and general shops and outlets	25–35

The division of sales according to economic type of outlet was approximately as follows:

	%
Multiple shops	10–15
Variety chain stores	10–15
Co-operatives and department stores	2–3
Unit retailers	67–78

Multiple shops include multiple chemists, hairdressers and grocers.

The cost of distribution

Practically all razors and blades were branded and, in most cases, price-maintained by the manufacturers.

The margins earned by wholesalers and retailers were as follows:

Wholesalers. The margins allowed or earned by wholesalers were usually 16–19% of the wholesale selling price, plus settlement discount of 2½% for payment in the month. In some instances no wholesale terms as such were quoted by manufacturers and the purchase price varied with the quantity bought.

Retailers purchasing direct from manufacturers obtained a margin ranging from 30–46%. The basic margin was usually 30–33% and on top of this special and volume discounts were given to retailers purchasing in large quantities. Settlement discounts to retailers purchasing direct varied from 2½–5%. Only retailers purchasing in large quantities, such as multiple organizations, would earn margins at the top end of the range. Where wholesale terms were quoted, multiple organizations usually bought at those terms. The average margin earned by retailers purchasing direct from manufacturers was 38–39%.

Retailers purchasing from wholesalers usually earned a margin of 30–33%, plus a settlement discount of up to 2½%.

Stock turn. Wholesalers' stock turn is estimated to have averaged 12 times a year and retailers' between 6 and 9 times a year. Variety chain stores and multiple organizations usually had a much higher stock turn.

Manufacturers' distribution costs. There were wide variations in manufacturers' distribution costs according to the policy of the individual manufacturer. The following estimates are an attempt to give a picture of the trade as a whole. Manufacturers' distribution costs are estimated at 15–20% of sales revenue. Of this total, delivery costs are estimated at 1–2%, selling costs at 4–5% and advertising at 10–15%.

The total costs of distribution are estimated at 51–54% of retail sales.

5. DENTIFRICE AND TOOTHBRUSHES

Consumers' expenditure and methods of distribution

Consumers' expenditure in 1938 on this group of goods, including dentifrices, toothbrushes and dental fixatives and cleaners, is estimated at £5 millions. Of this total, dentifrices accounted for about £3·25 millions—made up of 82–84% pastes, 11–12% solids and 5–6% powders—and toothbrushes for about £1·25 millions.

The methods of distribution. The proportions of total sales passing through the main channels of distribution in 1938 are estimated as follows:

	%
From manufacturer to retailer	53–57
From manufacturer to wholesaler to retailer	43–47

The channels of distribution of the two main groups of goods varied as follows: 55–60% of the sales of dentifrices went from manufacturer direct to retailer and the remainder through wholesalers, and 45–50% of the sales of toothbrushes went from manufacturer direct to retailer and the remainder through wholesalers.

Number of retail outlets. The number of retail outlets for these goods is estimated at between 75–100,000. The main trade types of outlet selling the products were chemists and drug stores numbering 17,500, approximately 25,000 grocers, and 10–15,000 hairdressers. In addition, department stores, most of the variety chain stores and a large number of general shops also sold these goods.

Sales by different types of retail outlet. The estimates of the proportions of total sales undertaken by the different trade outlets are as follows:

	%
Chemists and drug stores	60–65
Grocers	10–15
Variety chain stores	10–15
Hairdressers	3–7
Other outlets	5–10

For the two main groups of product there were small variations in the proportions sold by the different types of retail outlet. Dentifrices had a higher sale in grocers' shops and a smaller sale in hairdressers' than the average given above. Toothbrushes had a very small sale in grocers', while sales in chemists' and hairdressers' were higher than the average given above. In all about 20,000 outlets were responsible for three-quarters of the total trade.

The proportions of total sales made by the different types of economic outlet are estimated as follows:

	%
Multiple shops, including multiple chemists and grocers	19–23
Variety chain stores	10–15
Co-operative stores	4–5
Unit retailers	60–64

Again, there were variations for the two main groups. Dentifrices had a higher sale in multiple shops and variety chain stores and a smaller sale by unit retailers than the average for all dental preparations given above. Toothbrushes, on the other hand, had a higher sale by unit retailers and a smaller sale in multiple shops and variety chain stores.

The cost of distribution

Practically all dentifrices and about one-half of the toothbrushes were branded and price-maintained by manufacturers in 1938, but some of these goods were sold below the fixed prices. Approximately one-third of the remaining toothbrushes were branded by wholesalers and retailers.

The margins allowed or earned by wholesalers and retailers in 1938 were approximately as follows:

Dentifrices. Manufacturers who concentrated on selling direct to retailers usually quoted rates according to the volume of goods bought, irrespective of whether they were bought by wholesalers or retailers. In some cases, however, to encourage retail purchases, the higher rates were given for window display instead of for size of purchase.

The terms allowed, expressed as discounts off the retail selling price, ranged between 25 and 37½%, including volume and window display discounts. Wholesalers usually bought at the highest discount and retailers buying from them could usually obtain a discount of 27–28% off the retail price. Wholesalers' margins, therefore, were 12½–14% on sales and this was the usual margin allowed to wholesalers in those cases where separate terms were allowed to them by manufacturers. In a few cases, large retailers, purchasing direct, obtained margins up to 42–43%, but in these instances the retailers usually bore carriage charges.

The margins allowed on powders and solids were slightly lower than those for toothpastes, though the same practice of additional discounts for volume purchases or window display obtained.

Settlement discounts, which were not always given, were usually 2½% for payment within the month.

Toothbrushes. The wholesalers' margins ranged from 15–25% on sales plus, in some cases, a 5% turnover discount. Some manufacturers gave special discounts in particular periods of the year, for example a bonus of, say, 2 free brushes for each 12 ordered, i.e. an additional discount of 14–15%. On unbranded brushes the usual margins earned by wholesalers were 25–30%. The average wholesale margin, including discounts for quantity purchases, special discounts and margins on unbranded brushes, was 22–24% on sales. In addition, most wholesalers received a settlement discount of 2½% for payment within the month.

Retailers buying from wholesalers usually obtained a margin of 33% of the retail selling price, plus a settlement discount of 1½–2½%. Retailers purchasing direct from manufacturers received a margin of 33% of the retail selling price and were entitled to the same cash and volume discounts and special annual bonus terms as were given to wholesalers, that is a range of margins from 33–47%. Large buyers purchasing direct from manufacturers often bought on wholesale terms and obtained a margin of up to 57% of the retail price. Sometimes the retailers purchasing on these terms paid the carriage cost.

Manufacturers' distribution costs. The distribution costs of the dentifrice manufacturer who sold mainly direct to retailers and advertised his products were of the order of 40–50% on sales revenue. Of this, selling costs were 5–7%, carriage outwards 2–3% and advertising 33–40%.

Other manufacturers who sold mainly through wholesalers and did little advertising had distribution costs of 8–10% on sales revenue.

The distribution costs of toothbrush manufacturers ranged from 7–20% on turnover, with an average of approximately 12–13%. Advertising costs represented over one-half of total selling costs.

The total costs of distribution of dental preparations are estimated at 58–61% and of toothbrushes at 55–58% of retail sales.

6. PROPRIETARY AND NON-PROPRIETARY MEDICINES AND DRUGS

Consumers' expenditure and methods of distribution

Consumers' expenditure on proprietary and non-proprietary medicines and drugs in 1938 is estimated at £22–24 millions. This estimate includes the sales of medicines in shops other than chemists', but endeavours to exclude dispensing by chemists, whether under the National Health Insurance scheme or private dispensing, and the sales of medicines and drugs by either manufacturers, wholesalers or retail chemists to doctors, hospitals and other institutions. Expenditure on infant and invalid foods and on health food beverages is also excluded as the distribution of these products is discussed elsewhere. One-half of the expenditure is estimated to have represented the sale of proprietary medicines and drugs and the remainder the sale of non-proprietary medicines and drugs of various kinds.

These goods were manufactured by four different types of firm. Firstly, the manufacturer with no retail interests who sold his products to wholesalers and retailers. Secondly, multiple retail chemists' organizations which possessed manufacturing facilities and sold the greater part of their output in their own retail shops but also sold a small proportion to wholesalers and other retailers. Thirdly, the many firms who were designated wholesalers but who had manufacturing departments which either undertook the whole process of manufacture or re-packed and labelled goods produced by other firms. Fourthly, retail chemists who undertook some manufacturing themselves and sold products under their 'own name' brand. The nationally advertised and distributed products were manufactured mainly by the first group and partly by the third group referred to above.

The methods of distribution. The proportions of total sales passing through the main channels of distribution in 1938 are estimated as follows:

	%
From manufacturer to wholesaler to retailer	50–60
From manufacturer direct to retailer	40–50

Included in the sales direct to retailers are the sale of goods produced by manufacturing establishments linked with multiple retail organizations and sold in the retail branches, the sale of goods manufactured by wholesalers, the sale by retail chemists of 'own name' medicines and drugs and the sales by co-operative wholesale societies to retail co-operative societies. The independent chemists and other shops selling proprietary medicines are estimated to have purchased between three-quarters and four-fifths of their supplies through wholesalers.

Number of wholesalers and retailers. The number of specialist chemist wholesalers in 1938 is estimated at 60. A large proportion of these, as suggested above, undertook some manufacturing or branding of medicines and drugs. In addition there were a number of wholesalers, 150–200, who carried these goods but who did not normally stock a complete range of chemist's goods. A number of grocery wholesalers and general wholesalers carried some proprietary medicines.

The specialist chemist wholesaler for the most part operated on a large scale and the important ones maintained depots in different parts of the country. Some had as many as a thousand purchasing accounts and 6–8,000 selling accounts, and carried a stock of 8–10,000 different lines of proprietary medicines and drugs.

The number of retail chemists in 1938 is estimated at 16,000, including chemist departments in co-operative stores 450–500, and in department stores 200–250. There were a further 1,500 drug stores selling some of these goods. Approximately 3,250–3,750 of the chemists and drug stores were branches of multiple organizations, that is organizations having five or more branches. Proprietary medicines were sold through a wide range of retail outlets in addition to chemists and drug stores, and the total number of outlets in 1938 is estimated at 150–160,000.

Sales by different types of retail outlet. The proportions of the total sales of proprietary medicines and drugs undertaken by the different trade types of retail outlet are estimated as follows:

	%
Chemists and drug stores	80–85
Grocers, variety chain stores, hairdressers, public-houses and general shops and outlets	15–20

Almost all the non-proprietary medicines and drugs were sold by chemists and drug stores while between one-quarter and one-third of the sales of proprietary medicines and drugs are estimated to have been made by shops other than chemists.

The proportions of sales undertaken by the different economic types of outlet for 1938 are estimated as follows:

	%
Multiple shops, including variety chain stores	33–35
Co-operative and department stores	5–7
Unit retailers	58–62

Between one-quarter and one-third of the sales of medicines and drugs made by multiple shops were the product of their own manufacturing establishments.

The cost of distribution

Approximately 50–60% of the sales of proprietary medicines in 1938 were made at prices agreed between the manufacturers, wholesalers and retailers through the Proprietary Articles Trade Association. Many products not listed by the P.A.T.A. were also price-maintained.

Margins of wholesalers on proprietary medicines and drugs ranged between 10% and up to 17½% on sales. The average margin earned by wholesalers on these goods was 12½–15%. Some manufacturers gave special terms to wholesalers but a number offered the same sliding-scale terms to retailers as to wholesalers. The return earned by wholesalers depended on the size of the extra discounts they obtained for bulk purchases and on the quantities and terms of re-sale to retailers. In these cases the margins earned by wholesalers were usually similar to those given above, 12–15% on sales. Wholesalers' margins on non-proprietary medicines and drugs ranged between 10–15% and sometimes 17½% on sales. The wholesalers earned the higher discount when purchasing in bulk quantities from manufacturers.

The retailers' margins on proprietary medicines and drugs ranged from 20–33⅓% on sales. Within this range two main practices were common. On the nationally advertised and distributed products retailers' margins usually ranged from 20–27½%, while on the products which were less advertised and in some cases not nationally distributed the margin ranged from 27½–33%. In each case the range of margins suggested relates to 'basic' margins. In addition, on practically all brands of proprietary medicines and drugs retailers were able to obtain higher margins by placing orders over a certain amount, or by ordering at certain times of the year, or by giving window or counter displays or by various other methods designed by the manufacturers to encourage the sale of their products. These discounts took the form of a lower purchasing price, a straight discount of 7½% or 10%, or bonuses of 13 or 14 to the dozen. Retailers were also entitled to settlement discounts, which were usually 2½% for payment in the month but rose in some cases to 5–6% for payment in 7 days or by return. The size of these additional display, window, volume and settlement discounts tended to be related inversely to the size of the initial discount. That is, in those instances where a basic retail margin of 20% was given, the retailer could by purchasing in quantities and by providing window displays increase this margin by a further 15%, while in those cases where the initial discount of 27½% or 30% was given the additional quantity rebates were on a smaller scale and might only yield 5–7½% in addition. The combined basic margins and discounts for display, quantity and settlement on proprietary medicines and drugs ranged between 27½–50% on sales. Most retailers were able to obtain some additional discounts as well as the basic margin, and the average retail margin, including all discounts on proprietary medicines and drugs, both on nationally advertised and on less advertised goods, was between 29–31%.

Retailers' margins on non-proprietary medicines and drugs ranged between 20–25% on sales. On purchases from wholesalers or in small quantities from manufacturers the margin earned was at the lower end of the scale but on purchases in quantity direct from manufacturers retailers would usually earn 25% and an additional 1½–2½% for purchases over a certain quantity or as settlement discounts. The average margin earned by retailers was 23–25%.

Multiple retailers in practically every case purchased both proprietary and non-proprietary medicines and drugs from manufacturers at wholesale terms. Where no wholesale terms were quoted but merely terms for quantities, these firms usually obtained the highest discounts offered. The retail margin of multiple firms on the sale of these goods averaged 33–35% on sales.

In the case of medicines and drugs sold by multiple retail chemists which were the product of a manufacturing establishment connected with the multiple firm, the price-spread between the manufacturing cost and the retail price was of the order of 50–60% of the retail price. This spread includes, of course, the cost of the wholesaling function which was performed by the manufacturing multiple organizations. In the case of the unit retailer making and selling his 'own name' products the margin is estimated to have ranged between 40–50% of the retail price.

Manufacturers and wholesalers paid the cost of carriage to retailers on drugs and medicines in all cases of orders over a certain quantity, usually £2 of one product or of assorted lots.

The stock turn of specialist wholesalers is estimated at 12–14 times a year, and the average stock turn of the chemist of proprietary and non-proprietary medicines and packed drugs at 4–6 times a year.

Manufacturers' distribution costs on proprietary medicines and drugs, excluding the costs of distributing the goods produced by the manufacturing establishments of multiple retail organizations, are estimated to have averaged 35–40% of sales revenue. Of this, selling costs, administrative charges, salesmen's salaries, etc., averaged 3–5%, carriage and transport costs between 2–4% and advertising 28–32%. There were important variations between different firms, and it was usual for those manufacturers with relatively high advertising costs and who advertised on a national scale to give lower retail margins and smaller quantity discounts and special bonuses than the manufacturers who had lower advertising costs and who did little national advertising.

Manufacturers' distribution costs on non-proprietary medicines and drugs averaged 6–8% of sales revenue.

The total costs of distribution of proprietary medicines and drugs are estimated at 58–62% and of non-proprietary medicines and drugs at 39–43% of retail sales.

7. INFANT AND INVALID FOODS

Consumers' expenditure and methods of distribution

Consumers' expenditure on infant and invalid foods in 1938 is estimated at £3–4 millions. This estimate attempts to exclude the purchases of these goods by hospitals, the medical profession and child welfare departments of public authorities. The goods covered include all infant and invalid foods, essences, powders and liquids except health food beverages with milk and cereal base.

The methods of distribution. The proportions of total sales passing through the main channels of distribution in 1938 are estimated as follows:

	%
From manufacturer to wholesaler to retailer	55–65
From manufacturer direct to retailer	35–45

Included in the sales direct to retailer are the sales of co-operative wholesale societies to co-operative retail societies.

Number of wholesalers and retailers. The number of wholesalers regularly handling and stocking these goods in 1938 is estimated at 100–150 and the number of retail outlets at 15–20,000. The majority of these retail outlets were chemists and these shops did over three-quarters of the trade, but some grocers and general shops also stocked a small range of these goods. Multiple shops including variety chain stores are estimated to have been responsible for 27–33% of the total trade.

The cost of distribution

Most of these products were branded and price-maintained in 1938 and nearly all the manufacturers were members of the Proprietary Articles Trade Association.

The margins allowed to wholesalers and retailers were as follows:

Wholesalers were given special terms by some manufacturers, usually 10–12½% on sales, but in most cases retailers and wholesalers could buy on the same terms. These were based on a sliding scale according to quantity, and the difference between the purchase and selling price usually yielded a wholesaler 11–12% on sales. In a few cases the margin could rise to 15% on sales.

Retailers purchasing from wholesalers usually earned 20–23% on sales. Retailers purchasing direct from manufacturers earned varying margins according to the quantities purchased, ranging from 20–33% on sales. The usual margins earned on direct purchases were 27–33⅓% on sales but on some popular brands the margins rarely rose above 25% on sales.

Settlement discounts were not given by a number of firms. Where however the practice was followed, usually in the case of firms giving a low initial margin, the rate was 2½% for payment in the month.

The stock turn of retailers of these products averaged 6–7 times a year, and that of wholesalers 10–12 times a year.

Manufacturers' distribution costs, including carriage and packing, selling costs, salesmen's salaries, and advertising are estimated to have averaged about 25% of sales revenue. Of this, selling costs, salesmen's salaries, samples and administrative selling costs averaged 5–7%, carriage and packing 6–7%, and advertising 10–15%.

The total costs of distribution are estimated at 47–51% of retail sales.

8. CONTRACEPTIVES

Consumers' expenditure and methods of distribution

Consumers' expenditure on contraceptives in 1938 is estimated at between £2–2·5 millions. This estimate includes expenditure on chemical contraceptives as well as rubber goods, the latter representing approximately four-fifths of total sales. Over three-quarters of these goods, mainly rubber products, were imported. The distribution of contraceptives through the medical profession and clinics is excluded from this estimate.

The methods of distribution. The proportions of the total sales of these goods passing through the main channels of distribution in 1938 are estimated as follows:

	%
From manufacturer or importer direct to retailer	52–62
From manufacturer or importer to wholesaler to retailer	38–48

In the majority of cases importers acted as wholesalers or were importer/wholesalers and occasionally specialist retailers of these goods imported direct. There was an important difference in the methods of distribution employed as between rubber goods and chemical contraceptives. While over three-fifths of the former passed from the importer direct to retailer only one-fifth of the latter was distributed directly from manufacturer to retailer, the remainder going through wholesalers.

Number of retail outlets. Most chemists' wholesalers handled these goods and so did a number of wholesalers in other trades such as hairdressers' sundriesmen and general wholesalers. The number of wholesalers specializing in contraceptives were very few and were usually importing houses. The number of shops selling these goods is not known with accuracy but is estimated at between 15–20,000. The majority of chemists handled the whole range or a part of the range of these goods as did some hairdressers and general shops, and there were between 750–1,000 specialist retailers.

Sales by different types of outlet. The proportions of the total sales in 1938 made by the different trade types of retail outlet are estimated as follows:

	%
Chemists' shops	40–50
Specialist retailers	40–45
Hairdressers' and general shops and other outlets	10–15

A higher than average proportion of the imported rubber goods was sold by the specialist retailers, and hairdressers and general shops rarely sold chemical contraceptives.

The proportions of total sales made by the different economic types of retail outlet in 1938 are estimated as follows:

	%
Multiple shops including multiple chemists and multiple specialist retailers	25–35
Unit retailers	65–75

The cost of distribution

Imported contraceptives were not usually price-maintained, though in many instances the importer or wholesaler who re-packed and branded the goods under his own name would put forward a suggested retail selling price. In the case of home-manufactured products the majority were price-maintained.

The margins earned by wholesalers and retailers on the sale of these goods varied widely between the imported and home-manufactured products and also according to the methods of purchase. The estimated ranges were as follows:

The importer earned a margin ranging from 15–50% on returns; when selling to wholesalers he usually earned 15–20% on sales and when combining the importing and wholesaling functions and selling direct to retailers 33–50% on sales.

The wholesaler purchasing home-manufactured products and selling to retailers earned a margin ranging from 12½–17½% on sales with an average of 15%. On imported goods a margin ranging from 20–33⅓% on sales was earned.

The retailer earned a margin ranging from 30–45% on sales on home-manufactured goods. The margin actually earned by the retailer would depend on the additional bonuses he earned by quantity purchases. While the larger retailers and multiple firms would usually earn a margin at the top of this range the smaller chemists usually did not purchase in quantities to allow a large volume rebate. In these instances margins ranged between 33⅓–35%. On imported rubber goods the retailer's margins varied slightly with the source of purchase and ranged from 50–85% on sales. When the retailer purchased from the wholesaler the margin was usually lower than when he purchased direct from importers. The size of the retail margin would to a large extent depend on whether the wholesaler or importer undertook the re-packing and testing of the goods or whether this was done by the retailer. The specialist retailer usually undertook this function himself, and it is estimated that there was a loss of approximately 5% due to damaged goods.

The settlement discount in the trade was usually 2½% for payment in the month, but in a number of instances terms were net.

The stock turn of wholesalers of chemical contraceptives averaged 9–12 times a year and of retailers 12–15 times a year. The stock turn of retailers of rubber contraceptives varied between 12–24 times a year.

Manufacturers' distribution costs. The specialist retailers usually undertook extensive advertising in the form of display, catalogues and literature, and a significant proportion of their sales was done by post. In the case of home-manufactured products, this form of sales promotion was usually the responsibility of the manufacturer and the distribution costs incurred, including advertising, catalogues, brochures, salesmen's salaries, carriage and packing, and administrative selling costs are estimated at 35–40% of sales revenue. Advertising and sales promotion represented about three-quarters of manufacturers' total selling costs.

The total costs of distribution are estimated at 74–78% of retail sales.

9. PHOTOGRAPHIC GOODS

Consumers' expenditure and methods of distribution

Consumers' expenditure on photographic goods in 1938 is estimated at £2–3 millions. This relates to purchases by 'amateurs' and endeavours to exclude all purchases by industrial and commercial undertakings and purchases by schools and institutions. Also excluded is consumers' expenditure on developing and printing, which can be classed as a service. Of the total expenditure, sales of photographic materials, films and plates accounted for 80–85% and the sales of photographic apparatus, mainly still cameras, for the remainder. Both roll film and cameras were imported to some extent in 1938, but the imports of film were usually handled by manufacturers in the United Kingdom and resold by them.

The methods of distribution. The main channels of distribution of photographic film and cameras in 1938 and the proportions of total sales passing through each are estimated as follows:

	%
From manufacturer or importer direct to retailer	80–85
From manufacturer or importer to wholesaler to retailer	15–20

Some imported cameras were purchased by retailers direct from foreign manufacturers through agents and these sales have been included in the manufacturer direct to retailer sales.

Number of wholesalers and retailers. There were approximately 20 wholesalers of photographic goods in 1938, but these wholesalers did not deal in photographic goods alone but in a range of other goods as well; they usually handled chemists' sundries.

There were approximately 20,000 retail selling points of photographic goods in 1938. Of these some 500 were specialist photographic dealers, about 2,000 were photographic dealers/chemists and/or opticians who did about one-half or more of their trade in photographic goods,

10–12,000 were chemists selling mainly films but some box cameras and the remaining 6–7,000 were general shops, tobacconists, variety chain stores and kiosks selling films only.

Sales by different types of retail outlet. The proportions of total sales undertaken by the different trade types of outlet are estimated as follows:

	%
Specialist retailers	27–33
Chemists and opticians	55–65
Other retailers	8–12

Multiple shops, mainly chemists and including variety chain stores, are estimated to have undertaken 15–20% of the total retail turnover of these goods.

The cost of distribution

The bulk of the goods sold to the amateur photographer were price-maintained by the manufacturer in 1938.

The margins allowed to wholesalers and retailers were as follows:

Cameras and apparatus. The wholesaler received a discount off the retail price of 33⅓% plus 12½%. The retailer earned a margin of 33⅓% on sales.

Roll films. The wholesaler received a discount off the retail price of 30% plus 10–12½% and sometimes 15%. The average gross margin earned by wholesalers was 11% on sales. The retailer earned a margin of 30% on sales.

In the case of non-price-maintained goods the average on-costs used by wholesalers and retailers yielded a similar range of gross margins on sales.

Most of the goods were sold under these rates of discount although in a few instances additional discounts of up to 10% were given to retailers who advertised or promoted the sale of a particular brand of photographic apparatus. Multiple organizations received the same discounts as independent retailers.

Settlement discounts. Both wholesalers and retailers were entitled to an additional discount of 2½% for payment within the month.

Stock turn. The sale of photographic goods to amateur photographers was highly seasonal and the average stock turn of retailers was between 3–4 times a year. In the summer the stock turn of film would be monthly.

Manufacturers' distribution costs[1] varied with the differing sales policies, but for the large manufacturers selling direct to between 12–18,000

[1] See page 164.

retailers, distribution costs as a percentage of sales revenue, including transport, salesmen's salaries, administrative selling costs and advertising costs, amounted to between 15–18% of sales revenue. Advertising costs are estimated to have represented between one-third and one-half of these costs.

The total costs of distribution are estimated at 44–46% of retail sales.

CHAPTER XXVII

OTHER MANUFACTURED GOODS

I. SEWING MACHINES

Consumers' expenditure and methods of distribution

The expenditure by the private domestic consumer on sewing machines in 1938 is estimated at £1·3 millions, over nine-tenths of which was spent on machines manufactured in this country.

The method of distribution was almost entirely from manufacturers to their own shops and direct to other retailers. The wholesaler handled only a very small proportion of the trade, probably about 5%, and dealt mostly in imported machines.

Retail outlets. Sales through manufacturers' own shops represented approximately 84–86% of total retail sales. These specialist shops, numbering about 1,000, also sold accessories and replacement parts and provided instructional and maintenance services.

The remainder of the direct sales were to shops such as ironmongers, cycle shops and clothing shops, which acted as agencies for the branded products of manufacturers in districts where manufacturers had no shops of their own, and to co-operative wholesale societies, multiple shops and department stores which generally sold the machines under their own brand names.

Approximately 87–90% of the total trade was undertaken by multiple shops, the great majority of which were owned by the manufacturers, about 3% by the retail co-operative and department stores, and the remainder by unit retailers.

The cost of distribution

The machines sold under the manufacturers' brand names were sold at prices fixed by the manufacturers' distributing organizations. The price-spread between factory value and retail price is estimated to have ranged between 60–70% of retail price. This covered manufacturers' total distribution costs including the upkeep of their retail shops and repair and maintenance services.[1]

Retail margins. In the case of the small proportion of machines sold through independent retailers acting as agents for the manufacturers, the margin allowed the retailer was between 25 and 33⅓% of the fixed retail price, the average being nearer the 33⅓%.

[1] See page 164.

The small number of unbranded machines sold to department stores were bought by them at a discount of $33\frac{1}{3}$% off the usual retail price of similar branded machines. The store was free to fix its own mark-up so long as the manufacturer's brand name was not used.

Hire purchase. It is estimated that 70–75% of the total sales were made under hire-purchase arrangements.

The total costs of distribution are estimated at 58–62% of retail sales.

2. PERAMBULATORS AND BABY CARRIAGES

Consumers' expenditure and methods of distribution

Consumers' expenditure on perambulators and baby carriages in 1938 is estimated at approximately £1·5–2 millions.

The methods of distribution. The proportions of total sales passing through the main channels of distribution in 1938 are estimated as follows:

	%
From manufacturer direct to retailer	80–90
From manufacturer to factor or wholesaler to retailer	5–10
From manufacturer to factor to the consumer and from manufacturer direct to the consumer	5–10

The sales of manufacturers direct to retailers include the sales by manufacturers in their own or tied retail shops and the sales through the co-operative wholesale societies to retail societies.

Number of retail outlets. The number of wholesalers in the trade was very small. The goods were bulky and subject to damage and thus a great deal of intermediary handling was not possible. There were approximately 2,500 selling points for perambulators, of which some 750 were specialist shops handling perambulators and other children's equipment including toys and the remainder included department stores, some co-operative stores, and other shops doing a small trade in children's equipment.

A few retail shops were owned by manufacturers but it is thought that these shops did only 2–5% of the total trade, and the department store trade is estimated at 10–15% of the total sales. The bulk of the sales were undertaken by the specialist retailer.

The cost of distribution

The majority of manufacturers in 1938 fixed retail prices for their perambulators and the margins allowed to wholesalers or factors and to retailers were as follows:

Wholesalers or factors obtained a discount off the invoice price ranging from 5–15%. In some cases factors who were in practice acting as retailers received no wholesale discount at all.

Retailers usually received a $33\frac{1}{3}$% margin off the selling price or, in cases where the goods were not price-maintained, put 50% on cost. This is an average, and in some cases, owing to competition between manufacturers, higher retail margins were earned. Additions to the basic margin sometimes took the form of special discounts of up to 5% for large purchases, and sometimes of cheaper supplies of other goods.

Settlement discounts. Both factors and retailers were entitled to $3\frac{3}{4}$% cash discount for payment within a month and the majority of retailers qualified for this discount.

Manufacturers' distribution costs were relatively heavy owing to direct selling and the bulky character of the goods. Including transport and carriage costs, packing, selling costs, advertising and administration, manufacturers' selling costs averaged between 13–15% of their turnover. Advertising represented about one-tenth of these costs. There were, of course, variations between particular manufacturers.

Hire purchase and club trading existed in the trade in 1938 but not to a very great extent. It is thought that perhaps 10% of the perambulators in 1938 were sold on hire-purchase terms and the addition to the retail price of purchases made in this fashion was in the region of 15%. Club trading accounted for between 5–10% of the perambulators sold and the discount to members of clubs ranged between 5–10%.

The total costs of distribution are estimated to have averaged 46–49% of retail sales.

3. PORTABLE TYPEWRITERS

Consumers' expenditure and methods of distribution

Consumers' expenditure on portable typewriters was between £275–300,000. Other types of machines are excluded from this study, as in practically all cases they were sold to industrial and commercial users. Imported machines represented some 40% of the total sales.

The methods of distribution. The channels of distribution of portable typewriters varied slightly according to whether they were home-manufactured or imported. Certain British manufacturers had their own retail branches in London and, in some cases, in the provinces, but generally the British companies distributed their products through accredited agents. Some overseas manufacturers also made similar arrangements through accredited agents in the United Kingdom, but the overseas manufacturers with the largest sales in the United Kingdom maintained retail branches in London and in the provinces.

The proportions of total sales of portable typewriters passing through the main channels of distribution in 1938 were approximately as follows:

	%
From manufacturer through own retail branch to consumer	55–65
From manufacturer to accredited retail agent, stationer or department store	35–45

Number of outlets. The number of accredited agents, dealers and retailers of portable typewriters in 1938 is estimated at 2–3,000. These agents were usually dealers in office equipment, although there were a number of firms whose main business was stationery. Some of the larger department stores did some trade in portable typewriters, amounting approximately to 2–4% of total sales of these goods.

The cost of distribution

The re-sale price of portable typewriters was, in the majority of cases, fixed by the manufacturers, and the margins allowed to agents or dealers in 1938 ranged between 30–33⅓% on sales. The most usual discount was 33⅓%.

Manufacturers' distribution costs. It is almost impossible to distinguish manufacturers' distribution costs on portable typewriters from the costs of distributing other types of machines and from the cost of running and maintaining retail branches and depots. An approximate estimate of manufacturers' distribution costs, excluding expenses of maintaining branches and depots, is 6–9% of sales revenue. The spread between the landed cost of imported machines and the price charged to the purchaser in retail branches maintained by the overseas manufacturers was in the region of 45–55% of the retail price.

The total costs of distribution are estimated to have averaged 44–46% of retail sales.

GLOSSARY

The definitions and classifications of the terms used in this book are set out below. They refer only to the practice adopted in this enquiry, and as they are in part determined by the information available they are not intended to have universal application.

PRODUCERS, WHOLESALERS AND RETAILERS

Producers. Growers, manufacturers and processors.

Producer/retailers. Producers selling direct to the public from farm, delivery vehicle or market stall, or through a unit shop. Multiple and co-operative organizations which sell through their own retail outlets goods produced by linked productive units, however, have not been classified as producer/retailers.

Wholesalers. All intermediaries between producers or importers and retailers who assume physical and/or financial ownership of the goods in question, with the exception of the wholesaling organizations linked with producers and with multiple and co-operative outlets. Included therefore are higglers, jobbers, factors, dealers, merchants, distributors, primary wholesalers (except where they undertake processing and have been classified as producers), secondary wholesalers and other intermediaries where they fulfil the functions described above in respect of the particular commodities discussed. Commission agents, so-called 'brass-platers', import agents and others not taking financial or physical possession of the goods have not been classed as wholesalers.

Manufacturer/wholesalers. Producers selling both their own and bought-out commodities through a linked wholesaling organization.

Wholesaler/retailers. Firms which act both as wholesale distributors, selling to other retailers, and as retailers.

Mail order sales. Sales by producers direct to consumers by post. Sales by mail order by retailers or other organizations who are not the producers of the commodities are excluded from this category.

METHODS OF DISTRIBUTION

Three main methods of distribution have been distinguished. The types of sale which have been included under each main heading are given below.

From manufacturer, importer or grower to wholesaler and then to retailer.

1. Goods changing hands physically and financially between manufacturer, importer or grower and an intermediary who re-sells to retailers.

2. Goods changing hands in this way twice or more before reaching the retailer, that is where there are two or more such intermediaries. For the type of intermediaries classed as wholesalers see *Wholesalers.* In all cases it is assumed that there is no financial link between producer and wholesaler, or between wholesaler and retailer.

From manufacturer, importer or grower direct to retailer.

1. Goods sold by manufacturers, importers or growers direct to retailers including those sold through manufacturers' wholesaling organizations. (Goods bought-out by manufacturers and sold by the manufacturers' wholesaling organization, however, have been classed as sales through wholesalers.)
2. Goods sold by manufacturers, importers or growers to retailers through brokers, auctioneers, agents, commission agents and the like who do not take financial possession of the goods but act on behalf of producers or retailers.
3. Goods purchased direct from overseas by retailers.
4. Goods sold to retailers by importer/wholesalers.
5. Goods sold by producers or importers to the wholesale organizations of multiple, co-operative or department store concerns or imported directly by these concerns.
6. Goods produced by multiple and co-operative concerns for sale through their own retail outlets.
7. Goods sold by producers to wholesaler/retailers when sold through the latter's own retail outlets.
8. Goods sold direct to the public by wholesalers.

From manufacturer, importer or grower direct to consumers.

1. Sales by producer/retailers. See *Producer/retailers.*
2. Goods sold to consumers by door-to-door salesmen employed by producers. (Goods sold by retailers on orders from producers' door-to-door salesmen, however, have been classed as sales direct to retailers.)
3. Goods sold by producers to consumers by mail order or by other direct means.

TYPES OF RETAIL OUTLET

Multiple shop. Shop owned by a firm which owns or controls five or more retail branches.

Department store. Store possessing five or more separate departments under one roof, usually with some physical barrier between one department and the next and a separate system of accounts for each department.

Co-operative store. Shop owned by a retail co-operative society. The wholesale co-operative societies have been classed as wholesaling organizations linked with the retail co-operatives.

Variety chain store. Multiple shop selling a large variety of goods under one roof but usually without any clear distinction between departments and often having a price limit.

Unit retailer. A residual term covering all retailers not by definition included in any of the above groups.

COSTS OF DISTRIBUTION

Gross margin. This is the estimated realized margin obtained after allowing for mark-downs, for all forms of stock losses, and for all discounts, rebates, bonuses, allowances, quantity or volume discounts, settlement discounts, etc., received less discounts given, and has been expressed as a percentage on sales. The gross margin therefore represents the difference between the actual cost of the goods to the wholesaler or retailer and the return from their sale shown as a percentage of the latter.

Margin. In the case studies the term margin has in some instances been used to refer to the initial mark-up, on-cost or margin on returns before allowance has been made for stock losses, etc.; in addition an estimate has usually been given of the realized margin before allowing for settlement discounts given and received, which have in most instances been shown separately.

Settlement discounts. Discounts given for payment within a specified time, expressed, usually, as a percentage of the invoice price.

Producers' distribution costs. These are taken to include the following expenses incurred by producers in distributing and marketing their products.

1. All expenses connected directly with selling and sales promotion, that is salesmen's salaries, commission and other payments, travelling expenses, advertising and sales promotion including free gifts, samples, catalogues and other material, and market research expenses. General selling office expenses including invoicing and stock control, and all payments made to agents, brokers and other intermediaries acting directly on behalf of the producer.

2. All expenses connected with the handling of the finished goods, that is warehousing and storage costs including the cost of maintaining depots, the packing of the finished goods and the cost of carriage and transport whether provided by the producer or by an outside contractor.

3. All expenses connected with indirect selling costs, that is general administrative costs and the costs of providing finance and credit.

4. The expenses and profit incurred by producers in selling through their own wholesaling organizations and in selling direct to the consumer by door-to-door salesmen, mail order and other direct methods are also included in producers' distribution costs except in the case of producer/retailer sales—see *Retailers' gross margin*—and of the sales of goods through multiple or co-operative outlets linked with the producing organization. In these instances the producers' distribution costs include only those expenses incurred under the above three headings, the wholesaling/retailing gross margins of multiple and co-operative organizations being included in retailers' gross margins.

Wholesalers' distribution costs or gross margin. The wholesalers' gross margin, as defined above, including the gross margin of importers and importer/wholesalers and the gross margin earned by producers when handling bought-out goods in their own wholesaling organization. The margin earned by large-scale retailing organizations when performing a wholesaling function and purchasing on wholesale terms has been included in retailers' gross margins as have the wholesaling margins of the co-operative wholesale societies.

Retailers' distribution costs or gross margin. The retailers' gross margin, as defined above, including the total wholesale and retail margins of retail organizations which performed a wholesaling function and purchased on wholesale terms, whether the purchases were made through a separate company or organization or not. The combined wholesale and retail margins of co-operative wholesale and retail societies. The difference between the cost of production and the profit on production of commodities sold by producer/retailers and of commodities sold by linked production and retailing organizations and the revenue obtained from the retail sale of the goods. Where the margins of unit retailers on goods purchased from wholesalers are considered, the wholesale and retail margins of the large-scale retail organizations are not, of course, included.

Total costs of distribution. The estimated difference between the return to producers less their distribution costs, or the value of goods on landing at the port, and the expenditure by consumers, expressed as a percentage of the latter. In other words this cost is the sum of producers' distribution costs and wholesalers' and retailers' realized margins, taken as percentages of retail sales.

OTHER TERMS

Rate of stock turn. The estimated average rate at which stock is turned over in the year calculated by dividing sales by stock at selling·price

Price-maintained goods. This is used to refer to goods the retail price of which is fixed or suggested by producers or wholesalers.

BIBLIOGRAPHY

The bibliography given below is limited to those books, pamphlets and articles which have been of direct value in this enquiry. It is not intended to be a comprehensive bibliography of studies on distribution questions. With one exception—the American study *Does Distribution Cost Too Much?*—all the sources given refer to conditions in the United Kingdom. But readers should be aware that a great number of studies have been published in the United States on both the practice and theory of the distribution of consumer goods.

The books, pamphlets and articles consulted have been arranged under three main headings. Firstly, those books and official reports which deal with general distribution questions. Secondly, those books and reports which deal with the distribution of articles of food and drink. Thirdly, those books and reports which deal with the distribution of clothing and other goods. A fourth section has been added listing some of the periodicals and trade papers which were of value. In these instances it is not possible to refer individually to all the articles and items which had a direct or indirect bearing on the subject under enquiry as often the reference was very oblique, confirming or revising information already obtained from other sources or suggesting a new method of approach, but the list may assist other workers in this field.

I. GENERAL STUDIES

(*a*) *Books, pamphlets and articles*

Association for Planning and Regional Reconstruction, *Retail Shops*, Report No. 23, London, 1943. (Typescript.)

Braithwaite, Dorothea and Dobbs, S. P., *The Distribution of Consumable Goods*, London, George Routledge and Sons, 1932.

British National Committee, The International Chamber of Commerce, *Trial Census of Distribution in Six Towns*, London, British National Committee, 1937.

Cadbury Brothers Ltd., *Industrial Record 1919–1939*, Bournville, Cadbury Brothers Ltd. [1945?].

Chisholm, Cecil (editor), *Marketing Survey of the United Kingdom*, London, Business Publications, second edition 1937, third edition 1939, first post-war edition 1948.

Dunlop, W. R., 'Retail Profits', *Economic Journal*, vol. XXXIX, no. 155, September 1929, p. 357.

The Economist, 27 April 1946, 'Britain's Shops', by a Correspondent.

Fabian Society, *Distribution: The Case for a National Census*, Research Series No. 108, London, Fabian Publications and Victor Gollancz, 1946.

Fogarty, M. P. (editor), *Further Studies in Industrial Organization*, London, Methuen and Co., 1948.

Ford, P., 'Excessive Competition in the Retail Trades. Changes in the Numbers of Shops, 1901–1931', *Economic Journal*, vol. XLV, no. 179, September 1935, p. 501.

Grether, Ewald T., *Re-sale Price Maintenance in Great Britain with an Application to the Problem in the United States*, Berkeley, University of California Publications in Economics, vol. II, no. 3, 1935.

Hoffman, P. C., *Shops and the State and State of the Shops*, London, The Shop Assistant Publishing Company, no date.

The Hulton Retailer Readership Studies, compiled by J. W. Hobson and H. Henry, Numbers 1–10: *The Grocery Trade; The Tobacco Trade; The Sugar Confectionery Trade; The Ironmongery Trade; The Women's Wear Trade; The Pharmaceutical Trade; The Electrical, Radio and Gramophone Trades; The Men's Wear Trade; The Hairdressing and Beauty Trades; The Garage and Car Accessory Trade*. London, Hulton Press, 1948.

Johnson-Davies, K. C., *Control in Retail Industry*, London, Trade and Publishing Company, 1945.

Kaldor, Nicholas and Silverman, Rodney, *A Statistical Analysis of Advertising Expenditure and of the Revenue of the Press*, National Institute of Economic and Social Research, Economic and Social Studies VIII, Cambridge University Press, 1948.

Leak, H. and Maizels, A., 'The Structure of British Industry', *Journal of the Royal Statistical Society*, vol. CVIII, Part II, 1945, p. 142.

Levy, Hermann, *Retail Trade Associations*, London, Kegan Paul, Trench, Trubner and Co., 1942.

Levy, Hermann, *The Shops of Britain*, London, Kegan Paul, Trench, Trubner and Co., 1948.

Lewis, W. Arthur, 'Competition in Retail Trade', *Economica*, New Series, vol. XII, no. 48, November 1945, p. 202.

Madge, Charles, 'War and the Small Retail Shop', Institute of Statistics, Oxford, *Bulletin*, vol. IV, Supplement no. 2, April 1942.

Manchester Guardian Commercial Weekly, series of articles, 1938 to July 1939 on the distributive trades.

Neal, Lawrence E., *Retailing and the Public*, London, George Allen and Unwin, 1932.

Plant, Arnold (editor), *Some Modern Business Problems*, London, Longmans, Green and Co., 1937.

Plant, Arnold and Fowler, R. F., 'The Analysis of Costs of Retail Distribution', *Transactions of the Manchester Statistical Society*, Session 1938–39.

Reddaway, W. B., 'Some Problems of Taking a Census of Distribution', *Transactions of the Manchester Statistical Society*, Session 1946–47.

Rothwell, Tom S., *A Nation of Shopkeepers*, London, Herbert Joseph [1947?].

Silverman, H. A. (editor), *Studies in Industrial Organization*, Nuffield College Social Reconstruction Survey, London, Methuen and Co., 1946.

Smith, Henry, *Retail Distribution*, Oxford University Press, 1948 (second edition).

Smith, Henry, *Wholesaling and Retailing*, Fabian Society Tract No. 272, London, Fabian Publications and Victor Gollancz, 1949.

Stewart, Paul W. and Dewhurst, J. Frederic, *Does Distribution Cost Too Much?* New York, The Twentieth Century Fund, 1939.

Urwick, L. and Valentine, F. P., *Europe—United States of America*, Trends in the Organisation and Methods of Distribution in the two Areas, Paris, International Chamber of Commerce, 1931.

Vallance, Aylmer, *Hire-Purchase*, London, Thomas Nelson and Sons, 1939.

(*b*) *Books on the Co-operative Movement*

Barou, N. (editor), *The Co-operative Movement in Labour Britain*, London, Victor Gollancz, 1948.

Carr-Saunders, A. M., Florence, P. Sargant, and Peers, Robert, *Consumers' Co-operation in Great Britain*, London, George Allen and Unwin, 1942 (third, revised, edition).

Census of Shops, A Census of Shops and Retail Outlets operated by Co-operative Societies in 1946, Manchester, Co-operative Union, 1947.

Cole, G. D. H., *A Century of Co-operation*, Manchester, Co-operative Union, 1946.

Elliott, Sidney R., *England, Cradle of Co-operation*, London, Faber and Faber, 1937.

Hough, J. A., *Report of the Economic Survey of the Services Provided by Retail Co-operative Societies*, Manchester, Co-operative Union, 1938.

Hough, J. A., *Dividend on Co-operative Purchases*, Manchester, Co-operative Union, 1936.

The People's Year Book 1939, prepared by the Publicity Department, Co-operative Society. Manchester, C.W.S. Ltd., 1939; also *The People's Year Book 1940*.

Redfern, P., *The New History of the C.W.S.*, London, J. M. Dent and Sons, 1938.

Report of the Seventy-First Annual Co-operative Congress, 1939, edited by R. A. Palmer, Manchester, Co-operative Union, 1939; also the *Report of the Seventy-Second Annual Congress, 1940*.

(*c*) *Official Reports*

Board of Trade, *Report of the Committee appointed by the Lord Chancellor and the President of the Board of Trade to consider certain Trade Practices* (Restraint of Trade), H.M.S.O., 1931.

Board of Trade, *Second Interim Report of the Retail Trade Committee: The Impact of the War on the Retail Trades in Goods other than Food*, H.M.S.O., 1942.

Board of Trade, *Third Report of the Retail Trade Committee: Concentration in the Retail Non-Food Trades*, H.M.S.O., 1942.

Report of the Census of Distribution Committee, Cmd. 6764, H.M.S.O., 1946.

II. THE DISTRIBUTION OF FOOD AND DRINK

(*a*) *Books, pamphlets and articles*

Agricultural Register, 1938–9, Oxford, Agricultural Economics Research Institute, 1939.

Atkins, John, *The Distribution of Fish*, London, Fabian Society, Research Series No. 60, 1941.

Baxter, J., *The Organisation of the Brewing Trade*, unpublished Ph.D. thesis, University of London, 1945.

Brewers' Society, *The Brewers' Almanack and Wine and Spirit Trade Annual, 1939*, London, The Brewers' Society, 1939, and 1940 and 1941 issues.

British Agriculture, a Report of an Enquiry organized by Viscount Astor and B. Seebohm Rowntree, London, Longmans, Green and Co., 1938.

Coles, R., *An Account of the Organization of the Egg Industry with Special Reference to England and Wales*, unpublished M.Sc. thesis, University of London, 1938.

Cripps, John, *The Distribution of Milk: A Study of Town Delivery Costs*, Oxford, Agricultural Economics Research Institute, 1938.

Darling, George, *The Politics of Food*, London, George Routledge and Sons, 1941.

Dobbs, S. P., *Report on the Operating Expenses of Retail Confectionery Shops*, prepared for the Manufacturing Confectioners' Alliance Incorporated, London, 1932.

Drake, W., *The Organization of Wholesale Distribution in Great Britain of Fruit, Flowers and Vegetables of Domestic and Foreign Origin*, unpublished M.Com. thesis, University of London, 1941.

Dunlop, W. R., 'A Contribution to the Study of London's Retail Meat Trade', *Economic Journal*, vol. xxxv, no. 139, September 1925, p. 416.

Enock, A. G., *This Milk Business*, London, H. K. Lewis and Co., 1943.

Murray, K. A. H., and Rutherford, R. S. G., *Milk Consumption Habits*, Oxford, Agricultural Economics Research Institute, 1941.

National Association of Master Bakers, Confectioners and Caterers, *Bread Costs in War-Time*, London, 1944.

Pepperall, R. A., *The Milk Marketing Board*, Wells, Somerset: Clare, Son and Co., 1948.

Shaw, T. J., *The Marketing and Distribution of Home-Produced Meat and Livestock*, paper read to the British Society of Animal Production, 21 February 1945.

Smith, Charles, *Britain's Food Supplies in Peace and War:* a survey prepared for the Fabian Society, London, George Routledge and Sons, 1940.

Vinter, P., and Bulmer, J., *Milk: from Cow to Consumer*, London, Fabian Society, Research Series No. 41, 1938.

Walworth, George, *Feeding the Nation in Peace and War*, London, George Allen and Unwin, 1940.

Williams, F. H. B., *The Tea Trade*, unpublished M.Sc. thesis, University of London, 1938.

Witney, D., 'A Retail Butcher's Business', *Journal of Proceedings of the Agricultural Economics Society*, vol. v, no. 4, June 1939, p. 337.

(*b*) *Official reports*

Board of Trade, *Report of the Food Council on the Costs and Profits of Retail Milk Distribution in Great Britain*, H.M.S.O., 1937.

Board of Trade, *Report of the Food Council for the year 1938*, H.M.S.O., 1939.

First Report of the Royal Commission on Food Prices, Cmd. 2390, H.M.S.O., 1925.

The Herring Industry, First Report of the Sea-Fish Commission for the United Kingdom, Cmd. 4677, H.M.S.O., 1934.

Ministry of Agriculture, various publications in the *Economic Series* (Orange Books) on the marketing of agricultural products.

Ministry of Agriculture and Fisheries, *Interim and Final Reports of the Departmental Committee on the Distribution and Prices of Agricultural Produce* (the Linlithgow Committee), H.M.S.O., 1924.

Ministry of Agriculture and Fisheries, *Report of the Committee appointed to review the Working of the Agricultural Marketing Acts* (the Lucas Committee), Economic Series No. 48, H.M.S.O., 1947.

Ministry of Food, *Analysis of the Grocery and Provisions Retail Distributive Trade*, London, 1947. (Typescript.)

Ministry of Food, *How Britain was Fed in War-time: Food Control 1939 to 1945*, H.M.S.O., 1946.

Ministry of Food, *Report of the Select Committee appointed to examine the Cost of Milk Distribution*, H.M.S.O., 1940.

Ministry of Food, *Personal Points Rationing, Analysis of the Chocolate and Sugar Confectionery Distributive Trade*, London, 1947. (Typescript.)

Potato Marketing Board, *Report on the Operation of the Potato Marketing Scheme, 1938*, London, Potato Marketing Board, 1938.

Report of the Joint Committee of Enquiry into the Anglo-Argentine Meat Trade, Cmd. 5839, H.M.S.O., 1938.

Report of the Committee on Milk Distribution, Cmd. 7414, H.M.S.O., 1948.

The White Fish Industry, Second Report of the Sea-Fish Commission for the United Kingdom, Cmd. 5130, H.M.S.O., 1936.

III. CLOTHING AND OTHER GOODS

(a) Books, pamphlets and articles

The British Photographic Industry, Home Trade and Export Groups, *A Survey of the British Photographic Industry*, London, 1945.

Brunner, Christopher T., *The Problem of Oil*, London, Ernest Benn, 1930.

Drapers' Chamber of Trade and Retail Furnishers' Chamber of Trade, *Report of the Post-War Reconstruction Committee*, London, 1945.

Electrical Fair Trading Council, *British Electrical Industry Fair Trading Policy for the Home Trade*, London, Edition 3, 1945.

The Pharmaceutical Society of Great Britain, *Report of the Committee of Enquiry*, London, Part I 1939, Part II 1940.

Political and Economic Planning, *Report on the British Coal Industry*, London, P E P, 1936.

Political and Economic Planning, *The British Fuel and Power Industries*, London, P E P, 1947.

Political and Economic Planning, *The Market for Household Appliances*, London, P E P, 1945.

Proprietary Articles Trade Association, *Protected List and Year Book, 1940*, London, P.A.T.A., 1940.

Raymond, Harold, *Publishing and Bookselling*, a Survey of Post-War Developments and Present-Day Problems, London, J. M. Dent and Sons, 1938.

Reynolds, P. A., *Motor Trade Practice*, London, Methuen and Co., 1937.

Sanders, F. D. (editor), *British Book Trade Organisation*, a Report of the Work of the Joint Committee, London, George Allen and Unwin, 1939.

Smith, Norman, *Your Coal and You*, Fabian Tract No. 259, London, Fabian Society, 1942.

The Society of Motor Manufacturers and Traders Ltd., *The Motor Industry of Great Britain, 1939*, London, S.M.M.T., 1939.

Wholesale Textile Association, *Textile Distribution in the Post-War World*, Third and Final Report issued by the Post-War Reconstruction Committee, London, 1945.

Williams, G. S., 'Book Trade Policy', *The Publisher and Bookseller*, 15 September 1933.

Unwin, Sir Stanley, *The Truth About Publishing*, London, George Allen and Unwin, 1946 (fourth, revised, edition).

(b) Official reports

Board of Trade Journal, 3 June 1944, 'Retail Outlets for Rationed Clothing, Footwear and Textiles'.

Board of Trade Journal, 29 September 1945, 'Production and Employment in the Clothing Industry'.

Board of Trade, *Working Party Reports* on *Cotton* (1946), *Boots and Shoes* (1946), *Furniture* (1946), *Pottery* (1946), *Hosiery* (1946), *Jewellery and Silverware* (1946), *Linoleum and Felt Base* (1947), *Hand-blown Domestic Glassware* (1947), *Heavy Clothing* (1947), *Light Clothing* (1947), *Carpets* (1947), *Cutlery* (1947), *Rubber-Proofed Clothing* (1947).

Mines Department, *Minutes of Evidence to the Departmental Committee on the Distribution of Coal, Coke and Manufactured Fuel* (the Monckton Committee), 1938–39, H.M.S.O. 1939.

Report of the Select Committee on Medicine Stamp Duties, together with the Proceedings of the Committee, Minutes of Evidence and Index, also Proceedings of the Select Committee on Medicine Stamp Duties, 1935–6. H.M.S.O., 1937.

IV. PERIODICALS AND TRADE JOURNALS

The Baker and Confectioner
The Bookseller
The Bookseller and Stationer
The Brewers' Guardian
The Brewers' Journal and Hop and Malt Trades Review
The Brewing Trade Review
The British Baker
The British Jeweller
British Millinery
The British Pharmacist
The British Stationer
Brushes and Toilet Goods

The Chain and Multiple Store
The Chemist and Druggist
The Cigar and Tobacco World
The Confectioner, Baker and Restaurateur
The Confectionery Journal
The Confectionery News and Ice Cream and Soda Fountain News

The Dairyman
The Drapers' Record
Drug Merchandising

The Economist
Electrical Trading and Radio Marketing

The Fish Trades Gazette
The Food Trade Review
Fruit, Flower and Vegetable Marketing
The Fur Record
The Furniture Record
The Furnishing World

Games and Toys
The Grocers' Gazette and Provision Trades News
The Grocer and Oil Trades Review
Grocery
Grocery and Branch Store Management

The Hairdresser and Beauty Trade
The Hardware Trade Journal
Harper's Wine and Spirit Gazette
The Hatters' Gazette
The Hosiery Trade Journal

The Ironmongers' Weekly

Labour Research
Leather Goods
The Licensing World

The Manufacturing Clothier
Marketing, The Official Journal of the Incorporated Sales Managers' Association
The Meat Trades Journal
Men's Wear
Men's Wear Merchandising
The Milk Industry

Modern Meat Marketing
The Motor Cycle and Cycle Trader
The Motor Trader

The National Association Review of Master Bakers, Confectioners and Caterers
The New Dawn
N.U.R.C. News Letter, The Official Journal of the National Union of Retail Confectioners
The Off-Licence Journal
The Outfitter

The Perfumery and Essential Oils Record
The Petroleum Times
The Pharmaceutical Journal
The Photographic Dealer
The Pottery Gazette and Glass Trade Review
The Publishers' Circular and Publisher and Bookseller

The Retail Chemist

Scope
The Shoe and Leather News
The Shoe and Leather Record
Smallwares, Novelties and Dress Accessories
The Small Trader
Store
Soap, Perfumery and Cosmetics

The Textile Weekly
Tobacco
The Tobacconist and Confectioner

The Watchmaker, Jeweller and Silversmith
The Wine and Spirit Trade Record
The Wireless and Electrical Trader

INDEX

Notes: n=note; t=Table; tn=Table note. The arabic numerals refer throughout to pages and not to Tables.

Printed in the United States
By Bookmasters